THE CANTOS
OF
EZRA POUND

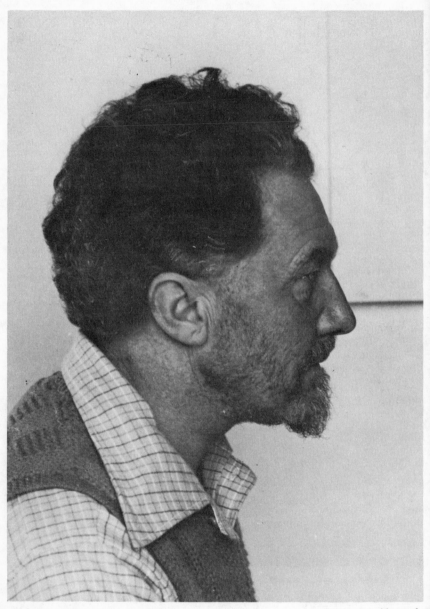

EZRA POUND

THE CANTOS
OF
EZRA POUND

A NEW DIRECTIONS BOOK

LIBRARY OF CONGRESS CATALOG CARD NUMBER: 70-117217

ACKNOWLEDGMENTS

Part of Canto 113 first appeared in *Poetry* in 1962, and part first appeared in *The New Yorker* in 1968.

FRONTISPIECE PHOTOGRAPH BY ARNOLD GENTHE.

MANUFACTURED IN THE UNITED STATES OF AMERICA.

PUBLISHED IN CANADA BY MC CLELLAND & STEWART, LIMITED.

FIRST PRINTING OF *Cantos 1–117* IN ONE VOLUME, 1970

SECOND PRINTING, 1971

New Directions Books are published for James Laughlin by New Directions Publishing Corporation, 333 Sixth Avenue, New York 10014.

CONTENTS

A Draft of XXX Cantos (1930)   1

Eleven New Cantos XXXI–XLI (1934)   151

The Fifth Decad of Cantos XLII–LI (1937)   207

Cantos LII–LXXI (1940)   253

The Pisan Cantos LXXIV–LXXXIV (1948)   423

Section: Rock-Drill De Los Cantares LXXXV–XCV
     (1955)   541

Thrones de los Cantares XCVI–CIX (1959)   649

Drafts and Fragments of Cantos CX–CXVII (1969)   775

A DRAFT OF
XXX CANTOS

I

AND then went down to the ship,
  Set keel to breakers, forth on the godly sea, and
  We set up mast and sail on that swart ship,
  Bore sheep aboard her, and our bodies also
Heavy with weeping, and winds from sternward
Bore us out onward with bellying canvas,
Circe's this craft, the trim-coifed goddess.
Then sat we amidships, wind jamming the tiller,
Thus with stretched sail, we went over sea till day's end.
Sun to his slumber, shadows o'er all the ocean,
Came we then to the bounds of deepest water,
To the Kimmerian lands, and peopled cities
Covered with close-webbed mist, unpierced ever
With glitter of sun-rays
Nor with stars stretched, nor looking back from heaven
Swartest night stretched over wretched men there.
The ocean flowing backward, came we then to the place
Aforesaid by Circe.
Here did they rites, Perimedes and Eurylochus,
And drawing sword from my hip
I dug the ell-square pitkin;
Poured we libations unto each the dead,
First mead and then sweet wine, water mixed with white flour.
Then prayed I many a prayer to the sickly death's-heads;
As set in Ithaca, sterile bulls of the best
For sacrifice, heaping the pyre with goods,
A sheep to Tiresias only, black and a bell-sheep.
Dark blood flowed in the fosse,
Souls out of Erebus, cadaverous dead, of brides
Of youths and of the old who had borne much;
Souls stained with recent tears, girls tender,

Men many, mauled with bronze lance heads,
Battle spoil, bearing yet dreory arms,
These many crowded about me; with shouting,
Pallor upon me, cried to my men for more beasts;
Slaughtered the herds, sheep slain of bronze;
Poured ointment, cried to the gods,
To Pluto the strong, and praised Proserpine;
Unsheathed the narrow sword,
I sat to keep off the impetuous impotent dead,
Till I should hear Tiresias.
But first Elpenor came, our friend Elpenor,
Unburied, cast on the wide earth,
Limbs that we left in the house of Circe,
Unwept, unwrapped in sepulchre, since toils urged other.
Pitiful spirit.   And I cried in hurried speech:
" Elpenor, how art thou come to this dark coast?
" Cam'st thou afoot, outstripping seamen? "
            And he in heavy speech:
" Ill fate and abundant wine.   I slept in Circe's ingle.
" Going down the long ladder unguarded,
" I fell against the buttress,
" Shattered the nape-nerve, the soul sought Avernus.
" But thou, O King, I bid remember me, unwept, unburied,
" Heap up mine arms, be tomb by sea-bord, and inscribed:
" *A man of no fortune, and with a name to come.*
" And set my oar up, that I swung mid fellows."

And Anticlea came, whom I beat off, and then Tiresias Theban,
Holding his golden wand, knew me, and spoke first:
" A second time? why? man of ill star,
" Facing the sunless dead and this joyless region?
" Stand from the fosse, leave me my bloody bever
" For soothsay. "
            And I stepped back,
And he strong with the blood, said then: " Odysseus

4

" Shalt return through spiteful Neptune, over dark seas,
" Lose all companions. " And then Anticlea came.
Lie quiet Divus. I mean, that is Andreas Divus,
In officina Wecheli, 1538, out of Homer.
And he sailed, by Sirens and thence outward and away
And unto Circe.
        Venerandam,
In the Cretan's phrase, with the golden crown, Aphrodite,
Cypri munimenta sortita est, mirthful, orichalchi, with golden
Girdles and breast bands, thou with dark eyelids
Bearing the golden bough of Argicida. So that:

II

Hang it all, Robert Browning,
   there can be but the one "Sordello."
But Sordello, and my Sordello?
Lo Sordels si fo di Mantovana.
So-shu churned in the sea.
Seal sports in the spray-whited circles of cliff-wash,
Sleek head, daughter of Lir,
      eyes of Picasso
Under black fur-hood, lithe daughter of Ocean;
And the wave runs in the beach-groove:
"Eleanor, ἑλέναυς and ἑλέπτολις!"
      And poor old Homer blind, blind, as a bat,
Ear, ear for the sea-surge, murmur of old men's voices:
"Let her go back to the ships,
Back among Grecian faces, lest evil come on our own,
Evil and further evil, and a curse cursed on our children,
Moves, yes she moves like a goddess
And has the face of a god
      and the voice of Schoeney's daughters,
And doom goes with her in walking,
Let her go back to the ships,
      back among Grecian voices."
And by the beach-run, Tyro,
      Twisted arms of the sea-god,
Lithe sinews of water, gripping her, cross-hold,
And the blue-gray glass of the wave tents them,
Glare azure of water, cold-welter, close cover.
Quiet sun-tawny sand-stretch,
The gulls broad out their wings,
      nipping between the splay feathers;

Snipe come for their bath,
                bend out their wing-joints,
Spread wet wings to the sun-film,
And by Scios,
                to left of the Naxos passage,
Naviform rock overgrown,
                algæ cling to its edge,
There is a wine-red glow in the shallows,
                a tin flash in the sun-dazzle.

The ship landed in Scios,
                men wanting spring-water,
And by the rock-pool a young boy loggy with vine-must,
                " To Naxos? Yes, we'll take you to Naxos,
Cum' along lad. " " Not that way! "
" Aye, that way is Naxos."
                And I said: " It's a straight ship."
And an ex-convict out of Italy
                knocked me into the fore-stays,
(He was wanted for manslaughter in Tuscany)
                And the whole twenty against me,
Mad for a little slave money.
                And they took her out of Scios
And off her course...
                And the boy came to, again, with the racket,
And looked out over the bows,
                and to eastward, and to the Naxos passage.
God-sleight then, god-sleight:
                Ship stock fast in sea-swirl,
Ivy upon the oars, King Pentheus,
                grapes with no seed but sea-foam,
Ivy in scupper-hole.
Aye, I, Accœtes, stood there,
                and the god stood by me,
Water cutting under the keel,

7

Sea-break from stern forrards,
> wake running off from the bow,
And where was gunwale, there now was vine-trunk,
And tenthril where cordage had been,
> grape-leaves on the rowlocks,
Heavy vine on the oarshafts,
And, out of nothing, a breathing,
> hot breath on my ankles,
Beasts like shadows in glass,
> a furred tail upon nothingness.
Lynx-purr, and heathery smell of beasts,
> where tar smell had been,
Sniff and pad-foot of beasts,
> eye-glitter out of black air.
The sky overshot, dry, with no tempest,
Sniff and pad-foot of beasts,
> fur brushing my knee-skin,
Rustle of airy sheaths,
> dry forms in the *æther*.
And the ship like a keel in ship-yard,
> slung like an ox in smith's sling,
Ribs stuck fast in the ways,
> grape-cluster over pin-rack,
> void air taking pelt.
Lifeless air become sinewed,
> feline leisure of panthers,
Leopards sniffing the grape shoots by scupper-hole,
Crouched panthers by fore-hatch,
And the sea blue-deep about us,
> green-ruddy in shadows,
And Lyæus: "From now, Accœtes, my altars,
Fearing no bondage,
> fearing no cat of the wood,
Safe with my lynxes,
> feeding grapes to my leopards,

8

Olibanum is my incense,
>   the vines grow in my homage."

The back-swell now smooth in the rudder-chains,
Black snout of a porpoise
>   where Lycabs had been,
Fish-scales on the oarsmen.
>   And I worship.
I have seen what I have seen.
>   When they brought the boy I said:
" He has a god in him,
>   though I do not know which god."
And they kicked me into the fore-stays.
I have seen what I have seen:
>   Medon's face like the face of a dory,
Arms shrunk into fins.   And you, Pentheus,
Had as well listen to Tiresias, and to Cadmus,
>   or your luck will go out of you.
Fish-scales over groin muscles,
>   lynx-purr amid sea...
And of a later year,
>   pale in the wine-red algæ,
If you will lean over the rock,
>   the coral face under wave-tinge,
Rose-paleness under water-shift,
>   Ileuthyeria, fair Dafne of sea-bords,
The swimmer's arms turned to branches,
Who will say in what year,
>   fleeing what band of tritons,
The smooth brows, seen, and half seen,
>   now ivory stillness.

And So-shu churned in the sea, So-shu also,
>   using the long moon for a churn-stick...
Lithe turning of water,
>   sinews of Poseidon,

Black azure and hyaline,
        glass wave over Tyro,
Close cover, unstillness,
        bright welter of wave-cords,
Then quiet water,
        quiet in the buff sands,
Sea-fowl stretching wing-joints,
        splashing in rock-hollows and sand-hollows
In the wave-runs by the half-dune;
Glass-glint of wave in the tide-rips against sunlight,
        pallor of Hesperus,
Grey peak of the wave,
        wave, colour of grape's pulp,

Olive grey in the near,
        far, smoke grey of the rock-slide,
Salmon-pink wings of the fish-hawk
        cast grey shadows in water,
The tower like a one-eyed great goose
        cranes up out of the olive-grove,

And we have heard the fauns chiding Proteus
        in the smell of hay under the olive-trees,
And the frogs singing against the fauns
        in the half-light.
And...

III

I SAT on the Dogana's steps
For the gondolas cost too much, that year,
And there were not " those girls ", there was one face,
And the Buccentoro twenty yards off, howling " Stretti ",
And the lit cross-beams, that year, in the Morosini,
And peacocks in Koré's house, or there may have been.
        Gods float in the azure air,
Bright gods and Tuscan, back before dew was shed.
Light: and the first light, before ever dew was fallen.
Panisks, and from the oak, dryas,
And from the apple, mælid,
Through all the wood, and the leaves are full of voices,
A-whisper, and the clouds bowe over the lake,
And there are gods upon them,
And in the water, the almond-white swimmers,
The silvery water glazes the upturned nipple,
        As Poggio has remarked.
Green veins in the turquoise,
Or, the gray steps lead up under the cedars.

My Cid rode up to Burgos,
Up to the studded gate between two towers,
Beat with his lance butt, and the child came out,
Una niña de nueve años,
To the little gallery over the gate, between the towers,
Reading the writ, voce tinnula:
That no man speak to, feed, help Ruy Diaz,
On pain to have his heart out, set on a pike spike
And both his eyes torn out, and all his goods sequestered,
" And here, Myo Cid, are the seals,
The big seal and the writing."
And he came down from Bivar, Myo Cid,

11

With no hawks left there on their perches,
And no clothes there in the presses,
And left his trunk with Raquel and Vidas,
That big box of sand, with the pawn-brokers,
To get pay for his menie;
Breaking his way to Valencia.
Ignez da Castro murdered, and a wall
Here stripped, here made to stand.
Drear waste, the pigment flakes from the stone,
Or plaster flakes, Mantegna painted the wall.
Silk tatters, " Nec Spe Nec Metu."

IV

PALACE in smoky light,
  Troy but a heap of smouldering boundary stones,
ANAXIFORMINGES! Aurunculeia!
  Hear me. Cadmus of Golden Prows!
The silver mirrors catch the bright stones and flare,
Dawn, to our waking, drifts in the green cool light;
Dew-haze blurs, in the grass, pale ankles moving.
Beat, beat, whirr, thud, in the soft turf
        under the apple trees,
Choros nympharum, goat-foot, with the pale foot alternate;
Crescent of blue-shot waters, green-gold in the shallows,
A black cock crows in the sea-foam;

And by the curved, carved foot of the couch,
        claw-foot and lion head, an old man seated
Speaking in the low drone... :
            Ityn!
Et ter flebiliter, Ityn, Ityn!
And she went toward the window and cast her down,
      " All the while, the while, swallows crying:
Ityn!
      " It is Cabestan's heart in the dish."
      " It is Cabestan's heart in the dish?
      " No other taste shall change this."
And she went toward the window,
          the slim white stone bar
Making a double arch;
Firm even fingers held to the firm pale stone;
Swung for a moment,
          and the wind out of Rhodez
Caught in the full of her sleeve.
      . . . the swallows crying:

13

'Tis. 'Tis. Ytis!
            Actæon...
            and a valley,
The valley is thick with leaves, with leaves, the trees,
The sunlight glitters, glitters a-top,
Like a fish-scale roof,
            Like the church roof in Poictiers
If it were gold.
            Beneath it, beneath it
Not a ray, not a slivver, not a spare disc of sunlight
Flaking the black, soft water;
Bathing the body of nymphs, of nymphs, and Diana,
Nymphs, white-gathered about her, and the air, air,
Shaking, air alight with the goddess,
            fanning their hair in the dark,
Lifting, lifting and waffing:
Ivory dipping in silver,
            Shadow'd, o'ershadow'd
Ivory dipping in silver,
Not a splotch, not a lost shatter of sunlight.
Then Actæon: Vidal,
Vidal. It is old Vidal speaking,
            stumbling along in the wood,
Not a patch, not a lost shimmer of sunlight,
            the pale hair of the goddess.

The dogs leap on Actæon,
            " Hither, hither, Actæon,"
Spotted stag of the wood;
Gold, gold, a sheaf of hair,
            Thick like a wheat swath,
Blaze, blaze in the sun,
            The dogs leap on Actæon.

14

Stumbling, stumbling along in the wood,
Muttering, muttering Ovid:
   " Pergusa... pool... pool!... Gargaphia,
" Pool... pool of Salmacis."
   The empty armour shakes as the cygnet moves.

Thus the light rains, thus pours, *e lo soleills plovil*
The liquid and rushing crystal
   beneath the knees of the gods.
Ply over ply, thin glitter of water;
Brook film bearing white petals.
The pine at Takasago
   grows with the pine of Isé!
The water whirls up the bright pale sand in the spring's mouth
" Behold the Tree of the Visages! "
Forked branch-tips, flaming as if with lotus.
   Ply over ply
The shallow eddying fluid,
   beneath the knees of the gods.

Torches melt in the glare
   set flame of the corner cook-stall,
Blue agate casing the sky (as at Gourdon that time)
   the sputter of resin,
Saffron sandal so petals the narrow foot: Hymenæus Io!
   Hymen, Io Hymenæe! Aurunculeia!
One scarlet flower is cast on the blanch-white stone.

   And Sō-Gyoku, saying:
" This wind, sire, is the king's wind,
   This wind is wind of the palace,
Shaking imperial water-jets."
   And Hsiang, opening his collar:
" This wind roars in the earth's bag,
   it lays the water with rushes."

No wind is the king's wind.
          Let every cow keep her calf.
     "This wind is held in gauze curtains..."
          No wind is the king's...

The camel drivers sit in the turn of the stairs,
          Look down on Ecbatan of plotted streets,
"Danaë!   Danaë!
          What wind is the king's? "
Smoke hangs on the stream,
The peach-trees shed bright leaves in the water,
Sound drifts in the evening haze,
          The bark scrapes at the ford,
Gilt rafters above black water,
          Three steps in an open field,
Gray stone-posts leading...

Père Henri Jacques would speak with the Sennin, on Rokku,
Mount Rokku between the rock and the cedars,
Polhonac,
As Gyges on Thracian platter set the feast,
Cabestan, Tereus,
          It is Cabestan's heart in the dish,
Vidal, or Ecbatan, upon the gilded tower in Ecbatan
Lay the god's bride, lay ever, waiting the golden rain.
By Garonne.   " Saave! "
The Garonne is thick like paint,
Procession, — " Et sa'ave, sa'ave, sa'ave Regina! " —
Moves like a worm, in the crowd.
Adige, thin film of images,
Across the Adige, by Stefano, Madonna in hortulo,
As Cavalcanti had seen her.
          The Centaur's heel plants in the earth loam.
And we sit here...
          there in the arena...

V

GREAT bulk, huge mass, thesaurus;
  Ecbatan, the clock ticks and fades out
  The bride awaiting the god's touch; Ecbatan,
  City of patterned streets; again the vision:
Down in the viæ stradæ, toga'd the crowd, and arm'd,
Rushing on populous business,
and from parapet looked down
and North was Egypt,
        the celestial Nile, blue deep,
        cutting low barren land,
Old men and camels
                working the water-wheels;
Measureless seas and stars,
Iamblichus' light,
        the souls ascending,
Sparks like a partridge covey,
        Like the " ciocco ", brand struck in the game.
" Et omniformis ": Air, fire, the pale soft light.
Topaz I manage, and three sorts of blue;
        but on the barb of time.
The fire? always, and the vision always,
Ear dull, perhaps, with the vision, flitting
And fading at will. Weaving with points of gold,
Gold-yellow, saffron... The roman shoe, Aurunculeia's
And come shuffling feet, and cries " Da nuces!
" Nuces! " praise, and Hymenæus " brings the girl to her man "
Or " here Sextus had seen her."
Titter of sound about me, always.
        and from " Hesperus..."
Hush of the older song: " Fades light from sea-crest,
" And in Lydia walks with pair'd women
" Peerless among the pairs, that once in Sardis

" In satieties...
          Fades the light from the sea, and many things
" Are set abroad and brought to mind of thee,"
And the vinestocks lie untended, new leaves come to the shoots,
North wind nips on the bough, and seas in heart
Toss up chill crests,
          And the vine stocks lie untended
And many things are set abroad and brought to mind
Of thee, Atthis, unfruitful.
          The talks ran long in the night.
And from Mauleon, fresh with a new earned grade,
In maze of approaching rain-steps, Poicebot—
The air was full of women,
          And Savairic Mauleon
Gave him his land and knight's fee, and he wed the woman.
Came lust of travel on him, of *romerya;*
And out of England a knight with slow-lifting eyelids
Lei fassa furar a del, put glamour upon her...
And left her an eight months gone.
          " Came lust of woman upon him,"
Poicebot, now on North road from Spain
(Sea-change, a grey in the water)
          And in small house by town's edge
Found a woman, changed and familiar face;
Hard night, and parting at morning.

And Pieire won the singing, Pieire de Maensac,
Song or land on the throw, and was *dreitz hom*
And had De Tierci's wife and with the war they made:
          Troy in Auvergnat
While Menelaus piled up the church at port
He kept Tyndarida.   Dauphin stood with de Maensac.

John Borgia is bathed at last.   (Clock-tick pierces the vision)
Tiber, dark with the cloak, wet cat gleaming in patches.

18

Click of the hooves, through garbage,
Clutching the greasy stone. " And the cloak floated."
Slander is up betimes.
        But Varchi of Florence,
Steeped in a different year, and pondering Brutus,
Then " Σίγα μαλ' αὖθις δευτέραν!
" Dog-eye!! " (to Alessandro)
        " Whether for love of Florence," Varchi leaves it,
Saying " I saw the man, came up with him at Venice,
" I, one wanting the facts,
" And no mean labour... Or for a privy spite? "
Our Benedetto leaves it,
But: " I saw the man. Se pia?
" O empia? For Lorenzaccio had thought of stroke in the open
But uncertain (for the Duke went never unguarded)
" And would have thrown him from wall
" Yet feared this might not end him," or lest Alessandro
Know not by whom death came, O se credesse
" If when the foot slipped, when death came upon him,
" Lest cousin Duke Alessandro think he had fallen alone,
" No friend to aid him in falling."
                    Caina attende.
The lake of ice there below me.
And all of this, runs Varchi, dreamed out beforehand
In Perugia, caught in the star-maze by Del Carmine,
Cast on a natal paper, set with an exegesis, told,
All told to Alessandro, told thrice over,
Who held his death for a doom.
In abuleia. But Don Lorenzino
Whether for love of Florence ... but
" O se morisse, credesse caduto da sè "
Σίγα, σίγα
Schiavoni, caught on the wood-barge,
Gives out the afterbirth, Giovanni Borgia,
Trails out no more at nights, where Barabello

Prods the Pope's elephant, and gets no crown, where Mozarello
Takes the Calabrian roadway, and for ending
Is smothered beneath a mule,
            a poet's ending,
Down a stale well-hole, oh a poet's ending.   " Sanazarro
" Alone out of all the court was faithful to him "
For the gossip of Naples' trouble drifts to North,
Fracastor (lightning was midwife) Cotta, and Ser D'Alviano,
Al poco giorno ed al gran cerchio d'ombra,
Talk the talks out with Navighero,
Burner of yearly Martials,
            (The slavelet is mourned in vain)
And the next comer says " Were nine wounds,
" Four men, white horse. Held on the saddle before him..."
Hooves clink and slick on the cobbles.
Schiavoni... cloak... " Sink the damn thing! "
Splash wakes that chap on the wood-barge.
Tiber catching the nap, the moonlit velvet,
A wet cat gleaming in patches.
            " Se pia," Varchi,
" O empia, ma risoluto
" E terribile deliberazione."
            Both sayings run in the wind,
Ma se morisse!

VI

WHAT you have done, Odysseus,
    We know what you have done...
    And that Guillaume sold out his ground rents
    (Seventh of Poitiers, Ninth of Aquitain).
" Tant las fotei com auzirets
" Cen e quatre vingt et veit vetz..."
The stone is alive in my hand, the crops
    will be thick in my death-year...
Till Louis is wed with Eleanor
And had (He, Guillaume) a son that had to wife
The Duchess of Normandia whose daughter
Was wife to King Henry e maire del rei jove...
Went over sea till day's end (he, Louis, with Eleanor)
Coming at last to Acre.
" Ongla, oncle " saith Arnaut
    Her uncle commanded in Acre,
That had known her in girlhood
        (Theseus, son of Aegeus)
And he, Louis, was not at ease in that town,
And was not at ease by Jordan
As she rode out to the palm-grove
Her scarf in Saladin's cimier.
Divorced her in that year, he Louis,
        divorcing thus Aquitaine.
And that year Plantagenet married her
        (that had dodged past 17 suitors)
Et quand lo reis Lois lo entendit
        mout er fasché.
Nauphal, Vexis, Harry joven
In pledge for all his life and life of all his heirs
Shall have Gisors, and Vexis, Neufchastel
But if no issue Gisors shall revert...

" Need not wed Alix... in the name
Trinity holy indivisible... Richard our brother
Need not wed Alix once his father's ward and...
But whomso he choose...for Alix, etc...

Eleanor, domna jauzionda, mother of Richard,
Turning on thirty years (wd. have been years before this)
By river-marsh, by galleried church-porch,
Malemorte, Correze, to whom:
                    " My Lady of Ventadour
" Is shut by Eblis in
" And will not hawk nor hunt
                    nor get her free in the air
" Nor watch fish rise to bait
" Nor the glare-wing'd flies alight in the creek's edge
" Save in my absence, Madame.
              ' Que la lauzeta mover '
" Send word I ask you to Eblis
                    you have seen that maker
" And finder of songs so far afield as this
" That he may free her,
                    who sheds such light in the air."

E lo Sordels si fo di Mantovana,
Son of a poor knight, Sier Escort,
And he delighted himself in chançons
And mixed with the men of the court
And went to the court of Richard Saint Boniface
And was there taken with love for his wife
                         Cunizza, da Romano,
That freed her slaves on a Wednesday
Masnatas et servos, witness
Picus de Farinatis
and Don Elinus and Don Lipus
              sons of Farinato de' Farinati

" free of person, free of will
" free to buy, witness, sell, testate."
A marito subtraxit ipsam...
        dictum Sordellum concubuisse:
        " Winter and Summer I sing of her grace,
        As the rose is fair, so fair is her face,
        Both Summer and Winter I sing of her,
        The snow makyth me to remember her."

And Cairels was of Sarlat...
                        Theseus from Troezene
And they wd. have given him poison
But for the shape of his sword-hilt.

VII

ELEANOR (she spoiled in a British climate)
　　　'Ελανδρος and 'Ελέπτολις, and
　　　poor old Homer blind,
　　　blind as a bat,
Ear, ear for the sea-surge;
　　　rattle of old men's voices.
And then the phantom Rome,
　　　marble narrow for seats
" Si pulvis nullus " said Ovid,
" Erit, nullum tamen excute."
Then file and candles, e li mestiers ecoutes;
Scene for the battle only, but still scene,
Pennons and standards y cavals armatz
Not mere succession of strokes, sightless narration,
And Dante's " ciocco," brand struck in the game.

Un peu moisi, plancher plus bas que le jardin.

" Contre le lambris, fauteuil de paille,
" Un vieux piano, et sous le baromètre..."

The old men's voices, beneath the columns of false marble,
The modish and darkish walls,
Discreeter gilding, and the panelled wood
Suggested, for the leasehold is
Touched with an imprecision... about three squares;
The house too thick, the paintings
a shade too oiled.
And the great domed head, *con gli occhi onesti e tardi*
Moves before me, phantom with weighted motion,
Grave incessu, drinking the tone of things,
And the old voice lifts itself
　　　　weaving an endless sentence.

We also made ghostly visits, and the stair
That knew us, found us again on the turn of it,
Knocking at empty rooms, seeking for buried beauty;
And the sun-tanned, gracious and well-formed fingers
Lift no latch of bent bronze, no Empire handle
Twists for the knocker's fall; no voice to answer.
A strange concierge, in place of the gouty-footed.
Sceptic against all this one seeks the living,
Stubborn against the fact. The wilted flowers
Brushed out a seven year since, of no effect.
Damn the partition! Paper, dark brown and stretched,
Flimsy and damned partition.
                Ione, dead the long year
My lintel, and Liu Ch'e's lintel.
Time blacked out with the rubber.

            The Elysée carries a name on
And the bus behind me gives me a date for peg;
Low ceiling and the Erard and the silver,
These are in " time." Four chairs, the bow-front dresser,
The panier of the desk, cloth top sunk in.
            " Beer-bottle on the statue's pediment!
" That, Fritz, is the era, to-day against the past,
" Contemporary." And the passion endures.
Against their action, aromas. Rooms, against chronicles.
Smaragdos, chrysolithos; De Gama wore striped pants in Africa
And " Mountains of the sea gave birth to troops ";

Le vieux commode en acajou:
            beer-bottles of various strata,
But *is* she dead as Tyro? In seven years?
   Ἐλέναυς, ἔλανδρος, ἐλέπτολις
The sea runs in the beach-groove, shaking the floated pebbles,
Eleanor!
            The scarlet curtain throws a less scarlet shadow;

Lamplight at Buovilla, e quel remir,
        And all that day
Nicea moved before me
And the cold grey air troubled her not
For all her naked beauty, bit not the tropic skin,
And the long slender feet lit on the curb's marge
And her moving height went before me,
        We alone having being.
And all that day, another day:
        Thin husks I had known as men,
Dry casques of departed locusts
        speaking a shell of speech...
Propped between chairs and table...
Words like the locust-shells, moved by no inner being;
        A dryness calling for death;

Another day, between walls of a sham Mycenian,
" Toc " sphinxes, sham-Memphis columns,
And beneath the jazz a cortex, a stiffness or stillness,
        Shell of the older house.
Brown-yellow wood, and the no colour plaster,
Dry professorial talk...
        now stilling the ill beat music,
House expulsed by this house.

        Square even shoulders and the satin skin,
Gone cheeks of the dancing woman,
        Still the old dead dry talk, gassed out —
It is ten years gone, makes stiff about her a glass,
A petrefaction of air.
        The old room of the tawdry class asserts itself;
The young men, never!
        Only the husk of talk.
O voi che siete in piccioletta barca,
Dido choked up with sobs, for her Sicheus

Lies heavy in my arms, dead weight
        Drowning, with tears, new Eros,

And the life goes on, mooning upon bare hills;
Flame leaps from the hand, the rain is listless,
Yet drinks the thirst from our lips,
        solid as echo,
Passion to breed a form in shimmer of rain-blur;
But Eros drowned, drowned, heavy-half dead with tears
        For dead Sicheus.

Life to make mock of motion:
For the husks, before me, move,
        The words rattle: shells given out by shells.
The live man, out of lands and prisons,
        shakes the dry pods,
Probes for old wills and friendships, and the big locust-casques
Bend to the tawdry table,
Lift up their spoons to mouths, put forks in cutlets,
And make sound like the sound of voices.
        Lorenzaccio
Being more live than they, more full of flames and voices.
Ma se morisse!
        Credesse caduto da sè, ma se morisse.
And the tall indifference moves,
        a more living shell,
Drift in the air of fate, dry phantom, but intact.
O Alessandro, chief and thrice warned, watcher,
        Eternal watcher of things,
Of things, of men, of passions.
        Eyes floating in dry, dark air,
E biondo, with glass-grey iris, with an even side-fall of hair
The stiff, still features.

VIII

THESE fragments you have shelved (shored).
"Slut!" "Bitch!" Truth and Calliope
Slanging each other sous les lauriers:
That Alessandro was negroid. And Malatesta
Sigismund:
> *Frater tamquam*

Et compater carissime: tergo
>> *...hanni de*
>> *..dicis*
>> *...entia*

Equivalent to:
> Giohanni of the Medici,
> Florence.

Letter received, and in the matter of our Messire Gianozio,
One from him also, sent on in form and with all due dispatch,
Having added your wishes and memoranda.
As to arranging peace between you and the King of Ragona,
So far as I am concerned, it wd.
Give me the greatest possible pleasure,
At any rate nothing wd. give me more pleasure
or be more acceptable to me,
And I shd. like to be party to it, as was promised me,
either as participant or adherent.
As for my service money,
Perhaps you and your father wd. draw it
And send it on to me as quickly as possible.
And tell the *Maestro di pentore*
That there can be no question of
His painting the walls for the moment,
As the mortar is not yet dry
And it wd. be merely work chucked away
> (*buttato via*)

But I want it to be quite clear, that until the chapels are ready
I will arrange for him to paint something else
So that both he and I shall
Get as much enjoyment as possible from it,
And in order that he may enter my service
And also because you write me that he needs cash,
I want to arrange with him to give him so much per year
And to assure him that he will get the sum agreed on.
You may say that I will deposit security
For him wherever he likes.
And let me have a clear answer,
For I mean to give him good treatment
So that he may come to live the rest
Of his life in my lands —
Unless you put him off it —
And for this I mean to make due provision,
So that he can work as he likes,
Or waste his time as he likes
(*affatigandose per suo piacere o no
non gli manchera la provixione mai*)

                                   never lacking provision.

           SIGISMUNDUS PANDOLPHUS DE MALATESTIS
           *In campo Illus. Domini Venetorum die 7
           aprilis 1449 contra Cremonam*

    . . . . . and because the aforesaid most illustrious
Duke of Milan
Is content and wills that the aforesaid Lord Sigismundo
Go into the service of the most magnificent commune
of the Florentines
For alliance defensive of the two states,
Therefore between the aforesaid Illustrious Sigismund
And the respectable man Agnolo della Stufa,
                ambassador, sindic and procurator
Appointed by the ten of the baily, etc., the half

Of these 50,000 florins, free of attainder,
For 1400 cavalry and four hundred foot
To come into the terrene of the commune
                    or elsewhere in Tuscany
As please the ten of the Baily,
And to be himself there with them in the service
of the commune
With his horsemen and his footmen
            (*gente di cavallo e da pie*) etc.
            Aug. 5 1452, *register of the Ten of the Baily.*

From the forked rocks of Penna and Billi, on Carpegna
with the road leading under the cliff,
                    in the wind-shelter into Tuscany,
And the north road, toward the Marecchia
                    the mud-stretch full of cobbles.

Lyra:
" Ye spirits who of olde were in this land
Each under Love, and shaken,
Go with your lutes, awaken
The summer within her mind,
Who hath not Helen for peer
            Yseut nor Batsabe."

With the interruption:
            Magnifico, compater et carissime
            (Johanni di Cosimo)
Venice has taken me on again
            At 7,000 a month, *fiorini di Camera.*
For 2,000 horse and four hundred footmen,
And it rains here by the gallon,
We have had to dig a new ditch.
In three or four days
I shall try to set up the bombards.

Under the plumes, with the flakes and small wads of colour
Showering from the balconies

30

With the sheets spread from windows,
> with leaves and small branches pinned on them,
Arras hung from the railings; out of the dust,
With pheasant tails upright on their forelocks,
> The small white horses, the
Twelve girls riding in order, green satin in pannier'd habits;
Under the baldachino, silver'd with heavy stitches,
Bianca Visconti, with Sforza,
The peasant's son and the duchess,
To Rimini, and to the wars southward,
Boats drawn on the sand, red-orange sails in the creek's mouth,
For two days' pleasure, mostly " *la pesca*," fishing,
Di cui in the which he, Francesco, *godeva molto.*
> To the war southward
In which he, at that time, received an excellent hiding.
And the Greek emperor was in Florence
> (Ferrara having the pest)
And with him Gemisthus Plethon
Talking of the war about the temple at Delphos,
And of POSEIDON, *concret Allgemeine,*
And telling of how Plato went to Dionysius of Syracuse
Because he had observed that tyrants
Were most efficient in all that they set their hands to,
But he was unable to persuade Dionysius
To any amelioration.
And in the gate at Ancona, between the foregate
And the main-gates
Sigismundo, ally, come through an enemy force,
To patch up some sort of treaty, passes one gate
And they shut it before they open the next gate, and he says:
" Now you have me,
> Caught like a hen in a coop."
And the captain of the watch says: " Yes Messire Sigismundo,
But we want this town for ourselves."

With the church against him,
With the Medici bank for itself,
With wattle Sforza against him
Sforza Francesco, wattle-nose,
Who married him (Sigismundo) his (Francesco's)
Daughter in September,
Who stole Pèsaro in October (as Broglio says " *bestialmente* "),
Who stood with the Venetians in November,
With the Milanese in December,
Sold Milan in November, stole Milan in December
Or something of that sort,
Commanded the Milanese in the spring,
    the Venetians at midsummer,
The Milanese in the autumn,
And was Naples' ally in October,
        He, Sigismundo, *templum ædificavit*
In Romagna, teeming with cattle thieves,
        with the game lost in mid-channel,
And never quite lost till' 50,
        and never quite lost till the end, in Romagna,
So that Galeaz sold Pèsaro " to get pay for his cattle."

And Poictiers, you know, Guillaume Poictiers,
        had brought the song up out of Spain
With the singers and viels. But here they wanted a setting,
By Marecchia, where the water comes down over the cobbles
And Mastin had come to Verucchio,
        and the sword, Paolo il Bello's,
        caught in the arras
And, in Este's house, Parisina
Paid
For this tribe paid always, and the house
Called also Atreides',
And the wind is still for a little

And the dusk rolled
        to one side a little
And he was twelve at the time, Sigismundo,
And no dues had been paid for three years,
And his elder brother gone pious;
And that year they fought in the streets,
And that year he got out to Cesena
        And brought back the levies,
And that year he crossed by night over Foglia, and...

IX

One year floods rose,
      One year they fought in the snows,
      One year hail fell, breaking the trees and walls.
      Down here in the marsh they trapped him
in one year,
And he stood in the water up to his neck
      to keep the hounds off him,
And he floundered about in the marsh
      and came in after three days,
That was Astorre Manfredi of Faenza
      who worked the ambush
      and set the dogs off to find him,
In the marsh, down here under Mantua,
And he fought in Fano, in a street fight,
      and that was nearly the end of him;
And the Emperor came down and knighted us,
And they had a wooden castle set up for fiesta,
And one year Basinio went out into the courtyard
      Where the lists were, and the palisades
      had been set for the tourneys,
And he talked down the anti-Hellene,
      And there was an heir male to the seignor,
      And Madame Ginevra died.
And he, Sigismundo, was Capitan for the Venetians.
And he had sold off small castles
      and built the great Rocca to his plan,
And he fought like ten devils at Monteluro
      and got nothing but the victory
And old Sforza bitched us at Pesaro;
      (*sic*) March the 16th:
" that Messire Alessandro Sforza
      is become lord of Pesaro

through the wangle of the Illus. Sgr. Mr. Fedricho d'Orbino
Who worked the wangle with Galeaz
        through the wiggling of Messer Francesco,
Who waggled it so that Galeaz should sell Pesaro
        to Alex and Fossembrone to Feddy;
and he hadn't the right to sell.
And this he did *bestialmente;* that is Sforza did *bestialmente*
as he had promised him, Sigismundo, *per capitoli*
        to see that he, Malatesta, should have Pesaro "
And this cut us off from our south half
        and finished our game, thus, in the beginning,
And he, Sigismundo, spoke his mind to Francesco
        and we drove them out of the Marches.

And the King o' Ragona, Alphonse le roy d'Aragon,
        was the next nail in our coffin,
And all you can say is, anyway,
that he Sigismundo called a town council
And Valturio said " as well for a sheep as a lamb "
        and this change-over (*hæc traditio*)
As old bladder said "*rem eorum saluavit* "
Saved the Florentine state; and that, maybe, was something.
And " Florence our natural ally " as they said in the meeting
        for whatever that was worth afterward.
And he began building the TEMPIO,
        and Polixena, his second wife, died.
And the Venetians sent down an ambassador
And said " speak humanely,
But tell him it's no time for raising his pay."
And the Venetians sent down an ambassador
        with three pages of secret instructions
To the effect: Did he think the campaign was a joy-ride?
And old Wattle-wattle slipped into Milan
But he couldn't stand Sidg being so high with the Venetians
And he talked it over with Feddy; and Feddy said " Pesaro "

35

And old Foscari wrote " *Caro mio*
" If we split with Francesco you can have it
" And we'll help you in every way possible."
But Feddy offered it sooner.
And Sigismundo got up a few arches,
And stole that marble in Classe, " stole " that is,
Casus est talis:
Foscari doge, to the prefect of Ravenna
" Why, what, which, thunder, damnation???? "

Casus est talis:
Filippo, commendatary of the abbazia
Of Sant Apollinaire, Classe, Cardinal of Bologna
That he did one night (*quadam nocte*) sell to the
Illmo D°, D° Sigismund Malatesta
Lord of Arimininum, marble, porphyry, serpentine,
Whose men, Sigismundo's, came with more than an hundred
two wheeled ox carts and deported, for the beautifying
of the *tempio* where was Santa Maria in Trivio
Where the same are now on the walls.   Four hundred
ducats to be paid back to the *abbazia* by the said swindling
Cardinal or his heirs.
grnnh! rrnnh, pthg.
wheels, plaustra, oxen under night-shield,
And on the 13th of August: Aloysius Purtheo,
The next abbot, to Sigismundo, receipt for 200 ducats
Corn-salve for the damage done in that scurry.

And there was the row about that German-Burgundian female
And it was his messianic year, Poliorcetes,
but he was being a bit too POLUMETIS
And the Venetians wouldn't give him six months vacation.

And he went down to the old brick heap of Pesaro
and waited for Feddy

36

And Feddy finally said " I am coming!...
          ... to help Alessandro."
And he said: " This time Mister Feddy has done it."
He said: " Broglio, I'm the goat.   This time
          Mr. Feddy has done it (*m'l'ha calata*)."
And he'd lost his job with the Venetians,
And the stone didn't come in from Istria:
And we sent men to the silk war;
And Wattle never paid up on the nail
          Though we signed on with Milan and Florence;
And he set up the bombards in muck down by Vada
          where nobody else could have set 'em
          and he took the wood out of the bombs
          and made 'em of two scoops of metal
And the jobs getting smaller and smaller,
          Until he signed on with Siena;
          And that time they grabbed his post-bag.
And what was it, anyhow?
          Pitigliano, a man with a ten acre lot,
Two lumps of tufa,
          and they'd taken his pasture land from him,
And Sidg had got back their horses,
          and he had two big lumps of tufa
          with six hundred pigs in the basements.
And the poor devils were dying of cold.
And this is what they found in the post-bag:
          Ex Arimino die xxii Decembris
     " *Magnifice ac potens domine, mi singularissime*
" I advise yr. Lordship how
" I have been with master Alwidge who
" has shown me the design of the nave that goes in the middle,
" of the church and the design for the roof and..."
" JHesus,
" *Magnifico exso.*   Signor Mio
" Sence to-day I am recommended that I have to tel you my

37

"father's opinium that he has shode to Mr. Genare about the
" valts of the cherch... etc ...

"Giovane of Master alwise P. S.   I think it advisabl that
" I shud go to rome to talk to mister Albert so as I can no
" what he thinks about it rite.

" Sagramoro..."

" Illustre signor mio, Messire Battista..."

" First: Ten slabs best red, seven by 15, by one third,
" Eight ditto, good red, 15 by three by one,
" Six of same, 15 by one by one.
" Eight columns 15 by three and one third
               etc... with carriage, danars 151

" MONSEIGNEUR:
    " Madame Isotta has had me write today about Sr. Galeazzo's
" daughter.   The man who said young pullets make thin
" soup, knew what he was talking about.   We went to see the
" girl the other day, for all the good that did, and she denied
" the whole matter and kept her end up without losing her
" temper.   I think Madame Ixotta very nearly exhausted the
" matter. *Mi pare che avea decto hogni chossia.* All the
" children are well.   Where you are everyone is pleased and
" happy because of your taking the chateau here we are the
" reverse as you might say drifting without a rudder.   Madame
" Lucrezia has probably, or should have, written to you, I
" suppose you have the letter by now.   Everyone wants to be
" remembered to you.   21 Dec.   D. de M."

" ... *sagramoro* to put up the derricks.   There is a supply of
" beams at..."

" MAGNIFICENT LORD WITH DUE REVERENCE:
    " Messire Malatesta is well and asks for you every day.   He
" is so much pleased with his pony, It wd. take me a month
" to write you all the fun he gets out of that pony.   I want to
" again remind you to write to Georgio Rambottom or to his

" boss to fix up that wall to the little garden that madame Isotta
" uses, for it is all flat on the ground now as I have already told
" him a lot of times, for all the good that does, so I am writing
" to your lordship in the matter I have done all that I can, for
" all the good that does as noboddy hear can do anything
" without you.
"   " your faithful
LUNARDA DA PALLA.
20 Dec. 1454."

" ... gone over it with all the foremen and engineers. And
" about the silver for the small medal..."

" *Magnifice ac potens*...
"   " because the walls of..."

" *Malatesta de Malatestis ad Magnificum Dominum Patremque*
" *suum*.

" Ex^{so} D^{no} et D^{no} sin D^{no} Sigismundum Pandolfi Filium
"   " Malatestis Capitan General

"Magnificent and Exalted Lord and Father in especial my
" lord with due recommendation: your letter has been pre-
" sented to me by Gentilino da Gradara and with it the bay
" pony (ronzino baiectino) the which you have sent me, and
" which appears in my eyes a fine caparison'd charger, upon
" which I intend to learn all there is to know about riding, in
" consideration of yr. paternal affection for which I thank
" your excellency thus briefly and pray you continue to hold
" me in this esteem notifying you by the bearer of this that
" we are all in good health, as I hope and desire your Ex^{ct}
" Lordship is also: with continued remembrance I remain
"   " Your son and servant
MALATESTA DE MALATESTIS.
*Given in Rimini, this the 22nd day of December
anno domini 1454 "*
(*in the sixth year of his age*)

39

" ILLUSTRIOUS PRINCE:

" Unfitting as it is that I should offer counsels to Hannibal..."

" *Magnifice ac potens domine, domine mi singularissime,* " *humili recomendatione premissa* etc. This to advise your " M^{gt} Ld^{shp} how the second load of Veronese marble has " finally got here, after being held up at Ferrara with no end " of fuss and botheration, the whole of it having been there " unloaded.

" I learned how it happened, and it has cost a few florins to " get back the said load which had been seized for the skipper's " debt and defalcation; he having fled when the lighter was " seized. But that Y^r M^{gt} Ld^{shp} may not lose the moneys " paid out on his account I have had the lighter brought here " and am holding it, against his arrival. If not we still have " the lighter.

" As soon as the Xmas fêtes are over I will have the stone " floor laid in the sacresty, for which the stone is already cut. " The wall of the building is finished and I shall now get the " roof on.

" We have not begun putting new stone into the martyr " chapel; first because the heavy frosts wd. certainly spoil " the job; secondly because the aliofants aren't yet here and " one can't get the measurements for the cornice to the columns " that are to rest on the aliofants.

" They are doing the stairs to your room in the castle... I " have had Messire Antonio degli Atti's court paved and the " stone benches put in it.

" Ottavian is illuminating the bull. I mean the bull for " the chapel. All the stone-cutters are waiting for spring " weather to start work again.

" The tomb is all done except part of the lid, and as soon as " Messire Agostino gets back from Cesena I will see that he " finishes it, ever recommending me to y^r M^{gt} Ld^{shp}

" believe me y^r faithful
PETRUS GENARIIS."

That's what they found in the post-bag
And some more of it to the effect that
       he " lived and ruled "

" *et amava perdutamente Ixotta degli Atti* "
e " *ne fu degna* "
        " *constans in proposito*
" *Placuit oculis principis*
" *pulchra aspectu* "
" *populo grata* (*Italiaeque decus*)
" and built a temple so full of pagan works "
       i. e. Sigismund
and in the style " Past ruin'd Latium "
The filigree hiding the gothic,
       with a touch of rhetoric in the whole
And the old sarcophagi,
       such as lie, smothered in grass, by San Vitale.

X

AND the poor devils dying of cold, outside Sorano,
And from the other side, from inside the château,
Orsini, Count Pitigliano, on the 17th of November:
"Siggy, darlint, wd. you not stop making war on
"insensible objects, such as trees and domestic vines, that have
"no means to hit back... but if you will hire yourself out to a
"commune (Siena) which you ought rather to rule than
"serve..."
                which with Trachulo's damn'd epistle...
And what of it *any*how? a man with a ten acre lot,
Pitigliano... a lump of tufa,
                And S. had got back their horses
And the poor devils dying of cold...
(And there was another time, you know,
He signed on with the Fanesi,
                and just couldn't be bothered...)
And there were three men on a one man job
                And Careggi wanting the baton,
And not getting it just then in any case.

And he, Sigismundo, refused an invitation to lunch
                In commemoration of Carmagnola
                (vide Venice, between the two columns
                where Carmagnola was executed.)
                Et
                "*anno messo a saccho el signor Sigismundo*"
As Filippo Strozzi wrote to Zan Lottieri, then in Naples,
                "I think they'll let him through at Campiglia"

                Florence, Archivio Storico, 4th Series t. iii, e
                "*La Guerra dei Senesi col conte di Pitigliano.*"

And he found Carlo Gonzaga sitting like a mud-frog
                in Orbetello

42

And he said:
　　　" *Caro mio,* I can not receive you
It really *is* not the moment."
And Broglio says he ought to have tipped Gorro Lolli.
But he got back home here somehow,
And Piccinino was out of a job,
And the old row with Naples continued.

And what he said was all right in Mantua;
And Borso had the pair of them up to Bel Fiore,
The pair of them, Sigismundo and Federico Urbino,
Or perhaps in the palace, Ferrara, Sigismund upstairs
And Urbino's gang in the basement,
And a regiment of guards in, to keep order,
　　　For all the good that did:
" *Te cavero la budella del corpo!* "
El conte levatosi:
　　　" *Io te cavero la corata a te!* "
And that day Cosimo smiled,
That is, the day they said:
　　　" Drusiana is to marry Count Giacomo..."
(Piccinino) *un sorriso malizioso.*
Drusiana, another of Franco Sforza's;
It would at least keep the row out of Tuscany.
And he fell out of a window, Count Giacomo,
Three days after his death, that was years later in Naples,
For trusting Ferdinando of Naples,
And old Wattle could do nothing about it.

　　　　Et:

. . . .

INTEREA PRO GRADIBUS BASILICAE S. PIETRI EX ARIDA MATERIA
INGENS PYRA EXTRUITUR IN CUJUS SUMMITATE IMAGO SIGIS-
MUNDI COLLOCATUR HOMINIS LINEAMENTA, ET VESTIMENTI
MODUM ADEO PROPRIE REDDENS, UT VERA MAGIS PERSONA,
QUAM IMAGO VIDERETUR; NE QUEM TAMEN IMAGO FALLERET,

ET SCRIPTURA EX ORE PRODIIT, QUAE DICERET:
     SIGISMUNDUS HIC EGO SUM
MALATESTA, FILIUS PANDULPHI, REX PRODITORUM,
DEO ATQUE HOMINIBUS INFESTUS, SACRI CENSURA SENATUS
IGNI DAMNATUS;

               SCRIPTURAM

MULTI LEGERUNT. DEINDE ASTANTE POPULO, IGNE IMMISSO,
ET PYRA SIMULACRUM REPENTE FLAGRAVIT.

           Com. Pio II, Liv. VII, p. 85.
           Yriarte, p. 288.

. . . .

So that in the end that pot-scraping little runt Andreas
      Benzi, da Siena
Got up to spout out the bunkum
That that monstrous swollen, swelling s. o. b.
      Papa Pio Secundo
      Æneas Silvius Piccolomini
      da Siena
Had told him to spout, in their best bear's-greased latinity;

Stupro, cæde, adulter,
homocidia, parricidia ac periurus,
presbitericidia, audax, libidinosus,
wives, jew-girls, nuns, necrophiliast, *fornicarium ac sicarium,*
proditor, raptor, incestuosus, incendiarius, ac
concubinarius,
and that he rejected the whole symbol of the apostles,
and that he said the monks ought not to own property
and that he disbelieved in the temporal power,
neither christian, jew, gentile,
      nor any sect pagan, *nisi forsitan epicureæ.*

And that he did among other things
Empty the fonts of the chiexa of holy water
And fill up the same full with ink

That he might in God's dishonour
Stand before the doors of the said chiexa
Making mock of the inky faithful, they
Issuing thence by the doors in the pale light of the sunrise
Which might be considered youthful levity
            but was really a profound indication;

" Whence that his, Sigismundo's, fœtor filled the earth
And stank up through the air and stars to heaven
Where — save they were immune from sufferings —
It had made the emparadisèd spirits pewk "
            from their jeweled terrace.

" *Lussurioso incestuoso, perfide, sozzure ac crapulone,*
assassino, ingordo, avaro, superbo, infidele
fattore di monete false, sodomitico, uxoricido "

and the whole lump lot
given over to...

I mean after Pio had said, or at least Pio says that he
Said that this was elegant oratory " *Orationem*
Elegantissimam et ornatissimam
Audivimus venerabilis in Xti fratres ac dilectissimi
filii... (stone in his bladder
            testibus idoneis)
The lump lot given over
To that kid-slapping fanatic il cardinale di San Pietro in Vincoli
            To find him guilty, of the lump lot
As he duly did, calling rumour, and Messire Federico d'Urbino
And other equally unimpeachable witnesses.

So they burnt our brother in effigy
A rare magnificent effigy costing 8 florins 48 bol
(i.e. for the pair, as the first one wasn't a good enough likeness)
And Borso said the time was ill-suited
            to *tanta novità,* such doings or innovations,

45

God's enemy and man's enemy, *stuprum, raptum*
   I. N. R. I. Sigismund Imperator, Rex Proditorum.

And old Pills who tried to get him into a front rank action
In order to drive the rear guard at his buttocks,
Old Pills listed among the murdered, although he
Came out of jail living later.

Et les angloys ne povans desraciner... venin de hayne
Had got back Gisors from the Angevins,

And the Angevins were gunning after Naples
And we dragged in the Angevins,
And we dragged in Louis Eleventh,
And the *tiers Calixte* was dead, and Alfonso;
And against us we had " this Æneas " and young Ferdinando
That we had smashed at Piombino and driven out of the
Terrene of the Florentines;
And Piccinino, out of a job;
And he, Sidg, had had three chances of
Making it up with Alfonso, and an offer of
Marriage alliance;

And what he said was all right there in Mantua;
But Pio, sometime or other, Pio lost his pustulous temper.
And they struck alum at Tolfa, in the pope's land,
   To pay for their devilment.
And Francesco said:
   I also have suffered.
When you take it, give me a slice.
   And they nearly jailed a chap for saying
The job was *mal hecho;* and they caught poor old Pasti
In Venice, and were like to pull all his teeth out;
And they had a bow-shot at Borso
As he was going down the Grand Canal in his gondola
   (the nice kind with 26 barbs on it)

46

And they said: Novvy'll sell any man
       for the sake of Count Giacomo.
(Piccinino, the one that fell out of the window).

And they came at us with their ecclesiastical legates
Until the eagle lit on his tent pole.
And he said: The Romans would have called that an augury
E gradment li antichi cavaler romanj
       davano fed a quisti annutii,
All I want you to do is to follow the orders,
They've got a bigger army,
       but there are more men in this camp.

XI

EGRADMENT *li antichi cavaler romanj*
          davano fed a quisti annutii
          And he put us under the chiefs,
          and the chiefs went back to their squadrons:
Bernardo Reggio, Nic Benzo, Giovan Nestorno,
Paulo Viterbo, Buardino of Brescia,
          Cetho Brandolino,
And Simone Malespina, Petracco Saint Archangelo,
Rioberto da Canossa,
And for the tenth Agniolo da Roma
          And that gay bird Piero della Bella,
And to the eleventh Roberto,
And the papishes were three thousand on horses,
dilly cavalli tre milia,
And a thousand on foot,
And the Lord Sigismundo had but mille tre cento cavalli
And hardly 500 fanti (and one spingard),
And we beat the papishes and fought
them back through the tents
And he came up to the dyke again
And fought through the dyke-gate
And it went on from dawn to sunset
And we broke them and took their baggage
          and mille cinquecento cavalli
E li homini di Messire Sigismundo
non furono che mille trecento

And the Venetians sent in their compliments
And various and sundry sent in their compliments;
But we got it next August;
And Roberto got beaten at Fano,
And he went by ship to Tarentum,

I mean Sidg went to Tarentum
And he found 'em, the anti-Aragons,
           busted and weeping into their beards.
And they, the papishes, came up to the walls,
And that nick-nosed s.o.b. Feddy Urbino
Said: " *Par che è fuor di questo... Sigis... mundo.*" "
" They say he dodders about the streets
" And can put his hand to neither one thing nor the other,"
And he was in the sick wards, and on the high tower
And everywhere, keeping us at it.
And, thank God, they got the sickness outside
As we had the sickness inside,
And they had neither town nor castello
But dey got de mos' bloody rottenes' peace on us —
Quali lochi sono questi:
           Sogliano,
Torrano and La Serra, Sbrigara, San Martino,
Ciola, Pondo, Spinello, Cigna and Buchio,
Prataline, Monte Cogruzzo,
           and the villa at Rufiano
Right up to the door-yard
And anything else the Rev^{mo} Monsignore could remember.
And the water-rights on the Savio.
(And the salt heaps with the reed mats on them
           Gone long ago to the Venetians)
And when lame Novvy died, they got even Cesena.

And he wrote to young Piero:
           Send me a couple of huntin' dogs,
They may take my mind off it.
And one day he was sitting in the chiexa,
On a bit of cornice, a bit of stone grooved for a cornice,
Too narrow to fit his big beam,
           hunched up and noting what was done wrong,

And an old woman came in and giggled to see him
          sitting there in the dark
She nearly fell over him,
          And he thought:
Old Zuliano is finished,
If he's left anything we must see the kids get it,
Write that to Robert.
And Vanni must give that peasant a decent price for his horses,
Say that I will refund.

And the writs run in Fano,
For the long room over the arches
Sub annulo piscatoris, palatium seu curiam OLIM *de Malatestis.*
Gone, and Cesena, Zezena *d'''e b'''e colonne,*
And the big diamond pawned in Venice,
And he gone out into Morea,
Where they sent him to do in the Mo'ammeds,
With 5,000 against 25,000,
          and he nearly died out in Sparta,
Morea, Lakedæmon,
          and came back with no pep in him
And we sit here.   I have sat here
          For forty four thousand years,
And they trapped him down here in the marsh land,
          in '46 that was;
And the poor devils dying of cold, that was Rocca Sorano;
And he said in his young youth:
          Vogliamo,
che le donne, we will that they, *le donne,* go ornate,
As be their pleasure, for the city's glory thereby.

And Platina said afterward,
          when they jailed him
And the Accademia Romana,
For singing to Zeus in the catacombs,

Yes, I saw him when he was down here
Ready to murder fatty Barbo, "Formosus,"
And they want to know what we talked about?
          " *de litteris et de armis, praestantibusque ingeniis,*
Both of ancient times and our own; books, arms,
And of men of unusual genius,
Both of ancient times and our own, in short the usual subjects
Of conversation between intelligent men."

And he with his luck gone out of him
64 lances in his company, and his pay 8,000 a *year,*
64 and no more, and he not to try to get any more
And all of it down on paper
sexaginta quatuor nec tentatur habere plures
But leave to keep 'em in Rimini
          i.e. to watch the Venetians.

Damn pity he didn't
          (i.e. get the knife into him)
Little fat squab " Formosus "
Barbo said " Call me Formosus "
But the conclave wouldn't have it
          and they called him Paolo Secondo.

And he left three horses at one gate
          And three horses at the other,
And Fatty received him
          with a guard of seven cardinals " whom he could trust."
And the castelan of Montefiore wrote down,
" You'd better keep him out of the district.
" When he got back here from Sparta, the people
" Lit fires, and turned out yelling: ' PANDOLFO '! "

In the gloom, the gold gathers the light against it.

And one day he said: Henry, you can have it,
On condition, you can have it: for four months
You'll stand any reasonable joke that I play on you,
And you can joke back
              provided you don't get too ornry.
And they put it all down in writing:
For a green cloak with silver brocade
Actum in Castro Sigismundo, presente Roberto de Valturibus
.. sponte et ex certa scienta... to Enricho de Aquabello.

XII

AND we sit here
            under the wall,
            Arena romana, Diocletian's, les gradins
            quarante-trois rangées en calcaire.
Baldy Bacon
            bought all the little copper pennies in Cuba:
Un centavo, dos centavos,
            told his peons to " bring 'em in."
" Bring 'em to the main shack," said Baldy,
And the peons brought 'em;
" to the main shack brought 'em,"
As Henry would have said.
            Nicholas Castano in Habana,
He also had a few centavos, but the others
Had to pay a percentage.
            Percentage when they wanted centavos,
Public centavos.
            Baldy's interest
Was in money business.
            " No interest in any other kind uv bisnis,"
Said Baldy.
            Sleeping with two buck niggers chained to him,
Guardia regia, chained to his waist
To keep 'em from slipping off in the night;
Being by now unpopular with the Cubans;
            By fever reduced to lbs. 108.
Returned to Manhattan, ultimately to Manhattan.
24 E. 47th, when I met him,
Doing job printing, i.e., agent,
            going to his old acquaintances,
His office in Nassau St., distributing jobs to the printers,

Commercial stationery,
            and later, insurance,
Employers' liability,
            odd sorts of insurance,
Fire on brothels, etc., commission,
Rising from 15 dollars a week,
            Pollon d'anthropon iden,
Knew which shipping companies were most careless;
            where a man was most likely
To lose a leg in bad hoisting machinery;
Also fire, as when passing a whore-house,
Arrived, miraculous Hermes, by accident,
Two minutes after the proprietor's *angelos*
Had been sent for him.
Saved his people 11,000 in four months
            on that Cuba job,
But they busted,
Also ran up to 40,000 bones on his own,
    Once, but wanted to " eat up the whole'r Wall St."
And dropped it all three weeks later.
Habitat cum Quade, damn good fellow,
Mons Quade who wore a monocle on a wide sable ribbon.
            (Elsewhere recorded).
Dos Santos, José Maria dos Santos,
Hearing that a grain ship
Was wrecked in the estuary of the Tagus,
Bought it at auction, nemo obstabat,
No one else bidding. " Damn fool! " " Maize
Spoiled with salt water,
No use, can't do anything with it." Dos Santos.
All the stuff rotted with sea water.
Dos Santos Portuguese lunatic bought it,
Mortgaged then all his patrimony,
            e tot lo sieu aver,
And bought sucking pigs, pigs, small pigs,

54

Porkers, throughout all Portugal,
          fed on the cargo,
First lot mortgaged to buy the second lot, undsoweiter,
Porkers of Portugal,
          fattening with the fulness of time,
And Dos Santos fattened, a great landlord of Portugal
Now gathered to his fathers.
          Did it on water-soaked corn.
(Water probably fresh in that estuary)
Go to hell Apovitch, Chicago aint the whole punkin.
     Jim X...
          in a bankers' meeting,
          bored with their hard luck stories,
Bored with their bloomin' primness
          and the little white rims
They wore around inside the edge of their vests
To make 'em look as if they had on two waistcoats,
Told 'em the Tale of the Honest Sailor.
Bored with their proprieties,
          as they sat, the ranked presbyterians,
Directors, dealers through holding companies,
Deacons in churches, owning slum properties,
Alias usurers in excelsis,
          the quintessential essence of usurers,
The purveyors of employment, whining over their 20 p. c.
          and the hard times,
And the bust-up of Brazilian securities
          (S. A. securities),
And the general uncertainty of all investment
Save investment in new bank buildings,
          productive of bank buildings,
And not likely to ease distribution,
Bored with the way their mouths twitched
          over their cigar-ends,

Said Jim X... :
There once was a pore honest sailor, a heavy drinker,
A hell of a cuss, a rowster, a boozer, and
The drink finally sent him to hospital,
And they operated, and there was a poor whore in
The woman's ward had a kid, while
They were fixing the sailor, and they brought him the kid
When he came to, and said:
   " Here! this is what we took out of you."

An' he looked at it, an' he got better,
And when he left the hospital, quit the drink,
And when he was well enough
   signed on with another ship
And saved up his pay money,
   and kept on savin' his pay money,
And bought a share in the ship,
   and finally had half shares,
Then a ship
   and in time a whole line of steamers;
And educated the kid,
   and when the kid was in college,
The ole sailor was again taken bad
   and the doctors said he was dying,
And the boy came to the bedside,
   and the old sailor said:
" Boy, I'm sorry I can't hang on a bit longer,
" You're young yet.
   I leave you re-sponsa-bilities.
" Wish I could ha' waited till you were older,
" More fit to take over the bisness..."
   " But, father,
" Don't, don't talk about me, I'm all right,
" It's you, father."
   " That's it, boy, you said it.

" You called me your father, and I ain't.
" I ain't your dad, no,
" I am not your fader but your moder," quod he,
" Your fader was a rich merchant in Stambouli."

XIII

KUNG walked
             by the dynastic temple
         and into the cedar grove,
                 and then out by the lower river,
And with him Khieu, Tchi
             and Tian the low speaking
And " we are unknown," said Kung,
" You will take up charioteering?
             Then you will become known,
" Or perhaps I should take up charioteering, or archery?
" Or the practice of public speaking? "
And Tseu-lou said, " I would put the defences in order,"
And Khieu said, " If I were lord of a province
I would put it in better order than this is."
And Tchi said, " I would prefer a small mountain temple,
" With order in the observances,
             with a suitable performance of the ritual,"
And Tian said, with his hand on the strings of his lute
The low sounds continuing
             after his hand left the strings,
And the sound went up like smoke, under the leaves,
And he looked after the sound:
             " The old swimming hole,
" And the boys flopping off the planks,
" Or sitting in the underbrush playing mandolins."
             And Kung smiled upon all of them equally.
And Thseng-sie desired to know:
             " Which had answered correctly? "
And Kung said, " They have all answered correctly,
" That is to say, each in his nature."
And Kung raised his cane against Yuan Jang,
             Yuan Jang being his elder,

For Yuan Jang sat by the roadside pretending to
            be receiving wisdom.
And Kung said
            " You old fool, come out of it,
Get up and do something useful."
            And Kung said
" Respect a child's faculties
" From the moment it inhales the clear air,
" But a man of fifty who knows nothing
            Is worthy of no respect."
And " When the prince has gathered about him
" All the savants and artists, his riches will be fully employed."
And Kung said, and wrote on the bo leaves:
            If a man have not order within him
He can not spread order about him;
And if a man have not order within him
His family will not act with due order;
            And if the prince have not order within him
He can not put order in his dominions.
And Kung gave the words " order "
and " brotherly deference "
And said nothing of the " life after death."
And he said
            " Anyone can run to excesses,
It is easy to shoot past the mark,
It is hard to stand firm in the middle."

And they said: If a man commit murder
            Should his father protect him, and hide him?
And Kung said:
            He should hide him.

And Kung gave his daughter to Kong-Tch'ang
            Although Kong-Tch'ang was in prison.
And he gave his niece to Nan-Young
            although Nan-Young was out of office.

And Kung said " Wan ruled with moderation,
                In his day the State was well kept,
And even I can remember
A day when the historians left blanks in their writings,
I mean for things they didn't know,
But that time seems to be passing."
And Kung said, " Without character you will
                be unable to play on that instrument
Or to execute the music fit for the Odes.
The blossoms of the apricot
                blow from the east to the west,
And I have tried to keep them from falling."

XIV

Io venni in luogo d'ogni luce muto;
    The stench of wet coal, politicians
. . . . e and . . . . . n, their wrists bound to
      their ankles,
Standing bare bum,
Faces smeared on their rumps,
      wide eye on flat buttock,
Bush hanging for beard,
    Addressing crowds through their arse-holes,
Addressing the multitudes in the ooze,
      newts, water-slugs, water-maggots,
And with them . . . . . . r,
      a scrupulously clean table-napkin
Tucked under his penis,
      and . . . . m
Who disliked colloquial language,
Stiff-starched, but soiled, collars
      circumscribing his legs,
The pimply and hairy skin
      pushing over the collar's edge,
Profiteers drinking blood sweetened with sh-t,
And behind them . . . . . . f and the financiers
      lashing them with steel wires.

And the betrayers of language
      . . . . . . n and the press gang
And those who had lied for hire;
the perverts, the perverters of language,
      the perverts, who have set money-lust
Before the pleasures of the senses;

howling, as of a hen-yard in a printing-house,
      the clatter of presses,

the blowing of dry dust and stray paper,
fœtor, sweat, the stench of stale oranges,
dung, last cess-pool of the universe,
mysterium, acid of sulphur,
the pusillanimous, raging;
plunging jewels in mud,
                and howling to find them unstained;
sadic mothers driving their daughters to bed with decrepitude,
sows eating their litters,
and here the placard ΕΙΚΩΝ ΓΗΣ,
            and here: THE PERSONNEL CHANGES,

melting like dirty wax,
                decayed candles, the bums sinking lower,
faces submerged under hams,
And in the ooze under them,
reversed, foot-palm to foot-palm,
                hand-palm to hand-palm, the agents provocateurs
The murderers of Pearse and MacDonagh,
                Captain H. the chief torturer;
The petrified turd that was Verres,
                bigots, Calvin and St. Clement of Alexandria!
black-beetles, burrowing into the sh-t,
The soil a decrepitude, the ooze full of morsels,
lost contours, erosions.

                Above the hell-rot
the great arse-hole,
                broken with piles,
hanging stalactites,
                greasy as sky over Westminster,
the invisible, many English,
                the place lacking in interest,
last squalor, utter decrepitude,

the vice-crusaders, fahrting through silk,
        waving the Christian symbols,
. . . . frigging a tin penny whistle,
Flies carrying news, harpies dripping sh-t through the air,

The slough of unamiable liars,
        bog of stupidities,
malevolent stupidities, and stupidities,
the soil living pus, full of vermin,
dead maggots begetting live maggots,
        slum owners,
usurers squeezing crab-lice, pandars to authority,
pets-de-loup, sitting on piles of stone books,
obscuring the texts with philology,
        hiding them under their persons,
the air without refuge of silence,
        the drift of lice, teething,
and above it the mouthing of orators,
        the arse-belching of preachers.
        And Invidia,
the corruptio, fœtor, fungus,
liquid animals, melted ossifications,
slow rot, fœtid combustion,
    chewed cigar-butts, without dignity, without tragedy,
. . . . .m Episcopus, waving a condom full of black-beetles,
monopolists, obstructors of knowledge,
        obstructors of distribution.

XV

THE saccharescent, lying in glucose,
    the pompous in cotton wool
            with a stench like the fats at Grasse,
    the great scabrous arse-hole, sh-tting flies,
            rumbling with imperialism,
ultimate urinal, middan, pisswallow without a cloaca,
. . . . . . r less rowdy, ... Episcopus
        . . . . sis,
            head down, screwed into the swill,
his legs waving and pustular,
            a clerical jock strap hanging back over the navel
his condom full of black beetles,
            tattoo marks round the anus,
and a circle of lady golfers about him.

the courageous violent
            slashing themselves with knives,
the cowardly inciters to violence
. . . . . n and. . . . . . .h eaten by weevils,
. . . . ll like a swollen fœtus,
            the beast with a hundred legs, USURA
and the swill full of respecters,
            bowing to the lords of the place,
explaining its advantages,
            and the laudatores temporis acti
claiming that the sh-t used to be blacker and richer
and the fabians crying for the petrification of putrefaction,
for a new dung-flow cut in lozenges,
the conservatives chatting,
            distinguished by gaiters of slum-flesh,
and the back-scratchers in a great circle,
            complaining of insufficient attention,

the search without end, counterclaim for the missing scratch
the litigious,
a green bile-sweat, the news owners, ... s
        the anonymous
. . . . ffe, broken
        his head shot like a cannon-ball toward the glass gate,
peering through it an instant,
        falling back to the trunk, epileptic,
et nulla fidentia inter eos,
        all with their twitching backs,
with daggers, and bottle ends, waiting an
        unguarded moment;

a stench, stuck in the nostrils;
beneath one
        nothing that might not move,
mobile earth, a dung hatching obscenities,
        inchoate error,
boredom born out of boredom,
british weeklies, copies of the . . . . c,
a multiple . . . . . . nn,
and I said, " How is it done? "
        and my guide:
This sort breeds by scission,
This is the fourmillionth tumour.
In this *bolge* bores are gathered,
Infinite pus flakes, scabs of a lasting pox.

skin-flakes, repetitions, erosions,
endless rain from the arse-hairs,
as the earth moves, the centre
      passes over all parts in succession,
a continual bum-belch
       distributing its productions.

Andiamo!
>One's feet sunk,
the welsh of mud gripped one, no hand-rail,
the bog-suck like a whirl-pool,
and he said:
>>Close the pores of your feet!
And my eyes clung to the horizon,
>>oil mixing with soot;
and again Plotinus:
>>To the door,
Keep your eyes on the mirror.
Prayed we to the Medusa,
>>petrifying the soil by the shield,
Holding it downward
>>he hardened the track
Inch before us, by inch,
>>the matter resisting,
The heads rose from the shield,
>>hissing, held downwards.
Devouring maggots,
>>the face only half potent,
The serpents' tongues
>>grazing the swill top,
Hammering the souse into hardness,
>>the narrow rast,
Half the width of a sword's edge.
>>By this through the dern evil,
now sinking, now clinging,
>>Holding the unsinkable shield.
Oblivion,
>>forget how long,
sleep, fainting nausea.
>>" Whether in Naishapur or Babylon "
I heard in the dream.
>>Plotinus gone,

And the shield tied under me, woke;
The gate swung on its hinges;
Panting like a sick dog, staggered,
Bathed in alkali, and in acid.
Ἠέλιον τ' Ἠέλιον
      blind with the sunlight,
Swollen-eyed, rested,
      lids sinking, darkness unconscious.

XVI

AND before hell mouth; dry plain
            and two mountains;
        On the one mountain, a running form,
            and another
In the turn of the hill; in hard steel
The road like a slow screw's thread,
The angle almost imperceptible,
        so that the circuit seemed hardly to rise;
And the running form, naked, Blake,
Shouting, whirling his arms, the swift limbs,
Howling against the evil,
        his eyes rolling,
Whirling like flaming cart-wheels,
        and his head held backward to gaze on the evil
As he ran from it,
        to be hid by the steel mountain,
And when he showed again from the north side;
        his eyes blazing toward hell mouth,
His neck forward,
        and like him Peire Cardinal.
And in the west mountain, Il Fiorentino,
Seeing hell in his mirror,
        and lo Sordels
Looking on it in his shield;
And Augustine, gazing toward the invisible.

And past them, the criminal
        lying in blue lakes of acid,
The road between the two hills, upward
        slowly,
The flames patterned in lacquer, crimen est actio,
The limbo of chopped ice and saw-dust,

And I bathed myself with the acid to free myself
         of the hell ticks,
Scales, fallen louse eggs.
         Palux Laerna,
the lake of bodies, aqua morta,
of limbs fluid, and mingled, like fish heaped in a bin,
and here an arm upward, clutching a fragment of marble,
And the embryos, in flux,
         new inflow, submerging,
Here an arm upward, trout, submerged by the eels;
         and from the bank, the stiff herbage
the dry nobbled path, saw many known, and unknown,
for an instant;
         submerging,
The face gone, generation.

         Then light air, under saplings,
the blue banded lake under æther,
         an oasis, the stones, the calm field,
the grass quiet,
         and passing the tree of the bough
The grey stone posts,
         and the stair of gray stone,
the passage clean-squared in granite:
         descending,
and I through this, and into the earth,
         patet terra,
entered the quiet air
         the new sky,
the light as after a sun-set,
         and by their fountains, the heroes,
Sigismundo, and Malatesta Novello,
         and founders, gazing at the mounts of their cities.

The plain, distance, and in fount-pools
         the nymphs of that water

rising, spreading their garlands,
        weaving their water reeds with the boughs,
In the quiet,
        and now one man rose from his fountain
and went off into the plain.

Prone in that grass, in sleep;
        et j'entendis des voix:...
                       wall . . . Strasbourg
Galliffet led that triple charge. . . Prussians
and he said   [*Plarr's narration*]
        it was for the honour of the army.
And they called him a swashbuckler.
        I didn't know what it was
But I thought: This is pretty bloody damn fine.
And my old nurse, he was a man nurse, and
He killed a Prussian and he lay in the street
there in front of our house for three days
And he stank. . . . . . .
        Brother Percy,
And our Brother Percy...
        old Admiral
He was a middy in those days,
And they came into Ragusa
. . . . . . place those men went for the Silk War. . . . .
And they saw a procession coming down through
A cut in the hills, carrying something
The six chaps in front carrying a long thing
        on their shoulders,
And they thought it was a funeral,
        but the thing was wrapped up in scarlet,
And he put off in the cutter,
        he was a middy in those days,
To see what the natives were doing,
And they got up to the six fellows in livery,

70

And they looked at it, and I can still hear the old admiral,
" Was it? it was
Lord Byron
Dead drunk, with the face of an A y n . . . .
He pulled it out long, like that:
the face of an a y n . . . . gel."

And because that son of a bitch,
Franz Josef of Austria. . . . . .
And because that son of a bitch Napoléon Barbiche...
They put Aldington on Hill 70, in a trench
dug through corpses
With a lot of kids of sixteen,
Howling and crying for their mamas,
And he sent a chit back to his major:
I can hold out for ten minutes
With my sergeant and a machine-gun.
And they rebuked him for levity.
And Henri Gaudier went to it,
and they killed him,
And killed a good deal of sculpture,
And ole T.E.H. he went to it,
With a lot of books from the library,
London Library, and a shell buried 'em in a dug-out,
And the Library expressed its annoyance.
And a bullet hit him on the elbow
...gone through the fellow in front of him,
And he read Kant in the Hospital, in Wimbledon,
in the original,
And the hospital staff didn't like it.

And Wyndham Lewis went to it,
With a heavy bit of artillery,
and the airmen came by with a mitrailleuse,
And cleaned out most of his company,
and a shell lit on his tin hut,

While he was out in the privvy,
        and he was all there was left of'that outfit.

Windeler went to it,
        and he was out in the Ægæan,
And down in the hold of his ship
        pumping gas into a sausage,
And the boatswain looked over the rail,
        down into amidships, and he said:
        Gees! look a' the Kept'n,
The Kept'n's a-gettin' 'er up.

And Ole Captain Baker went to it,
        with his legs full of rheumatics,
So much so he couldn't run,
        so he was six months in hospital,
Observing the mentality of the patients.

And Fletcher was 19 when he went to it,
And his major went mad in the control pit,
    about midnight, and started throwing the 'phone about
And he had to keep him quiet
        till about six in the morning,
And direct that bunch of artillery.

And Ernie Hemingway went to it,
        too much in a hurry,
And they buried him for four days.

Et ma foi, vous savez,
        tous les nerveux. Non,
Y a une limite; les bêtes, les bêtes ne sont
Pas faites pour ça, c'est peu de chose un cheval.
Les hommes de 34 ans à quatre pattes
        qui criaient " maman." Mais les costauds,
La fin, là à Verdun, n'y avait que ces gros bonshommes
        Et y voyaient extrêmement clair.

Qu'est-ce que ça vaut, les généraux, le lieutenant,
on les pèse à un centigramme,
        n'y a rien que du bois,
Notr' capitaine, tout, tout ce qu'il y a de plus renfermé
        de vieux polytechnicien, mais solide,
La tête solide.   Là, vous savez,
Tout, tout fonctionne, et les voleurs, tous les vices,
Mais les rapaces,
        y avait trois dans notre compagnie, tous tués.
Y sortaient fouiller un cadavre, pour rien,
        y n'seraient sortis pour rien que ça.
Et les boches, tout ce que vous voulez,
        militarisme, et cætera, et cætera.
Tout ça, mais, MAIS,
        l'français, i s'bat quand y a mangé.
Mais ces pauvres types
A la fin y s'attaquaient pour manger,
        Sans ordres, les bêtes sauvages, on y fait
Prisonniers; ceux qui parlaient français disaient:
        " Poo quah?   Ma foi on attaquait pour manger."

C'est le corr-ggras, le corps gras,
        leurs trains marchaient trois kilomètres à l'heure,
Et ça criait, ça grincait, on l'entendait à cinq kilomètres.
(Ça qui finit la guerre.)

        Liste officielle des morts 5,000,000.

I vous dit, bè, voui, tout sentait le pétrole.
Mais, Non! je l'ai engueulé.
Je lui ai dit: T'es un con!   T'a raté la guerre.

O voui! tous les hommes de goût, y conviens,
Tout ça en arrière.
        Mais un mec comme toi!

C't homme, un type comme ça!
            Ce qu'il aurait pu encaisser!
Il était dans une fabrique.
What, burying squad, terrassiers, avec leur tête
            en arrière, qui regardaient comme ça,
On risquait la vie pour un coup de pelle,
Faut que ça soit bien carré, exact...

Dey vus a bolcheviki dere, und dey dease him:
Looka vat youah Trotzsk is done, e iss
            madeh deh zhamefull beace!!
" He iss madeh deh zhamefull beace, iss he?
            " He is madeh de zhamevul beace?
" A Brest-Litovsk, yess? Aint yuh herd?
            " He vinneh de vore.
" De droobs iss released vrom de eastern vront, yess?
" Un venn dey getts to deh vestern vront, iss it
            " How many getts dere?
" And dose doat getts dere iss so full off revolutions
" Venn deh vrench is come dhru, yess,
" Dey say, " Vot? " Un de posch say:
            " Aint yeh heard? Say, ve got a rheffolution."

That's the trick with a crowd,
            Get 'em into the street and get 'em moving.
And all the time, there were people going
Down there, over the river.

        There was a man there talking,
To a thousand, just a short speech, and
Then move 'em on. And he said:
Yes, these people, they are all right, they
Can do everything, everything except act;
And go an' hear 'em, but when they are through,
Come to the bolsheviki...

And when it broke, there was the crowd there,
And the cossacks, just as always before,
But one thing, the cossacks said:
   " Pojalouista."
And that got round in the crowd,
And then a lieutenant of infantry
Ordered 'em to fire into the crowd,
   in the square at the end of the Nevsky,
In front of the Moscow station,
And they wouldn't,
And he pulled his sword on a student for laughing,
And killed him,
And a cossack rode out of his squad
On the other side of the square
And cut down the lieutenant of infantry
And that was the revolution...
   as soon as they named it.

And you can't make 'em,
Nobody knew it was coming. They were all ready, the old gang,
Guns on the top of the post-office and the palace,
But none of the leaders knew it was coming.

And there were some killed at the barracks,
But that was between the troops.

So we used to hear it at the opera,
That they wouldn't be under Haig;
   and that the advance was beginning;
That it was going to begin in a week.

XVII

So that the vines burst from my fingers
        And the bees weighted with pollen
        Move heavily in the vine-shoots:
            chirr — chirr — chir-rikk — a purring sound,
And the birds sleepily in the branches.
                ZAGREUS! IO ZAGREUS!
With the first pale-clear of the heaven
And the cities set in their hills,
And the goddess of the fair knees
Moving there, with the oak-woods behind her,
The green slope, with white hounds
                leaping about her;
And thence down to the creek's mouth, until evening,
Flat water before me,
                and the trees growing in water,
Marble trunks out of stillness,
On past the palazzi,
                    in the stillness,
The light now, not of the sun.
                    Chrysophrase,
And the water green clear, and blue clear;
On, to the great cliffs of amber.
                        Between them,
Cave of Nerea,
    she like a great shell curved,
And the boat drawn without sound,
Without odour of ship-work,
Nor bird-cry, nor any noise of wave moving,
Nor splash of porpoise, nor any noise of wave moving,
Within her cave, Nerea,
                she like a great shell curved

In the suavity of the rock,
                                cliff green-gray in the far,
In the near, the gate-cliffs of amber,
And the wave
                    green clear, and blue clear,
And the cave salt-white, and glare-purple,
                cool, porphyry smooth,
                    the rock sea-worn.
No gull-cry, no sound of porpoise,
Sand as of malachite, and no cold there,
                the light not of the sun.

Zagreus, feeding his panthers,
                the turf clear as on hills under light.
And under the almond-trees, gods,
                with them, *choros nympharum*.   Gods,
Hermes and Athene,
                    As shaft of compass,
Between them, trembled —
To the left is the place of fauns,
                    sylva nympharum;
The low wood, moor-scrub,
                the doe, the young spotted deer,
                leap up through the broom-plants,
                        as dry leaf amid yellow.
And by one cut of the hills,
                the great alley of Memnons.
Beyond, sea, crests seen over dune
Night sea churning shingle,
To the left, the alley of cypress.
                            A boat came,
One man holding her sail,

Guiding her with oar caught over gunwale, saying:
"   There, in the forest of marble,
"   the stone trees — out of water —
"   the arbours of stone —
"   marble leaf, over leaf,
"   silver, steel over steel,
"   silver beaks rising and crossing,
"   prow set against prow,
"   stone, ply over ply,
"   the gilt beams flare of an evening "
Borso, Carmagnola, the men of craft, *i vitrei*,
Thither, at one time, time after time,
And the waters richer than glass,
Bronze gold, the blaze over the silver,
Dye-pots in the torch-light,
The flash of wave under prows,
And the silver beaks rising and crossing.
            Stone trees, white and rose-white in the darkness,
Cypress there by the towers,
            Drift under hulls in the night.

            " In the gloom the gold
Gathers the light about it."...

Now supine in burrow, half over-arched bramble,
One eye for the sea, through that peek-hole,
Gray light, with Athene.
Zothar and her elephants, the gold loin-cloth,
The sistrum, shaken, shaken,
            the cohorts of her dancers.
And Aletha, by bend of the shore,
            with her eyes seaward,
            and in her hands sea-wrack
Salt-bright with the foam.
Koré through the bright meadow,
            with green-gray dust in the grass:

" For this hour, brother of Circe."
Arm laid over my shoulder,
Saw the sun for three days, the sun fulvid,
As a lion lift over sand-plain;
                    and that day,
And for three days, and none after,
Splendour, as the splendour of Hermes,
And shipped thence
                    to the stone place,
Pale white, over water,
                    known water,
And the white forest of marble, bent bough over bough,
The pleached arbour of stone,
Thither Borso, when they shot the barbed arrow at him,
And Carmagnola, between the two columns,
Sigismundo, after that wreck in Dalmatia.
    Sunset like the grasshopper flying.

XVIII

A<small>ND</small> of Kublai:
>"I have told you of that emperor's city in detail
And will tell you of the coining in Cambaluc
    that hyght the secret of alchemy:
They take bast of the mulberry-tree,
That is a skin between the wood and the bark,
And of this they make paper, and mark it
Half a tornesel, a tornesel, or a half-groat of silver,
Or two groats, or five groats, or ten groats,
Or, for a great sheet, a gold bezant, 3 bezants,
        ten bezants;
And they are written on by officials,
And smeared with the great khan's seal in vermilion;
And the forgers are punished with death.
And all this costs the Kahn nothing,
And so he is rich in this world.
And his postmen go sewed up and sealed up,
Their coats buttoned behind and then sealed,
In this way from the voyage's one end to its other.
And the Indian merchants arriving
Must give up their jewels, and take this money
        in paper,
(That trade runs, in bezants, to 400,000 the year.)
And the nobles must buy their pearls"
— thus Messire Polo; prison at Genoa —
"Of the Emperor."
        There was a boy in Constantinople,
And some britisher kicked his arse.
"I hate these french," said Napoleon, aged 12,
To young Bourrienne, "I will do them all the harm
        that I can."
In like manner Zenos Metevsky.

And old Biers was out there, a greenhorn,
To sell cannon, and Metevsky found the back door;
And old Biers sold the munitions,
And Metevsky died and was buried, *i. e.* officially,
And sat in the Yeiner Kafé watching the funeral.
About ten years after this incident,
He owned a fair chunk of Humbers.
   " Peace!   Pieyce!! " said Mr. Giddings,
" Uni-ver-sal?   Not while yew got tew billions ov money,"
Said Mr. Giddings, " invested in the man-u-facture
" Of war machinery.   Haow I sold it to Russia —
" Well we tuk 'em a new torpedo-boat,
" And it was all electric, run it all from a
" Little bit uv a keyboard, about like the size ov
" A typewriter, and the prince come aboard,
" An' we sez wud yew like to run her?
" And he run damn slam on the breakwater,
" And bust off all her front end,
" And he was my gawd scared out of his panties.
" Who wuz agoin' tew pay fer the damage?
" And it was my first trip out fer the company,
" And I sez, yer highness, it is nothing,
" We will give yew a new one.   And, my Christ!
" The company backed me, and did we get a few orders? "
So La Marquesa de las Zojas y Hurbara
Used to drive up to Sir Zenos's place
   in the Champs Elysées
And preside at his dinners, and at *las once*
She drove away from the front door, with her footmen
And her coachman in livery, and drove four blocks round
To the back door, and her husband was the son of a bitch,
And Metevsky, " the well-known philanthropist,"
Or " the well-known financier, better known,"
As the press said, " as a philanthropist,"
Gave — as the Este to Louis Eleventh, —

A fine pair of giraffes to the nation,
And endowed a chair of ballistics,
And was consulted before the offensives.

And Mr. Oige was very choleric in a first-class
From Nice to Paris, he said: " Danger!
" Now a sailor's life is a life of danger,
" But a mine, why every stick of it is numbered,
" And one time we missed one, and there was
" Three hundred men killed in the 'splosion."
He was annoyed with the strikers, having started himself
As engineer and worked up, and losing,
By that coal strike, some months after the paragraph:

: Sir Zenos Metevsky has been elected President
Of the Gethsemane Trebizond Petrol.
And then there came out another: 80 locomotives
On the Manchester Cardiff have been fitted with
New oil-burning apparatus...
Large stocks of the heavier varieties of which (*i. e.* oil)
Are now on hand in the country.

So I said to the old quaker Hamish,
I said: " I am interested."   And he went putty colour
And said: " He don't advertise. No, I don't think
You will learn much."   That was when I asked
About Metevsky Melchizedek.
He, Hamish, took the tractors up to
King Menelik, 3 rivers and 140 ravines.

" Qu'est-ce qu'on pense...? " I said: " On don't pense.
" They're solid bone. You can amputate from just above
The medulla, and it won't alter the life in that island."
But he continued, " Mais, qu'EST-CE qu'ON pense,
" De la metallurgie, en Angleterre, qu'est-ce qu'on
" Pense de Metevsky? "

And I said: "They ain't heard his name yet.
"Go ask at MacGorvish's bank."

The Jap observers were much amused because
The Turkish freemasons hadn't bothered to
Take the..... regimental badges off their artillery.
And old Hamish: Menelik
Had a hunch that machinery...and so on...
But he never could get it to work,
            never could get any power.
The Germans wd. send him up boilers, but they'd
Have to cut 'em into pieces to load 'em on camels,
And they never got 'em together again.
And so old Hamish went out there,
And looked at the place, 3 rivers
And a hundred and forty ravines,
And he sent out two tractors, one to pull on the other
And Menelik sent down an army, a 5000 black army
With hawsers, and they all sweated and swatted.

And the first thing Dave lit on when they got there
Was a buzz-saw,
And he put it through an ebony log: whhsssh, t ttt,
Two days' work in three minutes.

War, one war after another,
Men start 'em who couldn't put up a good hen-roost.

Also sabotage...

XIX

SABOTAGE? Yes, he took it up to Manhattan,
      To the big company, and they said: Impossible.
      And he said: I gawt ten thousand dollars tew mak 'em,
      And I am a goin' tew mak 'em, and you'll damn well
Have to install 'em, awl over the place.
And they said: Oh, we can't have it.
So he settled for one-half of one million.
And he has a very nice place on the Hudson,
And that invention, patent, is still in their desk.
And the answer to that is: Wa'al he had the ten thousand.
And old Spinder, that put up the 1870 gothick memorial,
He tried to pull me on Marx, and he told me
About the " romance of his business ":
How he came to England with something or other,
                              and sold it.
Only he wanted to talk about Marx, so I sez:
Waal haow is it you're over here, right off the
                              Champz Elyza?
And how can yew be here? Why don't the fellers at home
Take it all off you? How can you leave your big business?
" Oh," he sez, " I ain't had to rent any money...
" It's a long time since I ain't had tew rent any money."
Nawthin' more about Das Kapital,
Or credit, or distribution.
And he " never finished the book,"
That was the other chap, the slender diplomatdentist
Qui se faisait si beau.

So we sat there, with the old kindly professor,
And the stubby little man was up-stairs.
And there was the slick guy in the other

84

corner reading The Tatler,
Not upside down, but never turning the pages,
And then I went up to the bed-room, and he said,
The stubby fellow: Perfectly true,
" But it's a question of feeling,
" Can't move 'em with a cold thing, like economics."
And so we came down stairs and went out,
And the slick guy looked out of the window,
And in came the street " Lemme-at-'em "
          like a bull-dog in a mackintosh.
          O my Clio!
Then the telephone didn't work for a week.

Ever seen Prishnip, little hunchback,
Couldn't take him for *any* army.
And he said: I haf a messache from dh' professor,
" There's lots of 'em want to go over,
" But when they try to go over,
" Dh' hRussian boys shoot 'em, and they want to know
" How to go over."

Vlettmann?...was out there, and that was,
Say, two months later, and he said:
" Jolly chaps," he said; " they used to go by
" Under my window, at two o'clock in the morning,
" All singing, all singing the *Hé Sloveny!* "

Yes, Vlettmann, and the Russian boys didn't shoot'em.
      Short story, entitled, the Birth of a Nation.
And there was that squirt of an Ausstrrian
        with a rose in his button-hole,
And how the hell he stayed on here,
        right through the whole bhloody business,
Cocky as Khristnoze, and enjoying every Boche victory.
Naphtha, or some damn thing for the submarines,

Like they had, just *had,* to have the hemp
                    via Rotterdam.
Das thust du nicht, Albert?
That was in the old days, all sitting around in arm-chairs,
And that's gone, like the cake shops in the Nevsky.
" No use telling 'em anything, revolutionaries,
Till they're at the *end,*
Oh, absolootly, AT the end of their tether.
Governed.   Governed the place from a train,
Or rather from three trains, on a railway,
And he'd keep about three days ahead of the lobby,
I mean he had his government on the trains,
And the lobby had to get there on horseback;
And he said: Bigod it's damn funny,
Own half the oil in the world, and can't get enough
To run a government engine! "
And then they jawed for two hours,
And finally Steff said: Will you fellows show me a map?
And they brought one, and Steff said:
" Waal what are those lines? "   " Yes, those straight lines."
" Those are roads."   And " what are those lines,
" The wiggly ones? "   " Rivers."
And Steff said: " Government property? "

So two hours later an engine went off with the order:
How to dig without confiscation.

And Tommy Baymont said to Steff one day:
" You think we run it, lemme tell you,
" We bought a coalmine, I mean the mortgage fell in,
" And you'd a' thought we could run it.

" Well I had to go down there meself, and the manager
" Said: " Run it, of course we can run it,
" We can't sell the damn coal."

86

So I said to the X. and B. Central,
— you'd say we boss the X. and B. Central? —
I said: You buy your damn coal from our mine.
And a year later they hadn't; so I had up the directors,
And they said:...well anyhow, they couldn't
                              buy the damn coal.
And next week ole Jim came, the big fat one
With the diamonds, and he said: "Mr. Baymont,
You just *must* charge two dollars more
A ton fer that coal. And the X. and B. will
Take it through us."

" So there was my ole man sitting,
They were in arm-chairs, according to protocol,
And next him his nephew Mr. Wurmsdorf,
And old Ptierstoff, for purely family reasons,
Personal reasons, was held in great esteem
                              by his relatives,
And he had his despatches from St. Petersburg,
And Wurmsdorf had his from Vienna,
And he knew, and they knew, and each knew
That the other knew that the other knew he knew,
And Wurmsdorf was just reaching into his pocket,
That was to start things, and then my ole man
Said it:
          Albert, and the rest of it.
Those days are gone by for ever."

" Ten years gone, ten years of my life,
Never get those ten years back again:
Ten years of my life, ten years in the Indian army;
But anyhow, there was that time in Yash (Jassy):
That was something, 14 girls in a fortnight."
" Healthy but verminous? " " That's it, healthy but verminous.
                    And one time in Kashmir,

In the houseboats, with the turquoise,
A pile three feet high on the boat floor,
And they'd be there all day at a bargain
For ten bobs' worth of turquoise."

XX

SOUND slender, quasi tinnula,
 Ligur' aoide: Si no'us vei, Domna don plus mi cal,
 Negus vezer mon bel pensar no val."
 Between the two almond trees flowering,
The viel held close to his side;
And another: s'adora ".
" Possum ego naturae
non meminisse tuae! "   Qui son Properzio ed Ovidio.

The boughs are not more fresh
where the almond shoots
take their March green.
And that year I went up to Freiburg,
And Rennert had said: Nobody, no, nobody
Knows anything about Provençal, or if there is anybody,
It's old Lévy."
And so I went up to Freiburg,
And the vacation was just beginning,
The students getting off for the summer,
Freiburg im Breisgau,
And everything clean, seeming clean, after Italy.

And I went to old Lévy, and it was by then 6.30
in the evening, and he trailed half way across Freiburg
before dinner, to see the two strips of copy,
Arnaut's, settant'uno R. superiore (Ambrosiana)
Not that I could sing him the music.
And he said: Now is there anything I can tell you? "
And I said: I dunno, sir, or
" Yes, Doctor, what do they mean by *noigandres?* "
And he said: Noigandres! NOIgandres!

" You know for seex mon's of my life
" Effery night when I go to bett, I say to myself:
" Noigandres, eh, *noi*gandres,
" Now what the DEFFIL can that mean! "
Wind over the olive trees, ranunculae ordered,
By the clear edge of the rocks
The water runs, and the wind scented with pine
And with hay-fields under sun-swath.
Agostino, Jacopo and Boccata.
You would be happy for the smell of that place
And never tired of being there, either alone
Or accompanied.
Sound: as of the nightingale too far off to be heard.
Sandro, and Boccata, and Jacopo Sellaio;
The ranunculæ, and almond,
Boughs set in espalier,
Duccio, Agostino; *e l'olors* —
The smell of that place — *d'enoi ganres*.
Air moving under the boughs,
The cedars there in the sun,
Hay new cut on hill slope,
And the water there in the cut
Between the two lower meadows; sound,
The sound, as I have said, a nightingale
Too far off to be heard.
And the light falls, *remir*,
from her breast to thighs.

He was playing there at the palla.
Parisina — two doves for an altar — at the window,
" *E'l Marchese*
Stava per divenir pazzo
after it all." And that was when Troy was down
And they came here and cut holes in rock,
Down Rome way, and put up the timbers;

And came here, condit Atesten...
          " Peace! keep the peace, Borso."
And he said: Some bitch has sold us
          (that was Ganelon)
" They wont get another such ivory."
And he lay there on the round hill under the cedar
A little to the left of the cut (Este speaking)
By the side of the summit, and he said:
          "I have broken the horn, bigod, I have
" Broke the best ivory, l'olofans."   And he said:
" Tan mare fustes! "
          pulling himself over the gravel,
" Bigod! that buggar is done for,
" They wont get another such ivory."
And they were there before the wall, Toro, las almenas,
(Este, Nic Este speaking)
                    Under the battlement
(Epi purgo) peur de la hasle,
And the King said:
          " God what a woman!
My God what a woman " said the King telo rigido.
" Sister! " says Ancures, " 's your sister! "
Alf left that town to Elvira, and Sancho wanted
It from her, Toro and Zamora.
                    " Bloody spaniard!
Neestho, le'er go back...
                    in the autumn."
" Este, go' damn you." between the walls, arras,
Painted to look like arras.
                    Jungle:
Glaze green and red feathers, jungle,
Basis of renewal, renewals;
Rising over the soul, green virid, of the jungle,
Lozenge of the pavement, clear shapes,
Broken, disrupted, body eternal,

Wilderness of renewals, confusion
Basis of renewals, subsistence,
Glazed green of the jungle;
Zoe, Marozia, Zothar,
                              loud over the banners,
Glazed grape, and the crimson,
HO BIOS,
                  cosi Elena vedi,
In the sunlight, gate cut by the shadow;
And then the faceted air:
Floating.   Below, sea churning shingle.
Floating, each on invisible raft,
On the high current, invisible fluid,
Borne over the plain, recumbent,
The right arm cast back,
                  the right wrist for a pillow,
The left hand like a calyx,
Thumb held against finger, the third,
The first fingers petal'd up, the hand as a lamp,
A calyx.
            From toe to head
The purple, blue-pale smoke, as of incense;
Wrapped each in burnous, smoke as the olibanum's,
Swift, as if joyous.
Wrapped, floating; and the blue-pale smoke of the incense
Swift to rise, then lazily in the wind
            as Aeolus over bean-field,
As hay in the sun, the olibanum, saffron,
As myrrh without styrax;
Each man in his cloth, as on raft, on
            The high invisible current;
On toward the fall of water;
And then over that cataract,
In air, strong, the bright flames, V shaped;
            Nel fuoco

D'amore mi mise, nel fuoco d'amore mi mise...
Yellow, bright saffron, croceo;
And as the olibanum bursts into flame,
The bodies so flamed in the air, took flame,
          "...Mi mise, il mio sposo novello."
Shot from stream into spiral,

Or followed the water. Or looked back to the flowing;
Others approaching that cataract,
As to dawn out of shadow, the swathed cloths
Now purple and orange,
And the blue water dusky beneath them,
          pouring there into the cataract,
With noise of sea over shingle,
               striking with:
               hah hah ahah thmm, thunb, ah
               woh woh araha thumm, bhaaa.
And from the floating bodies, the incense
     blue-pale, purple above them.
Shelf of the lotophagoi,
Aerial, cut in the aether.
                    Reclining,
With the silver spilla,
The ball as of melted amber, coiled, caught up, and turned.
Lotophagoi of the suave nails, quiet, scornful,
Voce-profondo:
          " Feared neither death nor pain for this beauty;
If harm, harm to ourselves."
And beneath: the clear bones, far down,
Thousand on thousand.
          " What gain with Odysseus,
" They that died in the whirlpool
" And after many vain labours,
" Living by stolen meat, chained to the rowingbench,
" That he should have a great fame

" And lie by night with the goddess?
" Their names are not written in bronze
            " Nor their rowing sticks set with Elpenor's;
" Nor have they mound by sea-bord.
            " That saw never the olives under Spartha
" With the leaves green and then not green,
            " The click of light in their branches;
" That saw not the bronze hall nor the ingle
" Nor lay there with the queen's waiting maids,
" Nor had they Circe to couch-mate, Circe Titania,
" Nor had they meats of Kalüpso
" Or her silk skirts brushing their thighs.
" Give!   What were they given?
                              Ear-wax.
" Poison and ear-wax,
                  and a salt grave by the bull-field,
" *neson amumona,* their heads like sea crows in the foam,
" Black splotches, sea-weed under lightning;
" Canned beef of Apollo, ten cans for a boat load."
Ligur' aoide.

And from the plain whence the water-shoot,
Across, back, to the right, the roads, a way in the grass,
The Khan's hunting leopard, and young Salustio
And Ixotta; the suave turf
Ac ferae familiares, and the cars slowly,
And the panthers, soft-footed.
Plain, as the plain of Somnus,
            the heavy cars, as a triumph,
Gilded, heavy on wheel,
            and the panthers chained to the cars,
Over suave turf, the form wrapped,
Rose, crimson, deep crimson,
And, in the blue dusk, a colour as of rust in the sunlight,
Out of white cloud, moving over the plain,

Head in arm's curve, reclining;
The road, back and away, till cut along the face of the rock,
And the cliff folds in like a curtain,
The road cut in under the rock
Square groove in the cliff's face, as chiostri,
The columns crystal, with peacocks cut in the capitals,
The soft pad of beasts dragging the cars;
Cars, slow, without creak,
And at windows in inner roadside:
        le donne e i cavalieri
         smooth face under hennin,
The sleeves embroidered with flowers,
Great thistle of gold, or an amaranth,
Acorns of gold, or of scarlet,
Cramoisi and diaspre
        slashed white into velvet;
Crystal columns, acanthus, sirens in the pillar heads;
And at last, between gilded barocco,
Two columns coiled and fluted,
Vanoka, leaning half naked,
        waste hall there behind her.
" Peace!
      Borso..., Borso! "

XXI

EEP the peace, Borso! " Where are we?
    " Keep on with the business,
               That's made me,
     " And the res publica didn't.
" When I was broke, and a poor kid,
" They all knew me, all of these *cittadini*,
" And they all of them cut me dead, della gloria."
Intestate, 1429, leaving 178,221 florins *di sugello*,
As is said in Cosimo's red leather note book. Di sugello.
And " with his credit emptied Venice of money "—
That was Cosimo —
" And Naples, and made them accept his peace."
And he caught the young boy Ficino
And had him taught the greek language;
" With two ells of red cloth per person
I will make you ", Cosimo speaking, " as many
Honest citizens as you desire."
Col credito suo...
Napoli e Venezia di danari...
Costretti... Napoli e Venezia... a quella pace...
Or another time... oh well, pass it.
And Piero called in the credits,
(Diotisalvi was back of that)
And firms failed as far off as Avignon,
And Piero was like to be murdered,
And young Lauro came down ahead of him, in the road,
And said: Yes, father is coming.

Intestate, '69, in December, leaving me 237,989 florins,
As you will find in my big green account book
In carta di capretto;

And from '34 when I count it, to last year,
We paid out 600,000 and over,
That was for building, taxes and charity.
Nic Uzano saw us coming.   Against it, honest,
And warned 'em.   They'd have murdered him,
And would Cosimo, but he bribed 'em;
And they did in Giuliano.   E difficile,
A Firenze difficile viver ricco
Senza aver lo stato.
" E non avendo stato Piccinino
" Doveva temerlo qualunque era in stato; "
And " that man sweated blood to put through that railway ";
" Could you ", wrote Mr. Jefferson,
" Find me a gardener
Who can play the french horn?
The bounds of American fortune
Will not admit the indulgence of a domestic band of
Musicians, yet I have thought that a passion for music
Might be reconciled with that economy which we are
Obliged to observe.   I retain among my domestic servants
A gardener, a weaver, a cabinet-maker, and a stone-cutter,
To which I would add a vigneron.   In a country like yours
(id est Burgundy) where music is cultivated and
Practised by every class of men, I suppose there might
Be found persons of these trades who could perform on
The french horn, clarionet, or hautboy and bassoon, so
That one might have a band of two french horns, two
Clarionets, two hautboys and a bassoon, without enlarging
Their domestic expenses.   A certainty of employment for
Half a dozen years
                    (affatigandose per suo piacer o non)
And at the end of that time, to find them, if they
Choose, a conveyance to their own country, might induce
Them to come here on reasonable wages.   Without meaning to
Give you trouble, perhaps it might be practicable for you

In your ordinary intercourse with your people to find out
Such men disposed to come to America. Sobriety and good
Nature would be desirable parts of their characters "

June 1778 Montecello

And in July I went up to Milan for Duke Galeaz
To sponsor his infant in baptism,
Albeit were others more worthy,
And took his wife a gold collar holding a diamond
That cost about 3000 ducats, on which account
That signor Galeaz Sforza Visconti has wished me
To stand sponsor to all of his children.

Another war without glory, and another peace without, quiet.

And the Sultan sent him an assassin, his brother;
And the Soldan of Egypt, a lion;
And he begat one pope and one son and four daughters,
And an University, Pisa; (Lauro Medici)
And nearly went broke in his business,
And bought land in Siena and Pisa,
And made peace by his own talk in Naples.
And there was grass on the floor of the temple,
Or where the floor of it might have been;
          Gold fades in the gloom,
               Under the blue-black roof, Placidia's,
Of the exarchate; and we sit here
By the arena, *les gradins...*
And the palazzo, baseless, hangs there in the dawn
With low mist over the tide-mark;·
And floats there nel tramonto
With gold mist over the tide-mark.
The tesserae of the floor, and the patterns.
Fools making new shambles;
               night over green ocean,
And the dry black of the night.

Night of the golden tiger,
And the dry flame in the air,
Voices of the procession,
Faint now, from below us,
And the sea with tin flash in the sun-dazzle,
Like dark wine in the shadows.
" Wind between the sea and the mountains "
The tree-spheres half dark against sea
half clear against sunset,
The sun's keel freighted with cloud,
And after that hour, dry darkness
Floating flame in the air, gonads in organdy,
Dry flamelet, a petal borne in the wind.
Gignetei kalon.
Impenetrable as the ignorance of old women.
In the dawn, as the fleet coming in after Actium,
Shore to the eastward, and altered,
And the old man sweeping leaves:
" Damned to you Midas, Midas lacking a Pan! "
And now in the valley,
Valley under the day's edge:
" Grow with the Pines of Ise;
" As the Nile swells with Inopos.
" As the Nile falls with Inopos."
Phoibos, turris eburnea,
ivory against cobalt,
And the boughs cut on the air,
The leaves cut on the air,
The hounds on the green slope by the hill,
water still black in the shadow.
In the crisp air,
the discontinuous gods;
Pallas, young owl in the cup of her hand,
And, by night, the stag runs, and the leopard,
Owl-eye amid pine boughs.

Moon on the palm-leaf,
                    confusion;
Confusion, source of renewals;
Yellow wing, pale in the moon shaft,
Green wing, pale in the moon shaft,
Pomegranate, pale in the moon shaft,
White horn, pale in the moon shaft, and Titania
By the drinking hole,
                    steps, cut in the basalt.
Danced there Athame, danced, and there Phæthusa
With colour in the vein,
Strong as with blood-drink, once,
With colour in the vein,
Red in the smoke-faint throat.   Dis caught her up.

And the old man went on there
          beating his mule with an asphodel.

XXII

AN' that man sweat blood
        to put through that railway,
        And what he ever got out of it?
        And he said one thing: As it costs,
As in any indian war it costs the government
20,000 dollars per head
To kill off the red warriors, it might be more humane
And even cheaper, to educate.
And there was the other type, Warenhauser,
That beat him, and broke up his business,
Tale of the American Curia that gave him,
Warenhauser permission to build the Northwestern railway
And to take the timber he cut in the process;
So he cut a road through the forest,
Two miles wide, an' perfectly legal.
Who wuz agoin' to stop him!

And he came in and said: Can't do it,
Not at that price, we can't do it."
That was in the last war, here in England,
And he was making chunks for a turbine
In some sort of an army plane;
An' the inspector says: " How many rejects? "
" What you mean, rejects? "
And the inspector says: " How many do you get? "
And Joe said: " We don't get *any* rejects, our..."
And the inspector says: " Well then of course
                            you can't do it."
Price of life in the occident.
And C. H. said to the renowned Mr. Bukos:
" What is the cause of the H. C. L.? " and Mr. Bukos,

The economist consulted of nations, said:
                    " Lack of labour."
And there were two millions of men out of work.
And C. H. shut up, he said
He would save his breath to cool his own porridge,
But I didn't, and I went on plaguing Mr. Bukos
Who said finally: " I am an orthodox
" Economist."
                Jesu Christo!
Standu nel paradiso terrestre
Pensando come si fesse compagna d'Adamo!!

And Mr. H. B. wrote in to the office:
I would like to accept C. H.'s book
But it would make my own seem so out of date.
            Heaven will protect
The lay reader.   The whole fortune of
Mac Narpen and Company is founded
Upon Palgrave's Golden Treasury.   Nel paradiso terrestre

And all the material was used up, Jesu Christo,
And everything in its place, and nothing left over
To make una compagna d'Adamo.   Come si fesse?
E poi ha vishtu una volpe
And the tail of the volpe, the vixen,
Fine, spreading and handsome, e pensava:
That will do for this business;
And la volpe saw in his eye what was coming,
Corre, volpe corre, Christu corre, volpecorre,
Christucorre, e dav' un saltu, ed ha preso la coda
Della volpe, and the volpe wrenched loose
And left the tail in his hand, e di questu
Fu fatta,
            e per questu
E la donna una furia,
Una fuRRia-e-una rabbia.

102

And a voice behind me in the street.
" Meestair Freer!   Meestair..."
And I thought I was three thousand
Miles from the nearest connection;
And he'd known me for three days, years before that,
And he said, one day a week later: Woud you lak
To meet a wholley man, yais he is a veree wholley man.
So I met Mohamed Ben Abt el Hjameed,
And that evening he spent his whole time
Queering the shirt-seller's business,
And taking hot whiskey.   The sailors
Come in there for two nights a week and fill up the café
And the rock scorpions cling to the edge
Until they can't jes' nacherly stand it
And then they go to the Calpe (Lyceo)

NO MEMBER OF THE MILITARY
OF WHATEVER RANK
IS PERMITTED WITHIN THE WALLS
OF THIS CLUB

That fer the governor of Gibel Tara.
" Jeen-jah!   Jeen-jah! " squawked Mohamed,
" O-ah, geef heem sax-pence."
And a chap in a red fez came in, and grinned at Mohamed
Who spat across four metres of tables
At Mustafa.   That was all there was
To that greeting; and three nights later
Ginger came back as a customer, and took it out of Mohamed.
He hadn't sold a damn shirt on the Tuesday.
And I met Yusuf and eight men in the calle,
So I sez: Wot is the matter?
And Yusuf said: Vairy foolish, it will

Be sefen an' seex for the summons
— Mohamed want to sue heem for libel —
To give all that to the court!
          So I went off to Granada
And when I came back I saw Ginger, and I said:
What about it?
          And he said: O-ah, I geef heem a
Seex-pence.   Customs of the sha-ha-reef.
And they were all there in the lyceo,
Cab drivers, and chaps from tobacco shops,
And Edward the Seventh's guide, and they were all
For secession.
Dance halls being closed at two in the morning,
By the governor's order.   And another day on the pier
Was a fat fellah from Rhode Island, a-sayin':
" Bi Hek!   I been all thru Italy
          An' ain't never been stuck! "
" But this place is plumb full er scoundrels."
And Yusuf said: Yais? an' the reech man
In youah countree, haowa they get their money;
They no go rob some poor pairsons?
And the fat fellah shut up, and went off.
And Yusuf said: Woat, he iss all thru Eetaly
An' ee is nevair been stuck, ee ees a liar.
W'en I goa to some forain's country
I am stuck.
          W'en yeou goa to some forain's country
You moss be stuck; w'en they come 'ere I steek thaim.
And we went down to the synagogue,
All full of silver lamps
And the top gallery stacked with old benches;
And in came the levite and six little choir kids
And began yowling the ritual
As if it was crammed full of jokes,
And they went through a whole book of it;

And in came the elders and the scribes
About five or six and the rabbi
And he sat down, and grinned, and pulled out his snuff-box,
And sniffed up a thumb-full, and grinned,
And called over a kid from the choir, and whispered,
And nodded toward one old buffer,
And the kid took him the snuff-box and he grinned,
And bowed his head, and sniffed up a thumb-full,
And the kid took the box back to the rabbi,
And he grinned, e faceva bisbiglio,
And the kid toted off the box to
   another old bunch of whiskers,
And he sniffed up his thumb-full,
And so on till they'd each had his sniff;
And then the rabbi looked at the stranger, and they
All grinned half a yard wider, and the rabbi
Whispered for about two minutes longer,
An' the kid brought the box over to me,
And I grinned and sniffed up my thumb-full.
And then they got out the scrolls of the law
And had their little procession
And kissed the ends of the markers.
And there was a case on for rape and blackmail
Down at the court-house, behind the big patio
   full of wistaria;
An' the nigger in the red fez, Mustafa, on the boat later
An' I said to him: Yusuf, Yusuf's a damn good feller.
And he says:
   " Yais, he ees a goot fello,
" But after all a chew
     ees a chew."
And the judge says: That veil is too long.
And the girl takes off the veil
That she has stuck onto her hat with a pin,
" Not a veil," she says, " 'at's a scarf."

And the judge says:
          Don't you know you aren't allowed all those buttons?
And she says: Those ain't buttons, them's bobbles.
Can't you see there ain't any button-holes?
And the Judge says: Well, anyway, you're not allowed ermine.
" Ermine? " the girl says, " Not ermine, that ain't,
" 'At's lattittzo."
And the judge says: And just what is a lattittzo?
And the girl says:
                    " It'z a animal."

Signori, *you* go and enforce it.

XXIII

E^T omniformis," Psellos, " omnis
    " Intellectus est." God's fire. Gemisto:
    " Never with this religion
    " Will you make men of the greeks.
" But build wall across Peloponesus
" And organize, and...
              damn these Eyetalian barbarians."
And Novvy's ship went down in the tempest
Or at least they chucked the books overboard.

How dissolve Irol in sugar... Houille blanche,
Auto-chenille, destroy all bacteria in the kidney,
Invention-d'entités-plus-ou-moins-abstraits-
en-nombre-égal-aux-choses-à-expliquer...
    La Science ne peut pas y consister. " J'ai
Obtenu une brulure " M. Curie, or some other scientist
" Qui m'a coûté six mois de guérison."
          and continued his experiments.
Tropismes! "We believe the attraction is chemical."

With the sun in a golden cup
        and going toward the low fords of ocean
Ἄλιος δ' Ὑπεριονίδας δέπας ἐσκατέβαινε χρύσεον
Ὄφρα δἰ ὠκεανοῖο περάσας
      ima vada noctis obscurae
Seeking doubtless the sex in bread-moulds
ἥλιος, ἅλιος, ἅλιος = μάταιος
(" Derivation uncertain." The idiot
Odysseus furrowed the sand.)
alixantos, aliotrephès, eiskatebaine, down into,
descended, to the end that, beyond ocean,
pass through, traverse

107

$$\pi o \tau \grave{\iota} \ \beta \acute{\epsilon} \nu \theta \epsilon a$$

$\nu \nu \kappa \tau \grave{o} s \ \grave{\epsilon} \rho \epsilon \mu \nu \hat{a} s,$

$\pi o \tau \grave{\iota} \ \mu a \tau \acute{\epsilon} \rho a, \ \kappa o \nu \rho \iota \delta \acute{\iota} a \nu \ \tau' \ddot{a} \lambda o \chi o \nu$

$\pi a \hat{\iota} \delta \acute{a} s \ \tau \epsilon \ \phi \acute{\iota} \lambda o \nu s \ \dots \ \ \breve{\epsilon} \beta a \ \delta \acute{a} \phi \nu a \iota \sigma \iota \ \kappa a \tau \acute{a} \sigma \kappa \iota o \nu$

Precisely, the selv' oscura

And in the morning, in the Phrygian head-sack

Barefooted, dumping sand from their boat

'Yperionides!

        And the rose grown while I slept,

And the strings shaken with music,

Capriped, the loose twigs under foot;

We here on the hill, with the olives

Where a man might carry his oar up,

And the boat there in the inlet;

As we had lain there in the autumn

Under the arras, or wall painted below like arras,

And above with a garden of rose-trees,

Sound coming up from the cross-street;

As we had stood there,

Watching road from the window,

Fa Han and I at the window,

And her head bound with gold cords.

Cloud over mountain; hill-gap, in mist, like a sea-coast.

Leaf over leaf, dawn-branch in the sky

And the sea dark, under wind,

The boat's sails hung loose at the mooring,

        Cloud like a sail inverted,

And the men dumping sand by the sea-wall

Olive trees there on the hill

      where a man might carry his oar up.

And my brother De Mænsac

Bet with me for the castle,

And we put it on the toss of a coin,

And I, Austors, won the coin-toss and kept it,

And he went out to Tierci, a jongleur
And on the road for his living,
And twice he went down to Tierci,
And took off the girl there that was just married to Bernart.

And went to Auvergne, to the Dauphin,
And Tierci came with a posse to Auvergnat,
And went back for an army
And came to Auvergne with the army
But never got Pierre nor the woman.
And he went down past Chaise Dieu,
And went after it all to Mount Segur,
    after the end of all things,
And they hadn't left even the stair,
And Simone was dead by that time,
And they called us the Manicheans
Wotever the hellsarse that is.

And that was when Troy was down, all right,
            superbo Ilion...
And they were sailing along
Sitting in the stern-sheets,
Under the lee of an island
And the wind drifting off from the island.
" Tet, tet...
            what is it? " said Anchises.
" Tethnéké," said the helmsman, " I think they
" Are howling because Adonis died virgin."
" Huh! tet..." said Anchises,
        " well, they've made a bloody mess of that city."

" King Otreus, of Phrygia,
" That king is my father."
            and saw then, as of waves taking form,
As the sea, hard, a glitter of crystal,
And the waves rising but formed, holding their form.
No light reaching through them.

XXIV

THUS the book of the mandates:

We desire that you our factors give to Zohanne of
Rimini
our servant, six lire marchesini,
for the three prizes he has won racing our barbarisci,
at the rate we have agreed on. The races he has won
are the Modena, the San Petronio at Bologna
and the last race at San Zorzo.

(Signed) Parisina Marchesa

.. pay them for binding
un libro franxese che si chiama Tristano...

Carissimi nostri
Zohanne da Rimini
has won the palio at Milan with our horse and writes that
he is now on the hotel, and wants money.
Send what you think he needs,
but when you get him back in Ferrara find out
what he has done with the first lot, I think over 25 ducats
But send the other cash quickly, as I don't want him
there on the hotel.
... perfumes, parrot seed, combs, two great and two
small ones from Venice, for madama la marxesana...
... 20 ducats to
give to a friend of ours who paid a bill for us
on this trip to Romagna...
... verde colore predeletto, 25 ducats ziparello
silver embroidered for Ugo fiolo del Signore...

(27 nov. 1427)
PROCURATIO NOMINE PATRIS, Leonello Este

(arranging dot for Margarita his sister, to
Roberto Malatesta of Rimini)
natae praelibati margaritae
Ill. D. Nicolai Marchionis Esten. et Sponsae:
The tower of Gualdo
with plenary jurisdiction in civils; and in criminal:
to fine and have scourged all delinquents
as in the rest of their lands,
" which things
this tower, estate at Gualdo had the Illustrious
Nicolaus Marquis of Este received from the said
Don Carlo (Malatesta)
for dower
Illustrae Dominae Parisinae Marxesana."

under my hand D. Michaeli de Magnabucis
Not. pub. Ferr.
D. Nicolaeque Guiduccioli de Arimino.
Sequit bonorum descriptio.

And he in his young youth, in the wake of Odysseus
To Cithera (a. d. 1413) " dove fu Elena rapta da Paris "
Dinners in orange groves, prows attended of dolphins,
Vestige of Rome at Pola, fair wind as far as Naxos
Ora vela, ora a remi, sino ad ora di vespero
Or with the sail tight hauled, by the crook'd land's arm
Zefalonia
And at Corfu, greek singers; by Rhodos
Of the windmills, and to Paphos,
Donkey boys, dust, deserts, Jerusalem, backsheesh
And an endless fuss over passports;
One groat for the Jordan, whether you go there or not,
The school where the madonna in girlhood
Went to learn letters, and Pilate's house closed to the public;
2 soldi for Olivet (to the Saracens)
And no indulgence at Judas's tree; and

" Here Christ put his thumb on a rock
" Saying: hic est medium mundi."
    (That, I assure you, happened.
                        Ego, scriptor cantilenae.)
For worse? for better? but happened.
After which, the greek girls at Corfu, and the
Ladies, Venetian, and they all sang in the evening
Benche niuno cantasse, although none of them could,
Witness Luchino del Campo.
Plus one turkish juggler, and they had a bath
When they got out of Jerusalem
And for cargo: one leopard of Cyprus
And falcons, and small birds of Cyprus,
Sparrow hawks, and grayhounds from Turkey
To breed in Ferrara among thin-legged Ferrarese,
Owls, hawks, fishing tackle.

Was beheaded Aldovrandino (1425, vent'uno Maggio)
Who was cause of this evil, and after
The Marchese asked was Ugo beheaded. And the Captain:
" Signor... si."   and il Marchese began crying
" Fa me hora tagliar la testa
" dapoi cosi presto hai decapitato il mio Ugo."
Rodendo con denti una bachetta che havea in mani.
And passed that night weeping, and calling Ugo, his son.
Affable, bullnecked, that brought seduction in place of
Rape into government, ter pacis Italiae auctor;
With the boys pulling the tow-ropes on the river
Tre cento bastardi (or bombardi fired off at his funeral)
And the next year a standard from Venice
(Where they'd called off a horse race)
And the baton from the Florentine baily.
" Of Fair aspect, gentle in manner "
Forty years old at the time;
" And they killed a judge's wife among other,

That was a judge of the court and noble,
And called Madonna Laodamia delli Romei,
Beheaded in the pa della justicia;
And in Modena, a madonna Agnesina
Who had poisoned her husband,
" All women known as adulterous,
" That his should not suffer alone."
                    Then the writ ran no further.
And in '31 married Monna Ricarda.

CHARLES... scavoir faisans... et advenir... a haute
noblesse du Linage et Hostel... e faictz hautex...
vaillance... affection... notre dict Cousin...
puissance, auctorite Royal... il et ses hors yssus... et
a leur loise avoir doresenavant
A TOUSIUOURS EN LEURS ARMES ESCARTELURE
... trois fleurs Liz d'or... en champs a'asur dentelle...
ioissent et usent.
                    Mil CCCC trente et ung, conseil
à Chinon, le Roy, l'Esne de la Trimouill,
Vendoise, Jehan Rabateau.

And in '32 came the Marchese Saluzzo
To visit them, his son in law and his daughter,
And to see Hercules his grandson, piccolo e putino.
And in '41 Polenta went up to Venice
Against Niccolo's caution
And was swallowed up in that city.
E fu sepulto nudo, Niccolo,
Without decoration, as ordered in testament,
Ter pacis Italiae.
And if you want to know what became of his statue,
I had a rifle class in Bondeno
And the priest sent a boy to the hardware
And he brought back the nails in a wrapping,

And it was the leaf of a diary
And he got the rest from the hardware
            (Cassini, libraio, speaking)
And on the first leaf of the wrapping
Was how in Napoleon's time
Came down a load of brass fittings from Modena
Via del Po, all went by the river,
To Piacenza for cannon, bells, door-knobs
And the statues of the Marchese Niccolo and of Borso
That were in the Piazza on columns.
And the Commendatore has made it a monograph
Without saying I told him and sent him
The name of the priest.

After him and his day
Were the cake-eaters, the consumers of icing,
That read all day per diletto
And left the night work to the servants;
Ferrara, paradiso dei sarti, " feste stomagose."

" Is it likely Divine Apollo,
That I should have stolen your cattle?
A child of my age, a mere infant,
            And besides, I have been here all night in my crib."
" Albert made me, Tura painted my wall,
And Julia the Countess sold to a tannery...

XXV

THE BOOK OF THE COUNCIL MAJOR
    1255 be it enacted:
    That they mustn't shoot crap in the hall
    of the council, nor in the small court under
pain of 20 danari, be it enacted:
1266 no squire of Venice to throw dice
*any*where in the palace or
in the loggia of the Rialto under pain of ten soldi
or half that for kids, and if they wont pay
they are to be chucked in the water. be it enacted
In libro pactorum
To the things everlasting
memory both for live men and for the future et
quod publice innotescat
in the said date, dicto millessimo
of the illustrious lord, Lord John Soranzo
by god's grace doge of Venice in the Curia
of the Palace of the Doges,
neath the portico next the house of the dwelling of
the Castaldio and of the heralds of the Lord Doge.
being beneath same a penthouse or cages
or room timbered (trabesilis) like a cellar
one Lion male and one female *simul commorantes*
which beasts to the Lord Doge were transmitted small
by that serene Lord King Frederic of Sicily, the
said lion knew carnally and in nature the Lioness
aforesaid and impregnated in that manner that animals
leap on one another to know and impregnate
on the faith of several ocular witnesses
Which lioness bore pregnant for about three months
(as is said by those who saw her assaulted)

and in the said millessimo and month on a sunday
12th. of the month of September about sunrise on
St. Mark's day early but with the light already apparent
the said lioness as is the nature of animals
whelped per naturam three lion cubs vivos et pilosos
living and hairy which born at once began life and motion
and to go gyring about their mother throughout the
aforesaid room as saw the aforesaid Lord Doge and as it
were all the Venetians and other folk who were in
Venice that day that concurred all for this as it were
miraculous sight. And one of the animals is a male
and the other two female

>I John Marchesini Ducal notary of the
>Venetians as eyewitness saw the
>nativity of these animals thus by
>mandate of the said Doge wrote this
>and put it in file.

Also a note from Pontius Pilate dated the " year 33."

Two columns (a. d. 1323) for the church of St. Nicholas of the
palace 12 lire gross.
To the procurators of St. Marc for entrance to the
palace, for gilding the images and the lion over the door
... to be paid...

Be it enacted:
to Donna Sorantia Soranzo that she come for the
feast of Ascension by night in a covered boat and
alight at the ripa del Palazzo, and when first sees the
Christblood go at once up into the Palace and may
stay in the Palace VIII days to visit the Doge her
father not in that time leaving the palace, nor
descending the palace stair and when she descends it
that she return by night the boat in the like manner

being covered.   To be revoked at the council's pleasure.
                    accepted by 5 of the council

1335. 3 lire 15 groats to stone for making a lion.
1340. Council of the lords noble, Marc Erizio
Nic. Speranzo, Tomasso Gradonico:
                                    that the hall
be new built over the room of the night watch
and over the columns toward the canal where the walk is...

... because of the stink of the dungeons. 1344.
1409... since the most serene Doge can scarce
stand upright in his bedroom...
                    vadit pars, two gross lire
stone stair, 1415, for pulchritude of the palace

                        254 da parte
                         de non 23
                        4 non sincere
Which is to say: they built out over the arches
and the palace hangs there in the dawn, the mist,
in that dimness,
or as one rows in from past the murazzi
the barge slow after moon-rise
and the voice sounding under the sail.
Mist gone.
            And Sulpicia
green shoot now, and the wood
white under new cortex
" as the sculptor sees the form in the air
            before he sets hand to mallet,
" and as he sees the in, and the through,
                        the four sides
" not the one face to the painter
As ivory uncorrupted:
                    " Pone metum Cerinthe "

Lay there, the long soft grass,
          and the flute lay there by her thigh,
Sulpicia, the fauns, twig-strong,
                    gathered about her;
The fluid, over the grass
Zephyrus, passing through her,
               " deus nec laedit amantes."
Hic mihi dies sanctus;
And from the stone pits, the heavy voices,
Heavy sound:
                " Sero, sero...
" Nothing we made, we set nothing in order,
" Neither house nor the carving,
" And what we thought had been thought for too long;
" Our opinion not opinion in evil
" But opinion borne for too long.
" We have gathered a sieve full of water."
And from the comb of reeds, came notes and the chorus
Moving, the young fauns: Pone metum,
Metum, nec deus laedit.

And as after the form, the shadow,
Noble forms, lacking life, that bolge, that valley
the dead words keeping form,
and the cry: Civis Romanus.
The clear air, dark, dark,
The dead concepts, never the solid, the blood rite,
The vanity of Ferrara;

Clearer than shades, in the hill road
Springing in cleft of the rock: Phaethusa
There as she came among them,
Wine in the smoke-faint throat,
Fire gleam under smoke of the mountain,
Even there by meadows of Phlegethon

And against this the flute: pone metum.
Fading, that they carried their guts before them,
And thought then, the deathless,
Form, forms and renewal, gods held in the air,
Forms seen, and then clearness,
Bright void, without image, Napishtim,
Casting his gods back into the νοῦς.

" as the sculptor sees the form in the air...
" as glass seen under water,
" King Otreus, my father...
and saw the waves taking form as crystal,
notes as facets of air,
and the mind there, before them, moving,
so that notes needed not move.

... side toward the piazza, the worst side of the room
that no one has been willing to tackle,
and do it as cheap or much cheaper...
                    (signed) Tician, 31 May 1513

It being convenient that there be an end to
the painting of Titian, fourth frame from the door on
the right of the hall of the greater council, begun
by maestro Tyciano da Cadore since its being thus
unfinished holds up the decoration of said hall on
the side that everyone sees.   We
move that by authority of this Council maestro Tyciano
aforesaid be constrained to finish said canvas,
and if he have not, to lose the expectancy of the
brokerage on the Fondamenta delli Thodeschi
and moreover to restore all payments recd. on account of
said canvas.   11 Aug. 1522
Ser Leonardus Emo, Sapiens Consilij:
Ser Philippus Capello, Sapiens Terrae Firmae:

In 1513 on the last day of May was conceded to
Tician of Cadore painter a succession to a brokerage
on the Fondamenta dei Thodeschi, the first to be vacant
In 1516 on the 5th. of december was declared that
without further waiting a vacancy he shd. enter that
which had been held by the painter Zuan Bellin on
condition that he paint the picture of the land battle
in the Hall of our Greater Council on the side toward
the piazza over the Canal Grande, the which Tician after
the demise of Zuan Bellin entered into possession of the
said Sensaria and has for about twenty years profited by
it, namely to about 100 ducats a year not including the
18 to 20 ducats taxes yearly remitted him it being
fitting that as he has not worked he should not have
the said profits WHEREFORE

                                          be it moved that the said
Tician de Cadore, pictor, be by authority of this Council
obliged and constrained to restore to our government all the
moneys that he has had from the agency during the time he
has not worked on the painting in the said
hall as is reasonable

             ayes 102, noes 38,   37 undecided
                                         register of the senate
                                         terra 1537, carta 136.

XXVI

AND I came here in my young youth
and lay there under the crocodile
By the column, looking East on the Friday,
And I said: Tomorrow I will lie on the South side
And the day after, south west.
And at night they sang in the gondolas
And in the barche with lanthorns;
The prows rose silver on silver
taking light in the darkness.   " Relaxetur ! "
11th. December 1461: that Pasti be let out
with a caveat
" caveat ire ad Turchum, that he stay out of
Constantinople
" if he hold dear our government's pleasure.
" The book will be retained by the council
(the book being Valturio's " Re Militari ").

To Nicolo Segundino, the next year, 12th. October
" Leave no... omnem... as they say... volve lapidem...
" Stone unturned that he, Pio,
" Give peace to the Malatesta.
" Faithful sons (we are) of the church
(for two pages)...
" And see all the cardinals and the nephew...
" And in any case get the job done.

" Our galleys were strictly neutral
" And sent there for neutrality.
" See Borso in Ferrara."

To Bernard Justinian, 28th. of October:
" Segundino is to come back with the news
" Two or three days after you get this."

Senato Secreto, 28th of October,
Came Messire Hanibal from Cesena :
" Cd. they hoist the flag of St. Mark
" And have Fortinbras and our army? "
" They cd. not... but on the quiet, secretissime,
" Two grand... Sic : He may have
" Two thousand ducats; himself to hire the men
" From our army."
. . . .
... 8 barrels wine, to Henry of Inghilterra...
Tin, serges, amber to go by us to the Levant,
Corfu, and above Corfu...

. . . .
And hither came Selvo, doge,
          that first mosiac'd San Marco,
And his wife that would touch food but with forks,
Sed aureis furculis, that is
          with small golden prongs
Bringing in, thus, the vice of luxuria;
And to greet the doge Lorenzo Tiepolo,
Barbers, heads covered with beads,
Furriers, masters in rough,
Master pelters for fine work,
And the masters for lambskin
With silver cups and their wine flasks
And blacksmiths with the gonfaron
          et leurs fioles chargies de vin,
The masters of wool cloth
Glass makers in scarlet
Carrying fabrefactions of glass;

122

25th April the jousting,
The Lord Nicolo Este,
          Ugaccion dei Contrarini,
The Lord Francesco Gonzaga, and first
The goldsmiths and jewelers' company
Wearing *pellande* of scarlet,
          the horses in cendato —
And it cost three ducats to rent any horse
For three hundred and fifty horses, in piazza,
And the prize was a collar with jewels
And these folk came on horses to the piazza
In the last fight fourteen on a side,
And the prize went to a nigger from Mantua
That came with Messire Gonzaga.

And that year ('38) they came here
Jan. 2. The Marquis of Ferrara
     mainly to see the greek Emperor,
To take him down the canal to his house,
And with the Emperor came the archbishops:
The Archbishop of Morea Lower
And the Archbishop of Sardis
And the Bishops of Lacedæmon and of Mitylene,
Of Rhodos, of Modon Brandos,
And the Archbishops of Athens, Corinth, and of Trebizond,
The chief secretary and the stonolifex.
And came Cosimo Medici " almost as a Venetian to Venice "
(That would be four days later)
And on the 25th, Lord Sigismundo da Rimini
For government business
And then returned to the camp.
And in February they all packed off
To Ferrara to decide on the holy ghost
And as to the which begat the what in the Trinity. —
Gemisto and the Stonolifex,

And you would have bust your bum laughing
To see the hats and beards of those greeks.

And the guild spirit was declining.
Te fili Dux, tuosque successores
Aureo anulo, to wed the sea as a wife;
for beating the Emperor Manuel,
eleven hundred and seventy six.
1175 a. d. first bridge in Rialto.
" You may seal your acts with lead, Signor Ziani."

The jewelers company had their furs lined with scarlet
And silk cloth for the horses,
A silk cloth called cendato
That they still use for the shawls;
And at the time of that war against Hungary
Uncle Carlo Malatesta, three wounds.
Balista, sword and a lance wound;
And to our general Pandolfo, three legates,
With silk and with silver,
And with velvet, wine and confections, to keep him ⌐
Per animarla — in mood to go on with the fighting.

" That are in San Samuele (young ladies)
            are all to go to Rialto
And to wear yellow kerchief, as are also
Their matrons (ruffiane)."
" Ambassador, for his great wisdom and money,
" That had been here as an exile, Cosimo
" Pater."
" Lord Luigi Gonzaga, to be given Casa Giustinian."

" Bishops of Lampascus and Cyprus
" And other fifty lords bishops
                    that are the church of the orient."

March 8, " That Sigismundo left Mantua
Ill contented...

And they are dead and have left a few pictures.
" Albizi have sacked the Medici bank."
" Venetians may stand, come, depart with their families
Free by land, free by sea
            in their galleys,
Ships, boats, and with merchandise.
2% on what's actually sold.   No tax above that.
            Year 6962 of the world
            18th. April, in Constantinople."
Wind on the lagoon, the south wind breaking roses.

Illmo ac ex^{mo} (eccellentissimo) princeps et d^{no}
Lord, my lord in particular, Sforza:
In reply to 1st l^{tr} of yr. ld^{shp}
re mat^{r} of horses, there are some for sale here.
I said that I hdn't. then seen 'em all thoroughly.
Now I may say that I have, and think
There are eleven good horses and almost that number
Of hacks that might be used in necessity,
To be had at a reasonable price.
It is true that there are X or XI big horses
    from 80 to 110 ducats
That seem to me dearer at the price
Than those for 80 ducats and under
And I think that if yr. ld^{sp} wd. send from
1000 ducats to one thousand 500 it cd. be spent
On stuff that wd. suit yr. L^{dp} quite well.
Please Y. L. to answer quickly
As I want to take myself out of here,
And if you want me to buy them
Send the cash by Mr. Pitro the farrier
And have him tell me by mouth or letter

What yr. ld^p wants me to buy.
Even from 80 ducats up there are certain good horses.
I have nothing else to say to your Lordship
Save my salutations.
Given Bologna, 14th. of August 1453
     Servant of yr. Illustrious Lordship
                    PISANELLUS

1462, 12th December: " and Vittor Capello
Brought also the head of St. George the Martyr
From the Island of Siesina.
This head was covered with silver and
Taken to San Giorgio Maggiore.

To the Cardinal Gonzaga of Mantua, ultimo febbraio 1548
" 26th of feb. was killed in this city
Lorenzo de Medicis.   Yr. Illu^s L^{dshp} will understand
from the enc. account how the affair is said to have
gone off.   They say those who killed him have certainly
got away in a post boat with 6 oars.   But they don't
know which way they have gone, and as a guard may
have been set in certain places and passes, it wd.
be convenient if yr. Ill^s L^{dshp} wd. write at once
to your ambassador here, saying among other things
that the two men who killed Lorenzino have passed through
the city of Mantua and that no one knows which
way they have gone.   Publishing this information
from yr. Ldshp will perhaps help them to get free.
Although we think they are already in Florence, but
in any case this measure can do no harm.   So that
yr. Ldshp wd. benefit by doing it quickly and even
to have others send the same news.
May Our Lord protect yr. Ill^s and most Revnd person
with the increase of state you desire.
            Venice, last of Feb. 1548
            I kiss the hands of yr. Ill. Ld^{shp}
            Don In. Hnr. de Mendoça

To the Marquis of Mantova, Fran° Gonzaga
Illustrious my Lord, during the past few days
An unknown man was brought to me by some others
To see a Jerusalem I have made, and as soon as he
saw it he insisted that I sell it him, saying it
gave him the gtst. content and satisfac^{tn}
Finally the deal was made and he took it away,
without paying and hasn't since then appeared.
I went to tell the people who had brought him, one
of whom is a priest with a beard that wears a
grey berettino whom I have often seen with you in
the hall of the gtr. council and I asked him the
fellow's name, and it is a Messire Lorenzo, the
painter to your Lordship, from which I have easily
understood what he was up to, and on that account
I am writing you, to furnish you my name and the
work's.   In the first place illustrious m. lord, I am
that painter to the Seignory, commissioned to paint the
gt. hall where Yr. Lordship deigns to mount
on the scaffold to see our work, the history of Ancona,
and my name is Victor Carpatio.
As to the Jerusalem I dare say there is not another
in our time as good and completely perfect, or as
large. It is 25 ft. long by 5 1/2, and I know Zuane
Zamberti has often spoken of it to yr. Sublimity; I
know certainly that this painter of yours has carried
off a piece, not the whole of it. I can send you
a small sketch in aquarelle on a roll, or have it
seen by good judges and leave the price to your
Lordship.
XV. Aug 1511, Venetijs.

                              I have sent a copy of
this letter by another way to be sure you get one or the other.
      The humble svt. of yr. Sublimity
                               Victor Carpathio
                                    pictore.

To the supreme pig, the archbishop of Salzburg:
Lasting filth and perdition.
Since your exalted pustulence is too stingy
To give me a decent income
And has already assured me that here I have nothing to hope
And had better seek fortune elsewhere;
And since thereafter you have
Three times impeded my father and self intending departure
I ask you for the fourth time
To behave with more decency, and this time
Permit my departure.

Wolfgang Amadeus, august 1777
(*inter lineas*)

" As is the sonata, so is little Miss Cannabich."

XXVII

FORMANDO di disio nuova persona
    One man is dead, and another has rotted his end off
    Et quant au troisième
    Il est tombé dans le
De sa femme, on ne le reverra
Pas, oth fugol ouitbaer:
" Observed that the paint was
Three quarters of an inch thick and concluded,
As they were being rammed through, the age of that
Cruiser." " Referred to no longer as
The goddamned Porta-goose, but as
England's oldest ally." " At rests in calm zone
If possible, the men are to be fed and relaxed,
The officers on the contrary..."
Ten million germs in his face,
" That is part of the risk and happens
" About twice a year in tubercular research, Dr. Spahlinger..."
" J'ai obtenu " said M. Curie, or some other scientist
" A burn that cost me six months in curing,"
And continued his experiments.
England off there in black darkness,
Russia off there in black darkness,
The last crumbs of civilization...
And they elected a Prince des Penseurs
Because there were so damn many princes,
And they elected a Monsieur Brisset
Who held that man is descended from frogs;
And there was a cracked concierge that they
Nearly got into the Deputies,
To protest against the earthquake in Messina.
    The Bucentoro sang it in that year,

1908, 1909, 1910, and there was
An old washerwoman beating her washboard,
That would be 1920, with a cracked voice,
Singing " Stretti! " and that was the last
Till this year, '27, Hotel Angioli, in Milan,
With an air Clara d'Ellébeuse,
With their lakelike and foxlike eyes,
With an air " Benette joue la Valse des Elfes "
In the salotto of that drummer's hotel,
Two young ladies with their air de province:
" No, we are Croat merchants, commercianti,
" There is nothing strange in our history."
" No, not to sell, but to buy."

And there was that music publisher,
The fellow that brought back the shrunk Indian head
Boned, oiled, from Bolivia, said:
" Yes, I went out there. Couldn't make out the trade,
Long after we'd melt up the plates,
Get an order, 200 copies, Peru,
Or some station in Chile."
Took out Floradora in sheets,
And brought back a red-headed mummy.
With an air Clara d'Ellébeuse, singing " Stretti."

Sed et universus quoque ecclesie populus,
All rushed out and built the duomo,
Went as one man without leaders
And the perfect measure took form;
" Glielmo ciptadin " says the stone, " the author,
" And Nicolao was the carver "
Whatever the meaning may be.
And they wrote for year after year.
Refining the criterion,
Or they rose as the tops subsided;

Brumaire, Fructidor, Petrograd.
And Tovarisch lay in the wind
And the sun lay over the wind,
And three forms became in the air
And hovered about him,
               so that he said:
This machinery is very ancient,
               surely we have heard this before.
And the waves like a forest
Where the wind is weightless in the leaves
But moving,
       so that the sound runs upon sound.
       Xarites, born of Venus and wine.

Carved stone upon stone.
But in sleep, in the waking dream,
Petal'd the air;
       twig where but wind-streak had been;
Moving bough without root,
               by Helios.
So that the Xarites bent over tovarisch.
And these are the labours of tovarisch,
That tovarisch lay in the earth,
And rose, and wrecked the house of the tyrants,
And that tovarisch then lay in the earth
       And the Xarites bent over tovarisch.

These are the labours of tovarisch,
That tovarisch wrecked the house of the tyrants,
And rose, and talked folly on folly,
And walked forth and lay in the earth
       And the Xarites bent over tovarisch.

And that tovarisch cursed and blessed without aim,
       These are the labours of tovarisch,

Saying:
>   "Me Cadmus sowed in the earth
>   And with the thirtieth autumn
> I return to the earth that made me.
> Let the five last build the wall;

I neither build nor reap.
That he came with the gold ships, Cadmus,
That he fought with the wisdom,
Cadmus, of the gilded prows. Nothing I build
And I reap
Nothing; with the thirtieth autumn
I sleep, I sleep not, I rot
And I build no wall.
>   Where was the wall of Eblis
At Ventadour, there now are the bees,
And in that court, wild grass for their pleasure
That they carry back to the crevice
Where loose stone hangs upon stone.
I sailed never with Cadmus,
>   lifted never stone above stone."

" Baked and eaten tovarisch!
" Baked and eaten, tovarisch, my boy,
" That is your story. And up again,
" Up and at 'em. Laid never stone upon stone."

" The air burst into leaf."
" Hung there flowered acanthus,
" Can you tell the down from the up? "

XXVIII

AND God the Father Eternal (Boja d'un Dio!)
Having made all things he cd.
think of, felt yet
That something was lacking, and thought
Still more, and reflected that
The Romagnolo was lacking, and
Stamped with his foot in the mud and
Up comes the Romagnolo:
          " Gard, yeh bloudy 'angman! It's me ".
Aso iqua me. All Esimo Dottor Aldo Walluschnig
Who with the force of his intellect
With art and assiduous care
Has snatched from death by a most perilous operation
The classical Caesarean cut
Marotti, Virginia, in Senni of San Giorgio
At the same time saving her son.
May there move to his laud the applause of all men
And the gratitude of the family.
          S. Giorgio, 23d May. A.D. 1925.
Item: There are people that can swimme in the sea
Havens and rivers naked
Having bowes and shafts,
Coveting to draw nigh yr. shippe which if they find not
Well watched and warded they wil assault
Desirous of the bodies of men which they covet for meate,
If you resist them
          They dive and wil flee.
And Mr Lourpee sat on the floor of the pension dining-room
Or perhaps it was in the alcove
And about him lay a great mass of pastells,
That is, stubbs and broken pencils of pastell,

In pale indeterminate colours.
And he admired the Sage of Concord
     " Too broad ever to make up his mind ".
And the mind of Lourpee at fifty
Directed him into a room with a certain vagueness
As if he wd.
neither come in nor stay out
As if he wd.
go neither to the left nor the right
And his painting reflected this habit.
And Mrs Kreffle's mind was made up,
Perhaps by the pressure of circumstance,
She described her splendid apartment
In Paris and left without paying her bill
And in fact she wrote later from Sevilla
And requested a shawl, and received it
From the Senora at 300 pesetas cost to the latter
(Also without remitting) which
May have explained the lassitude of her daughter;
And the best paid dramatic critic
Arrived from Manhattan
And was lodged in a bordello (promptly)
Having trusted " his people "
Who trusted a Dutch correspondent,
And when they had been devoured by fleas
(Critic and family)
They endeavoured to break the dutchman's month's contract,
And the ladies from West Virginia
Preserved the natal aroma,
And in the railway feeding-room in Chiasso
She sat as if waiting for the train for Topeka
— That was the year of the strikes —
When we came up toward Chiasso
By the last on the narrow-gauge,
Then by tramway from Como

Leaving the lady who loved bullfights
With her eight trunks and her captured hidalgo,
And a dutchman was there who was going
To take the boat at Trieste,
Sure, he was going to take it;
Would he go round by Vienna? He would not.
Absence of trains wdnt. stop him.
So we left him at last in Chiasso
Along with the old woman from Kansas,
Solid Kansas, her daughter had married that Swiss
Who kept the buffet in Chiasso.
Did it shake her? It did not shake her.
She sat there in the waiting room, solid Kansas,
Stiff as a cigar-store indian from the Bowery
Such as one saw in " the nineties ",
First sod of bleeding Kansas
That had produced this ligneous solidness;
If thou wilt go to Chiasso wilt find that indestructable female
As if waiting for the train to Topeka
In the buffet of that station on the bench that
Follows the wall, to the right side as you enter.
And Clara Leonora wd. come puffing so that one
Cd. hear her when she reached the foot of the stairs,
Squared, chunky, with her crooked steel spectacles
And her splutter and her face full of teeth
And old Rennert wd. sigh heavily
And look over the top of his lenses and
She wd. arrive after due interval with a pinwheel
Concerning Grillparzer or — pratzer
Or whatever follow the Grill —, and il Gran Maestro
Mr Liszt had come to the home of her parents
And taken her on his prevalent knee and
She held that a sonnet was a sonnet
And ought never be destroyed,
And had taken a number of courses

And continued with hope of degrees and
Ended in a Baptist learnery
        Somewhere near the Rio Grande.

And they wanted more from their women,
Wanted 'em jacked up a little
And sent over for teachers (Ceylon)
So Loica went out and died there
After her time in the post-Ibsen movement.

And one day in Smith's room
Or may be it was that 1908 medico's
Put the gob in the fire-place
Ole Byers and Feigenbaum and Joe Bromley,
Joe hittin' the gob at 25 feet
Every time, ping on the metal
        (Az ole man Comley wd. say: Boys!...
        Never cherr terbakker! Hrwwkke tth!
        Never cherr terbakker!,
" Missionaries," said Joe, " I was out back of Jaffa,
I dressed in the costume, used to like the cafés,
All of us settin' there on the ground,
Pokes his head in the doorway: " Iz there any,"
He says, " Gar'
Damn
Man here
Thet kan speak ENGLISH? "
        Nobody said anything fer a while
And then I said: " Hu er' you? "
" I'm er misshernary I am "
He sez, " chucked off a naval boat in Shanghaï.
I worked at it three months, nothin' to live on."
Beat his way overland.
I never saw the twenty I lent him."

Great moral secret service, plan, Tribune is told
limit number to thirty thousand,

only highest type will be included,
propaganda within ranks of the veterans,
to keep within bounds when they come into
contact with personal liberty...with the french authorities...
that includes the Paris police...
Strengthen franco-american amity.

NARCOTIC CHARGE: Frank Robert Iriquois
gave his home Oklahoma City... Expelled July 24 th.

" Je suis...
(Across the bare planks of a diningroom in the Pyrenees)
          ... plus fort que...
                         ... le Boud-hah! "
(No contradiction)
" Je suis...
          ... plus fort que le...
                         ... Christ!
(No contradiction)
" J'aurais...
          aboli...
                    le poids! "
(Silence, somewhat unconvinced.)
And in his waste house, detritus,
As it were the cast buttons of splendours,
The harbour of Martinique, drawn every house, and in detail.
Green shutters on half the houses,
Half the thing still unpainted.
                         "... sont
" l'in.. fan... terie кон-
                    lon-
                         i-ale "
voce tinnula
" Ce sont les vieux Marsouins! "
He made it, feitz Marcebrus, the words and the music,

137

Uniform out for Peace Day
And that lie about the Tibetan temple
(happens by the way to be true,
they do carry you up on their shoulders) but
Bad for his medical practice.
" Retreat? " said Dr Wymans, " It was marrvelous...
Gallipoli...
Secret. Turks knew nothing about it.
Uh! Helped me to get my wounded aboard."
And that man sweat blood to put through that railway,
And what he ever got out of it?
And one day he drove down to the whorehouse
Cause all the farmers had consented
            and granted the right of way,
But the pornoboskos wdn't. have it at any price
And said he'd shoot the surveyors,
But he didn't shoot ole pop in the buckboard,
He giv him the right of way.
And they thought they had him flummox'd,
Nobody'd sell any rails;
Till he went up to the north of New York state
And found some there on the ground
And he had 'em pried loose and shipped 'em
And had 'em laid here through the forest.

Thing is to find something simple
As for example Pa Stadtvolk;
Hooks to hang gutters on roofs,
A spike and half-circle, patented 'em and then made 'em;
Worth a good million, not a book in the place;
Got a horse about twenty years after, seen him
            Of a Saturday afternoon
When they'd taken down an old fence,
Ole Pa out there knockin the nails out
(To *save* 'em). I hear he smoked good cigars.

And when the Prince Oltrepassimo died, saccone,
That follow the coffins,
He lay there on the floor of the chapel
On a great piece of patterned brocade
And the walls solid gold about him
And there was a hole in one of his socks
And the place open that day to the public,
Kids running in from the street
And a cat sat there licking himself
And then stepped over the Principe,
Discobolus upstairs and the main door
Not opened since '70
When the Pope shut himself into the Vatican
And they had scales on the table
To weigh out the food on fast days;
And he lay there with his hood back
And the hole in one of his socks.

" Buk! " said the Second Baronet, " eh...
" Thass a funny lookin' buk " said the Baronet
Looking at Bayle, folio, 4 vols. in gilt leather, " Ah...
" Wu... Wu... wot you goin' eh to do with ah...
" ... ah read-it? "
                    Sic loquitur eques.

And lest it pass with the day's news
Thrown out with the daily paper,
Neither official pet
Nor Levine with the lucky button
Went on into darkness,
Saw naught above but close dark,
Weight of ice on the fuselage
Borne into the tempest, black cloud wrapping their wings,
The night hollow beneath them
And fell with dawn into ocean

But for the night saw neither sky nor ocean
And found ship... why?... how?... by the Azores.
And she was a bathing beauty, Miss Arkansas or Texas
And the man (of course) quasi anonymous
Neither a placard for non-smokers or non-alcohol
Nor for the code of Peoria;
Or one-eyed Hinchcliffe and Elsie
Blackeyed bitch that married dear Dennis,
That flew out into nothingness
And her father was the son of one too
That got the annulment.

XXIX

PEARL, great sphere, and hollow,
 Mist over lake, full of sunlight,
 Pernella concubina
 The sleeve green and shot gold over her hand
Wishing her son to inherit
Expecting the heir ainé be killed in battle
He being courageous, poisoned his brother puiné
Laying blame on Siena
And this she did by a page
Bringing war once more on Pitigliano
And the page repented and told this
To Nicolo (ainé) Pitigliano
Who won back that rock from his father
" still doting on Pernella his concubine ".
        The sand that night like a seal's back
        Glossy beneath the lanthorns.
From the Via Sacra
        (fleeing what band of Tritons)
Up to the open air
Over that mound of the hippodrome:
Liberans et vinculo ab omni liberatos
As who with four hands at the cross roads
By king's hand or sacerdos'
        are given their freedom
— Save who were at Castra San Zeno...

Cunizza for God's love, for remitting the soul of her father
— May hell take the traitors of Zeno.
And fifth begat he Alberic
And sixth the Lady Cunizza.

In the house of the Cavalcanti

Free go they all as by full manumission
All serfs of Eccelin my father da Romano
Save those who were with Alberic at Castra San Zeno
And let them go also
The devils of hell in their body.

And sixth the Lady Cunizza
That was first given Richard St Boniface
And Sordello subtracted her from that husband
And lay with her in Tarviso
Till he was driven out of Tarviso
And she left with a soldier named Bonius
nimium amorata in eum
And went from one place to another
" The light of this star o'ercame me "
Greatly enjoying herself
And running up the most awful bills.
And this Bonius was killed on a sunday
and she had then a Lord from Braganza
and later a house in Verona.

And he looked from the planks to heaven,
Said Juventus: " Immortal...
He said: " Ten thousand years before now...
Or he said: " Passing into the point of the cone
You begin by making the replica.
Thus Lusty Juventus, in September,
In cool air, under sky,
Before the residence of the funeral director
Whose daughters' conduct caused comment.
But the old man did not know how he felt
Nor cd. remember what prompted the utterance.
He said: " What I know, I have known,
" How can the knowing cease knowing? "

By the lawn of the senior elder
He continued his ambulation:
" Matter is the lightest of all things,
" Chaff, rolled into balls, tossed, whirled in the aether,
" Undoubtedly crushed by the weight,
" Light also proceeds from the eye;
" In the globe over my head
" Twenty feet in diameter, thirty feet in diameter
" Glassy, the glaring surface —
" There are many reflections
" So that one may watch them turning and moving
" With heads down now, and now up.
He went on toward the amateur student of minerals
That later went bankrupt;
He went on past the house of the local funny man,
Jo Tyson that had a camera.   His daughter was bow-legged
And married the assembly-man's son.

       O-hon dit que-ke fois au vi'-a-ge...

Past the house of the three retired clergymen
Who were too cultured to keep their jobs.
Languor has cried unto languor
        about the marshmallow-roast
(Let us speak of the osmosis of persons)
The wail of the phonograph has penetrated their marrow
(Let us...
The wail of the pornograph....)
    The cicadas continue uninterrupted.
With a vain emptiness the virgins return to their homes
With a vain exasperation
The ephèbe has gone back to his dwelling,
The djassban has hammered and hammered,
The gentleman of fifty has reflected
       That it is perhaps just as well.
Let things remain as they are.

The mythological exterior lies on the moss in the forest
And questions him about Darwin.
And with a burning fire of phantasy
            he replies with "Deh! nuvoletta..."
So that she would regret his departure.
            Drift of weed in the bay:
She seeking a guide, a mentor,
He aspires to a career with honour
To step in the tracks of his elders;
            a greater incomprehension?
There is no greater incomprehension
Than between the young and the young.
The young seek comprehension;
The middleaged to fulfill their desire.
Sea weed dried now, and now floated,
            mind drifts, weed, slow youth, drifts,
Stretched on the rock, bleached and now floated;
Wein, Weib, TAN AOIDAN
Chiefest of these the second, the female
Is an element, the female
Is a chaos
An octopus
A biological process
            and we seek to fulfill...
TAN AOIDAN, our desire, drift...
            Ailas e que'm fau miey huelh
            Quar no vezon so qu'ieu vuelh.
Our mulberry leaf, woman, TAN AOIDAN,
" Nel ventre tuo, o nella mente mia,
" Yes, Milady, precisely, if you wd.
have anything properly made."

" Faziamo tutte le due...
" No, not in the palm-room ". The lady says it is
Too cold in the palm-room. Des valeurs,

Nom de Dieu, et
    encore des valeurs.

She is submarine, she is an octopus, she is
A biological process,
So Arnaut turned there
Above him the wave pattern cut in the stone
Spire-top alevel the well-curb
And the tower with cut stone above that, saying:
    "I am afraid of the life after death."
and after a pause:
"Now, at last, I have shocked him."
And another day or evening toward sundown by the arena
(les gradins)
A little lace at the wrist
And not very clean lace either...
And I, "But this beats me,
"Beats me, I mean that I do not understand it;
"This love of death that is in them."
        Let us consider the osmosis of persons
nondum orto jubare;
The tower, ivory, the clear sky
Ivory rigid in sunlight
And the pale clear of the heaven
Phoibos of narrow thighs,
The cut cool of the air,
Blossom cut on the wind, by Helios
Lord of the Light's edge, and April
Blown round the feet of the God,
Beauty on an ass-cart
Sitting on five sacks of laundry
That wd. have been the road by Perugia
That leads out to San Piero. Eyes brown topaz,
Brookwater over brown sand,
The white hounds on the slope,

Glide of water, lights and the prore,
Silver beaks out of night,
Stone, bough over bough,
          lamps fluid in water,
Pine by the black trunk of its shadow
And on hill black trunks of the shadow
The trees melted in air.

XXX

OMPLEYNT, compleynt I hearde upon a day,
Artemis singing, Artemis, Artemis
Agaynst Pity lifted her wail:
Pity causeth the forests to fail,
Pity slayeth my nymphs,
Pity spareth so many an evil thing.
Pity befouleth April,
Pity is the root and the spring.
Now if no fayre creature followeth me
It is on account of Pity,
It is on account that Pity forbideth them slaye.
All things are made foul in this season,
This is the reason, none may seek purity
Having for foulnesse pity
And things growne awry;
No more do my shaftes fly
To slay.   Nothing is now clean slayne
But rotteth away.

In Paphos, on a day
                    I also heard:
... goeth not with young Mars to playe
But she hath pity on a doddering fool,
She tendeth his fyre,
She keepeth his embers warm.

Time is the evil.   Evil.
                    A day, and a day
Walked the young Pedro baffled,
                    a day and a day

After Ignez was murdered.

Came the Lords in Lisboa
                    a day, and a day
In homage.   Seated there
                    dead eyes,
Dead hair under the crown,
The King still young there beside her.

Came Madame ϓΛΗ
Clothed with the light of the altar
And with the price of the candles.
" Honour?   Balls for yr. honour!
Take two million and swallow it."
                         Is come Messire Alfonso
And is departed by boat for Ferrara
And has passed here without saying " O."

Whence have we carved it in metal
Here working in Caesar's fane:
            To the Prince Caesare Borgia
            Duke of Valent and Aemelia
...and here have I brought cutters of letters
and printers not vile and vulgar
            (in Fano Caesaris)
notable and sufficient compositors
and a die-cutter for greek fonts and hebrew
named Messire Francesco da Bologna
not only of the usual types but he hath excogitated
a new form called cursive or chancellry letters
nor was it Aldous nor any other but it was
this Messire Francesco who hath cut all Aldous his letters
with such grace and charm as is known
            Hieronymous Soncinus 7th July 1503.
and as for text we have taken it

from that of Messire Laurentius
and from a codex once of the Lords Malatesta...

And in August that year died Pope Alessandro Borgia,
          Il Papa mori.

          Explicit canto
            XXX

ELEVEN NEW CANTOS
XXXI–XLI

XXXI

TEMPUS loquendi,
  Tempus tacendi.
  Said Mr Jefferson: It wd. have given us
    time.
" modern dress for your statue.....
" I remember having written you while Congress sat at An-
  napolis,
" on water communication between ours and the western
  country,
" particularly the information....of the plain between
" Big Beaver and Cayohoga, which made me hope that a canal
......navigation of Lake Erie and the Ohio. You must have had
" occasion of getting better information on this subject
" and if you have you wd. oblige me
" by a communication of it. I consider this canal,
" if practicable, as a very important work.
       T. J. to General Washington, 1787

.....no slaves north of Maryland district....
.....flower found in Connecticut that vegetates when suspended
  in air...
...screw more effectual if placed below surface of water.
Suspect that a countryman of ours, Mr Bushnell of Connecticut
is entitled to the merit of prior discovery.
Excellency Mr Adams. Excellency Dr. Franklin.
And thus Mr Jefferson (president) to Tom Paine:
" You expressed a wish to get a passage to this country
in a public vessel. Mr. Dawson is charged with orders
to the captain of the 'Maryland' to receive and accommodate
  you
with passage back, if you can depart on so short a warning....

in hopes you will find us returned to sentiments
worthy of former time.....in these you have laboured as
much as any man living. That you may long live to
continue your labours and to reap their fitting reward....
Assurances of my high esteem and attachment."

" English papers...their lies.....

in a few years...no slaves northward of Maryland...

" Their tobacco, 9 millions, delivered in port of France;
6 millions to manufacture
on which the king takes thirty million
that cost 25 odd to collect
so that in all it costs 72 millions livres to the
consumer......
persuaded (I am) in this branch of the revenue
the collection absorbs too much.

(from Paris, 1785)

......for our model, the Maison Quarrée of Nismes.....

With respect to his motives (Madison writing) I acknowledged
I had been much puzzled to divine any natural ones
without looking deeper into human nature
than I was willing to do.

(in re/ Mr Robert Smith)
So critical the state of that country
moneyed men I imagine are glad to place their money abroad.
Mr Adams could borrow there for us.
This country is really supposed to be on the eve of a XTZBK49HT
(*parts of this letter in cypher*)
Jefferson, from Paris, to Madison, Aug. 2, 1787
I hear that Mr Beaumarchais means to make himself heard..
...turn through the Potomac,..commerce of Lake Erie....
I can further say with safety there is not a crowned head

in Europe whose talents or merits would entitle him
to be elected a vestryman by any American parish.

>   T. J. to General Washington, May 2. '88.

" When Lafayette harangued you and me and John Quincy
>   Adams
" through a whole evening in your hotel in the Cul de Sac....
" ....silent as you were. I was, in plain truth as astonished
" at the grossness of his ignorance of government and history,
" as I had been for years before at that of Turgot,
" La Rochefoucauld, of Condorcet and of Franklin."

>   To Mr Jefferson, Mr John Adams.

...care of the letters now enclosed. Most of them are
of a complexion not proper for the eye of the police.

>   From Monticello, April 16th. 1811

>   To Mr Barlow departing for Paris.

...indebted to nobody for more cordial aid than to Gallatin...

" Adair too had his kink. He believed all the Indians of
" America to be descended from the jews."

>   Mr Jefferson to Mr Adams.

" But observe that the public were at the same time paying
on it an interest of exactly the same amount
(four million dollars). Where then is the gain to either
party which makes it a public blessing? "

>   to Mr Eppes, 1813

" Man, a rational creature! " said Franklin.
" Come, let us suppose a rational man.
" Strip him of all his appetites, especially his hunger and thirst.
" He is in his chamber, engaged in making experiments,
" Or in pursuing some problem.
" At this moment a servant knocks. ' Sir,
" ' dinner is on the table.'
" ' Ham and chickens? ' ' Ham! '

" ' And must I break the chain of my thoughts to
" ' go down and gnaw a morsel of damned hog's arse?
" ' Put aside your ham; I will dine tomorrow; '
Take away appetite, and the present generation would not
Live a month, and no future generation would exist;
and thus the exalted dignity of human nature etc. .....
       Mr Adams to Mr Jefferson, 15 Nov. 1813.

" ..wish that I cd. subjoin Gosindi's Syntagma
" of the doctrines of Epicurus.

                                  (Mr Adams.)

" ..this was the state of things in 1785..."

                                (Mr Jefferson.)

..met by agreement, about the close of the session—
Patrick Henry, Frank Lee and your father,
Henry Lee and myself...to consult..measures
circumstances of times seemed to call for...
produce some channel of correspondence...this was in '73.
                          Jefferson to D. Carr

..church of St. Peter.....human reason, human conscience,
though I believe that there are such things....

                           Mr Adams.

A tiel leis....en ancien scripture, and this
they have translated *Holy Scripture*...
                        Mr Jefferson

and they continue this error.
" Bonaparte...knowing nothing of commerce....
...or paupers, who are about one fifth of the whole...

    (on the state of England in 1814).

            Hic Explicit Cantus

XXXII

THE revolution," said Mr Adams,
" Took place in the minds of the people."
..........with sixty cannon, ten tons of powder,
10,000 muskets and bayonets, lead, bed-covers,
uniforms and a colonel, to affirm their neutrality...the Amphi-
trite
departed the tenth of March to her first destination...
and a fourth which orders the liquidation
and payment of what remains due to the Merchants of Morea
et des dettes des dites Echelles as you may
read *dans les arrêts principaux du Conseil, decembre, 'soixante
six.*
*armes et autres ustenciles qui ne peuvent être que pour
le compte du gouvernement...* Monsieur Saint-Libin
très au fait des langues du Pays, connu des Nababs
especially Hyder Ali
*...pour l'exciter, et à tailler des croupières to the Anglois...
peu délicat sur les moyens....*to break up our bonds
with the Portagoose....and as for the Amphitrite, M'lorrd
she fits under Beaumarchais' supervision, her cargo
mainly munitions.......
Witnesses will some of them prove that he (Burr) had
no interest in the Ohio canal....
                              coram non judice
as usual where an opinion is to be supported right or wrong,
dwells on smaller objections and passes over the solid.
Oryzia mutica, the upland or mountain rice...
seed of perennial succory....very famous turnip of Sweden....

I pray you place me rectus in curia in this business
with the Emperor (Alexander) and to assure him

that I carry into my retirement the highest veneration...for his
dispositions to better at least in some degree the
condition of man oppressed....
If you return to us, to bring me a couple
of shepherd dogs, true-bred......much desired that war be
     avoided.
type-founding to which antimony is essential, I therefore place
     Mr Ronaldson in your hands.
...be avoided, if circumstances will admit...
for civilizing the indians, great improvement on the
ancient ineffectual...which began with religious ministrations.
The following has been successful. First, to raise cattle
whereby to acquire a sense of the value of property...
arithmetic to compute that value, thirdly writing, to
keep accounts, and here they begin to labour;
enclose farms, and the women to weave and spin...
fourth to read Aesop's Fables, which are their first delight
along with Robinson Crusoe. Creeks, Cherokees, the latter
now instituting a government.
...and as many, just as respectable, swore to the contrary
all of whom present at the sermon....
...deem it necessary to keep them down by hard labour, poverty,
     ignorance,
and to take from them, as from bees, so much of their earnings
as that unremitting labour shall be necessary to obtain a
     sufficient surplus
barely to sustain a scant life. And these earnings
they apply to maintain their privileged orders in splendour and
     idleness
to fascinate the eyes of the people...as to an order of superior
     beings...   June 12, '23 to Judge Johnson...

whether in a stye, stable or state-room,
let everything bend before them and banish whatever might
lead them to think...and thus are become as mere animals....

Cannibals of Europe are eating one another again....

out of his case, to say what the law in a moot case would be,
Judge Marshall is irregular....
...animal is entirely without thought
            if deprived of that organ...
                    Mr. Adams to Mr. Jefferson...

..whether in a stye, a stable or in a stateroom....
            Louis Sixteenth was a fool
The King of Spain was a fool, the King of Naples a fool
they despatched two courriers weekly to tell each other, over a
        thousand miles
            what they had killed...the King of Sardinia
was, like all the Bourbons, a fool, the
Portuguese Queen a Braganza and therefore by nature an idiot,
The successor to Frederic of Prussia, a mere hog
in body and mind, Gustavus and Joseph of Austria
were as you know really crazy, and George 3d was in
a straight waistcoat,

there remained none but old Catherine, too lately picked
up.........

by which we are in the constant practice of changing the
characters and propensities of the animals we raise for
our purposes....

            a guisa de leon
The cannibals of Europe are eating one another again
            quando si posa.

XXXIII

Is that despotism
or absolute power...unlimited sovereignty,
is the same in a majority of a popular assembly,
..... an aristocratical council, an oligarchical junto,
and a single emperor, equally arbitrary, bloody,
and in every respect diabolical. Wherever it has resided
has never failed to destroy all records, memorials,
all histories which it did not like, and to corrupt
those it was cunning enough to preserve.....

If the troops cd. be fed upon long letters, I believe the gent. at
the head of that dept. (in this country) wd. be the best
commissary on earth. But till I see him determined to act,
not to write; to sacrifice his domestic ease to the duties
of his appointment, and apply the resources of this country,
wheresoever they are to be had, I must entertain a different
opinion of him.

T. J. to P. Henry, March '79.

.....over five and twenty millions of people, when four and
twenty millions and five hundred thousand of them can
neither read nor write...as impracticable as it wd. be over
elephants in the Menagerie at Versailles.
Napoleon has invented a word, Ideology, which expresses my
opinion.
.....how far advanced we were in the science of aristocracy since
the stallions of Theognis...Have not Chancellor Livingston
and Major General Humphries introduced an aristocracy
of Merino sheep...entailed upon us and forever....of land
jobbers and stock jobbers to endless generations.

..multiplication of officers and salaries merely to make par-
tisans....

That this possessor be kalos k'àgathos, theocrat, baron, bojar or
rich man matters very little.

..difference ascribed to our superiority in taking aim when we
fire..

" I speak of the Grand Duke of Tuscany (T. J. to J. A. '77)
somewhat avaricious in his nature...crowns lying dead in
his coffers,...application perhaps from Dr. Franklin wd. be
prudent to sound well before hand...."

Condorcet has let the cat out of the bag. He has made precious
confessions. I regret that I have only an English translation
of his " Outline of the Historical View of the Progress of
the Human Mind." But in pages 247, 248 and 249 you will
find it frankly acknowledged that the philosophers of the
eighteenth century adopted all the arts of the Pharisees.

....was in the minds of the people, and this was effected from
1760 to 1775 in the course of fifteen years..before Lex-
ington.....

removal wd. be necessary to more able commissaries rather than
to a more plentiful country. (T. J. on provisions.)

Bonaparte, Poor Devil! what has and what will become of him
....Cromwell, Wat Tyler, Jack Cade, i.e. to a bad end.
And Wellington, envied, despised by all the barons, earls,
viscounts, as an upstart, a parvenue elated over their heads.
(Mr Adams to Thomas Jefferson.)

Litterae nihil sanantes....whether serpents' teeth sprang up men..
cannot appease my melancholy commiseration for our

armies in this furious snow storm (Quincey, November 15th.)

But two things I did learn from him (Plato): That Franklin's idea of exempting husbandmen and mariners etc. from the depredations of war was borrowed from him
and (secondly) that sneezing is a cure for the hickups.

but to keep in countenance the funding and banking system... orations, prayers, sermons...not that they loved General Washington, but merely to disgrace the old Whigs...

$75,000 equal to 1,000 specie. (Feb. 1781) settler will be worth to the public 20 times as much every year, as in our old plan he would have paid in a single payment.

limits of his individuality (cancels) and develops his power as a specie. (Das Kapital) denounced in 1842 still continue (today 1864) report of '42 was merely chucked into the archives and remained there while these boys were ruined and became fathers of this generation...for workshops remained a dead letter down to 1871 when was taken from control of municipal...and placed in hands of the factory inspectors, to whose body they added eight (8) assistants to deal with over one hundred thousand workshops and over 300 tile yards.

Rogier (minister) told me that this government (Brussels) had been intending to introduce such a law but found itself (re/ child labour not limited to 12 hours per day) always blocked by the jealous uneasiness that met any law tampering with the absolute freedom of labour.
Lord H. de Walden from Brussels. 1862

They (the owners) denounced the inspectors as a species of revolutionary commissar pitilessly sacrificing the unfortu-

nate labourers to their humanitarian fantasies (re/ the law
of 1848).

that no factory-owner shall sit as a magistrate in cases concern-
ing the spinning of cotton...(Factory Act of John
Hobhouse)
nor shall his father, brother, or son.

And if the same small boys are merely shifted from the spinning
room to the weaving room or from one factory to another,
how can the inspector verify the number of hours they
are worked? (1849, Leonard Horner).

Case where the jury ('62) was to decide whether soot adul-
terated with 90% of dust and sand was " adulterated-in-
the-legal-sense " soot or in the commercial " real soot." As
friends of commerce decided (the jury decided) it was
" real soot " against the plaintiff with costs.

avénement révolution allemande posait des problèmes nouveaux,
routine commercial être remplacée par création de deux
fonds or et blé destinés au proletariat victorieux (allemand)
to functionaries of legation in Berlin who are members
of the party (1923)

bureaucrat paisible, Van Tzin Vei se montra, tout à fait incap-
able d'assumer le rôle de chef d'une révolution sanguinaire.
(according to Monsieur Bessedovsky)

for ten years our (Russian) ambassadors have enquired what
theories are in fashion in Moscow and have reported their
facts to fit. (idem)
Bills discounted at exhorbitant rates, four times or three times
those offered by the Midland....
150 millions

yearly, merely in usurious discounts...

and he even

(to change the subject)

put into the mouths of the directors of the Federal Reserve banks the words that they should say..." You have got more than your share, we want you to reduce, we can not let you have any more."

(Mr Brookhart)

page 34 of the minutes then they adopted another resolution page 42 committee of interstate commerce, ask increase of railroad rates, said to them: wd. suggest, gentlemen, you be careful not to give out anything about any discussion of discount rates disturbs everybody immediate rush never discuss in the newspapers.....

.......& Company's banker was in that meeting, and next day he was out after a loan of 60 millions, and got it. Swift-amoursinclair but the country at large did not know it. The meeting decided we were over-inflated.

XXXIV

OILS, beasts, grasses, petrifactions, birds, incrustations,
Dr. Mitchell's conversation was various.....
And a black manservant, to embark on a voyage to
Russia...
Consistent with their peace and their separation from Europe....
English pretentions, exclusive, auf dem Wasser..... (a.d. 1809)
En fait de commerce ce (Bonaparte) est un étourdi," said
Romanzoff...
Freedom of admission for ships, freedom of departure, freedom
of purchase and sale...
Are the only members of the corps diplomatique who have any
interest in literature, conversation..
we talked of Shakespeare, Milton, Virgil and of the Abbé
Delille....
" Monsieur Adams " said the Emperor, " il y a cent ans que je
ne vous ai vu."
June 4th. 1811:
The idea occurred to me of a treaty of commerce.
Told him his government wd. probably make our peace.
" How? " said the ambassador (french).
" By not keeping her word."
And he, Bonaparte, said to Romanzoff:
" After the peace of Tilsit, where cd. I go but Spain? "
For he must always be *going*.
It is reported that the two empresses will return to the city
As is said to be customary
At least in wars *un peu interessantes*, which war Alexander
Has done all he can to prevent.
French army 500 thousand, the Russian 300 thousand,
But counting on space and time.

" The fifth element: mud." said Napoleon.

A black, Claud Gabriel, in the emperor's service

Was very ill used in America. Aug. 14th. to Oranienbaum.

Where was Ld. Cathcart (that is, at Madame de Stael's)

And she wanted to know how she cd.

Receive her interest from United States funds

While in England, and a war on between them.

Here the nobility have given one man to the army

From every ten of their peasants.

   Qu'il fit la sottise de Moscou

and he, Bonaparte had to borrow six shirts from

his minister, and four thousand louis...Mr Gallatin,

Mr Bayard...answer from Romanzoff...Mr Gallatin

did not think that " they cd." (did not

think that our actions in Florida could be justified).

Against rights on the Mississippi....our

Rights to fish, dry fish and cure...off Newfoundland.

At the opera: Tamerlan, and the ballet of Télémaque.

1815, March 18th. was expected (Bonaparte)

   last night at Auxerre,

Ney to be here (Paris) tomorrow, because it is the

King of Rome's birthday...

March twentieth: The King, Bourbon, left the Tuilleries,

To take, they say, the road going toward Beauvais...

At the Seance Royale last Thursday he had talked of

His death in defence of the country.

And when they wish to make the troops cheer, the

Soldiers say: Ah, voui, Vive le Roi.

Newspaper this morning headed *Journal de l'Empire*.

.....arrived last evening with the troops that had been sent out

  against him....

which is due to Bourbon misconduct.

I told him (Sir James Mackintosh) that I

Did not believe Dr Franklin or Washington

Had wanted the revolution....He asked if any leading man had.
I said, my father, perhaps, Samuel Adams, James Otis...

(And on his return was recd. by Gouverneur Morris and Mr
    Astor with a pubk. dinner at Tammany Hall.)
And one night a dead fowl was tied to Mr Onis's bell rope,
As (in his eyes) a gt. dishonour to Spain.
Mr Jefferson remarked that fond as he was of agriculture
He knew nothing about it tho' Mr Madison did.
Mr Madison was very efficient in the convention of '87.
" Mr Bagot has been a much better minister
" than a much abler man wd. have been, better
" for the interest of England, better
" for the tranquillity of this country." DeWitt Clinton
Never more low and discredited
Than just before being elected (comma)
Without opposition (comma) Governor of New York State.

" a misanthropist, an unsocial savage " J.Q.A. on himself.
Banks breaking all over the country,
Some in a sneaking, some in an impertinent manner...
prostrate every principle of economy.
Jan 18th. 1820. I (J.Q.A.) called at the President's
And the President said: Colonel Johnson
might have been more worthily occupied than in acting as
medium for proposal of
furnishing ten thousand stand of arms to Venezuela
in order to make a job for Duane.
                    a.d. 1820
.....is that moral considerations seldom
appear to have much weight in
                the minds of statesmen
unless connected with popular feelings....
while professing neutrality
            (himself to hire men from our army

167

secretissime, on the quiet) Monroe admits it.
No one else seems to mind.

    ....but the vice-presidency is—
to call things by their proper names—in the market.
" Defective in elementary knowledge and with a very
undigested system of ethics, Mr Clay (Henry) ".

After conversing with Mr Calhoun, Adams reflected:
Paper currency...reductions of fictitious capital....
Accumulation of debts as long as credit can be strained....
Mr Noah has a project for colonizing jews in this country
And wd. like a job in Vienna....
Xmas, 1820, read aloud after breakfast
From Pope's " Messiah." Not one of my family
Except George,
     appeared to take the least interest,
Nor is there any one of them
     who has a relish for literature.
I have been a lawyer for bread,
     a statesman at the call of my country.
Plain modest and tasteless monuments to George Clinton
and Elbridge Gerry....we have neither forefathers nor posterity,
     a few years will efface them.
....half educated, like almost all eminent men in this country..
..Calhoun thought we ought in no case
     attend a congress of the allies.
England more by her interest than
     from principle of general liberty...
We shd. separate from all European concerns.
Who have followed (maiden ladies have followed)
General Lafayette from Europe to Lisses. Oct. 2. '24.
So that when Washington left the senate chamber he said he
Wd. be damned if he ever went there again.

They (congress) wd. do nothing for
the education of boys but to make soldiers, they

wd. not endow a university (in 1826).
Black walnut, almond planted in spring
take two months precisely to vegetate to the surface.

This has been (May 26th) a harassing day
but I perceived a tamarind heaving up the earth
in tumbler number 2, and in tumbler number one, planted....

Interfere with official duty? I said
I thought that it wd. as the U.S. was interested in
the Canal Company by their subscription of one million dollars.
Reading Evelyn's " Sylva " and making
Trivial observations upon the vegetation of trees until dark.

Some sensibility at parting? Clay expressed a wish to
            hear from me now and again...
" There is something strange, and which wd. now be
            thought very affected in the language of Shakespeare
Whose common thoughts are expressed in uncommon words."
            (diary, March 1829)
But of late years have lost relish for fiction...
December 13th.: Mrs Eaton....
and accordingly she (Mrs Calhoun) remains in the untainted
atmosphere of S. Carolina.
English " Quarterly Review " for November,
            two articles of vilification...
Calhoun heads the moral party, Mr Van Buren....
President Jackson's spittin' box and a broken pipe on the floor..
I called upon Nicholas Biddle...and recd. two dividends
of my bank stock.....as I might be called to take part in
public measures.....I wished to divest myself
of all personal interest....Nov. 9. '31.

" I took seat Number 203." J. Q. Adams.
....asked him (Mr Webster) his views on
            the diminution in the tariff.

169

I said I had no desire that the interruption of social
intercourse between Gen Jackson and me shd.
continue (March second) so far, so good...a
restitution of it cd. not fail to expose me to obloquy
March the third: Dined with
            Mr Webster upon salmon sent from New York.
Miss Martineau....author of *Conversations upon Political
    Economy*
..a young woman...deaf..and hearing only through an ear-
    trumpet
Her conversation is lively and easy....
The reasoning of Mr Clay, Mr Calhoun, Mr Webster
is shallow, they speak to popular prejudice.
The old states will so sacrifice
            all their rights to the public lands...
L'ami de tout le monde, Martin Van Buren...
Mr Webster, a man of straw...in the yard of the
President's house. It is said that their object
was to remonstrate against working more
than ten hours a day (April 13th. '37).
At the President's house and had with him conversation
respecting the climate, Queen Victoria and the weather....

Legaré wd. retort upon them by preaching to the labourers
Insurrection against the capitalists of the North.

Senate Chamber where I found him (J. Calhoun)
discoursing to his own honour and glory and
vituperating Mr Clay.
.....after battling with each other on the atonement,
Christ and the Trinity....phrenology and animal magnetism....
Tippecanoe clubs..students of colleges, schoolboys...

The world, the flesh, the devils in hell are
Against any man who now in the North American Union
shall dare to join the standard of Almighty God to
Put down the African slave trade...what can I

Seventy-four years, verge of my birthday, shaking hand
...for the suppression of the African slave trade.....

Van Buren...against more than ten hours a day...
Harrison on a mean-looking horse...
            was amiable and benevolent...
Administration will waddle along...
            haec sunt infamiae...
                wrongs of the Cherokee nation..
These are the sins of Georgia
These are the lies
These are the infamies
These are the broken contracts...
Buchanan the shade of a shade,
            Scott a daguerreotype of a likeness
Mr Dan Webster spouting, Tyler's nose outreaching the
    munyment

Gun barrels, black walnut...

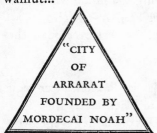

"CITY
OF
ARRARAT
FOUNDED BY
MORDECAI NOAH"

These words I read on a pyramid, written
            in English and Hebrew.
The firemen's torchlight procession,
Firemen's torchlight procession,
Science as a principle of political action

            Firemen's torchlight procession!
Proportioned to free inhabitants (Dec. 21. '43)
Electro-magnetic (Morse)

            Constans proposito....
            Justum et Tenacem

171

XXXV

So this is (may we take it) Mitteleuropa:

    Mr Corles was in command of machine guns
    but when the time came to fire
      he merely lit a cigarette and walked away from his
  battery and seated himself in a field,
So some subaltern gave the order to fire
and Mr Corles did not suffer the extreme penalty
because his family
was a very good bourgeois family in Vienna
and he was therefor sent to a mind sanatorium.
Mr Fidascz
explained to me
the horrors of playing the fiddle while that ass Nataanovitch,
or some other better known -ovitch
whose name we must respect because of the
law of libel,
was conducting
in particular the Mattias Passion, after requesting that
the audience come in black clothes;
And the Fraulein Doktor nearly wept over the Tyrol,
being incapable of seeing that the century-old joke on Italia
was now on somebody else
though if they cd. sentimentalize over that lousy old
bewhiskered sonvabitch François Giuseppe of whom nothing
good is recorded—in fact with the most patient research—
nothing good is recorded......and so forth....
this is Mitteleuropa
        and Tsievitz
has explained to me the warmth of affections,
the intramural, the almost intravaginal warmth of

hebrew affections, in the family, and nearly everything else....
pointing out that Mr Lewinesholme has suffered by deprivation
of same and exposure to American snobbery..." I am a product,"
said the young lady, " of Mitteleuropa,"
but she seemed to have been able to mobilize
and the fine thing was that the family did not
wire about papa's death for fear of disturbing the concert
which might seem to contradict the general indefinite wobble.
It must be rather like some internal organ,
some communal life of the pancreas....sensitivity
without direction...this is...
Oh yes, there are nobles, still interested in polo
said the whoring countess of course there were nobles.
Mister Axon the usually so intelligent was
after two lunches with Dortmund unable, in fact he was
quite unable to play respectable chess and the younger
Alexi after living with Murphy
was observed to be gray in the gills
through a presumed loss of vitality we have said that
stupidity is contagious, the divorce of Potemkin
was impeded by the death of his grandmother
and a resurgence of family feeling. His
wife now acts as his model and the Egeria
has, let us say, married a realtor. Having resigned overt
intention to remarry, the widow, once the rose,
spends her time now plaguing her daughter, and
Mr Elias said to me:
            " How do you get inspiration?
" Now my friend Hall Caine told me he came on a case
" a very sad case of a girl in the East End of London
" and it gave him an i n s p i r a t i o n . The only
" way I get inspiration is occasionally from a girl, I
" mean sometimes sitting in a restaurant and
            looking at a pretty girl I

" get an i-de-a, I-mean-a biz-nis i-de-a? "
        dixit sic felix Elias?
The tale of the perfect schnorrer: a peautiful chewisch poy
wit a vo-ice dot woult
meldt dh heart offa schtone
and wit a likeing for to make arht-voiks
and ven dh oldt ladty wasn't dhere any more
and dey didn't know why, tdhere ee woss in the
oldt antique schop and nobodty knew how he got dhere
and venn hiss brudder diet widout any bapers
he vept all ofer dh garpet so much he
had to have his clothes aftervards pressed
and he orderet a magnifficent funeral
and tden zent dh pill to dh vife.
        But when they have high cheek-bones
they are supposed to be Mongol. Eljen! Eljen Hatvany!
He had ideals and he said to the general at the conference,
" I introduce to you the head of the bakers' union.
" I introduce to you the head of the brick-layers' union.."
" Comment! Vous êtes tombés si bas? "
        replied General Franchet de Whatshisname
on the part of the french royalist party, showing thus
the use of ideals to a jewish Hungarian baron
with a library (naturally with a library)
and a fine collection of paintings? " We find the land over-
    brained."
said the bojars or whatever the old savages call it
as they hung their old huntsman friend to his chandelier
in his dining hall after the usual feasting and flagons
VIRTUSCH!! it must be one helluva country. Item:
That there be made a *fontego* (a chamber)
to lend money on cloth so that they cease not to
labour for lack of money..Item: that there be made a *scaven-
    zaria*
and it be furnished with cloth thus pledged

to be sold *a schavezo* at a price as if wholesale
plus only the proportion of the tax for the retail so that
Mantua cloth being cheap as in countries circumjacent and that
Brescians, Cremonesi, Parmenesi, Resanesi
who now go to Verona where it is cheaper as also
our own townsfolk go there, they wd. then come here or
stay here to the augment of industry and increase in
the retail tax and all of the other taxes.
Item: for the increase of this art
shd. be a man stationed in Venice...to sell what we
can't sell here...Item: a dye works...that they can dye
the pledged cloth...and that finding here cloth well coloured
....inficit umbras....
the Romagnols wd. come here to Mantua, and the March folk
who now go to Verona to buy...all of which wd.
be gain to this industry, bring more people to live here
and be of great use to yr. taxes.

                    Mantua 1401, una grida.

When the stars fall from the olive
Or with four points or with five
Toward St John's eve
Came this day Madame ὕλη, Madame la Porte Parure
Adorned with the Romancero,
foot like a flowery branch. That
Venice be *luogo di contratto* may we
say the place where the deal is made
and the profits
most assuredly from the pocket
of the last man who buys / ·exempt from customs
be food stuffs and nothing else so exempted
9 per cent in, and 9 out, for the upkeep of " The Dominant "
and De Gama (Vasco) a great inconvenience in fact the
worst news that there could be but:

            Can Portugal keep it up?
omnes de partibus ultramarinis

needing salt, made their peace with Venice
" who commands sea, commands trade "
let the rest provide for " The Dominant," " Victoria?
" Where 'ave I 'eard that nayme? "
Undersell, overbuy, maintain defence of the sea route
            a.d. 1423 et cetera
9% in and 9 out, no export of sand, alkali, rags.

Quality. So that our goods please the buyer.
Tell the Wazir that that stuff is ours only in name
it is made by damned jews in exile, made by damned jews in
Ragusa and sold with Venetian labels. Goods in
Venetian bottoms
no ship to be built out of Venice.
            Mocenigo. Fourteen twenty-three.
Have a load-line, no heavy deck cargo. Tola, octroi and decime.

XXXVI

Alady asks me
   I speak in season
  She seeks reason for an affect, wild often
   That is so proud he hath Love for a name
Who denys it can hear the truth now
Wherefore I speak to the present knowers
Having no hope that low-hearted
   Can bring sight to such reason
Be there not natural demonstration
   I have no will to try proof-bringing
Or say where it hath birth
What is its virtu and power
Its being and every moving
Or delight whereby 'tis called " to love "
Or if man can show it to sight.

Where memory liveth,
   it takes its state
Formed like a diafan from light on shade
Which shadow cometh of Mars and remaineth
Created, having a name sensate,
Custom of the soul,
   will from the heart;
Cometh from a seen form which being understood
Taketh locus and remaining in the intellect possible
Wherein hath he neither weight nor still-standing,
Descendeth not by quality but shineth out
Himself his own effect unendingly
Not in delight but in the being aware
Nor can he leave his true likeness otherwhere.

He is not vertu but cometh of that perfection
Which is so postulate not by the reason
But 'tis felt, I say.
Beyond salvation, holdeth his judging force
Deeming intention to be reason's peer and mate,
Poor in discernment, being thus weakness' friend
Often his power cometh on death in the end,
Be it withstayed
                and so swinging counterweight.
Not that it were natural opposite, but only
Wry'd a bit from the perfect,
Let no man say love cometh from chance
Or hath not established lordship
Holding his power even though
                Memory hath him no more.

Cometh he to be
                when the will
From overplus
Twisteth out of natural measure,
Never adorned with rest Moveth he changing colour
Either to laugh or weep
Contorting the face with fear
                resteth but a little
Yet shall ye see of him That he is most often
With folk who deserve him
And his strange quality sets sighs to move
Willing man look into that forméd trace in his mind
And with such uneasiness as rouseth the flame.
Unskilled can not form his image,
He himself moveth not, drawing all to his stillness,
Neither turneth about to seek his delight
Nor yet to seek out proving
Be it so great or so small.

He draweth likeness and hue from like nature
So making pleasure more certain in seeming
Nor can stand hid in such nearness,
Beautys be darts tho' not savage
Skilled from such fear a man follows
Deserving spirit, that pierceth.
Nor is he known from his face
But taken in the white light that is allness
Toucheth his aim
Who heareth, seeth not form
But is led by its emanation.
Being divided, set out from colour,
Disjunct in mid darkness
Grazeth the light, one moving by other,
Being divided, divided from all falsity
Worthy of trust
From him alone mercy proceedeth.

Go, song, surely thou mayest
Whither it please thee
For so art thou ornate that thy reasons
Shall be praised from thy understanders,
With others hast thou no will to make company.

" Called thrones, balascio or topaze "
Eriugina was not understood in his time
" which explains, perhaps, the delay in condemning him "
And they went looking for Manicheans
And found, so far as I can make out, no Manicheans
So they dug for, and damned Scotus Eriugina
" Authority comes from right reason,
          never the other way on "
Hence the delay in condemning him
Aquinas head down in a vacuum,
          Aristotle which way in a vacuum?

179

Sacrum, sacrum, inluminatio coitu.
Lo Sordels si fo di Mantovana
            of a castle named Goito.
" Five castles!
" Five castles! "
            (king giv' him five castles)
" And what the hell do I know about dye-works?! "
His Holiness has written a letter:
            " CHARLES the Mangy of Anjou....
..way you treat your men is a scandal...."
Dilectis miles familiaris...castra Montis Odorisii
Montis Sancti Silvestri pallete et pile...
In partibus Thetis....vineland
                        land tilled
                        the land incult
                        pratis nemoribus pascuis
                        with legal jurisdiction
his heirs of both sexes,
...sold the damn lot six weeks later,
Sordellus de Godio.
            Quan ben m'albir e mon ric pensamen.

XXXVII

THOU shalt not," said Martin Van Buren, " jail 'em for
     debt."
          " that an immigrant shd. set out with good banknotes
          and find 'em at the end of his voyage
but waste paper....if a man have in primeval forest
set up his cabin, shall rich patroon take it from him?
High judges? Are, I suppose, subject to passions
as have affected other great and good men, also
subject to esprit de corps.
The Calhouns " remarked Mr Adams
" Have flocked to the standard of feminine virtue "
" Peggy Eaton's own story " (Headline 1932)
Shall we call in the world to conduct our
municipal government?
Ambrose (Mr.) Spencer, Mr Van Renselaer
were against extension of franchise.
" Who work in factories and are employed by the wealthy
(State Convention 1821) dixit Spencer:
" Man who feeds, clothes, lodges another
has absolute control over his will."
Kent said they wd. " deplore in sackcloth and ashes
if they preserved not a senate
to represent landed interest, and did they
jeopard property rights? " To whom Mr Somebody Tompkins:
" Filled your armies
" while the priests were preaching sedition
" and men of wealth decrying government credit."
" ...in order to feed on the spoils."
Two words, said Mr Van Buren, came in with our revolution
and, as a matter of fact, why are we sent here?
" as for you Mr Chief Justice Spencer

" if they vote as they are bid by their employers
they will vote for the property which you so wish to protect."
.....when a turnpike depends upon congress
            local supervision is lost...
not surrender our conduct to foreign associations...
working classes
            who mostly
have no control over paper, and
derive no profit from bank stock....
merchants will not confess over trading
            nor speculators the disposition to speculate...
revenue for wants of the government
            to be kept under public control....do they pour
national revenue
            into banks of deposit
in seasons of speculation?
..diminish government patronage...sailor
not to be lashed save by court..   ....land
to actual settler (as against Mr Clay)
And when her father went broke, Mr Eaton..gave rise to
Washington gossip....loose morals of Mr Jefferson,
Servility of Martin Van Buren, said Adams (J. Quincy)
when everyone else is uncivil.
" No where so well deposited as in the pants of the people,
Wealth ain't," said President Jackson.
They give the union five years...
Bank did not produce uniform currency..
they wd. import grain rather than grow it...
Bank of England failed to prevent uses of credit...

" In Banking corporations " said Mr Webster " the
" interests of the rich and the poor are happily blended."
Said Van Buren to Mr Clay: " If you will give me
" A pinch of your excellent Maccoboy snuff..."

In Europe often by private houses, without assistance of banks
Relief is got not by increase
                    but by diminution of debt.
......as Justice Marshall, has gone out of his case...

Tip an' Tyler
We'll bust Van's biler......
brought in the vice of luxuria sed aureis furculis,
which forks were
bought back in the time of President Monroe
by Mr Lee our consul in Bordeaux.
"The man is a dough-face, a profligate,"
won't say he agrees with his party.

Authorized its (the bank's) president to use funds at
discretion (its funds, his discretion) to
influence press...
veto power, with marked discretion, used no further than
in objecting to bank under charter existing.
"Friendly feeling toward our bank in
"the mind of the President (Jackson
whose autograph was sent to the Princess Victoria)
                    wrote Biddle to Lennox Dec. 1829
"Counter rumours without foundation, I had
"a full and frank talk with the President who was
"most kind about its (the bank's) services to the country"
                    Biddle to Hamilton in November.

"To which end, largely increased line of discounts
1830, October, 40 million
May, 1837 seventy millions and then some.
Remembered this in Sorrento" in the vicinage of Vesuvius
near exhumed Herculaneum...
"30 million" said Mr Dan Wester "in states on the Mississippi
"will all have to be called in, in three

" years and nine months, if the charter be not extended..
" I hesertate nawt tew say et will dee-precierate
" everyman's prorperty from the etcetera
" to the kepertal ov Missouri, affect the price of
" crawps, leynd en the prordewce ov labour, to the
embararsement......"
de mortuis wrote Mr Van Buren
don't quite apply in a case of this character.

4 to 5 million balance in the national treasury
Receipts 31 to 32 million
Revenue 32 to 33 million
The Bank 341 million, and in deposits
6 millions of government money
(and a majority in the Senate)
Public Money in control of the President
from 15 to 20 thousand (id est, a fund for the secret service)

" employing means at the bank's disposal
in deranging the country's credits, obtaining by panic
control over public mind " said Van Buren
" from the real committee of Bank's directors
the government's directors have been excluded.
Bank president controlling government's funds
to the betrayal of the nation....
government funds obstructing the government...
and has sequestered the said funds of the government...
(with chapter, date, verse and citation)
acting in illegal secret
pouring oil on the press
giving nominal loans on inexistent security "
            in the eighteen hundred and thirties
" on precedent that Mr Hamilton has
never hesitated to jeopard the general
for advance of particular interests."

" Bank curtailed
17 million on a line of
64 million credits.

" Had not Mr Taney (of the treasury) prevented
that branch (in New York) from then collecting
8 million 700 thousand and armed our city with
9 million to defend us (the whole country)
in this war on its trade and commerce,
                    Cambreling, Globe Extra 1834
Peggy Eaton's Own Story. And if Marietta
Had not put on her grandmother's dress
She might have lasted, a mystery. If Dolores
Had not put on a hat shaped like a wig
She might have remained an exotic.
Placuit oculis, and did not mind strong cigars.

Irritable and unstable,
Is formed, is destroyed,
Recomposes to be once more decomposed
            (thus, descending to plant life)

Sorrento, June 21st. Villa Falangola
In the vicinage of Vesuvius, in the mirror of memory
Mr Van Buren:
                Judge Yeats, whom I remember etc...
Warded off scrutiny of his mental capacities
By a dignified and prudent reserve which
..long practice had made second nature...
Alex Hamilton had been blackmailed but
preferred, in the end, private scandal to shade on his
public career.
Marshall, said Roane, undermined the U.S. Constitution.
No man before Tom Jefferson in my house

Said one of the wool-buyers:
          " Able speech by Van Buren
" Yes, very able."
" Ye-es, Mr Knower, an' on wich side ov the tariff was it?
" Point I was in the act of considering "
          replied Mr Knower
In the mirror of memory: have been told I rendered
the truth a great service by that speech on the tariff
but directness on all points wd. seem not
to have been its conspicuous feature.
                    I thanked him
(James Jones, brother in law of Mr Clinton)
for his kind offer but
said my fortunes were too low in ebb
for me at that moment to compromise.
Lacked not who said that John Adams
disliked not so much the idea of a monarch
as preferred Braintree House over Hanover...
and his son, seeking light from the stars
deplored that representatives be paralyzed
by the will of constituents.
" I publicly answered more questions
than all other presidents put together "
          signed Martin Van Buren.
" Mr Webster in debt to the bank "
          Damned yellow rascal, said Clay
" Unnecessary, therefore injurious...
interference on the part of the government.
And they and their gang in congress
          debated three months without introducing
one solitary proposition to reverse Taney's decision
or in any way to relieve any distress.
                    HIC
                    JACET
          FISCI LIBERATOR

186

XXXVIII

il duol che sopra Senna
Induce, falseggiando la moneta.
Paradiso XIX, 118.

A N' that year Metevsky went over to America del Sud
(and the Pope's manners were so like Mr Joyce's,
got that way in the Vatican, weren't like that before)
Marconi knelt in the ancient manner
like Jimmy Walker sayin' his prayers.
His Holiness expressed a polite curiosity
as to how His Excellency had chased those
electric shakes through the a'mosphere.
Lucrezia
Wanted a rabbit's foot,
and he, Metevsky said to the one side
(three children, five abortions and died of the last)
he said: the other boys got more munitions
(thus cigar-makers whose work is highly repetitive
can perform the necessary operations almost automatically
and at the same time listen to readers who are hired
for the purpose of providing mental entertainment while they
work; Dexter Kimball 1929.)

Don't buy until you can get ours.
And he went over the border
and he said to the other side:
The *other* side has more munitions. Don't buy
until you can get ours.
And Akers made a large profit and imported gold into England
Thus increasing gold imports.
The gentle reader has heard this before.
And that year Mr Whitney

187

Said how useful short sellin' was,
          We suppose he meant to the brokers
And no one called him a liar.
And two Afghans came to Geneva
To see if they cd. get some guns cheap,
As they had heard about someone's disarming.
And the secretary of the something
Made some money from oil wells
          (In the name of God the Most Glorious Mr D'Arcy
is empowered to scratch through the sub-soil of Persia
until fifty years from this date...)
Mr Mellon went over to England
and that year Mr Wilson had prostatitis
And there was talk of a new Messiah
(that must have been a bit sooner)
And Her Ladyship cut down Jenny's allowance
Because of that bitch Agot Ipswich
And that year (that wd. be 20 or 18 years sooner)
They began to kill 'em by millions
Because of a louse in Berlin
          and a greasy basturd in Ausstria
By name François Giuseppe.

" Will there be war? " " No, Miss Wi'let,
" On account of bizschniz relations."
          Said the soap and bones dealer in May 1914
And Mr Gandhi thought:
          if we don't buy any cotton
And at the same time don't buy any guns......
Monsieur Untel was not found at the Jockey Club
...but was, later, found in Japan
And So-and-So had shares in Mitsui.
" The wood (walnut) will always be wanted for gunstocks "
And they put up a watch factory outside Muscou
And the watches kept time....Italian marshes

been waiting since Tiberius' time...
" Marry " said Beebe, " how do the fish live in the sea."
Rivera, the Spanish dictator, dictated that the
Infante was physically unfit to inherit...
    gothic type still used in Vienna
because the old folks are used to that type.
                              And Schlossmann
suggested that I stay there in Vienna
As stool-pigeon against the Anschluss
        Because the Ausstrians needed a Buddha
(Seay, brother, I leev et tuh yew!)
The white man who made the tempest in Baluba
Der im Baluba das Gewitter gemacht hat...
        they spell words with a drum beat,
" The country is overbrained " said the hungarian nobleman
in 1923. Kosouth (Ku' shoot) used, I understand
To sit in a café—all done by conversation—
It was all done by conversation,
        possibly because one repeats the point when conversing:
" Vienna contains a mixture of races."
        wd. I stay and be Bhudd-ha?
" They are accustomed to having an Emperor. They must have
Something to worship. (1927)"
But their humour about losing the Tyrol?
Their humour is not quite so broad.
The ragged arab spoke with Frobenius and told him
The names of 3000 plants.
        Bruhl found some languages full of detail
Words that half mimic action; but
generalization is beyond them, a white dog is
not, let us say, a dog like a black dog.
Do not happen, Romeo and Juliet...unhappily
I have lost the cutting but apparently
such things do still happen, he
suicided outside her door while

the family was preparing her body for burial,
and she knew that this was the case.

Green, black, December. Said Mr Blodgett:
" Sewing machines will never come into general use.

" I have of course never said that the cash is constant
(Douglas) and in fact the population (Britain 1914)
was left with 800 millions of " *deposits* "
after all the cash had been drawn, and
these deposits were satisfied by the
                    printing of treasury notes.
A factory
has also another aspect, which we call the financial aspect
It gives people the power to buy (wages, dividends
which are power to buy) but it is also the cause of prices
or values, financial, I mean financial values
It pays workers, and pays *for* material.
What it pays in wages and dividends
stays fluid, as power to buy, and this power is less,
per forza, damn blast your intellex, is less
than the total payments made by the factory
(as wages, dividends AND payments for raw material
bank charges, etcetera)
and all, that is the whole, that is the total
of these is added into the total of prices
caused by that factory, any damn factory
and there is and must be therefore a clog
and the power to purchase can never
(under the present system) catch up with
prices at large,

            and the light became so bright and so blindin'
in this layer of paradise
            that the mind of man was bewildered.

Said Herr Krupp (1842): guns are a merchandise
I approach them from the industrial end,
I approach them from the technical side,
1847 orders from Paris and Egypt....
            orders from the Crimea,
Order of Pietro il Grande,
                and a Command in the Legion of Honour...
500 to St Petersburg and 300 to Napoleon Barbiche
from Creusot. At Sadowa
        Austria had some Krupp cannon;
        Prussia had some Krupp cannon.
" The Emperor ('68) is deeply in'erested in yr. catalogue
and in yr. services to humanity "
                            (signed) Leboeuf
who was a relative of Monsieur Schneider
1900 fifty thousand operai,
        53 thousand cannon, about half for his country,
Bohlem und Halbach,
        Herr Schneider of Creusot
Twin arse with one belly.
Eugene, Adolf and Alfred " more money from guns than from
    tractiles "
Eugene was sent to the deputies;
        (Soane et Loire) to the Deputies, minister;
Later rose to be minister,
    " guns coming from anywhere,
but appropriations from the Chambers of Parliaments "
In 1874 recd. license for free exportation
Adopted by 22 nations
1885/1900 produced ten thousand cannon
to 1914, 34 thousand
one half of them sent out of the country
always in the chamber of deputies, always a conservative,
Schools, churches, orspitals fer the workin' man
Sand piles fer the children.

Opposite the Palace of the Schneiders
　　　　Arose the monument to Herr Henri
Chantiers de la Gironde, Bank of the Paris Union,
The franco-japanese bank
　　　　François de Wendel, Robert Protot
To friends and enemies of tomorrow
" the most powerful union is doubtless
　　　　that of the Comité des Forges,"
'' And God take your living " said Hawkwood
15 million: Journal des Débats
30 million paid to Le Temps
Eleven for the Echo de Paris
Polloks on Schneider patents
Our bank has bought us
　　　　a lot of shares in Mitsui
Who arm 50 divisions, who keep up the Japanese army
and they are destined to have a large future
" faire passer ces affaires
　　　　avant ceux de la nation."

XXXIX

ESOLATE is the roof where the cat sat,
Desolate is the iron rail that he walked
And the corner post whence he greeted the sunrise.
In hill path: " thkk, thgk "
of the loom
" Thgk, thkk " and the sharp sound of a song
under olives
When I lay in the ingle of Circe
I heard a song of that kind.
Fat panther lay by me
Girls talked there of fucking, beasts talked there of eating,
All heavy with sleep, fucked girls and fat leopards,
Lions loggy with Circe's tisane,
Girls leery with Circe's tisane
κακὰ φάρμακ᾽ ἔδωκεν
kaka pharmak edōken
The house of smooth stone that you can see from a distance
λύκοι ὀρέστεροι, ἠδὲ λέοντες
lukoi oresteroi ede leontes
wolf to curry favour for food
—born to Helios and Perseis
That had Pasiphae for a twin
Venter venustus, cunni cultrix, of the velvet marge
ver novum, canorum, ver novum
Spring overborne into summer
late spring in the leafy autumn
καλὸν ἀοιδιάει
KALON AOIDIAEI
"Η θεὸς, ἠὲ γυνή.....φθεγγώμεθα θᾶσσον
e theos e guné....ptheggometha thasson

193

First honey and cheese
      honey at first and then acorns
Honey at the start and then acorns
honey and wine and then acorns
Song sharp at the edge, her crotch like a young sapling
illa dolore obmutuit, pariter vocem

    Ἀλλ' ἄλλην χρὴ πρῶτον 'οδον τελέσαι, καὶ 'ικεσθαι 490/5
Εἰς Ἀΐδαο δόμους και επαινῆς Περσεφονείης'
ψυχῇ χρησομένους θηβαίου Τειρεοίαο
Μάντηος 'αλαοῦ του τε φρένες ἔμπεδοί εἰσι·
Τῷ καὶ τεθνηῶτι νόον πόρε Περσεφόνεια

When Hathor was bound in that box
    afloat on the sea wave
Came Mava swimming with light hand lifted in overstroke
sea blossom wreathed in her locks,
" What are you box? "
      " I am Hathor."
Che mai da me non si parte il diletto
Fulvida di folgore
Came here with Glaucus unnoticed, nec ivi in harum
Nec in harum ingressus sum.
    Discuss this in bed said the lady
Euné kai philoteti ephata Kirkh
Εὐνῇ καὶ φιλότητι, ἔφατα Κίρκη
es thalamon
Ἐs θάλαμόν
Eurilochus, Macer, better there with good acorns
Than with a crab for an eye, and 30 fathom of fishes
Green swish in the socket,
      Under the portico Kirké:......
" I think you must be Odysseus....
      feel better when you have eaten....

Always with your mind on the past....
Ad Orcum autem quisquam?
            nondum nave nigra pervenit.....
Been to hell in a boat yet?

Sumus in fide
Puellaeque canamus
sub nocte....
            there in the glade
To Flora's night, with hyacinthus,
With the crocus (spring
            sharp in the grass,)
Fifty and forty together
            ERI MEN AI TE KUDONIAI
Betuene Aprile and Merche
            with sap new in the bough
With plum flowers above them
            with almond on the black bough
With jasmine and olive leaf,
To the beat of the measure
From star up to the half-dark
From half-dark to half-dark
            Unceasing the measure
Flank by flank on the headland
            with the Goddess' eyes to seaward
By Circeo, by Terracina, with the stone eyes
            white toward the sea
With one measure, unceasing:
            " Fac deum! " " Est factus."
Ver novum!
            ver novum!
Thus made the spring,
Can see but their eyes in the dark
            not the bough that he walked on.

Beaten from flesh into light
Hath swallowed the fire-ball
A traverso le foglie
His rod hath made god in my belly
      Sic loquitur nupta
      Cantat sic nupta

Dark shoulders have stirred the lightning
A girl's arms have nested the fire,
Not I but the handmaid kindled
      Cantat sic nupta
I have eaten the flame.

XL

ESPRIT de corps in permanent bodies
    " Of the same trade," Smith, Adam, " men
    " never gather together
    " without a conspiracy against the general public."
Independent use of money (our OWN)
toward holding OUR bank, own bank
and in it the deposits, received, where received.
            De banchis cambi tenendi....
                Venice 1361,
'62..shelved for a couple of centuries..
" whether by privates or public...
            currency OF (O, F, of) the nation.
Toward producing that wide expanse of clean lawn
Toward that deer park toward
the playing fields, congeries, swimming pools, undsoweiter:
Sword-fish, seven marlin, world's record
extracted in 24 hours.
Wd. make the loan, sterling, eight hundred thousand
if Peabody wd. quit business.
            England 1858
IN THE NAME OF GOD THE MOST GLORIOUS MR.
    D'ARCY
is permitted for 50 years to dig up the subsoil of
Persia.
'62, report of committee:
Profit on arms sold to the government: Morgan
(Case 97) sold to the government the government's arms...
I mean the government owned 'em already
at an extortionate profit
Dollars 160 thousand, one swat, to Mr Morgan
for forcing up gold.

197

" Taking advantage of emergency " (that is war)
After Gettysburg, down 5 points in one day—
Bulls on gold and bears on the Union
" Business prospered due to war's failures."

" If a nation will master its money "

Boutwell decided bonds shd. be sold direct by the treasury.
Mr Morgan: contributions to the Republican Party, largely
to the republican party.
　　　　　　Beecher's church organized by realty agents—
Belmont representing the Rothschilds
" specie payment's resumption
" enriched a small group of holders."
stock subscription (railway construction)
seldom over 30 percent...
in '76 default 39% of the total
that is 39 per cent of the
bonds for railway construction
Said Mr Corey " there being no central institution
as in London "
Pujo investigation: Said Mr Morgan:
　　　　　　" never sold short in my life "
having learned that a high degree of liquidity....
1907 " cd. not have been done without Mr Baker
" we cdnt. have stopped it (the panic).
As to the government's arms: they were bought by
one government office before they had been sold
(as condemned) by another ditto (i.e. government office)
passing through a species of profit sieve.
" A greek," said Ionides or some other Hellene,
" honest after he has cleaned up 20 thousand "
meaning twenty thousand pund sterling.
　　　　　　With our eyes on the new gothic residence, with our
eyes on Palladio, with a desire for seignieurial splendours

(ÀGALMA, haberdashery, clocks, ormoulu, brocatelli,
tapestries, unreadable volumes bound in tree-calf,
half-morocco, morocco, tooled edges, green ribbons,
flaps, farthingales, fichus, cuties, shorties, pinkies
et cetera
            Out of which things seeking an exit

PLEASING TO CARTHEGENIANS: HANNO

that he ply beyond pillars of Herakles
60 ships of armada to lay out Phoenecian cities
to each ship 50 oars, in all
30 thousand aboard them with water, wheat in provision.
Two days beyond Gibel Tara layed in the wide plain
Thumiatehyon, went westward to Solois
an headland covered with trees
Entha hieron Poseidōnos, against the sun half a day
is seabord marshland high-murmuring rushes.
In that place great elephant herds
        and beasts many other amongst them
So laid we house: Karikon, Gutta, Akra, Meli, Arambo
These are the cities, then Lixos
Pours down from out of High Libya
The lixitae friendly cowboys and herders
Up country be aethiopians living with untamed beasts
shut in by the Lixtus mountain
whereon are misshapen men swifter than horses.

Men of Lixtae came with us to interpret
for 12 days sailing southward, southward by desert
one day sailed against sun, there is an harbour
with an island 15 miles in circumference,
We built there, calling it Cyrne
believing it opposite Carthage as our sailing time
was the same as from Carthage to the Pillars.

Past Xrestes, a great river,
        a lagoon with three largish islands
a day onward great hills end an inlet,
Their folk wear the hides of wild beasts
and threw rocks to stone us,
        so prevented our landing.
Next is a river wide, full of water
crocodiles, river horses, Thence we turned back to Cyrne
for 12 days coasted the shore
Aethiops fled at our coming
Our Lixtae cd. not understand them.
12th day rose the woody mountain
with great soft smell from the trees
all perfumes many-mingling.
Two days, the wide bayou or inlet
Lay flatland above it busy by night with fires.
Filled our tanks, sailed 5 days along shore
Came then West Horn, the island that closes its harbour
And by day we saw only forest,
        by night their fires
With sound of pipe against pipe
The sound ply over ply; cymbal beat against cymbal,
The drum, wood, leather, beat, beat noise to make terror.
The diviners told us to clear.
Went from that fire fragrance,
flames flowed into sea,
Fearing and swiftly, the land by night decked with flame
One pillar of light above others
Scorched at the sky and stars
By day this stood an high mountain
That they call the gods' carroch.
By flame for three days to South Horn, the bayou,
the island of folk hairy and savage
whom our Lixtae said were Gorillas.
We cd. not take any man, but three of their women.

Their men clomb up the crags,
Rained stone, but we took three women
who bit, scratched, wd. not follow their takers.
Killed, flayed, brought back their pelts into Carthage.
Went no further that voyage,
        as were at end of provisions.
Out of which things seeking an exit
To the high air, to the stratosphere, to the imperial
calm, to the empyrean, to the baily of the four towers
the NOUS, the ineffable crystal:
Karxèdoniōn Basileos
        hung this with his map in their temple.

XLI

MA QVESTO,"
    said the Boss, " è divertente."
catching the point before the aesthetes had got
    there;
    Having drained off the muck by Vada
From the marshes, by Circeo, where no one else wd. have
    drained it.
Waited 2000 years, ate grain from the marshes;
Water supply for ten million, another one million " *vani* "
that is rooms for people to live in.
    XI of our era.
Story told by the mezzo-yit:
That they were to have a consortium
and one of the potbellies says:
    will come in for 12 million "
And another: three millyum for my cut;
And another: we will take eight;
And the Boss said: but what will you
    DO with that money? "
" But! but! signore, you do not ask a man
what he will *do* with his money.
That is a personal matter.
And the Boss said: but what will you do?
You won't really need all that money
because you are all for the *confine*."
" Noi ci facciam sgannar per Mussolini "
    said the commandante della piazza.
" Popolo " said Cici " ignorante!
" And the worst of 'em all is my " donna "
    (In the third year of his age)

" Where the Pope goes is lack of money
Because of the mass of clerics
            who bring cheques for the banks to cash,
And for these the banks must pay money.
And you must know how they pay, and
when and on what days there are markets
and in which seasons are the fairs, and
when they need money in which where
and what are the rates of exchange
            (Messire Uzzano in 1442)
To have shortage neither in time nor in place
but to have money there ready
for sailing of ships, wangles of merchants
and for the due pay for soldiers
            both from commune or overlord,
and you must work day and night
to keep up with your letters.

Eleven hours the day, 32 centimes the hour
" And you stole it "
            said the employer at Orbe
After the boss had worn out his best only shoes.
Monday 14th, in the morning.
After six days in the training corps
They sent him back to the front
            (documento)
Geschichte und Lebensbilder
Temperature of enormous importance
Erneuerung des Religiosen Lebens
more especially in mountain warfare
In den Deutschen Befreiungskriegen, by Wilhelm Baur
This remarkable work was presented
            to the young Uhlan officer
by her imperial majesty Augusta Victoria
with a tender and motherly dedication

Renewal of higher life
in the struggle for German freedom, 19 hundred and 8,
in mountain warfare,
ordine, contrordine e disordine
" una pace qualunque "
            social content to the war.
The young Uhlan was never out of uniform from his
eighth year till the end of the war
            contrordine e disordine
Trees, hedges of white thorn, toward San Casciano
were stiff frosted with silver—
20 metres between the trenches
" was identified as the hospital where Mussolini...from
photo in Corriere di Domenica, and then bombed...

Feldmarschall Hindenburg in the imperial box
Heard for the first time Mozart and asked what the noise was
all this god damned cultural nonsense.
But Fritz' father had kept the letter
That he, Herr Nvon so Forth, shd. back up
his, Hindenburg's application
for a seven dollar per year increase in pension—
fees due him for having participated in the
Battle of Waffenschlag, in the seventies or whenever.
Una pace qualunque. Over Udine...
wd. have called that eagle a portent
" Yes, sir, we will file that "
            said the seventh under cat's dogkeeper
when he rec'd the Hun ultimatum,
The rest being nacherly on french vacation... 1914
" At any rate, he had the fleet out."
            remarked Winston's mama.
" Never " said Winston to his cousin
            " waste time making munitions.
Be a GUN, and shoot other's munitions.

Don't waste time having ideas."
(cousin deeply impressed..but
did not achieve lasting preeminence)
in that world which M. Crevel has depicted
in the world of Esperanza, Primrose and Augusta;
of fat fussy old women and of fat fussy old men.
" Sure they want war," said Bill Yeats,
" They want all the young gals fer themselves."
That llovely unconscious world
              slop over slop, and blue ribbons
" Pig and Piffle " they called it in private
10 pence per copy to make, 6 pence on the stands
and each year 20 thousand in profits
Pays to control the Times, for its effect on the market
" where there is no censorship by the state
there is a great deal of manipulation..."
              and news sense?
Cosimo First guaranteed it.
To pay 5% on its stock, Monte dei Paschi
and to lend at 5 and ½
Overplus of all profit, to relief works
and the administration on moderate pay..
              that stood even after Napoleon.
Said C.H. " To strangle the bankers...? "
And Woergl in our time?

To the Count de Vergennes. Paris, August. 1785
Consumption tobacco, esteemed in francs
15 to 30 million pounds, let us say it may be 24
delivered in ports of France @ 8 sous
                     9 million 600 thousand
at the rate 6 sous to manufacture
                     7 million and something
revenue to the King   30 million
to the consumer   72

expense of the tax in collection is therefore
                    say 25 million
presumptuous to assume

Twenty million ȷrenchmen, 19 millions accursed, Mrs. Trist,
In every material circumstance.....
Public debt increasing at about one million a year
You will see by Gallatin's speeches....
Saddled by bank, led by a bridle
National property being increased...
must furnish adequate representation...
all imported commodities are raised about 50 percent
Vol. IX. 337, Lands rose in a vortex of paper,
          not here where the banks do not reach
Mechanics get 1.50 a day
But are worse off than with the old wages....
Independent use of our money...toward holding our bank.
          Mr Jefferson to Colonel Monroe
120 million german fuses used by the allies to kill Germans
British gunsights from Jena
Schneider Creusot armed Turkey
Copper from England thru Sweden...Mr Hatfield
Patented his new shell in eight countries.

          ad interim 1933

THE FIFTH DECAD
OF CANTOS
XLII-LI

XLII

W̲E̲ ought, I think, to say in civil terms: You be
damned '
(Palmerston, to Russell re/ Chas. H. Adams)
' And how this people CAN in this the fifth
et cetera year of the war, leave that old etcetera up
there on that monument! ' H.G. to E.P. 1918
Lex salica! lex Germanica, Antoninus
said law rules at sea

FIXED in the soul, nell' anima, of the Illustrious College
They had been ten years proposing such a Monte,
That is a species of bank—damn good bank, in Siena

A mount, a bank, a fund a bottom an
institution of credit
a place to send cheques in and out of
and yet not yet a banco di giro, and the Bailey
sought views from the Senate ' With paternal affection
justice convenience of city what college had with such
foresight wherefore S.A. (Your Highness) as in register
Nov. 1624
following details: as third, a Yearly balance
as 5th that any citizen shall have right to deposit
and to fruits therefrom resultant at five percent annual interest
and that borrowers pay a bit over that
for services (dei ministri) that is for running expenses
and book keeping which shall be counted a half scudo
per hundred per year
(All of this is important)
and 6thly that the Magistrate
give his chief care that the specie

be lent to whomso can best use it USE IT
(*id est, più utilmente*)
to the good of their houses, to benefit of their business
as of weaving, the wool trade, the silk trade
And that (7thly) the overabundance every five years shall the
                                        Bailey
distribute to workers of the contrade (the wards) holding in
reserve a prudent proportion as against unforeseen losses
though there shd. be NO such losses
and 9th that the borrowers can pay up before the end of their
term whenso it be to their interest. No debt to run more than
five years.
July 1623
Loco Signi
✠   [a cross in the margin]
That profit on deposits should be used to cover all losses
and the distributions on the fifth year be made from remaining
profits, after restoration of losses no (*benché*) matter how
small
with sane small reserve against future idem
I, Livio Pasquini, notary, citizen of Siena, most faithfully copied
July 18th. 1623
Consules, Iudices, and notary public pro serenissimo
attest Livio's superscript next date being November.
              wave falls and the hand falls
Thou shalt not always walk in the sun
        or see weed sprout over cornice
Thy work in set space of years, not over an hundred.

That the Mount of Pity (or Hock Shop)
municipal of Siena has lent only on pledges
that is on stuff actually hocked...wd be we believe useful
and beneficent that there be place to lend licitly
MONEY to receive licitly money
at moderate and legitimate interest

was sent months ago to YYour HHighness AA VV a memorial
to erect a New Mountain
could accept specie from Universities (id est congregations)
and individuals and from Luoghi
i.e. companies and persons both public and private
                                        WHOMSOEVER
not requiring that they have special privilege
because of their state or conditions but to folk of
ANY CONDITION
            that the same Mount cd/lend on good Mallevadoria
(that is security) at the same rate plus a little over
to cover current expenses of supervisors and employees
& being sent to YY. HHighnesses (AA. VV. = YY HH)
that you might understand it
that it be brought to consideration with certain details
discussed first orally and then put into writing
(in what wd. seem to have been 1622)
Stating that Siena had no income and Their Highnesses
had provided credit from customs
and from miscellaneous taxes
and that the Grand Duke hadn't lost anything by it
Plus a list of Sienese assets (coolish)
Plus a lien on ' The Abundance '
And knowing that all this is but a little
Pledge the persons and goods of the laity
And leave open door to other towns in the state
who care to give similar pledges
And that whoso puts in money shall have lots in the Monte
that yield 5% interest
and that these shareholders shall receive their due fruit
And that the Gd Duke make known at Siena
to the same deputies of the Bailey...
but that it be separate from the Pawn Shop
and have its own magistrates and employees
and that YYour HHighnesses send approbation

commanding their will, we humbly with reverence
...the 29th day of Xember 1622...
                  servants of YYour HHighnesses

                                          Nicolo de Antille
                                          Horatio Gionfiglioli
                                          Sebastiano Cellesi

            TTheir HHighnesses gratified
            the city of this demand to
            erect a New Monte
            for good public and private and to facilitate...
            ..agreed to accommodate
            ......and to lend the fund against the Gd Duke's
            public entries to the sum of
            200,000 scudi
            capital for fruit at 5% annual
            which is 10,000 a year
            assigned on the office of grazing
            on caution of said security offered
            leaving ground for other towns that
            wish to participate
                              with TTheir HHighnesses
                              approbations as follows:
            Maria Maddalena Tutrice
                        Hor° della Rena   30 Xembre   1622
Needs a stamp
refer to
the Governor
Fabbizio bollo
      vedo
Governatore   the illustrious Bailey
executed in toto & as per true rescript of
                        TTheir HHighnesses

      2 Jan 1622
                  Cenzio Grcolini
which date goes in the Sienese calendar

whereof December was the x th month and
                March was the New Year
                                    ACTUM SENIS, the
Parish of San Joannij in the Gd Ducal Palace
present the Marquis Joanne Christophoro   the
illustrious Marquis Antony Mary of Malaspina
and the most renowned Johnny something or other de Binis
Florentine Senator, witness and I notary undersigned
Ego Livius Pasquinus of Marius
(deceased) filius Apostolic Imperial and Pontifical notary
public Judge Ordinary, Citizen of Siena
WHEREFORE
            let all sundry and whoever be
satisfied that the said MOUNT may be created.
so that the echo turned back in my mind: Pavia:
Saw cities move in one figure, Vicenza, as depicted
San Zeno by Adige...
                    I Nicolaus Ulivis
de Cagnascis citizen of Pistoja Florentine notary public
countersigning
                    Senatus Populusque Senensis
OB PECUNIAE SCARCITATEM
                    borrowing, rigging exchanges,
licit consumption impeded
                    and it is getting steadily WORSE
others with specie abundant do not use it in business
(to be young is to suffer.
                    Be old, and be past that)
do not use it in business and everyone remains here
without work
few come to buy in the market
                    fewer still work the fields
Monte non vacabilis publico
shares not to expire with death...will TTheir HHighnesses
against public entries

get that straight—capital two hundred thousand
which wd. correspond to 10,000 income
on the entries of the office of grazing
with precautions (cauteles)
to guarantee their same Highnesses against any possible loss
Which idea dates at least to July 1623
die decima ottava
and other copies 1624, 1622
which seems to have been approved ' last October '
by Della Rena and M. Magdalene the She Guardian,
tutrice, more or less regent
Don Ferdinandus Secundus   Dux Magnus
and his Serenest she tutrices
with public documentation
for public and private utility
foreseeing erection
legitimate and just, such a MOUNTAIN

Chigi, Soffici, Marcellus de? Illuri,
no, Marcellus Austini, Caloanes Marescotti and
Lord Mt Alban effected
that the officers of this Mountain
and in time to come all their successors
shares that shall be called Loca Montis—
Have you a place on the Hill, sir?
            out of sure knowledge and
ex certe scientia et in plenitude of their powers
inviolable for observance, so to be comprehended
10 thousand scudi
de libris septeno
? one scudo worth 7 lire
in respect to 200,000 (two hundred thousand).

XLIII

To the serenissimo D^{no} (pronounced Domino)
and his most serene aftercomers
things, persons et omnia alia juva
whatever
and the cash in the Pawn Shop
(Mount of Pity)
eiusdem civitatis Senén.
there being in the third place
2 thousand 310 there to the credit of
The Magnificent Magistrates and Lords Officers
and 3756 in the same Mount
described as to credit of citizens
and in common called money of Genova
and Most Serene M Dux
and serenest (feminine) tutrices
by the said Masters Deputies of the Bailey
as to the best mode and obligations and cautions
most ample dee-liberation
prayer, supplication as herewith and herefollowing
videlicet alligati
In the Name of Omnipotent God
and the Glorious Virgin our Advocate
to the Gd Duke's honour and exaltation
the Most Serene, Tuscanissimo Nostro Signore
in the Lord's year 1622
Saturday fourth day of March
at? VIth (hour? after sunrise or whatever)
called together assembled in general
council of the People of the City of Siena magnificent
Symbolic good of the Commune
and fatherland dilettissimo

having chief place and desire that the
citizens get satisfaction (siano soddisfatti) contentment
and be fully persuaded of
what for the common good is here being dealt with
as we have already been for ten years projecting this MONTE
for gt. future benefit to the city
          Worthy will to the chosen end.
Ob pecuniae scarsitatem
                         S. P. SENEN[sis] ac pro eo amplissim
Balia Collegium civices vigilantiae
totius civitatis
Urban VIIIth of Siena, Ferd. I mag duce d° n°
felicitatem dominante et Ferd. I
Roman Emperor as elected.
1251 of the Protocols marked also
X, I, I, F, and four arabic
OB PECUNIAE SCARSITATEM
because there was shortage of coin, in November
because of taxes, exchanges, tax layings and usuries
legitimate consumption impeded
ten thousand on the office of pasturage

to the end:
          four fat oxen
having their arses wiped
and in general being tidied up to serve god under my window
with stoles of Imperial purple
with tassels, and grooms before the carroccio
on which carroch six lion heads
          to receive the wax offering
Thus arrive the gold eagles, the banners of the contrade,
and boxes of candles
                    ' Mn-YAWWH!!! '
Said the left front ox, suddenly,
'pnAWH! ' as they tied on his red front band,

St George, two hokey-pokey stands and the unicorn
    ' Nicchio! Nicch-iO-né!! '
The kallipygous Sienese females
get that way from the *salite*
    that is from continual plugging up hill
One box marked ' 200 LIRE '
                    ' laudate pueri '
alias serve God with candles
with the palio and 17 banners
and when six men had hoisted up the big candle
a bit askew in the carroch and the fore ox had
been finally arse-wiped
they set off toward the Duomo, time
consumed 1 hour and 17 minutes.
                   on the security
mobile and immobile
of individual citizens
in the city or wheresoever REE-
sponsibility quocunque aliunde
and this *obligatio,* obligation shd/be divided
by portion of immobile goods
       thus deliberated in full meeting
in the name of the OMNIPOTENT, and of the glorious Virgin
M^a (meaning Maria) our Advocate
year of salvation 1622 on a Saturday
as was the 4th day of March
having already ten years ago started proposing
representatives of the whole people
and below written notaries public
two hundred thousand
             (scudi)
Maister Augustino Chisio equites
anointed of the order of Stephen (pope, holy)
ducatorum? no. ducentorum
a return of 10,000 scudi

in the parish of San Giovanni (Joannis)
To be or not to be tied up with the Pawn Shop
and his successors in the Great Duchy
    guarantee of the income from grazing
up to (illegible) said to mean, no...
libris septem, the sum of, summam, scutorum
ten thousand
On security mobile and immobile
                             REE-

sponsibility

      Out of Syracuse
not having money aboard
to Athens at creditors' risk
cut the sails, dumped oil at an island
      but the S.O. man
wouldnt swallow it.
Up to the quantity of 200,000
on the whole people's credit
for public and private utility
      shares to be called Loca Montis
which is to say sites on the Mountain
@ 100 scudi to give 5 scudi a year
as long as the MOUNT endure
      there first was the fruit of nature
there was the whole will of the people
serene M. Dux and His tutrices
and lords deputies of the Bailey, in name of Omnipotent God
      best mode etcetera, and the Glorious Virgin
convoked and gathered together 1622
general council there were 117 councillors
in the hall of World Map, with bells and with
voice of the Cryer (Il Banditore)
shares of Mount to yield five scudi on each hundred
per annum, and to be separate from the PITY

with its own magistrates, its own ministers
Ill^{us} Balia eseguisca in tutto
                        Rescript of TTheir HHighnesses

ACTUM SENIS in Parochia S. Giovannis
blank leaves at end up to the index
hoc die decim' octavo, from the Incarnation
year 1623. Celso had a wheat scheme
July to December, July to November
Grass nowhere out of place.
                        Pine cuts the sky into three
Thus BANK of the grassland was raised into Seignory
stati fatti Signoria, being present Paris Bolgarini
credit of the Commune of Siena
12 of the Bailey present...went into committee
I cancellarius wrote to His Highness
A New Mount that shall receive from all sorts of persons
from Luoghi public and private, privileged and non-privileged
a base, a fondo, a deep, a sure and a certain
the City having ' entrate '
                        the customs and public income

150 to $\dfrac{M}{200}$ scudi

to guarantee which
            wd/suffice 8 to 10 thousand yearly
on the *gabelle* and/or on the dogana
Tuesday 3 Jan to Wed. 6 Epifany 1622
a New Monte requested to bear @ 5% annual

1622 January, assigned on the Paschi
Off° de Paschi
March 1622 Donna Orsola of wherever   removed from the book
of the Sienese public women (motion approved by the Bailey)
March 24 again appeared black money from Florence
Monte de Firenze, vacabile, 1591,

payable every two months had been 8 and 1/2
gangsters admitted.

1621 to provide WORK for the populace.
register, rescript
                    O—
razio della Rena to be recognized
as illegitimate father of the bastards of Pietro de Medici
at 100 scudi per annum
            if you follow me, not as the
legitimate father of Pietro's illegitimate offspring

Orbem bellis, urbem gabellis, Urbanus octavus
implevit.

June 21st Friday or thereabouts 1624
agreed to magistrate's order that
Mrs Margurita de Pecora Gallo
be removed from the register of the town whores
of Siena, on charge of thievery
Friday the first day of July
Merchants spoke to the Bailey, action on Monte Nuovo
delayed
Jan. 1622 the Duke answered, and already spoke of the
grass land
16 July, Monte Nuovo, committee to arrange it.
New Mount approved by their Highnesses
Xbre Monte Paschale, fatto Signoria   notice served to the
Magistrates for Conservations and to the Magistracy of
the Grazing
May 1626 more stew about the black money (lead money)
rescript:
            that in the said place
be not put for the Lord Count nor his successors
any surety for bandits and criminals

but only for civil debts, that it serve not as safe cache for criminals
as did the Florentine Loan Office
anno domini 15 hundred an' whatever
remain obliged to take salt from Grosseto
at the same price as now ruling

1676 ambassadors to Firenze
when the Grand Duke said he did not understand economics
non intendeva di quella materia
being obliged to trust in his ministers
1679 for two years no one gaoled
for debts under 14 lire, those in for 30 or under
cd. be released on order of the Buonuomini
who shd/fix terms for arbitration
Monte to lend 4736 scudi
to the Tolomei foundation, and to take no interest on this sum
spent for the college
1680 to debtors 4% and one third
to creditors be paid 2/3rds of 1% under that, frozen assets

Dixbre '22 make responsible
all persons, and all goods of the laity
that the Mount have its fund secure
that whoso puts his coin in it shall hold his luoghi
bearing 5% fruitage per annum
Signed Nicolo de Antille
Horatio Gianfiglioli
Seb. Cellesi LL AA (Their Highnesses)
gratify this demand to set up a Monte
to Public Good and to private
to empower, facilitate, and be licit
were pleased to accommodate, and prestare
the fund on the Grand Duke's public income
to the sum as of capital 200,000
for 5% fruitage   that wd. be ten thousand the year

which attain to the Office of Grasslands
Paschi di detta Città
the said sum with cautele
that no one shd/suffer
                    Maria Maddalena, tutrice
                    Hor° della Rena
                                        (whose bastards)
1622 thirtieth of Xembre were not his natural bastards
that the Illustrious Bailey shall execute this order in all points
    (but only his bastards officially)
        faithful rescript of their Highnesses
2 Jan. 1622, Orazio Grcolini
Stile senese or the year beginning in March
Enacted Siena, in the Parish of S. Gionni, in palatio,
with witnesses above mentioned, apostolic, imperial, citizen
of Siena

Firenze 1749, 1000 scudi
    for draining the low land
2000 to fix Roman Road advance authorized up to 12,000

Public debt at the end of the Medici
scudi 14 million
or 80 million lira pre-war.

XLIV

ND thou shalt not, Firenze 1766, and thou shalt not
sequestrate for debt any farm implement
nor any yoke ox nor
any peasant while he works with the same.
                              Pietro Leopoldo
Heavy grain crop unsold
never had the Mount lacked for specie, cut rate to four and 1/3rd

creditors had always been paid,
that trade inside the Grand Duchy be free of impediments
shut down on grain imports
'83, four percent legal maximum interest
'85, three on church investments, motu proprio
Pietro Leopoldo
Ferdinando EVVIVA!!
                              declared against exportation
thought grain was to eat

Flags trumpets horns drums
and a placard
              VIVA FERDINANDO
and were sounded all carillons
with bombs and with bonfires and was sung TE DEUM
in thanks to the Highest for this so
provident law
and were lights lit in the chapel of Alexander
      and the image of the Madonna unveiled
and sung litanies and then went to St Catherine's chapel
in S. Domenico and by the reliquary
of the Saint's head sang prayers and
went to the Company Fonte Giusta

223

also singing the litanies
and when was this thanksgiving ended the cortege
and the contrade with horns drums
trumpets and banners went to the
houses of the various ambulant vendors, then were the sticks of the
flags set in the stanchions on the Palace of the Seignors
and the gilded placard between them
(thus ended the morning)
        meaning to start in the afternoon
and the big bell and all bells of the tower in the piazza
sounded from 8 a.m. until seven o'clock in the evening
without intermission and next day was procession
coaches and masks in great number
and of every description e di tutte le qualità
    to the sound always of drums and trumpets
crying VIVA FERDINANDO and in all parts of the piazza
were flames in great number and grenades burning
to sound of bombs and of mortaretti and the shooting of
guns and of pistols and in chapel of the Piazza
a great number of candles for the publication of this so
provident law and at sundown were dances
    and the masks went into their houses
and the captains of the ward companies,
the contrade, took their banners to the Piazza Chapel
where once more they sang litanies
and cried again Ferdinando EVVIVA
Evviva Ferdinado il Terzo
and from the contrade continued the drumming
and blowing of trumpets and hunting horns,
torch flares, grenades and they went to the Piazza del Duomo
with a new hullabaloo gun shots mortaretti and pistols
there were no streets not ablaze with the torches
or with wood fires and straw flares
and the vendors had been warned not to show goods for
    fear of disorder and stayed all that day within doors

or else outside Siena. This was a law called
Dovizia annonaria
               to be freed from the Yoke of Licence
From October 9th until the 3rd of November
was unforeseen jubilation, four lines of tablet in marble:
            Frumentorum licentia
      coercita de annonaria laxata Pauperum aeque
          divitium bono conservit
          FERDINANDI 1792
refused to take with him objects of small bulk which he
held to be the property of the nation. Ferd III. 1796
that the sovereign be il più galantuomo del paese

the citizen priest Fr Lenzini mounted the tribune
to join the citizen Abrâm
and in admiring calm sat there with them the citizen
the Archbishop
               from 7,50 a bushel to 12
   by the 26th April

and on June 28th came men of Arezzo
past the Porta Romana and went into the ghetto
there to sack and burn hebrews
part were burned with the liberty tree in the piazza
and for the rest of that day and night
1799 anno domini
Pillage stopped by superior order 3rd July was discovered a
    treason
in the cartridges given the troops
that is were full of semolina, not powder
    and cherry stone where shd/have been ball
and in others too little powder
Respectons les prêtres, remarked Talleyrand
1800 a good grain and wine year
       if you wd/get on well with the peasantry
of the peninsula.

Premier Brumaire:
Vous voudrez citoyen
turn over all sums in yr/ cash box
to the community, fraternité, greetings.

                              Delort
acting for Dupont Lieutenant General
Louis King of Etruria, Primus, absolute, without constitution.
taxes so heavy that are thought to be more than
paid by subjects of Britain.

                    Gen. Clarke to the Ministro degli Esteri
Whereas the fruits of the Mount were the 2/3rds of the one
                                                    percent
wherewith to pay all current expenses. Madame ma soeur et
                                                    cousine
I have received Your Majesty's letter of
November twenty-fourth I
suppose that in the actual circumstances
She will be in a hurry to get to Spain or at least to
leave a country where she can no longer
stay with the dignity befitting her rank.
I have given orders that she be
received in my kingdom of Italy
and in my French States with honours that are due her.
If your Majesty should be in Milan or Turin
before the 18th of december I should have the
advantage of seeing her. I am sending an officer my
aide de camp, General Reile who will deliver this letter.
He will be charged at the same time to take measures
for the security of the country and
to remove men who could trouble its quiet,
      since I learn that Your Majesty has already thought necessary
to import troops from Lisbon.
My troops shd have by now entered that capital
and taken possession of Portugal

Wherewith I pray God, Madam my sister and cousin,
he be pleased to have you in holy and worthy keeping

At Venice, december fifth 1807
          Your Majesty's kind brother and cousin
                    NAPOLEON
(his secretary mixing the pronouns
You, She, she all to Majesty)
And those men who ' with bestial enthusiasm ' took horse place
were, says the much lesser Bandini, paid by the prefect
and beforehand prepared.

" Artists high rank, in fact sole social summits
which the tempest of politics can not reach,"
          which remark appears to have been made by
                              Napoleon
And ' Semiramis ' 1814 departed from Lucca
          but her brother's law code remains.
monumento di civile sapienza
dried swamps, grew cotton, brought in merinos
mortgage system improved
          ' Thank god such men be but few '
though they build up human courage
And before him had been Pietro Leopoldo
that wished state debt brought to an end;
that put the guilds under common tribunal;
that left names only as vestige of feudal chain;
that lightened mortmain that princes and church be under tax
as were others; that ended the gaolings for debt;
that said thou shalt not sell public offices;
that suppressed so many *gabelle*;
that freed the printers of surveillance
          and wiped out the crime of lèse majesty;
that abolished death as a penalty and all tortures in prisons
which he held were for segregation;

227

that split common property among tillers;
roads, trees, and the wool trade,
the silk trade, and a set price, lower, for salt;
plus another full page of such actions Habsburg Lorraine
His son the Third Ferdinando, cut taxes by half,
improved tillage in Val di Chiana, Livorno porto franco.

and this day came Madame Letizia,
the ex-emperor's mother, and on the 13th departed.

' The foundation, Siena, has been to keep bridle on usury.'
Nicolò Piccolomini, Provveditore.

XLV

With *Usura*

With usura hath no man a house of good stone
each block cut smooth and well fitting
that design might cover their face,
with usura
hath no man a painted paradise on his church wall
harpes et luz
or where virgin receiveth message
and halo projects from incision,
with usura
seeth no man Gonzaga his heirs and his concubines
no picture is made to endure nor to live with
but it is made to sell and sell quickly
with usura, sin against nature,
is thy bread ever more of stale rags
is thy bread dry as paper,
with no mountain wheat, no strong flour
with usura the line grows thick
with usura is no clear demarcation
and no man can find site for his dwelling.
Stonecutter is kept from his stone
weaver is kept from his loom
WITH USURA
wool comes not to market
sheep bringeth no gain with usura
Usura is a murrain, usura
blunteth the needle in the maid's hand
and stoppeth the spinner's cunning. Pietro Lombardo
came not by usura
Duccio came not by usura

nor Pier della Francesca; Zuan Bellin' not by usura
nor was ' La Calunnia ' painted.
Came not by usura Angelico; came not Ambrogio Praedis,
Came no church of cut stone signed: *Adamo me fecit*.
Not by usura St Trophime
Not by usura Saint Hilaire,
Usura rusteth the chisel
It rusteth the craft and the craftsman
It gnaweth the thread in the loom
None learneth to weave gold in her pattern;
Azure hath a canker by usura; cramoisi is unbroidered
Emerald findeth no Memling
Usura slayeth the child in the womb
It stayeth the young man's courting
It hath brought palsey to bed, lyeth
between the young bride and her bridegroom
            CONTRA NATURAM
They have brought whores for Eleusis
Corpses are set to banquet
at behest of usura.

N.B. Usury: A charge for the use of purchasing power, levied
without regard to production; often without regard to the
possibilities of production. (Hence the failure of the Medici
bank.)

XLVI

ND if you will say that this tale teaches...
a lesson, or that the Reverend Eliot
has found a more natural language...you who think
you will
get through hell in a hurry...
That day there was cloud over Zoagli
And for three days snow cloud over the sea
Banked like a line of mountains.
Snow fell. Or rain fell stolid, a wall of lines
So that you could see where the air stopped open
and where the rain fell beside it
Or the snow fell beside it. Seventeen
Years on this case, nineteen years, ninety years
on this case
An' the fuzzy bloke sez (legs no pants ever wd. fit) ' IF
that is so, any government worth a damn can
pay dividends? '
The major chewed it a bit and sez: ' Y—es, eh...
You mean instead of collectin' taxes? '
' Instead of collecting taxes.' That office?
Didja see the Decennio?
?
Decennio exposition, reconstructed office of Il Popolo,
Waal, ours waz like that, minus the Mills bomb an' the teapot,
heavy lipped chap at the desk,
One half green eye and one brown one, nineteen
Years on this case, CRIME
Ov two CENturies, 5 millions bein' killed off
to 1919, and before that
Debts of the South to New York, that is to the
banks of the city, two hundred million,

war, I don't think (or have it your own way...)
about slavery?
Five million being killed off..couple of Max's drawings,
one of Balfour and a camel, an'
one w'ich fer oBviOus reasons haz
never been published, ole Johnny Bull with a 'ankerchief.
It has never been published..
    ' He ain't got an opinion.'
Sez Orage about G.B.S. sez Orage about Mr Xtertn.
Sez Orage about Mr Wells, ' he wont HAVE an opinion
trouble iz that you mean it, you never will be a journalist.'
19 years on this case, suburban garden,
' Greeks! ' sez John Marmaduke ' a couple of art tricks!
' What else? never could set up a NATION! '
' Wouldn't convert me, dwn't HAVE me converted,
' Said " I know I didn't *ask* you, your father sent you here
" to be trained. I know what I'd feel.
" send my son to England and have him come back a christian!
" what wd. I feel? " ' Suburban garden
Said Abdul Baha: " I said ' let us speak of religion.'
" Camel driver said: I must milk my camel.
" So when he had milked his camel I said ' let us speak of religion.'
And the camel driver said: It is time to drink milk.
' Will you have some? ' For politeness I tried to join him.
Have you ever tasted milk from a camel?
I was unable to drink camel's milk. I have *never* been able.
So he drank all of the milk, and I said: let us speak of religion.
' I have drunk my milk. I must dance.' said the driver.
We did not speak of religion." Thus Abdul Baha
Third vice-gerent of the First Abdul or whatever Baha,
the Sage, the Uniter, the founder of a religion,
in a garden at Uberton, Gubberton, or mebbe it was some
other damned suburb, but at any rate a suburban suburb
amid a flutter of teacups, said Mr Marmaduke:
" Never will understand us. They lie. I mean personally

" They are mendacious, but if the tribe gets together
" the tribal word will be kept, hence perpetual misunderstanding.
" Englishman goes there, lives honest, word is reliable,
" ten years, they believe him, then he signs terms for his
                                             government.
        " and, naturally, the treaty is broken, Mohammedans,
" Nomads, will never understand how we do this."
17 years on this case, and we not the first lot!
Said Paterson:
                Hath benefit of interest on all
the moneys which it, the bank, creates out of nothing.

                Semi-private inducement
Said Mr RothSchild, hell knows which Roth-schild
1861, '64 or there sometime, " Very few people
" will understand this. Those who do will be occupied
" getting profits. The general public will probably not
" see it's against their interest."
                Seventeen years on the case; here
Gents, is/are the confession.
        " Can we take this into court?
      " Will any jury convict on this evidence?
1694 anno domini, on through the ages of usury
On, right on, into hair-cloth, right on into rotten building,
Right on into London houses, ground rents, foetid brick work,
Will any jury convict 'um? The Foundation of Regius Professors
Was made to spread lies and teach Whiggery, will any
                JURY convict 'um?
The Macmillan Commission about two hundred and forty years
                                             LATE
with great difficulty got back to Paterson's
The bank makes it *ex nihil*
Denied by five thousand professors, will any
Jury convict 'um? This case, and with it
the first part, draws to a conclusion,

of the first phase of this opus, Mr Marx, Karl, did not
foresee this conclusion, you have seen a good deal of
the evidence, not knowing it evidence, is monumentum
look about you, look, if you can, at St Peter's
Look at the Manchester slums, look at Brazilian coffee
or Chilean nitrates. This case is the first case
Si requieres monumentum?
This case is not the last case or the whole case, we ask a
REVISION, we ask for enlightenment in a case
moving concurrent, but this case is the first case:
Bank creates it ex nihil. Creates it to meet a need,
Hic est hyper-usura. Mr. Jefferson met it:
No man hath natural right to exercise profession
of lender, save him who hath it to lend.
Replevin, estopple, what wangle which wangle, VanBuren met it.
Before that was tea dumped into harbour, before that was a
great deal still in the school books, placed there
NOT as evidence. Placed there to distract idle minds,
Murder, starvation and bloodshed, seventy four red revolutions
Ten empires fell on this grease spot.
' I rule the Earth ' said Antoninus ' but LAW rules the sea '
meaning, we take it, lex Rhodi, the Law Maritime
                         of sea lawyers.
usura and sea insurance
wherefrom no State was erected greater than Athens.
Wanting TAXES to build St Peter's, thought Luther beneath
                                        civil notice,
1527. Thereafter art thickened. Thereafter design went to hell,
Thereafter barocco, thereafter stone-cutting desisted.
' Hic nefas ' (narrator) ' commune sepulchrum.'

19 years on this case/first case. I have set down part of
The Evidence. Part/commune sepulchrum
Aurum est commune sepulchrum. Usura, commune sepulchrum.

234

helandros   kai heleptolis   kai helarxe.
Hic Geryon est. Hic hyperusura.

FIVE million youths without jobs
FOUR million adult illiterates
15 million ' vocational misfits ', that is with small chance for jobs
NINE million persons annual, injured in preventable industrial
accidents
One hundred thousand violent crimes. The Eunited States ov
America
3rd year of the reign of F. Roosevelt, signed F. Delano, his uncle.
CASE for the prosecution. That is one case, minor case
in the series/Eunited States of America, a.d. 1935
England a worse case, France under a foetor of regents.
' Mr Cummings wants Farley's job ' headline in current paper.

XLVII

WHO even dead, yet hath his mind entire!
This sound came in the dark
First must thou go the road
                              to hell
And to the bower of Ceres' daughter Proserpine,
Through overhanging dark, to see Tiresias,
Eyeless that was, a shade, that is in hell
So full of knowing that the beefy men know less than he,
Ere thou come to thy road's end.
                    Knowledge the shade of a shade,
Yet must thou sail after knowledge
Knowing less than drugged beasts. *phtheggometha*
thasson
φθεγγώμεθα θᾶσσον
            The small lamps drift in the bay
And the sea's claw gathers them.
Neptunus drinks after neap-tide.
Tamuz! Tamuz!!
The red flame going seaward.
            By this gate art thou measured.
From the long boats they have set lights in the water,
The sea's claw gathers them outward.
Scilla's dogs snarl at the cliff's base,
The white teeth gnaw in under the crag,
But in the pale night the small lamps float seaward
                              Τυ Διώνα
                              TU DIONA

Και Μοῖραι' Ἄδονιν
Kai MOIRAI' ADONIN
The sea is streaked red with Adonis,
The lights flicker red in small jars.

Wheat shoots rise new by the altar,
      flower from the swift seed.
Two span, two span to a woman,
Beyond that she believes not. Nothing is of any importance.
To that is she bent, her intention
To that art thou called ever turning intention,
Whether by night the owl-call, whether by sap in shoot,
Never idle, by no means by no wiles intermittent
Moth is called over mountain
The bull runs blind on the sword, *naturans*
To the cave art thou called, Odysseus,
By Molü hast thou respite for a little,
By Molü art thou freed from the one bed
      that thou may'st return to another
The stars are not in her counting,
      To her they are but wandering holes.
Begin thy plowing
When the Pleiades go down to their rest,
Begin thy plowing
40 days are they under seabord,
Thus do in fields by seabord
And in valleys winding down toward the sea.
When the cranes fly high
      think of plowing.
By this gate art thou measured
Thy day is between a door and a door
Two oxen are yoked for plowing
Or six in the hill field
White bulk under olives, a score for drawing down stone,
Here the mules are gabled with slate on the hill road.
Thus was it in time.
And the small stars now fall from the olive branch,
Forked shadow falls dark on the terrace
More black than the floating martin
      that has no care for your presence,

His wing-print is black on the roof tiles
And the print is gone with his cry.
So light is thy weight on Tellus
Thy notch no deeper indented
Thy weight less than the shadow
Yet hast thou gnawed through the mountain,
                    Scylla's white teeth less sharp.
Hast thou found a nest softer than cunnus
Or hast thou found better rest
Hast'ou a deeper planting, doth thy death year
Bring swifter shoot?
Hast thou entered more deeply the mountain?

The light has entered the cave. Io! Io!
The light has gone down into the cave,
Splendour on splendour!
By prong have I entered these hills:
That the grass grow from my body,
That I hear the roots speaking together,
The air is new on my leaf,
The forked boughs shake with the wind.
Is Zephyrus more light on the bough, Apeliota
more light on the almond branch?
By this door have I entered the hill.
Falleth,
Adonis falleth.
Fruit cometh after. The small lights drift out with the tide,
sea's claw has gathered them outward,
Four banners to every flower
The sea's claw draws the lamps outward.
Think thus of thy plowing
When the seven stars go down to their rest
Forty days for their rest, by seabord
And in valleys that wind down toward the sea

Καὶ Μοῖραι' "Αδονιν

KAI MOIRAI' ADONIN

When the almond bough puts forth its flame,
When the new shoots are brought to the altar,

Τυ Διώνα, Καὶ Μοῖραι

TU DIONA, KAI MOIRAI

Καὶ Μοῖραι' "Αδονιν

KAI MOIRAI' ADONIN

that hath the gift of healing,
that hath the power over wild beasts.

XLVIII

A ND if the money be rented
       Who shd pay rent on that money?
       Some fellow who has it on rent day,
        or some bloke who has not?
Died Mahomet VIth Yahid Eddin Han
    ' by profession ex-sultan '
65 years of age in San Remo (1926)
begotten of Abdul Mejid. At beatification
80 loud speakers were used. Subsequent to the
Turkish war Mr Kolschitzky
received for his services as a spy
five score sacks of coffee (de Banchiis cambi tenendi)
thus initiating the coffee-house facts of Vienna
sixteen hundred, I think, and whenever; Von Unruh
is rather good at imitating the sergeant
who jammed down the cadavers; there were cadavers
and the pit was not large enough to hold all the kadavers
so the sergeant jammed 'em down with his boots
to get the place smooth for the Kaiser.
Herr Von Unruh is rather good at miming that sergeant
vide Verdun; and what he wrote down; at Verdun.
Said Mr Charles Francis Adams
there was no good conversation. At no single entertainment
in London did I find any good conversation
They take Browning for an American,
he is unenglish in his opinions and carriage.
       Was put in the cellarage
Van Buren having written it down
' deface and obliterate ' wrote J. Adams
' become fathers of the next generation ' wrote Marx
..tuberculosis...Bismarck

blamed american civil war on the jews;
particularly on the Rothschild
one of whom remarked to Disraeli
that nations were fools to pay rent for their credit
Δίγονος
DIGONOS; lost in the forest; but are then known as leopards
after three years in the forest; they are known as ' twice-born '.
I am sorry, Your Highness   Cawdor, Sept 23
To have been so long in returning the
pedigree of yr cairn puppy
but when I wrote to the man you bought him from
I received a reply from his wife (or daughter)
saying he had just gone on a holiday
and that he wd write me when he returned.
        I find Dhu Achil (sire) has been registered
at the Kennel Club, but the dam is unregistered.
Dhu Achil has won a fair number of prizes at Scottish Shows
and there are some other good dogs in the pedigree
        (three senators; four bottles of whiskey)
so the puppy seems quite well bred   (and at)
For the sake of convenience I will write particulars
(four o'clock in the morning Mr Rhumby)
on a separate sheet of paper
        (waz Sekkertary) The little dog is doing
(Ov State) very well at Mr McLocherty's and is quite happy.
They are very fond of him and he is a most affectionate dog
                Yours respectfully
Galileo; pronounced ' Garry Yeo '
err' un' imbecille; ed ha imbecillito
(voice under my window) il mondo
No trustee of the Salem Museum, who had not doubled
both Good Hope and The Horn.
        Sea as if risen over the headland
and there are twin seas in the cloud
12% interest in Bithynia;

for home Romans interest 6. No man theign
said Athelstan who has not made three voyages
going hence off this land into other lands as a merchant
' A little more stock ' said the president over the telephone
To the printer ' we sold all that what you printed us '
        So the bond salesman went abroad.
They say, that is the Norse engineer told me, that out past Hawaii
they spread threads from gun'ale to gun'ale
in a certain fashion
and plot a course of 3000 sea miles
lying under the web, watching the stars
' while she bought 2 prs of shoes
2 veils; 2 parasols; an orchid (artificial)
for which I was presented with a new kind of net gloves
made like fishnet; so the day was not wholly wasted
The priest here
had una nuova messa
        (dodicesimo anno E.F.)
bella festa, because there was a priest here to say his
first mass
and all the mountains were full of fires, and
we went around through the village
        in giro per il paese
2 men and 2 horses
and then the music and on the sides
children carrying torches and the
carrozze with the priests, and the one that had to say
the new mass, and the carrozze were full of fine flowers
and there were a lot of people. I liked it,
all the houses were full of lights and
tree branches in the windows
covered with hand-made flowers and
the next day they had mass and a procession
Please may I go back there
and have a new pair of Sunday shoes? '

Velvet, yellow, unwinged
clambers, a ball, into its orchis
and the stair there still broken
the flat stones of the road, Mt Segur.
From Val Cabrere, were two miles of roofs to San Bertrand
so that a cat need not set foot in the road
where now is an inn, and bare rafters,
where they scratch six feet deep to reach pavement
where now is wheat field, and a milestone
an altar to Terminus, with arms crossed
back of the stone
Where sun cuts light against evening;
where light shaves grass into emerald
Savairic; hither Gaubertz;
                                     Said they wd. not be under Paris

Falling Mars in the air
bough to bough, to the stone bench
where was an ox in smith's sling hoisted for shoeing
where was spire-top a-level the grass yard
Then the towers, high over chateau—
Fell with stroke after stroke, jet avenger
bent, rolled, severed and then swallowed limb after limb
Hauled off the butt of that carcass, 20 feet up a tree trunk,
Here three ants have killed a great worm. There
Mars in the air, fell, flew.
Employed, past tense; at the Lido, Venezia
an old man with a basket of stones,
that was, said the elderly lady, when the beach costumes
were longer,
and if the wind was, the old man placed a stone.

XLIX

For the seven lakes, and by no man these verses:
    Rain; empty river; a voyage,
    Fire from frozen cloud, heavy rain in the twilight
    Under the cabin roof was one lantern.
The reeds are heavy; bent;
and the bamboos speak as if weeping.

Autumn moon; hills rise about lakes
against sunset
Evening is like a curtain of cloud,
a blurr above ripples; and through it
sharp long spikes of the cinnamon,
a cold tune amid reeds.
Behind hill the monk's bell
borne on the wind.
Sail passed here in April; may return in October
Boat fades in silver; slowly;
Sun blaze alone on the river.

Where wine flag catches the sunset
Sparse chimneys smoke in the cross light

Comes then snow scur on the river
And a world is covered with jade
Small boat floats like a lanthorn,
The flowing water clots as with cold. And at San Yin
they are a people of leisure.
Wild geese swoop to the sand-bar,
Clouds gather about the hole of the window
Broad water; geese line out with the autumn
Rooks clatter over the fishermen's lanthorns,

A light moves on the north sky line;
where the young boys prod stones for shrimp.
In seventeen hundred came Tsing to these hill lakes.
A light moves on the south sky line.

State by creating riches shd. thereby get into debt?
This is infamy; this is Geryon.
This canal goes still to TenShi
though the old king built it for pleasure

```
K E I    M E N   RAN   K E I
K I U    M A N   MAN   K E I
JITSU   GETSU   K O   KWA
T AN   FUKU   TAN   K A I
```

Sun up; work
sundown; to rest
dig well and drink of the water
dig field; eat of the grain
Imperial power is? and to us what is it?

The fourth; the dimension of stillness.
And the power over wild beasts.

R EVOLUTION ' said Mr Adams ' took place in the
            minds of the people
            in the fifteen years before Lexington ',
                    That wd have been in Peter Leopold's time
to his Lordship the Count Orso and his descendants
male legitimate and natural the administration of
civil and criminal justice in the said place

debt when the Medici took the throne was 5 million
and when they left was fourteen
and its interest ate up all the best income

the first folly was planting factories for wool spinning
in England and Flanders
            then England kept her raw wool, so that
damped down the exchanging
            the arts gone to hell by 1750
and Leopoldo cut down the taxes
found there was ' Un ' abbondanza che affamava '
says Zobi
            Leopold cut down the debt interest
and put the Jesuits out
                        and put end to the Inquisition
1782
      and they brought in Mr Locke's
essay on interest
                  but Genoa took our trade and Livorno
kept treaty with England to the loss of Livorno
that is to say Livorno trade took a loss
Te, admirabile, O VashinnnTTonn!
            Livorno stuff went in Genovese bottoms

246

because Tuscany kept her word and a treaty
Voi, popoli transatlantici admirabili!
saith Zobi, sixty years later.
   ' Pardon our brief digression ' saith Zobi:
America is our daughter and VashiNNtonn had civic virtues.
and Leopoldo meant to cut off two thirds of state debt,
to abolish it
         and then they sent him off to be Emperor
in hell's bog, in the slough of Vienna, in
     the midden of Europe in the black hole of all
mental vileness, in the privvy that stank Franz Josef,
in Metternich's merdery in the absolute rottenness,
among embastardized cross-breeds,

But Ferdinando staved off an Anschluss and Paris exploded

' certain practices called religious ' said Zobi
' lack of experience in economic affairs '
Pius sixth, vicar of foolishness, no Jew God
wd. have kept THAT in power.
So that about the time of MARENGO the First Consul
wrote: I left peace. I find war.
     I find enemies inside yr frontier
      Your cannon sold to yr enemies
1791, end of representative government
      18th Brumale, 10th of November
14th. June, 1800 MARENGO
Mars meaning, in that case, order
That day was Right with the victor
    mass weight against wrong
a.d. 1800
      interest at 24 to the hundred
and as they say ' commerce languished '
1801 the triumvirs wanted to go Leopoldine as was.
A thousand of the old guard at Portoferraio

and two million a year, one half of it
reversable to the Empress
from Elba
for the mildness of the climate
and the suavity of its denizens
from an English frigate descended
And Ferdinando Habsburg (but of the House of Lorraine)
which is the true name of the clean part of that family
got back a state free of debt
coffers empty
but the state without debt
England and Austria were for despots with commerce
considered
put back the Pope but
reset no republics: Venice, Genova, Lucca
and split up Poland in their soul was usura
and in their hand bloody oppression
and that son of a dog, Rospigliosi,
came into Tuscany to make serfs of old Tuscans.
S..t on the throne of England, s..t on the Austrian sofa
In their soul was usura and in their minds darkness
and blankness, greased fat were four Georges
Pus was in Spain, Wellington was a jew's pimp
and lacked mind to know what he effected.
' Leave the Duke, Go for gold! '
In their souls was usura and in their hearts cowardice
In their minds was stink and corruption
Two sores ran together,
and hell pissed up Metternich
Filth stank as in our day
' From the brigantine Incostante '
for a hundred days against hell belch
Hope spat from March into June
Ney out of his saddle

Grouchy delayed
          Bentinck's word was, naturally,
not kept by the English. Genova under Sardegna. Hope
spat from Cannes, March, into Flanders.
                    ' Not '
said Napoleon ' because of that league of lice
but for opposing the Zeitgeist! That was my ruin,
That I ran against my own time, turning backward '
OBIT, aetatis 57, five hundred years after D. Alighieri.
Not, certainly, for what most embellishes il sesso femminile
and causes us to admire it, they wrote of Marie de Parma
his widow.
Italy ever doomed with abstractions, 1850, wrote Zobi,
By following brilliant abstractions.
Mastai, Pio Nono, D'Azeglio went into exile
and so on the 30th of October Lord Minto
was in Arezzo (I think Bowring had preceded) and the
crowd cried EVVIVA
Evviva the Tariff League
and Minto yelled Evviva Leopoldo
Evviv' INDIPENDENZA, this was the new Leopoldo
though Minto was for slowness and sureness.
Lalage's shadow moves in the fresco's knees
She is blotted with Dirce's shadow
dawn stands there fixed and unmoving
                    only we two have moved.

LI

SHINES
in the mind of heaven God
who made it
more than the sun
in our eye.
Fifth element; mud; said Napoleon
With usury has no man a good house
made of stone, no paradise on his church wall
With usury the stone cutter is kept from his stone
the weaver is kept from his loom by usura
Wool does not come into market
the peasant does not eat his own grain
the girl's needle goes blunt in her hand
The looms are hushed one after another
ten thousand after ten thousand
Duccio was not by usura
Nor was ' La Calunnia ' painted.
Neither Ambrogio Praedis nor Angelico
had their skill by usura
Nor St Trophime its cloisters;
Nor St Hilaire its proportion.
Usury rusts the man and his chisel
It destroys the craftsman, destroying craft;
Azure is caught with cancer. Emerald comes to no Memling
Usury kills the child in the womb
And breaks short the young man's courting
Usury brings age into youth; it lies between the bride
and the bridegroom
Usury is against Nature's increase.
Whores for Eleusis;
Under usury no stone is cut smooth

Peasant has no gain from his sheep herd
            Blue dun; number 2 in most rivers
for dark days, when it is cold
A starling's wing will give you the colour
or duck widgeon, if you take feather from under the wing
Let the body be of blue fox fur, or a water rat's
or grey squirrel's. Take this with a portion of mohair
and a cock's hackle for legs.
12th of March to 2nd of April
Hen pheasant's feather does for a fly,
green tail, the wings flat on the body
Dark fur from a hare's ear for a body
a green shaded partridge feather
            grizzled yellow cock's hackle
green wax; harl from a peacock's tail
bright lower body; about the size of pin
the head should be. can be fished from seven a.m.
till eleven; at which time the brown marsh fly comes on.
As long as the brown continues, no fish will take Granham

That hath the light of the doer, as it were
a form cleaving to it.
Deo similis quodam modo
hic intellectus adeptus
Grass; nowhere out of place. Thus speaking in Königsberg
Zwischen die Volkern erzielt wird
a modus vivendi.
circling in eddying air; in a hurry;
the 12: close eyed in the oily wind
these were the regents; and a sour song from the folds
            of his belly
sang Geryone; I am the help of the aged;
I pay men to talk peace;
Mistress of many tongues; merchant of chalcedony
I am Geryon twin with usura,

You who have lived in a stage set.
A thousand were dead in his folds;
in the eel-fishers basket
Time was of the League of Cambrai:

CANTOS LII-LXXI

No one is going to be content with a transliteration of Chinese names. When not making a desperate effort at mnemonics or differentiating in vain hope of distinguishing one race from another, I mainly use the french form. Our European knowledge of China has come via latin and french and at any rate the french vowels as printed have some sort of uniform connotation.

Table

		PAGE
Rays idiogram from Fenollosa collection		254

CANTO

LII.	Li ki	257

LIII.	Great Emperors	262
	First dynasty HIA	
	Tching Tang of CHANG (second dynasty) b.c. 1766	
	Third dynasty TCHEOU b.c. 1122-255	
	Confucius (KUNG FU TSEU) 551-479	

LIV.	Fourth Dynasty TSIN, Burning of the Books 213	275
	Fifth Dynasty HAN b.c. 202	
	Eighth Dynasty SUNG a.d. 420	
	Thirteenth Dynasty TANG 618	

LV.	Tchun of TANG a.d. 805 Ngan's reforms	290
	Nineteenth Dynasty SUNG 960	

LVI.	Ghengis 1206	301
	Kublai 1260	
	Twentieth Dynasty YUEN (Mongol)	
	Lady Ouang Chi	
	HONG VOU died 1399	
	Twenty-first Dynasty MING 1368	

LVII.	Flight of Kien Ouen Ti	311

CANTO   PAGE

LVIII. Japan   316
        Tartar Horse Fairs
        Tai Tsong, son of Tai Tseu
        Twenty-second Dynasty MANCHU 1625

 LIX. The books into Manchu   324
        Russian treaty

  LX. Jesuits   328

 LXI. Yong Tching (Chi tsong hien Hoang Ti) 1723   334
        Kien Long 1736
In the text names of Emperors and of Dynasties are in CAPS.

LXII-LXXI. JOHN ADAMS   341
        Writs of assistance   354
        Defence of Preston   359
        The congress (Nomination of Washington)   364
        Voyage to France   371
            (not being diddled by Vergennes or plastered
            by Dr. Franklin)
        Saving the fisheries   377
        Plan of Government   392
        Recognition, loan from the Dutch, treaty with
            Holland   400-05
        London   412
        Avoidance of war with France   418

Note the final lines in greek, Canto 71, are from Hymn of
Cleanthes, part of Adams' *paideuma*: Glorious, deathless of
many names, Zeus aye ruling all things, founder of the inborn
qualities of nature, by laws piloting all things.

Other foreign words and ideograms both in these two decads
and in earlier cantos enforce the text but seldom if ever add
anything not stated in the english, though not always in lines
immediately contiguous to these underlinings.

LII

A ND I have told you of how things were under Duke
Leopold in Siena
And of the true base of credit, that is
the abundance of nature
with the whole folk behind it.
' Goods that are needed ' said Schacht (anno seidici)
commerciabili beni, deliverable things that are wanted.
neschek is against this, the serpent
And Vivante was there in his paradise, the mild air
the fields rolling eastward, and the tower half ruin'd
with a peasant complaining that her son was taken for war
and he said ' plutocracies were less violent '.
━━━━━ sin drawing vengeance, poor yitts paying for

paying for a few big jews' vendetta on goyim
I think wrote Miss Bell to her mama
that when not against the interests of Empire
we shd/ keep our pledges to Arabs.
Thus we lived on through sanctions, through Stalin
Litvinof, gold brokers made profit
rocked the exchange against gold
Before which entrefaites remarked Johnnie Adams (the elder)
IGNORANCE, sheer ignorance ov the natr ov money
sheer ignorance of credit and circulation.
Remarked Ben: better keep out the jews
or yr/ grand children will curse you
jews, real jews, chazims, and *neschek*
also super-neschek or the international racket

━━━━━━━━━━━━━━━━━━━━━━━
━━━━━━━━━━━━━━━━━
━━━━━━━━━━━━━━━
━━━━━━━━━━━━━━━━━━━━━━

governments full of their gun-swine, bankbuzzards, poppinjays.
Did commit, that he did in the Kingdom of Italy...
of the two usuries, the lesser is now put down.
that he did in the Kingdom of Britain etc/
      Between KUNG and ELEUSIS
Under the Golden Roof, la Dorata
      her baldacchino
Riccio on his horse rides still to Montepulciano
      the groggy church is gone toothless
No longer holds against *neschek*
      the fat has covered their croziers
The high fans and the mitre mean nothing
Once only in Burgos, once in Cortona
      was the song firm and well given
old buffers keeping the stiffness,
      Gregory damned, always was damned, obscurantist.
Know then:
      Toward summer when the sun is in Hyades
Sovran is Lord of the Fire
      to this month are birds.
with bitter smell and with the odour of burning
To the hearth god, lungs of the victim
      The green frog lifts up his voice
      and the white latex is in flower
In red car with jewels incarnadine
      to welcome the summer
In this month no destruction
      no tree shall be cut at this time
Wild beasts are driven from field
      in this month are simples gathered.
The empress offers cocoons to the Son of Heaven
      Then goes the sun into Gemini
Virgo in mid heaven at sunset
      indigo must not be cut
No wood burnt into charcoal

gates are all open, no tax on the booths.
Now mares go to grazing,
            tie up the stallions
Post up the horsebreeding notices
            Month of the longest days
Life and death are now equal
            Strife is between light and darkness
Wise man stays in his house
            Stag droppeth antlers
Grasshopper is loud,
            leave no fire open to southward.
Now the sun enters Hydra, this is the third moon of summer
Antares of Scorpio stands mid heaven at sunset
Andromeda is with sunrise
            Lord of the fire is dominant
To this month is SEVEN,
            with bitter smell, with odour of burning
Offer to gods of the hearth
            the lungs of the victims
Warm wind is rising, cricket bideth in wall
Young goshawk is learning his labour
            dead grass breedeth glow-worms.
In Ming T'ang HE bideth
            in the west wing of that house
Red car and the sorrel horses
            his banner incarnadine.
The fish ward now goes against crocodiles
To take all great lizards, turtles, for divination,
sea terrapin.
The lake warden to gather rushes
            to take grain for the *manes*
to take grain for the beasts you will sacrifice
to the Lords of the Mountains
            To the Lords of great rivers
Inspector of dye-works, inspector of colour and broideries

see that the white, black, green be in order
let no false colour exist here
black, yellow, green be of quality
                This month are trees in full sap
Rain has now drenched all the earth
                dead weeds enrich it, as if boil'd in a bouillon.
Sweet savour, the heart of the victim
yellow flag over Emperor's chariot
                yellow stones in his girdle.
Sagittarius in mid-course at sunset
                cold wind is beginning. Dew whitens.
Now is cicada's time,
                the sparrow hawk offers birds to the spirits.
Emperor goes out in war car, he is drawn by white horses,
white banner, white stones in his girdle
eats dog and the dish is deep.
                This month is the reign of Autumn
Heaven is active in metals, now gather millet
                and finish the flood-walls
Orion at sunrise.
                Horses now with black manes.
Eat dog meat. This is the month of ramparts.
Beans are the tribute, September is end of thunder
The hibernants go into their caves.
                Tolls lowered, now sparrows, they say, turn into oysters
The wolf now offers his sacrifice.
                Men hunt with five weapons,
They cut wood for charcoal.
                New rice with your dog meat.
First month of winter is now
                sun is in Scorpio's tail
at sunrise in Hydra, ice starting
The pheasant plunges into Houai (great water)
                and turns to an oyster
Rainbow is hidden awhile.

Heaven's Son feeds on roast pork and millet,
Steel gray are stallion.
        This month winter ruleth.
The sun is in archer's shoulder
        in crow's head at sunrise
Ice thickens. Earth cracks. And the tigers now move to mating.
Cut trees at solstice, and arrow shafts of bamboo.
Third month, wild geese go north,
        magpie starts building,
Pheasant lifteth his voice to the Spirit of Mountains
The fishing season is open,
        rivers and lakes frozen deep
Put now ice in your ice-house,
        the great concert of winds
Call things by the names. Good sovereign by distribution
Evil king is known by his imposts.
Begin where you are said Lord Palmerston
        began draining swamps in Sligo
Fought smoke nuisance in London. Dredged harbour in Sligo.

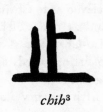

chih[3]

LIII

Yeou taught men to break branches
        Seu Gin set up the stage and taught barter,
        taught the knotting of cords
        Fou Hi taught men to grow barley
        2837 ante Christum
and they know still where his tomb is
by the high cypress between the strong walls.
the FIVE grains, said Chin Nong, that are
        wheat, rice, millet, *gros blé* and chick peas
and made a plough that is used five thousand years
Moved his court then to Kio-feou-hien
held market at mid-day
' bring what we have not here ', wrote an herbal
Souan yen bagged fifteen tigers
        made signs out of bird tracks
Hoang Ti contrived the making of bricks
and his wife started working the silk worms,
        money was in days of Hoang Ti.
He measured the length of Syrinx
        of the tubes to make tune for song
Twenty-six (that was) eleven ante Christum
        had four wives and 25 males of his making
His tomb is today in Kiao-Chan
Ti Ko set his scholars to fitting words to their music
        is buried in Tung Kieou
This was in the twenty fifth century a.c.
        YAO like the sun and rain,
saw what star is at solstice
saw what star marks mid summer
YU, leader of waters,
        black earth is fertile, wild silk still is from Shantung
Ammassi, to the provinces,

let his men pay tithes in kind.
' Siu-tcheou province to pay in earth of five colours
Pheasant plumes from Yu-chan of mountains
Yu-chan to pay sycamores
          of this wood are lutes made
Ringing stones from Se-choui river
and grass that is called Tsing-mo' or μῶλυ,
Chun to the spirit Chang Ti, of heaven
moving the sun and stars
          que vos vers expriment vos intentions,
          et que la musique conforme

YAO

CHUN

YU

KAO-YAO

阜
陶

abundance.
Then an Empress fled with Chao Kang in her belly.
Fou-hi by virtue of wood;
Chin-nong, of fire; Hoang Ti ruled by the earth,
Chan by metal.
Tchuen was lord, as is water.
CHUN, govern
YU, cultivate,
The surface is not enough,
      from Chang Ti nothing is hidden.
For years no waters came, no rain fell
      for the Emperor Tching Tang
grain scarce, prices rising
so that in 1760 Tching Tang opened the copper mine (ante
                                 Christum)
made discs with square holes in their middles
      and gave these to the people
wherewith they might buy grain
                  where there was grain
The silos were emptied
7 years of sterility
          der im Baluba das Gewitter gemacht hat
Tching prayed on the mountain and

264

wrote MAKE IT NEW
on his bath tub
      Day by day make it new
cut underbrush,
pile the logs
keep it growing.
Died Tching aged years an hundred,
in the 13th of his reign.
      ' We are up, Hia is down.'
Immoderate love of women
Immoderate love of riches,
Cared for parades and huntin'.
      Chang Ti above alone rules.
Tang not stinting of praise:
      Consider their sweats, the people's
If you wd/ sit calm on throne.

 hsin[1]

 jih[4]

jih[4]

 hsin[1]

 Hsia

Hia! Hia is fallen
      for offence to the spirits
For sweats of the people.
      Not by your virtue
      but by virtue of Tching Tang
Honour to YU, converter of waters
Honour Tching Tang
Honour to YIN
seek old men and new tools
      After five hundred years came then Wen Wang
B.C. 1231
Uncle Ki said: Jewels!
      You eat nothing but bears' paws.
In marble tower of Lou Tai doors were of jasper

that palace was ten years in the making
Tan Ki, palace, lit by day with torches and lanthorns
             Now Kieou's daughter
             was baked in an ox and served.
And they worked out the Y-king or changes
             to guess from
In plain of Mou Ye, Cheou-sin came as a forest moving
       Wu Wang entered the city
gave out grain till the treasures were empty
by the Nine vases of YU, demobilized army
             sent horses to Hoa-chan
             To the peach groves
Dated his year from the winter solstice.
             Red was his dynasty.
Kids 8 to 15 in the schools, then higher training
mottoes writ all over walls
             ' Use their ways and their music
             Keep form of their charts and banners
             Prepare soldiers in peace time
             All is lost in the night clubs
                    that was gained under good rule.'
Wagon with small box wherein was a needle
             that pointed to southward
and this was called the South Chariot.
             Lo Yang in the middle Kingdom and its length
was 17200 feet. Saith Tcheou Kong: True sage seeks not repose.
             Hope without work is crazy
Your forebear among the people
             dressed as one of the people
Caring for needs of the people,
             old when he came to the throne
Observing the solstice.
             Died eleven o six ante Christum
             are still bits of his writing
' A good governor is as wind over grass

A good ruler keeps down taxes.'
Tching-ouang kept lynx eye on bureaucrats
          lynx eye on the currency
weight of the tchu was one 24th of an ounce
          or one hundred grains of millet
cloth bolt and silk bolt
to be two feet two inches by four tchang (one Tchang equals
                              four feet)
reigned till 1079
          and was peace for the rest of his reign.
Called for his hat shaped as a mortar board
          set out the precious stones on his table
saying this is my will and my last will
          Keep peace
Keep the peace, care for the people.
          Ten lines, no more in his testament.
Chao Kong called the historians,
          laid out white and violet damask
For the table of jewels, as when Tching-ouang received princes.
On the table of the throne of the West
          laid out the charters
constitutions of antient kings and two sorts of stone
Hong-pi and Yuen-yen
And on the East table he put the pearls from Mt Hoa-chan
and pearls from the islands and the sphere of Chun
that showeth the places of heaven. And the dance robes of In
the old dynasty and the great drum that is 8 feet high
these he put in the place for music. The pikes, bows,
bamboo arrows and war gear he set to the East.
The mats of the first rank of rushes bordered with damask
of the second of bamboo and the third rank
of tree bark.
A gray fur cap for the crowning, and 20 ft halbards.
(Ten seven eight ante Christum)
' Left in my Father's orders, By the table of jewels

To administrate as in the law left us
Keep peace in the Empire
Ouen Ouang, and Wu Wang your fathers.'
Thus came Kang to be Emperor/.
White horses with sorrel manes in the court yard.
'I am pro-Tcheou' said Confucius
'I am' said Confutzius 'pro-Tcheou in politics'
Wen-wang and Wu-wang had sage men, strong as bears
Said young Kang-wang:
Help me to keep the peace!
Your ancestors have come one by one under our rule
for our rule.
Honour to Chao-Kong the surveyor.
Let his name last 3000 years
Gave each man land for his labour
not by plough-land alone
But for keeping of silk-worms
Reforested the mulberry groves
Set periodical markets
Exchange brought abundance, the prisons were empty.
'Yao and Chun have returned'
sang the farmers
'Peace and abundance bring virtue.' I am
'pro-Tcheou' said Confucius five centuries later.
With his mind on this age.

 Chou

In the 16th of Kang Ouang died Pé-kin
Prince of Lou, friend of peace, friend of the people
worthy son of Tcheou-kong
And in the 26th Kang Ouang, died Chao-Kong the tireless

on a journey he made for good of the state
and men never thereafter cut branches
         of the pear-trees whereunder he had sat deeming
                                                  justice
      deeming the measures of lands.
And you will hear to this day the folk singing
      Grow pear-boughs, be fearless
      let no man break twig of this tree
      that gave shade to Chao-Kong
      he had shadow from sun here;
               rest had he in your shade.
Died then Kang Wang in the 26th of his reign.   b.c. 1053
Moon shone in an haze of colours
Water boiled in the wells, and died Tchao-ouang
         to joy of the people.
Tchao-ouang that hunted across the tilled fields
And MOU-OUANG said:
         ' as a tiger against me,
               a man of thin ice in thaw
aid me in the darkness of rule '
         then fell into vanity
against council led out a myriad army and brought back
4 wolves and 4 deer
         his folk remained mere barbarians.
Yet when neared an hundred
         he wd/ have made reparation
Criminal law is from Chun,
         from necessity only
In doubt, no condemnation, rule out irrelevant evidence.
Law of MOU is law of the just middle, the pivot.
Riches that come of court fines and of judges' takings
         these are no treasure
as is said in the book *Lin hing* of the *Chu King*.
And the governor's daughters, three daughters,
came to the river King-Ho,

For ten months was the emperor silent
and in the twelfth month, he, KONG, burnt the town
and got over it
Song turned against Y-wang, great hail upon
Hiao wang
killing the cattle, Han-kiang was frozen over.
And in his time was the horse dealer Fei-tsei
industrious, of the fallen house of Pe-y
who became master of equerry, who became Prince of Tsin.
Li WANG avid of silver, to whom a memorial
' A Prince who wd/ fulfill obligation, takes caution
à ce que l'argent circule
that cash move amongst the people.
' Glory of HEOU-TSIE is clouded
Deathless his honour that saw his folk using their substance.
The end of your house is upon us.'

b.c. 860   Youi-leang-fou, in memorial.
Said Chao-kong: Talk of the people
is like the hills and the streams
Thence comes our abundance.
To be Lord to the four seas of China
a man must let men make verses
he must let people play comedies
and historians write down the facts
he must let the poor speak evil of taxes.
Interregnum of Cong-ho. Siuen went against the west tartars
His praise lasts to this day: Siuen-ouang contra barbaros
legat belli ducem Chaoumoukong,
Hoailand, fed by Hoai river
dark millet, Tchang wine for the sacrifice.
Juxta fluvium Hoai acies ordinatur nec mora
Swift men as if flyers, like Yangtse
Strong as the Yangtse,
they stand rooted as mountains
they move as a torrent of waters

Emperor not rash in council: agit considerate
HAN founded the town of Yuei
and taught men to sow the five grains
In the 4th year of Siuen,
Sié was founded.
and there were four years of dry summer.
RITE is:
Nine days before the first moon of spring time,
that he fast. And with gold cup of wheat-wine
that he go afield to spring ploughing
that he plough one and three quarters furrows
and eat beef when this rite is finished,
so did not Siuen
that after famine, called back the people
where are reeds to weave, where are pine trees
Siuen established this people hac loca fluvius alluit
He heard the wild geese crying sorrow
Campestribus locis
here have we fixed our dwelling
after our sorrow,
our grandsons shall have our estate
The Lady Pao Sse brought earthquakes. TCHEOU falleth,
folly, folly, false fires no true alarm
Mount Ki-chan is broken.
Ki-chan is crumbled in the 10th moon of the 6th year of
Yeou Ouang
Sun darkened, the rivers were frozen....
and at this time was Tçin rising, a marquis on the
Tartar border
Empire down in the rise of princes
Tçin drave the tartar, lands of the emperor idle
Tcheou tombs fallen in ruin
from that year was no order
No man was under another
9 Tcheou wd/ not stand together

                    were not rods in a bundle
Sky dark, cloudless and starless
            at midnight a rain of stars
                    Wars,
                        wars without interest
boredom of an hundred years' wars.
            And in Siang, the princes impatient
killed a bad king for a good one, and thus Ouen Kong
came to their rule in Sung land
            and they said Siang had been killed when hunting
Ouen cherished the people.
            States of Lou were unhappy
Their Richards poisoned young princes.
            All bloods, murders, all treasons
Sons of the first wife of Ouen Kong.
Ling Kong loved to shoot from the hedges
        you'd see him behind a wall with his arrows
For fun of winging pedestrians
            this prince liked eating bears' paws.
By the Nine Urns of Yu, King Kong
made an alliance at hearing the sound of Tcheou music
This was the year of the two eclipses
        And Cheou-lang that held up the portcullis
            was named ' hillock ' because of a lump on his head
Man of Sung, and his line of Lou land   Chung 仲
            and his second son was Kung-fu-tseu
Taught and the not taught. Kung and Eleusis
            to catechumen alone.
            And when Kung was poor, a supervisor of victuals 尼
            Pien's report boosted him   Ni
            so that he was made supervisor of cattle
In that time were banquets as usual, Kung was inspector of
                                                        markets
And that year was a comet in Scorpio
            and by night they fought in the boats on Kiang river

And King Wang thought to vary the currency
μεταθεμένων τε τῶν χρωμένων
against council's opinion,
and to gain by this wangling.
Honour to Fen-yang who resisted injustice
And King Kong said ' That idea is good doctrine '
But I am too old to start using it.
Never were so many eclipses.
Then Kungfutseu was made minister and moved promptly
against C. T. Mao
and had him beheaded
that was false and crafty of heart
a tough tongue that flowed with deceit
A man who remembered evil and was complacent in doing it.
LOU rose. Tsi sent girls to destroy it
Kungfutseu retired
At Tching someone said:
there is man with Yao's forehead
Cao's neck and the shoulders of Tsé Tchin
A man tall as Yu, and he wanders about in front of the
East gate
like a dog that has lost his owner.
Wrong, said Confucius, in what he says of those Emperors
but as to the lost dog, quite correct.
He was seven days foodless in Tchin
the rest sick and Kung making music
' sang even more than was usual '
Honour to Yng P the bastard
Tchin and Tsai cut off Kung in the desert
.   and Tcheou troops alone got him out
Tsao fell after 25 generations
And Kung cut 3000 odes to 300
Comet from Yng star to Sin star, that is two degrees long
in the 40th year of King Ouang
Died Kung aged 73

Min Kong's line was six centuries lasting
                and there were 84 princes
Swine think of extending borders
Decent rulers of internal order
                        Fan-li sought the five lakes
Took presents but made no highways
Snow fell in mid summer
                Apricots were in December, Mountains defend no state
nor swift rivers neither, neither Tai-hia nor Hoang-ho
Usurpations, jealousies, taxes
Greed, murder, jealousies, taxes and douanes
338 died Hao tse Kong-sung-yang
Sou-tsin, armament racket, war propaganda.
                and Tchan-y was working for Tsin
                brain work POLLON IDEN
and Tchao Siang called himself 'Emperor of the Occident'
Sou Tsi thought it badinage
Yo-Y reduced corvées and taxes.
Thus of Kung or Confucius, and of 'Hillock' his father
when he was attacking a city
his men had passed under the drop gate
And the warders then dropped it, so Hillock caught
the whole weight on his shoulder, and held till his
last man had got out.
                Of such stock was Kungfutseu.

Chou

274

LIV

So that Tien-tan chose bulls, a thousand
and covered them with great leather masks, making
dragons
and bound poignards to their horns
and tied torches, pitch-smeared, to their tails
and loosed them by night from ten points
on the camp of Ki-kié the besieger
lighting the torches
So died Ki-kié and that town (Tsié-mé) was delivered.   *b.c. 279*
For three hundred years, four hundred, nothing quiet,
WALL rose in the time of TSIN CHI
TCHEOU lasted eight centuries and then TSIN came
and of TSIN was CHI HOANG TI that united all China
who referred to himself as the surplus
or needless bit of the Empire
and jacked up astronomy
and after 33 years burnt the books
because of fool litterati   *b.c. 213*
by counsel of Li-ssé
save medicine and on field works
and HAN was after 43 years of TSIN dynasty.

some fishin' some huntin' some things cannot be
changed
some cook, some do not cook
some things can not be changed.

And when TSE-YNG had submitted, Siao-ho ran to the palace
careless of treasure, and laid hold of the records,
registers of the realm for Lord Lieou-pang
that wd/ be first HAN
Now after the end of EULH and the death of his eunuch

were Lieou-pang, and Hiang-yu
      who had taste for commanding
but made no progress in letters,
    saying they serve only to transmit names to posterity
and he wished to carve up the empire
      bloody rhooshun, thought in ten thousands
his word was worth nothing, he would not learn fencing. And
                             against him
Lieou-pang stored food and munitions

b.c. 202 so that he came to be emperor, KAO,
      brought calm and abundance
No taxes for a whole year,
               ' no taxes till people can pay 'em '
' When the quarry is dead, weapons are useless.'
' It appears to me ' said this Emperor, ' that it is
because I saw what each man cd/ put through.'
And Lou-kia was envoy to Nan-hai, with nobility,
and wished that the *king* (the books Chu king and Chi king)
                    be restored
to whom KAO: I conquered the empire on horseback.
to whom Lou: Can you govern it in that manner?
whereon Lou-kia wrote ' The New Discourse ' (Sin-yu)
    in 12 chapters, and the books were restored.
And KAO went to Kung fu tseu's tomb out of policy
    videlicet to please the writers and scholars
A hot lord and unlettered, that knew to correct his own faults
    as indeed when he had first seen palace women, their
                        splendour
      yet listened to Fan-kouai
and had gone out of Hien-yang the palace, aroused.
And he told Siao-ho to edit the law code

Thereon the men in the vaudevilles
      sang of peace and of empire
        Au douce temps de pascor

276

And Tchang-tsong wrote of music, its principles
        Sun-tong made record of rites
And this was written all in red-character, countersigned by
                                        the assembly
sealed with the Imperial Seal
        and put in the hall of the forebears
as check on successors.
                HIAO HOEI TI succeeded his father.
Rain of blood fell in Y-yang
        pear trees fruited in winter
LIU-HEOU was empress, with devilments,
        till the grandees brought Hiao OUEN   b.c. 179
        Prince of Tai to the throne
that was son of KAO TI and a concubine
        (no tribute for the first year of his reign)
And the chief of the Southern Barbarians complained
that his silver import was intercepted
        circulation of specie impeded
        the tombs of his ancestors ruin'd
' 49 years have I governed Nan-yuei
        my grandsons are now fit to serve
I am old, nigh blind, can scarce hear the drum-beats
        I give up title of Emperor.'
And Kia-Y sent in a petition that they store grain against
                                        famine
and HIAO OUEN TI the emperor published:
        Earth is the nurse of all men
        I now cut off one half the taxes
I wish to follow the sages, to honour Chang Ti by my furrow
Let farm folk have tools for their labour it is
        for this I reduce the said taxes
Gold is inedible. Let no war find us unready.
        Thus Tchao-tso of his ministry (war)
' Gold will sustain no man's life nor will diamonds

277

keep the land under culture....
by wise circulation. Bread is the base of subsistence.'

They ended mutilation as punishment
were but 400 men in all jails
Died HIAO OUEN TI, ante Cristum one fifty seven.
After 23 years of reign, that pensioned the elders.

b.c. 146 Great rebels began making lead money
grasshoppers came against harvest
And Li-kouang bluffed the tartars (the Hiong-nou)
in face of a thousand, he and his scouts dismounted
and unsaddled their horses, so the Hiong nou
thought Li's army was with him.
Virtue is the daughter of heaven, YU followed CHUN
and CHUN, YAO having one root of conduct
HIAO KING had a just man's blood on his conscience.

Sin
jih
jih
sin,

HIA'S fortune was in good ministers
The highbrows are full of themselves
learnèd, gay and irrelevant
on such base nothing stands
HAN OU was for huntin', huntin' tigers, bears, leopards
They said: you outride all yr/ huntsmen
no one else has such good horses.
The prince of Hoai-nan took to light reading
Prince of Ho-kien preferred histories, *Chu King*
and the *Tcheou-li* and the *Li-ki* of Mencius (Mong-tsé)
and the *Chi-king* or Odes of Mao-chi and the *Tchun-tsiou*
with the comment of Tso-kieou-min.
and the Li-yo with treatise on music.

278

HAN TCHAO TI opened the granaries
HAN SIEUN (or SIUN) was fed up with highbrows
         Preferred men who knew people's habits
' Writers are full of their own importance '
And when the tartar king came to Tchang-ngan
         all the troops stood before him
the great in ceremonial uniform waited before that city
and the EMPEROR
         came out of the Palace with
         foreign and chinese princes,
Mandarins of the army and the book mandarins
         as an hedge from the palace
             and He took his way between them
         mid cheering and acclamation
             Ouan-soui!! Ouan-soui!!
         10,000 Ouan Soui!! may he live for
                         ten thousand years!
They cried this for the Emperor and joy was in every voice.
And the Tartar ran from his car to HAN SIEUN
         held out his hand in friendship
         and then remounted his war horse
         And they came into the city, and to the palace
                                 prepared
And next day two imperial princes went to the Prince Tartar
         the Tchen-yu and brought him to the audience hall
         where all princes sat in their orders
         and the Tchen-yu knelt to HAN SIEUN
and stayed three days there in festival
         whereafter he returned to his border and province.
         He was the Prince of Hiong-nou
And the kings of Si-yu, that are from Tchang-ngan to the
                                 Caspian
         came into the Empire
to the joy of HAN SIEUN TI
         (Pretty manoeuvre but the technicians

279

watched with their hair standing on end
                    anno sixteen, Bay of Naples)
From Ngan to the Caspian all was under HAN SIEUN

b.c. 49 The text of *books* reëstablished. And he died in the 25th of
                                        his reign
And Fong-chi led the bear back to its cage
        which tale is as follows:
Fong-chi and Fou-chi had titles but only as Queens of
                            HAN YUEN
and in the imperial garden a bear forced the bars of his cage
and of the court ladies only Fong faced him
        who seeing this went back quietly to his cage.
And now was seepage of bhuddists. HAN PING
simple at table, gave tael to the poor
Tseou-kou and Tchong took the high road
The Prince of Ou-yen killed off a thousand,
        set troops to tilling the fields.
KOUANG OU took his risks as a common soldier
HAN MING changed nothing of OU's
        gave no posts to princesses' relatives
and Yang Tchong sent in a placet that food prices had risen
since the start of the Tartar war, taxes had risen
Year of drought 77 and the Empress MA CHI answered:
Until now few Empresses' relatives
        have been enriched without making trouble
When Ouang Chi's five brothers were lifted
        thick fog came on this Empire
' History is a school book for princes.'
HAN HO TI heard men's good counsel

a.d. 107 And in the third moon of the first year of HAN NGAN
the Empress' brother named Teng-tchi refused the honour
                                of princedom

But gathered scholars and finally heard of Yang-tchin
whom he made governor

and Yang-tchin refused gold of the mandarin
                                      Ouang-mi
      earthquakes and eclipses.
And they turned out 300 mandarins
            that were creations of Léang-ki
And HUON gave most of the swag to the people   *a.d. 159*
      500 million tael
            war, taxes, oppression
            backsheesh, taoists, bhuddists
            wars, taxes, oppressions
And some grandees formed an academy
and the eunuchs disliked the academy
            but they never got rid of the eunuchs
Téou-Chi brought back the scholars
            and the books were incised in stone   *a.d. 175*
46 tablets set up at the door of the college
            inscribed in 5 sorts of character
HAN HUON was run by eunuchs
HAN LING was governed by eunuchs
            wars, murders and crime news
HAN sank and there were three kingdoms
            and booze in the bamboo grove
where they sang: emptiness is the beginning of all things.
Lieou-Tchin died in hall of the forebears—
            when his father wd/ not die fighting—
by suicide, slaying his children and consort.
Down! HAN is down. Under TçIN
Tou-yu proposed a bridge over Hoang-ho   *a.d. 274*
TçIN OU TI mourned for Sir Yang-Hou
            that had planned the union of empire,
and had named Tou-yu to succeed him
Ouang-siun wrote to his MAJESTY: Wind was against us
at San-chan, we cd/ not sail up the Kiang
nor was there sense in returning.
Not I but Sun-hao's own men sacked his palace.

And TçIN OU exempted the conquered in OU from taxes.
Was an army and navy dog fight. And after the fall of Sun-hao
his ballet distracted the EMPEROR
               were five thousand ballet girls
               after the first Quindecennio
And Lieou-Y answered the Emperor:
           ' Difference, milorr ', is that HUON and LING TI
extracted and kept it in public vaults
              whereas YR Majesty keeps it in yr/ own private
TçIN OU dismissed too many troops
             and was complimented on dragons
             (two found in the soldiers' well, green ones)
and the country was run by Yang Siun
while the emperor amused himself in his park
             had a light car made, harnessed to sheep
The sheep chose which picnic he went to,
ended his days as a gourmet. Said Tchang, tartar:
             Are not all of his protégés flatterers?
             How can his county keep peace?
And the prince Imperial went into the cabaret business
             and read Lao Tse.

a.d. 317   HOAI TI was deposed, MIN TI taken by tartars
made lackey to Lieou-Tsong of Han
TçIN TCHING cared for the people.
TçIN NGAN died of tonics and taoists
TçIN HIAO told a girl she was 30
             and she strangled him
a.d. 396   (piquée de ce badinage) he drunk at the time
Now was therefore SUNG rising.
             When Lieou-yu's mother was buried
His dad couldn't hire a nurse for this babby
             KAO-TSOU.
             last TçIN down in a Bhud mess
KAO TSEU preferred distribution
No pomps in palatio, Made peace with the tartars

Li-Chan wd/ not leave his mountain
          Et les Indiens disent que Boudha
in the form of a white buck elephant
          slid into Queen Nana's bosom, she virgin,
and after nine months ingestion
               emerged on the dexter side
The Prince of Ouei put out hochangs
put out the shamen and Taotssé
a.d. 444, putt 'em OUT
          in the time of OUEN TI
          ' Let artisans teach their sons crafts '
Found great store of arms in a temple
Then To-pa-tao went after the shave-heads, the hochang
And the censor finally printed his placet
          against extortionate judgements and greed of
          the High Judge Yupingtchi   *a.d. 448*
OUEN TI reduced him (Yupingtchi)
And there was peace between Sung land and Oueï land
and they ordered more war machines à la Valturio
          conscriptions, assassins, taoists
          taxes still in the hands of the princes
OU TI had 'em centralized
Yen Yen was frugal. Oueï prince went pussyfoot
And the rites of *Tien*, that is Heaven
were ploughing and the raising of silk worms
OU TI ploughed his festival furrow   *a.d. 460*
          his Empress did rite of the silk worms
Then OU went gay and SUNG ended.
Thus was it with Kao's son that was Siao, that was called
                                        as Emperor
OU TI
          collecter of vases
               (Topas were in Ouei country, they were Tartar)
bhuddists, hochangs, serendipity
' Man's face is a flag ' said Tan Tchin

' Thought is to body as is its edge to a sword '
' Wheat is by sweat of the people '
So OU TI of LEANG had a renaissance
         Snow lay in Ping Tching till June
Emp'r'r huntin' and the Crown Prince full of saki
And Topa Hong came south under the rain
' No lack of students, few wise.
        Perhaps this is due to the colleges.'
And Topa, who was Lord of the Earth called himself Yuen
        and there was a hand-out to the aged
halls were re-set to Kung-fu-tseu
yet again, allus droppin' 'em and restorin' 'em
after intervals. And there was war on the Emperor OU TI
Hochang consider their own welfare only.
And the 46 tablets that stood still there in Yo Lang
were broken and built into Foé's temple (Foé's, that is
                    goddam bhuddists.)
this was under Hou-chi the she empress.
OU TI went into cloister
        Empire rotted by hochang, the shave-heads, and
Another boosy king died. Snow alone kept out the tartars
And men turned their thought toward Ouen Ti
        Yang-kien of Soui set men to revise his law code
Sou-ouei advised him, grain went into his granaries
HEOU raised the Three Towers
        sat late and wrote verses
His mandate was ended.

        Came the XIIth dynasty: SOUI
YANG-KIEN, rough, able, wrathy
        flogged a few every day
            and sacrificed on Mt Taï Chan
Built Gin Cheou the palace
        pardoned those who stood up to him.
Touli-Kahn, tartar, was given a princess
        now was contempt of scholars

OUEN kept up mulberry trees
                    and failed with his family
YANG (kouang) TI ordered more buildings
                    jobs for two millyum men
                    and filled his zoological gardens
1600 leagues of canals 40 ft wide for the
                    honour of YANG TI of SOUI
the stream Kou-choui was linked to Hoang Ho the river
                    great works by oppression
                    by splendid oppression
the Wall was from Yu-lin to Tsé-ho
                    and a million men worked on that wall.
Pei-kiu was tactful with traders,
                    knowing that YANG liked news from afar,
with what he learned of the Si-yu he mapped 48 kingdoms.
KONG sank in abuleia. TANG rising.
And the first TANG was KAO TSEU, the starter.   *a.d. 618*
And that year died Li-Chi that had come to his rescue
with a troop of 10,000. The war drums beat at her funeral
And her husband drove back the tartars, Tou-kou-hoen.
Fou stood against foé, damn bhuddists
When TAÏ TSONG came to be emperor he turned out 3000
                                        fancies
Built thus for two hundred years TANG
And there were ten thousand students.
          Fou-Y saying they use muzzy language
the more to mislead folk.
          Kung is to China as is water to fishes.
War, letters, to each a time.
          Provinces by mountain and rivers divided.
          ' A true prince wants his news straight '
TAÏ TSONG was no friend to taozers hochangs and foés.
Was observer of seasons, saying:
          Take not men from the plough
Let judges fast for three days before passing capital sentence
                    285

Oueï-Tching rock-like in council
                    made the Emperor put on his best clothes
Said: in war time we want men of ability
            in peace we want also character
300 were unjailed to do their spring ploughing
            and they all came back in October
' I grew with the people ' said TAÏ TSONG
            ' my son in the palace '
Died KAO TSEU the emperor's father
            635 anno domini
Died the Empress Tchang-sun CHI
            leaving ' Notes for Princesses '
And TAÏ in his law code cut 92 reasons for death sentence
            and 71 for exile
            as they had been under SOUI
And there were halls to Confucius and Tchéou-Kong
Ma-tchéou spoke against corvées
            that had been under SOUI
Grain price was high when TAÏ entered
            a small measure cost one bolt of silk, entire.
If a prince piles up treasure
            he shares only his surplus
Lock not up the people's subsistence. Said TAÏ TSONG:
            let a prince be cited for actions.
A measure of rice now cost three or four denars,
            that wd/ feed one man for one day.
Oueï-tching spoke his mind to the Emperor. Died a.d. 643.
            And there were plots in palatio.
TAÏ TSONG had a letch for Corea
And an embassy came from north of the Caspian
            from Koulihan of short nights
where there is always light over horizon
            and from the red-heads of Kieï-kou
Blue-eyed and their head man was Atchen or Atkins Chélisa

And the Emperor TAÏ TSONG left his son 'Notes on
                                        Conduct'
whereof the 3rd treats of selecting men for a cabinet
whereof the 5th says that they shd/ tell him his faults
the 7th: maintain abundance
The 10th a charter of labour
and the last on keepin' up kulchur
            Saying ' I have spent money on palaces
                too much on 'osses, dogs, falcons
but I have united the Hempire (and you 'aven't)
Nothing harder than to conquer a country
            and damn'd easy to lose one, in fact there
ain't anything heasier.
            Died TAÏ TSONG in the 23rd of his reign.
And left not more than fifty men in all jails of the empire
none of 'em complaining of judgement.
            And the tartars wanted to die at his funeral
            and wd/ have, if TAÏ hadn't foreseen it
                and writ expressly that they should not.
Then the Empress Ou-heou ran the country
                toward ruin
but TAÏ TSONG'S contraption still worked—   *a.d. 662*
        local administrations in order
Tching-gintai drove after tartars,
                        his men perished in snow storms
            and the hochang ran the old empress
the old bitch ruled by prescription and hochangs
who told her she was the daughter of Buddha
            Tartars remembering TAÏ TSONG
held up the state of TAÏ TSONG
            young TCHONG was run by his wife.
Honour to HIEUN ' to hell with embroideries,   *a.d.*
to hell with the pearl merchants '   *713-756*
HIEUN measured shadows at solstice
            polar star at 34.4

Measured it in different parts of the empire
  at Lang-tchéou was 29 and a half
  Tsiun-Y 34° and 8 lines
For five years no taxes in Lou-tchéou
  census 41 million, 726 anno domini
And HIEUN TSONG decreed Kung posthumous honours
That he shd/ be henceforth called prince not mere ' maistre '
             in all rites
and we were sad that the north cities, Chépoutching
   and Ngan-yong were in hands of the tartars
             (Tou-san)
And there came a taozer babbling of the elixir
   that wd/ make men live without end
and the taozer died very soon after that.
And plotters cried out against the Queen Koué-fei
a.d. 756   ' a rebel's daughter ' and killed her.
Tchang-siun fighting for SOU TSONG had need of arrows
and made then 1200 straw men which he set in dark
   under wall at Yong-kieu
and the tartars shot these full of arrows. And next night
Colonel Tchang set out real men, and the tartars withheld
           their arrows
   till Tchang's men were upon them.
To SOU TSONG they sent rhinoceri and elephants dancing
   and bowing, but when Li-yen
sent TÉ TSONG a memorial on the nuances of clouds our lord
TÉ TSONG replied that plentiful harvests were prognastics
           more to
his taste than strange animals
or even new botanical specimens and other natural what-nots
   Cock fighting wastes palace time
So they set up another tribunal
   to watch mandarins
   and no new temples to idols
700,000 men in the army

inkum 30 million tael silver
and in grain 20 million measures of 100 lbs each.
                Nestorians entered, General Kouo-tsé-y
is named in their monument.
                Such bravery and such honesty, 30 years without rest.
And more goddam Tartars bust loose again
                better war than peace with these tartars
Taxes rising, Li-ching had a liaison
And TÉ-TSONG rode apart from his huntsmen in the hunting
                                                by Sintien
and went into a peasant's house incognito
And said:
we had good crops for two years or three years
and no war.
And the peasant said: bé, if we have had
good crops for two years or three years
you've got no taxes to pay to the Emperor
                we used to pay twice a year and no extras
and now they do nothing but think up new novelties
        We pay the usual tithe, and if there's a full crop
They come round to squeeze more of it out of us
                and beat down our prices, and then
sell it back again to us
or else we have to get pack animals
or wear out our own, so that I can't keep a *tael* quiet.
Does this mean contentment? '
        Whereon TÉ TSONG did nothing
save exempt that one peasant from corvée.
                and then laid a tea tax
Empresses, rebels, tartars
                six months without rain.
Died TÉ-TSONG; the deceived.   *a.d. 805*

289

LV

Orbem bellis, urbem gabellis
> implevit
>> And the troops not even paid
>> And TCHUN the new Lord was dying
> but awoke to name Li-Chun his heir

And at this time died Ouei-Kao the just taxer

that set up pensions for widows
>> His temple stands to this day
>> that his soldiers built for him.
>> Honour to TCHUN-TSONG the sick man.

'Cut it! you bastard' said Lin-Yun
>> 'Do you take my neck for a whetstone?'

And the rebel Lieou Pi was delighted.

And the censors said Liki has hogged ten provinces' treasure

If these go to the national treasury
>> they will go out of circulation

the people thereby deprived,
>> so HIEN-TSONG threw this into commerce

仁者以財發身不

仁者以身發財

And yet he was had by the eunuchs,
　　　　the army 800 thousand
　　　　not tilling the earth
And half of the Empire tao-tse hochangs and merchants
so that with so many hochangs and mere shifters
　　　　three tenths of the folk fed the whole empire, yet
HIEN reduced the superfluous mandarins
　　　　and remitted taxes in Hoai
Li Kiang and Tien Hing were his ministers
　　　　remembering TCHING-OUANG, KANG,
　　　　　　　　HAN-OUEN and HAN KING TI
'Men are the basis of empire', said our lord HIEN-TSONG
　　　　yet he died of the elixir,
fooled by the eunuchs, and more Tou-san (tartars)　　　　*a.d.* 820
　　　　　　　　　　　　　　were raiding
MOU-TSONG drove out the taozers
　　　　but refused to wear mourning for HIEN his father.
The hen sang in MOU'S time, racin', jazz dancin'
and play-actors, Tartars still raidin'
MOU'S first son was strangled by eunuchs,
Came OUEN-TSONG and kicked out 3000 fancies
　　　　let loose the falcons
yet he also was had by the eunuchs after 15 years reign
OU-TSONG destroyed hochang pagodas,
　　　　spent his time drillin' and huntin'
Brass idols turned into ha'pence
　　　　chased out the bonzes from temples
　　　　46 thousand temples
chased out the eunuchs
　　　　and Tsaï-gin whom he had wished to make empress
　　　　　　　　hanged herself after his death
saying: I follow to the nine fountains'
So SIUEN decreed she shd/ be honoured as First Queen
　　　　　　　　　　of OU-TSONG

Ruled SIUEN with his mind on the 'Gold Mirror' of

a.d. 846   TAI TSONG
    Wherein is written: In time of disturbance
    make use of all men, even scoundrels.
    In time of peace reject no man who is wise.
HIEN said: no rest for an emperor. A little spark
    lights a great deal of straw.
SIUEN'S income was 18 million strings of a thousand
    on salt and wine only
not counting grain, silk etc.
        (calculated at french louis d'or 1770
            say about 90 millyun pund sterling)
A man who remembered faces
        and had by the taozers
tho' he stood for just price and sound paper
    13 years on the throne.

Y TSONG his son brought a jazz age HI-TSONG

a.d. 860   cock fights poverty archery
        Squabbles of governors, eunuchs
            Sun Te put out the Eunuchs
                and got himself murdered
Then came little dynasties, came by murder, by treason, with
the Prince of TçIN rising.
Li-ké-Yong is not dead' said Tchu
        ' for his son prolongs him '
whereas my sons are mere pigs and dogs.
HIU cut down taxes and douanes
            was hell on extorters
10 years chançons de gestes
        Khitans rising, Yeliou Apaoki and Chuliu, some gal,
HIU, gallant, pugnacious. So they said
        In the city of Tching-tcheou are women like clouds
                                            of heaven,
Silk, gold, piled mountain high.

292

Take it before Prince Tçin gets there.
Thus Ouang Yeou to the Khitan of Apaoki
     whose son was lost in the mulberry forest
Thus came TçIN into Empire
     calling themselves later TANG   *a.d. 923*
hunters and jongleurs. Comedians were the king's eyes
but unstable.
Took Chou land in 70 days without disorder
A Prince this was, but no Emperor, paladin, useless to rule.
Tartar Yuen ruled as protector
cut down taxes, analphabetic.
And yet he set all the hawks loose,
     said huntin' is hell on the crops
This Li-ssé Yuen, called MING TSONG, had eight years of
                                   good reign
Li Tsongkou ruled his troops by affection
     was Prince of Lou at this time   *a.d. 934*
that is Kungfutseu's country.
     The dowager empress chose him
          a great captain under MING TSONG
and they needed troops for defence against tartars
     in Chéking-Tang's department
Called Apaoki son of Chuliu to assist them
And Chéking Tang founded a dynasty
                coming up from the ranks
Dry spring, a dry summer
locusts and rain in autumn
     and beyond that, lack of specie
tax collectors inhuman.
     Chuliu a great Queen of the Tartar
Te Kouang put the emperor in a temple
     and supplied him with comforts
tartars put on chinese clothes
     Ouan soui!! ten thousand   *a.d. 947*
     evviva, evviva Lieou-Tchi-Yuen.

Turk of the horde of Chato, set his city at Caïfon fou
And the tartars called their dead emperor ' salted '
And it wd/ be now 13 years until SUNG.
Teoui-tchéou said: Lou land has produced only writers.
Said TAÏ-TSOU: KUNG is the master of emperors.
and they brought out Ou-tchao's edition, 953,
And TAÏ ordered himself a brick tomb with no flummery
no stone men sheep or tigers
CHI-TSONG in the thick by Tçé-tchéou, against Han
and tartars
sent reserve troops to the left wing
while he held firm on the right,
saying: now, that they think they have beaten us!
And CHI cleared out the temples and hochang
cleared out 30 thousand temples
and that left 26 hundred
with 60 thousand *bonzes* and *bonzesses.*
Chou coin was of iron
And CHI'S men drove the Tang boats from the
Hoaï-ho
all north of the great Kiang was to CHI-TSONG.
who lent grain to Hoaï-nan devast.
Died Ouang-po the advisor.
SUNG was for 300 years.
Light was in his birth room and fragrance
as if it were almond boughs
Red the robe of his dynasty
pourvou que ça doure, said his mother
He said: let brothers inherit
you are not here by virtush/
the last HAN was a minor
eunuchs, hochangs and taxers
princes get too much power
TCHAO KOUANG reviewed all capital sentences
took tax power from governors

and centered the army command
South Han was rotted with douanes
         was rotted with tortures
Tsiuenpiu in snow had all Chou
         and was sixty six days only in taking it. And the
                                                       emperor
Sent his own coonskin coat to this general
         who promptly went gay,
Five stars shone in Koué, five planets
TAI TSONG brought out the true BOOKS   *a.d. 978*
and there arose in the province of Ssétchuen a revolt
because of the greed of the mandarins.
         Not content with their salaries
         began to bleed merchants for licences
which new damn tax made money so scarce in that province
that men cdn't buy the necessities.   *a.d. 993*
         Therefore Ouang Siaopo of the people
demanded just distribution
         and they went against Tsing-chin city, and took
                                                       Pongchan
by violence and cut open the governor's belly
which they filled up with silver
         (bit of what he had extorted)
and TAI TSONG reigned 22 years
         caring for field work. Meanwhile Jelly Hugo
the tartar, a Khitan, freed his people of taxes
         and started old age relief. Ghengis rising
And Tchin-Song declined a present of sables (marte zibbeline)
saying it was just as cold for the soldiers.
and in ten four men cried once again Ouan Soui
may he live for 10 thousand years
         TCHIN-TSONG
ouan soui, may he live for ten thousand years
         who said: don't worry about coming ages
         the people need time to breathe.

And he made terms with the tartars, paid 'em in
      silk and in silver
to keep 'em quiet as far as the wall.
And the King of Khitan set court at Tchongking
our lord TCHIN going mumbo
      and they buried him with the tracts about heaven

      which had wrought his dishonour

and GIN TSONG cleaned out the *tao*zers
      and the tartars began using books
Han, Khitan, tartar wars, boredom of.
Money and all that, stabilization, probably racket
      1069
And now Fou-Pié to whom we owed the peace of 1042 with
                the tartars
returned and was kept and made minister
      and CHIN-TSONG lived soberly
with no splurge of table or costumes
      and at this time began Ngan
(or more fully Ouang-Ngan-ché) to demand that they reset
             the market tribunals,
posting every day what was on sale and what the right price
                  of it
      as had been under TCHEOU emperors
and that a market tax shd/ go to the emperor from this
      thereby relieving the poor of all douanes
giving them easy market for merchandise
      and enlivening commerce
by making to circulate the whole realm's abundance.
      and said he knew how hard it wd/ be to find
                personnel
to look after this, as when YAO had appointed Koen
      who could not, and then YU who had drawn off the
      flood water
And these changes annoyed, greatly, the bureaucrats

              whom he sent to *confino*
that is the most stubborn
                and got younger men to replace 'em.
And Liu-hoei said Ngan was a twister
                but the Emperor sent back Hoei's protest
So Hoei begged to retire, and
                was sent out to Tengtcheou as governor.
And Ngan saw land lying barren
                because peasants had nowt to sow there
whence said: Lend 'em grain in the spring time
                that they can pay back in autumn
with a bit of an increase, this wd/ augment the reserve,
This will need a tribunal
and the same tribunal shd/ seek
                            equity
for all lands and all merchandise
                according to harvest and soil
so that the emperor's tithes shd/ be proportionate
                to the rarity or the abundance of merchandise
to make commerce more easy, that the folk be not
                                            overburdened
nor yet the imperial revenue be made less.
and Ngan made yet a third point
that was to fix the value of money
                and to coin *enough* denars
that shd/ stay always on the same footing.
and Fan-chungin protested
                            but
Heoi-king argued for Ngan:
                no man is forced to borrow this grain in spring time
if peasants find it no advantage
                they will not come borrow it.
and Ssé-ma; said, all right in theory
                but the execution will be full of abuse
they'll take it, but not bring it back

TSONG of TANG put up granaries
somewhat like those you want to establish
a measure of ten or twelve pounds cost no more than ten pence
and when the price was put up
they went on buying
and the whole province was ruined
CHIN stayed pro-Ngan; and it was suggested that
drought was due to Ngan's reforms,
whereto Ngan said droughts had happened before.
and at the 12th moon of the 17th year of this Emperor
Ssé-ma Kouang, Fan Tsuyu and Lieou Ju offered the
HISTORY, called

a.d. 1084 *Tsé-tchi tong kien hang mou*
on the model of *Tso kieou ming*
and this began with the 23rd year of
OUEÏ-LIE of TCHEOU dynasty
and was in 294 books.
Honour to CHIN-TSONG the modest
Lux enim per se omnem in partem
Reason from heaven, said Tcheou Tun-y
enlighteneth all things
seipsum seipsum diffundit, risplende
Is the beginning of all things, et effectu,
Said Ngan: YAO, CHUN were thus in government
Died now the master of Nenuphar
Mandarins oppressing peasants to get back their grain loans,
and his dictionary is, they say, coloured with hochang
interpretations and Taozer, that is Ngan's.
and merchants in Caïfong put up their shutters in mourning
for Ssé-kouang
anti-tao, anti-bhud, anti-Ngan
whose rules had worked 20 years
till Ssé-kouang reversed 'em
Students went bhud rather than take Kung via Ngan,
Flood relief, due to Ngan?

298

joker somewhere?
came Tsaï King pro-Ngan, probably crooked
and they put Ngan's plaque in a temple
            HOEÏ went *taozer*, an' I suppose
Tsaï ran to state usury. The tartar lord
            wanted an alphabet
by name Akouta, ordered a written tongue for Kin tartars

And a fox walked into the Imperial palace
            and took his seat on the throne
a mad man ran shrieking: change, tartars more tartars
tartars pass over Hoang-ho
And they used paper notes when coin was too heavy for
                                                    transport
and redeemed those notes at one third/
And there were ever all sorts of disturbers
For there were the tartars, Khitan, that had
            taken the old Turk's country,
            and these tartars are called also Leao
And there are Kin tartars, that were under Akouta
            and these are called also Nutché, from north of Corea,
and there were the hordes of Ghengiz (TAI-TSOU, Témougin)
            of whom was CHI-TSOU or Koublai
Hoang ho, Hoang ho, tartars pass over Hoang ho.
SUNG died of taxes and gimcracks
Mongrels in fish-skin (shagreen, or shark's skin)
till 1157 the Kin used coin made in China
and Oulo stopped swapping silk for the toys of Hia,   *a.d. 1172*
said: men cannot eat jewels
Oulo of Kin, greatest of Kin, under him were books set
                                                    into Nutché
            in his reign were only 18 beheaded
but his brat was run by his missus
            and they had an ideological war
' mediocrity's childhood lasts into middle age '

they brought out a text book on music
GHINGIZ (Tchinkis) hearing of alphabets
    hearing of *mores*
and saw a green unicorn speaking
    fumée maligne in the underground 1219
said Yéliu Tchutsaï: tax; don't exterminate
    you will make more if you tax 'em.
this was a new idea to the mongols
who wanted to turn all land into grazing
    and saw no use for human inhabitants
these mongrels bein' 'orsemen
Ten percent tax on wine, three and 1/3rd on necessities
    mohammeds say different
make more anyhow if you tax 'em
    SUNG falling, Antzar went against Kin
    by Tang and Teng, let 'em pass.

LVI

Billets, biglietti, as coin was too heavy for transport,
        but redeemed the stuff at one third
    And Ou-Kiai had another swat at the tartars
        and licked 'em
And Yu-Tchong, governor of Kingtcheou in the Chensi
        said: my spies have told me etc/
        easy to start a war,
                not easy to finish one.
SUNG died of levying taxes
        gimcracks, SUNG died under HOEI the slider,
And there was a man named Tchinkis in Tartary
        hearing of alphabets, morals, mores
and a man named Yeliu-Tchutsai.
Yeliu apaoki Ouanyen akouta,
        of Kin, of Khitan, and Genghis of Yuen,
        hearing of alphabets
and Yeliu Tchutsai said to Ogotai:
                tax, don't exterminate
You'll make more by taxing the blighters
        thus saved several millyum lives of those chinamen
Bojars thought land was for grazing.
            ten percent tax on hooch, 3⅓rd on necessities
And they tried to stop the Tartars on Hoang Ho
        day falls like a fluttering flag
East princes went by the valley of box wood
        to cover Mt Kuai with a palace . . .
' There is ', said the Taozers,
' A medicine that gives immortality.'
        and ships sent (li Sao) to Japan.
Mt Tai Haku is 300 miles from heaven
        lost in a forest of stars,
Slept on the pine needle carpet

sprinkled horse blood
praying no brave man be born among Mongols
                Ouen yan Tchin hochang of Kin.

YAO, CHUN, YU controller of waters
Bridge builders, contrivers of roads
                gave grain to the people
                    kept down the taxes
Hochang, eunuchs, taoists and ballets
night-clubs, gimcracks, debauchery
                Down, down! Han is down
                Sung is down
Hochang, eunuchs, and taozers
empresses' relatives, came then a founder
saying nothing superfluous
cleared out the taozers and grafters, gave grain
                opened the mountains
Came taozers, hochang and debauchery
And litterati fought fiercer than other men to keep out the
                                                    mogul
drifting dung-dust from the North.
Hochang southward like rabbits
                half a million in one province only
mus ingens, ingens, noli meum granum comedere
                No slouch ever founded a dynasty
Died Kin Lusiang, historian and Confucian
                all mulberries frozen in Pa Yang
Where were two million trees and beyond that
Litterati fought fiercer than other men
Hail breaking the trees and walls
                    in I-Tching-tcheou
Crops gone.
Against Ogotai's catapults Nik-ia-su used powder
May the white birds remember this warrior, good at logistics
Ozin (Wodin) Youriak had 'em set out mulberry trees

Ghenso was for no taxes, grew up as a labourer
A hundred *chi* of rice for ten denars
   that is an 1/2 ounce of silver
ZinKwa observed that gold is inedible
Stored grain against famine
   observed that jade is inedible
And they used invisible writing
   in Ten Bou's time came a white phoenix
and in this time was Yeliu Tchutsai
   Meng Kong still held against Mogols.
   Han, Lang, Ouen, Kong,
   Mie, Kien, Tchong, King
   Fou, Pong, Chun King
         gone
Vendome, Beaugency, Notre Dame de Clery,
and they took law against Yeliu, but his leaving
was 13 flutes, his lute and his library
   to refute charge of embezzlement
And after him died Meng Kong.
   Kujak was crowned
And the first day they put on their white clothes
   and the second day red robes
and the third day were all lords in violet,
scarlet the fourth day, and Kujak went against Hungary
made war on Poland, on Prussia
   and Mengko took off taxes
And in Caï Fong they made a grain dividend
   and gave instruction in farming
     ploughs, money, ammassi

YAO, SHUN, YU, Kung
TCHIN OUANG, OUEN, Ghengiz Khan
And Mengko went into Bagdad, went into Kukano
   and died by the wall at Ho-tcheou
Ogotai reigned for nine years

Kublai ascended Mt Hianglou
              the Kiang full of war junks
              that SUNG thought security
LI TSONG believed his news service
                              wrongly
Kublai before him
        and about him damned rascals, courtezans, palace
                                                women
Cliques, easy wars without justice.
And Kublai said: Sung laws very beautiful
                    unlike their conduct
Kiassé harmed SUNG more than Mongols
North is the cradle of mongols
              Pasepa gave them their alphabet
              1000 words mongol, and 41 letters
SUNG sank by Yai island. The line of Ghengiz called YUEN

this dynasty mo'gol
              Hoang-ho's fount in a sea of stars.
Ouang tchi slew Ahama. Ouen Tiensiang was faithful.
War scares interrupt commerce. Money was now made of brass
and profit on arms went to the government
wine taxed high, settlers licensed.
Lou-chi brought back the grafters (Ahama's)
              and boosted the tea tax
Tchin-kin disgusted by the size of the tax receipts
              and L Sieuen staved off a war with Japan
              staved off a war on Annam
said: Taxes are not abundance
              Yeliu resumed the imperial college, gathering scholars
KUBLAI was a buggar for taxes
              Sangko stinking with graft
Ouantse made a law code
              eliminated 250 tribunals, that mostly did nowt but tax

KUBLAI died heavy with years
              his luck was good ministers, save for the treasury.

' As hunger alone drove them to brigandage
            they wd/ continue bandits till fed '
                This known in the time of TIMOUR
The last SUNG fled in what was left of a navy
            went down in sea waves, came mongols
of Ghengiz
            rose KUBLAI
HIA, CHANG, TCHEOU
            were great lines till Kungfutseu
Then were HAN   *b.c. 202*
        TÇIN   *a.d. 265*
            TANG   *a.d. 618*
                SUNG   *a.d. 950*
Then these mongols or YUEN
            Ghengiz, Ogotai, KUBLAI KHAN
                that came into Empire
From the Isle of Yai, no more SUNG counting
and mogols stood over all China
89 years more till MING came, 1368
that is from Ghengiz an hundred and 60 (Cambuskin)
And in south province Tchin Tiaouen had risen
and took the city of Tchang tcheou
offered marriage to Ouang Chi,
who said: It is an honour.
I must first bury Kanouen. His body is heavy.
His ashes were light to carry
Bright was the flame for Kanouen
            Ouang Chi cast herself into it, Faithful forever
                High the hall TIMOUR made her.

And in the 8th moon the public works and corvée department
presented GIN TSONG a volume on mulberry culture
by Miao Haokien where he explains in detail the
            growing of silk worms
            and of unwinding cocoons

305

and the Emperor had this engraved with all diagrams
                  and distributed throughout all China
nor had any emperor more care to find men of merit—
doing what KUBLAI had intended—

a.d.
1312/20   than had Aïulipata called GIN TSONG
          (Algiaptou khan) honouring Kung with the rites.
And his son died of assassins
                  died of the gang of Tiemoutier, lamas, foés,
shit and religion always stinking in concord
Came Jason against these assassins
came CHUNTI last of the mogul.
Two million families went down in famine
                  blood rained on the high land
                  green hair came down like rain
Hanjong levelled the temples
                  his folk burst into joy
                  to put land back under tillage
CHUNTI came to the college, as had not in 12 years of reign
gave a silver seal to Kung's epigon
                  but gangsters continued
a pirate declined to turn mandarin,
                  a comet exploded in Pleiades
Hoang-ho shifted its bed
                  and they said that the Milé Buddha
had come down to turn out the mogul,
                  pseudo-Sung put on red hats
Tienouan beat the rebels, Taipou was killed by rebels
                  Singki respected
and the lamas put on a ballet for CHUNTI
                  in ivory headgear
castagnettes crinkling and clacking, and a Tang dance
                  without fancy clothes
Kongpei said to Toto: Don't open dispatches.
                  Dragon barge drifted with music
Statue poured water amidship

Spirits struck the night watches
        they say CHUNTI invented this clockwork
The Red Caps called their candidate Ming Ouan
                as if emperor
Left monkhood and put manhood on
        to end the line of Ghengiz khan
Yuentchang ceased being hochang
        took Ito Yen without pillage
and passed over Kiang river
        conquered the Taiping province
Comet in Tchang star, over Tai Ming shone the meteor
                                  broom-shaped
Ming coming out of South Country, In 35 years' dissolution
        CHUNTI ceased from the throne.
Died Yukiou of more than ten wounds
Now in Chang-tou was ruin
        the high house of KUBLAI cast down
Came Ming slowly, a thousand, an hundred thousand
the pirate Kouetchin came to him
        At court, eunuchs and grafters
        among mongols no man trusted other
The empress' folk in Corea killed off king Peyen
Of MING were now 200,000
        that fought three days in the boat fight
there by lake Peyan
        to Hoang Ho the river
Yeougin and the Tching brothers
        till Leou Lean was arrowed.
And they left Tchin-li his father's treasure
        but took his grain for the people.
Came MING thus to KianKing, say 1368
For crime after TIMOUR the mandate
        left YUEN mongols
        No slouch ever founded a dynasty
From Ghengiz were 8 score years until MING time

Said now YUENTCHANG
          suis fils d'un pauvre laboureur
In a village of Ssetcheou in the province of Kiangnan
at seventeen was made shaveling
          then enrolled under Tsehing the captain
This is called Destiny
          Schicksal to bring peace to the Empire
Li, Su, Tong and I
          were four musketeers
We were workmen in the same village
          we were plain sojers together
If we can take Chantong province, we can take Pekin
          (and did so, 1368)
He said to Su Ta: Do as you deem
          CHANG, CHOU, and HAN rose by talents
Once we four were lucky to have even canvas coats
Mongols are fallen
          from losing the law of Chung Ni
                    (Confucius)
HAN came from the people
How many fathers and husbands are fallen
Make census
Give rice to their families
Give them money for rites
Let rich folk keep their goods by them
Let the poor be provided
I came not against YUEN
          but against grafters and rebels
I rebelled not against KUBLAI, not against Ghengizkhan
          but against lice that ate their descendants.
TAI TSONG
KAO TSEU
TAI TSOU
and now HONG VOU three hundred, three hundred

each had 300 years by the mandate
             five cycles of 60 years
Mongols were an interval

YAO

SHUN

HAN

TCHEU

' Once again war is over. Go talk to the savants.'
He gave fur coats to the troops in Ninghia
Showed no zenophobia. Moguls wd/ not have chinese in office.
In Pekin he paid the soldiers
To peasants he gave allotments
            gave tools and yoke oxen
No eunuchs to serve save as domestics
' Don't believe all you are told by officials
' I suggest ', said HONG VOU, ' that you get a faculty
      a good faculty before increasing the number of students.'

He declined arab cosmetics
   Capn Yé-ouang built an ice wall
to keep off the Yuen
   which they took for a real wall.
' Coreans are gentle by nature '.
     and that year the Emperor died.
Five planets were in conjunction.
In '84 died General Li-ouen, in '85 Su Ta
in 1386 peace
HONG VOU declined a treatise on Immortality
   offered by Taozers, Et
En l'an trentunième de son Empire
   l'an soixante de son eage
HONG VOU voyant ses forces affoiblir
   dict: Que la vertu t'inspire, Tchu-ouen.
Vous, mandarins fidèles, lettrés, gens d'armes
   Aidez mon petit-fils à soutenir
La dignité de cest pouvoir
   le poids de son office
Et comme au Prince OUEN TI
   jadis des HAN
Faictes moi mes funérailles.

LVII

AND when KIEN OUEN was throned
his uncle set to unthrone him, saying:
As Tcheou-kong looked after Tching-ouang his
nephew...
protect him from the guiles of his ministers.
And when the palace cd/ no more hold out
they remembered a box left by HONG VOU
wherein was written:
Go out by the gate of Kouémen
Under night dark, follow the aqueduct till you come to the
temple of Chin Lo-koan
And in the red chest was habit of hochang
and diploma of hochang
Nine men went with KIEN OUEN TI   *a.d. 1403*
and at Kouémen gate, messire Ouangchin, the taoist
beat with his head on the ground, crying Ouan Soui
may you live for 10,000 years
HONG VOU came to me in a vision
saying go to the gate at Kouémen
and that I row you to Chin-lo-koan.
Were nine mandarins, were Yang-long and Yé Hihien
that went thus with KIEN TI, took monkhood,
and he was wandering for 35 years until YNG-TSONG
from one hiding place to another.
YONG LO did 20 years heavy police work
To whom came an envoi from Bengal   *a.d. 1409*
And Malacca came into our Empire,   *a.d. 1415*
And YANG LO commanded a ' *summa* '
that is that the gist of the books be corrected.
And Mahamou sent in tribute of horses.
            GIN TSONG was ten months on the throne
Under tartars had all gone feudal. And in 1430 was peace

Came YNG-TSONG a child of eight years,
eunuchs as wet-rot in the palace
            HONG VOU restored Imperial order
yet now came again eunuchs, taozers and hochang
            Armourers worked day and night
YUKIEN burnt the forage round Pekin
            against tartar horses
this was in days of KING TI
            Fan-kuang took burning arrows
and lances of the sort that one throws
Yésien, Péyen, Tiémour came up under the walls at Pekin
Che-heng and Yukien were defenders
            ' no longer amused by their promises '
In '52 was Emperor's grain ration
            for famine in Honan, for famine in Shantung
a million six hundred thousand measures of grain
And for war they made 15 foot carrochs
            with a case slung below for provisions
                        (vide Valturio)
and a cannon to forrard, a turret bordered with lances
we had a thousand such carrochs
counting they wd/ fill a field of four *li*
and these were never brought into action

a.d. 1459 Died Yukien the restorer, that had so vile a reward
            by his own hand, in prison.
Ché-heng turned to magicians
            a man full of himself.
Now were the new maps published. There was a rebellion
                        of eunuchs
HIEN TSONG the idolater did posthumous honour to Yukien
decreed Kungfutseu was an Emperor
            to be so held in all rites,
            Drove out the taozers and hochang
yet for one eunuch, Hoai-ngan, one might forgive many
                        eunuchs

Tho' they tried a star chamber
            and held it all of four years
till HIEN TSONG removed them.
another Lord seeking elixir
seeking the transmutation of metals
seeking a word to make change

HOAI of SUNG was nearly ruined by taozers
HIEN of TANG died seeking elixir
and in '97 they made a law code
            a bear walked into Pekin unnoticed
though they strafed the watch for allowing it
and there were 53 million folk in the Empire
at tribute average of five measures
            of, say, 100 lbs each
' OU TI of LÉANG, HOEÏ-TSONG of SUNG
were more than all other Emperors
            Laoist and foéist, and came both to an evil end.
To hell with the pyramid
            YAO and SHUN lived without any such monument
TCHEOU KONG and Kungfutseu certainly wd/ not have
                                    ordered one
nor will it lengthen YR MAJESTY'S days
            It will shorten the lives of YR subjects
they will, many of 'em, die under new taxes.'
Died HIAO TSONG aged 36, after peace and his 18 years   *a.d. 1505*
      on the throne
And 8 bloody eunuchs conspired with Lieu,

thunderbolt fell, naturally, on the palace
From HONG VOU were an hundred and forty years
          till now OU TSONG, a minor,
and 140 would be till the MANCHU, new mongol.
And when Lieou-kin the castrat was arrested
they found in his buildings:
                gold bars 240 thousand, of about 10 tael each
                      15 millions in money
                      5 million bars silver, of about 50 tael each
                      2 measures of unset jewels
          thus shaking the Emperor's confidence
In 1512 came 'bachelors men', that were horse thieves.
Died OU TSONG the lazy
And the Empress chose CHI-TSONG successor
who was son (aîné) of the second son of the Emperor
                                HIEN TSONG
he was a writer of verses,
          in fact he said he wd/ like to resign
and she (TCHANG CHI) told them to lay hold of Kiang-ping
and they found in his cellarage
                70 caskets of gold
                2 thousand 200 caskets of silver
                500 caskets of mixed
                400 great plates, gold and silver
not to count silk of the first grade, pearls,
cut stones and jewels
Came again Mansour the tartar
          and tartars said they wanted a market for horses
Jap sailors drove chinks to embargo
                'no trade save with our *regnicoles*'
And were five planets in the constellation of Yng-che
a.d. 1536 CHI-TSONG did rites at the MING tombs
                on Mt Tien-cheou
Japs burnt the salt works at Hai men

Oua-chi led troops against them
           who called themselves ' wolves of our Lady '
And Japs feared only this lady Oua-chi
Pirates almost took Fou-kien.

LVIII

SINBU put order in Sun land, Nippon, in the beginning
                              of all things
     where were DAI till Shogun Joritomo
     These Dai were of heaven descended, so saying.
Gods were their forebears. Till the Shogun
or crown general put an end to internal wars
And DAI were but *reges sacrificioli* after this time
in Miaco, with formalities
          wearing gold-flowered robes.
At each meal was a new clay dish for their service
' Descended from Ten Seo DAISIN
          that had reigned for a million years.'
All these lords say they are of heaven descended
and they ran into debt to keep up appearance
they were there busy with sciences, poetry, history
dancing, in Miaco, and music, playing at jeu de paume and
                                        escrime
with a garrison to keep watch on 'em
          and to keep 'em from interfering with business.
So came a ' butler to a person of quality '
          Messire Undertree
a slave, in Sa Mo a fish-vendor
          a stud-keeper,
                    that made war on Corea
          and was called WAR GOD post mortem
And because of the hauteur of
     Portagoose prelates, they drove the Xtians out of Japan
till were none of that sect in the Island
a.d. 1578 And in the 5th moon of the 20th year of OUAN LI
with ships new conditioned
Messire Undertree went against the Lord Lipan
boozing king of Korea

316

and four towns opened their gates to the Nippons
and he, Undertree, came to Pinyang the chief city
destroying the royal tombs
and the Koreans ran yowling to China
   seeking help of the emperor OUAN LI
At this time were ' the pirates incorporate '
   Ku ching the imperial tutor said: I was seduced
             by imposters
CHIN SONG had come aged 10 to the throne

And on t'other side was the question of horse fairs, and tartars
of whom were Nutché or savage,
   these traded at Kaiyuen
and the other great hordes, Pe and Nan-koan
   that were beyond the great wall fighting each other
and the Nutché gave refuge to mongols
when the mongrels were driven from China by MING lords
and they were so poor they were driven to peddling
   ginseng, beaver pelts horse hair
   and fur of martes zibbeline
seven such hordes united, and drave MING before them
But Nutché of Nankoen, first fought the wild Nutché
   in the 4th year of Suen Te
They stopped paying tribute 1430 or thereabouts
and a diplomat said to the Tartars:
   You have lost yr/ market for ginseng
     you have lost horse fairs
     by fighting each other.
And on t'other side, was Undertree making war in Korea
and Père Ricci brought a clock to the Emperor
   that was set in a tower
And Ku Tchang wasn't safe, even buried,
   Court ladies in cabal, gangsters set to defame him.
till his son hanged himself from the worry.

And the eunuchs of Tientsin brought Père Mathieu to court
        where the Rites answered:
        Europe has no bonds with our empire
and never receives our law
As to these images, pictures of god above and a virgin
they have little intrinsic worth. Do gods rise boneless to heaven
that we shd/ believe your bag of their bones?
The Han Yu tribunal therefore considers it useless
to bring such novelties into the PALACE,
we consider it ill advised, and are contrary
to receiving either these bones or père Mathieu.
        The emperor CHIN TSONG received him.

ten thousand brave men, ten thousand
        desperate sieges
        like bells or a ghazel
treacheries, and romances,
and now the bull tanks didn't work
from the beginning of China, great generals, faithful adherents,
To echo, desperate sieges, sell outs
        bloody resistance, and now the bull tanks didn't work
sieges from the beginning of time until now.
sieges, court treasons and laziness.
Against order, lao, bhud and lamas,
        night clubs, empresses' relatives, and hoang miao,
poisoning life with mirages, ruining order; TO KALON
And Ti Koen heard cries from the forest
whence came the bull tanks
came great cars built like ships fifteen feet high
        by a hundred, three deckers.
                carried on great wheels of stone
                drawn each by an hundred or more hundred oxen
But Tchu-yé and his men
                made their sortie
Cast petards that frightened the oxen,

thereby war cars were turned over.
and Tchu-yé's men slaughtered the siegers

HOAI TSONG fell before tartars, 5 ly from Tsunhoa
TAI TSONG of Manchu took them the law from China
       forbad manchus marry their sisters
Yellow belt for the Emperor
      red belt for the princess of blood
Told all to cut off their pig tails
and south Ming had to fear more from rottenness inside
      than from the Manchu north and north east.
Li koen viceroy had spent all this money, *not* paying the
                            troops
who turned bandit.
And the Lord of MANCHU wrote to the MING lord saying:
      We took arms against oppression
          and from fear of oppression
not that we wish to rule over you
      When in Suen fou I met with YR officers
I sacrificed on this oath, a black bull to earth
a white horse to the Spirit of Heaven
      although they were quite subordinate officers
I did this from respect to YR PERSON
                      as peace oath
to show that we wanted peace
      Whereto all my actions have tended
I offered to extradite criminals
to give back droves stolen
And to this offer I had no answer
I don't mean no proper answer
I had no answer whatever
And Kong Yeou came to join TAI TSONG
      and Tai sent an hetman to greet this Kong, rebel,
who came with boats arms munitions and furniture,
an hundred thousand folk came with Kong Yeou

And TAI TSONG said: No tartars favoured of heaven
have stayed boxed within their own customs
                Moguls took letters from lamas
I a free lord without overlord
will adopt such law as I like, in my right to adopt it
I take letters from China
                which is not to say that I take orders from any man
I take laws, but not orders.
                Thereafter he graded his officers
Aba tchan, Maen tchan, Tihali tchan
                on mandarin system
and four more islands came to him
and he TAI set exams in the Chinese manner
                for 16 bachelors, first class
                    31 bachelors, seconds, and 181 thirds
and he made a Berlitz, Manchu, chinese and mongul
and gave prizes, and camped next year Kourbang tourha
Here Mongrels came to him, and thence into China southward
by gorges
                the gorges of Ho-che near Ton,
                and by Tai chen gorge west of Taitong
naming Chensi as next place of muster
(TAI TSONG, son of TAI TSOU, ruling from Mougden)
                1625/35
Chose learning from Yao, Shun and Kungfutseu,
                from Yu leader of waters.
And in the seventh moon this monarch of Tartary
coming near unto Suen-hoa-fou wrote to the governor:
                Your sovran treats me as enemy
without asking what forces my action
                you are, indeed, subjects of a great realm
but the larger that empire, the more shd/ it strive toward peace
If children are cut off from parents
                if wives can not see their husbands
if yr houses are devast and your riches carried away

this is not of me but of mandarins
        Not I but yr/ emperor slaughters you
and yr/ overlords who take no care of yr/ people
        and count soldiers as nothing.

And toward the end of the 8th moon
Tengyun sent in dispatches: I have beaten the tartars
        I have slaughtered great numbers. Which he had not.
Whereup TAI TSONG wrote him: I will send a thousand
                      to meet any ten thousand
If you fear to risk that, send a thousand
        I will meet them with an hundred
Hoping this will teach you not to lie to your Emperor.
And after the next raid offered peace.
        And after vain waiting an answer
His tartar folk again asked him to be Emperor
and he said: If the King of Corea accepts me
Whereon the Tartars wrote the King of Korea:
        Eight ROYAL PRINCES OF MANCHU
18 great lords of our banners to the King of Corea
As heaven appears to desire it
        we accept our King to be Emperor
having begged him to take this mandate.
        The Mogul princes have joined us
HONG VOU brought the land under one rule
Before him the Kin were united
and after them was YUEN, entirety
And the Mongols wrote to Corea:
49 PRINCES MOGUL; to the King of Corea
200 years under MING
        and now turn against them
because of the crimes of their mandarins
        we join Manchu to make end of oppression
The weakness of the Ming troops, the faithlessness
                  of their commanders

show that their MANDATE is fallen
we now recognize TAI TSONG of MANCHU
Our blood in his service
For two years we have besought him to take IMPERIAL title
Four hundred thousand Mogul, their quivers and arrows
are back of this.
And Corea replied in the negative
And next year TAI TSONG took throne
third moon, 1635 anno domini
Put the three races in office
as moguls after Ghengis had not done
and continued the raiding...
round Peking, into Shantung (gallice Chantong)
and into Kiangnan, returning with plunder.
Thus until Ousan invited them to put down the rebels.

Rice was at one mark silver the measure
in Kaï fong
and human meat sold in market
Litse's gangsters over all Honan
Li Sao: weep, weep over Kaïfong; Kientsong the bloody
and Litse called himself Emperor
Ming troops were unpaid
Eunuchs devoured the taxes; the Prime minister
could not get hold of them
And the castrats opened the gates of Pekin to rebels
till HOEI died hung in his belt
and there was blood in the palace. Li Sao; Li Sao,
wrong never ending
Likoue: faithful to death, and then after
and in this day Ousan asked in the Manchu
TAI TSONG was dead these two years;
his brothers ruling as counsel.
Atrox MING, atrox finis
the nine gates were in flame.

Manchu with Ousan put down many rebels
Ousan offered to pay off these Manchu
who replied then with courtesy:
we came for Peace not for payment.
   came to bring peace to the Empire
in Pekin they cried OUAN SOUI
    a thousand, ten thousand years, A NOI
eijen, ouan soui; Ousan, Ousan
    peace maker Ousan, in the river, reeds,
  flutes murmured Ousan
Brought peace into China; brought in the Manchu
Litse thought to gain Ousan,
    roused Ousan and Ousan
remembered his father
    dead by the hand of Litse.
$$\tau\acute{\alpha}\delta' \,\tilde{\omega}\delta' \,\check{\epsilon}\chi\epsilon\iota$$

LIX

De libro CHI-KING sic censeo
        wrote the young MANCHU, CHUN TCHI,
        less a work of the mind than of affects
        brought forth from the inner nature
here sung in these odes.
Urbanity in externals, virtu in internals
        some in a high style for the rites
some in humble;
for Emperors; for the people
all things are here brought to precisions
that we shd/ learn our integrity
that we shd/ attain our integrity
Ut animum nostrum purget, Confucius ait, dirigatque
ad lumen rationis
                perpetuale effecto/
That this book keep us in due bounds of office
        the norm
show what we shd/ take into action;
        what follow within and persistently
CHI KING ostendit incitatque. Vir autem rectus
et libidinis expers ita domine servat
with faith, never tricky, obsequatur parentis
nunquam deflectat
all order comes into such norm
igitur meis encomiis, therefor this preface
                CHUN TCHI anno undecesimo

                                (a.d. 1655)

periplum, not as land looks on a map
but as sea bord seen by men sailing.
Now tarters in the murk night
sent great numbers of sojers with lanthorns
which they held up very high

324

and thus spread light on proceedings
causing great fear in Nanking.
        so the last mingsters fled out by the Tchinkiang road.
And the ammiral put to sea thinking perhaps that
a few minutes more resistance
        wd/ be of no mortal use.
And on the tenth came an officer
        to say that the port was in tartar hands
But MiLord the Prince and his eating companions
were in no shape to take in the message
        They weren't sober till the following midnight
whereon they skedaddled
        And the Nankings set up a new emperor   *a.d.* 1645
And the order to off pigtails stiffened resistance
put new guts into mingsters
Kouei born to ill fortune
no mingster cd/ trust any other; cd/ agree with any six others
        utilité publique, motif trop élevé
for vile courtiers
and when the young MANCHU was 14 they gave him to
                                        wife a mogul
and took in Galileo's astronomy,
        chucked the mohametan
And there came a hong-mao or red-headed Dutchman
And the portagoose to Macao
        and they say that the Emperor CHUN TCHI
died of sorrow, for the death of one of his queens
        an officer's wife who had risen.
And the four regents put eunuchs out of high office
a thousand purged out of palace
and a half ton block of iron inscribed
        Let there be no Eunuch in office hereafter.
And in '64 they putt out the Xtians
Portageese were confined to Macao
        Thus KANG HI
                    325

who played the spinet on Johnnie Bach's birthday
do not exaggerate/ he at least played on some such instrument
and learned to pick out several tunes (european)
and were demarked the borders of Russia
with a portagoose and a frog priest to interpret
to whom each a robe brocaded with dragons
but not embroidered

> and short coats of martin, satin lining, gold buttons
> Pereira and Gerbillon
> made mandarins second order

And that embassy went out via Mt Paucity

> and paid visit to the *ho fo,* the lama who dies not

as he sat on a pair of great cushions
one brocade and the other plain yellow
who blessed them with tea and a luncheon

> and in another room assez mal propre
> singing his prayers was another

and in yet another temple apartment another said frankly
he didn't see how he cd/ have lived in another body
before this and in any case had no such remembrance
but only the *ho fo's* word

> and they went on toward the Hans of Kalkas

where they got order to turn about and come home
was a war on between Eleutes and Kalkas
and to tell the Oros (the O Rossians) to meet 'em at Selinga
or some other place on the frontier

> to determine frontiers.

which they accomplished next year at Nipchou.

> With these ambassadors were a lot of domestics

five thousand 800 sojers
and a spot of artillery

> who all passed the gt wall at Cha houkoen.

And KANG walked to his grandmother's funeral
a distance of 500 ly from the capital.

326

And this embassy was concerning the Amur frontier
coming from Petersburg
but we wanted our martin sables, our huntin'
that was on the north side of the Amur
where are mountains and great lakes in the valleys.
Year 28th of KANG HI, under the 7th moon
was this treaty in latin with copies in tartar and muscovite
and the chinks swore by the god of Xtians
thinking nothing else wd/ have more force with the muscovites
' To spare further bloodshed on our frontiers
we here near the town of Nipchou
                            swear peace solid, eternal
state that boundary stones shall be set.
                    Pray we to the GOD of all things
                        who seeth our hearts
                    that if any man here have reservation
                    or plot his own profit
                            in violence to this treaty
                    he die before he reach a ripe age
                                        So the envoys
embraced to the music of instruments
and the rhoosians (Orosians) served a sort of lunch
to the chinese ambassadors
                    confitures and three sorts of wine
                    vintage of europe
and this was due to the frog and the portagoose
                    Gerbillon and Pereira
            to Gerbillon in the most critical moment
that he kept their tempers till they came to conclusion.

LX

So the Jesuits' brought in astronomy
     (Galileo's, an heretic's)
     music and physics from Europe,
     Grimaldi, Intorcetta, Verbiest,
Koupelin. Subject of yr/ Majesty,
        prescribed of the tribune of rites:
True that the Europeans have passed zealously many dangers
and have brought us astronomy, and founded cannon
which have served us in civil wars,
and that one shd/ reward their services in negotiating with
                      the ORosians.
They have not made any trouble.
     We permit lamas, hochangs and taotsés to go to
                their churches
It wd/ seem unwarranted to forbid only these Europeans
to go to their temples. We deem therefore
that they be so permitted
indiscriminate to pray and burn perfumes.
       3rd day 2nd moon of the 31st year of KANG HI
17 grandees of the Empire, whereof eleven cabinet ministers
                of this EMPEROR
Les pères Gerbillon, Fourtères, Bournat
took quinine to the palace, anno domini 1693
Hence the Jesuit church in Pekin in the Hoang Tchang
       that is the palace enclosure.
And Feyenkopf in the Kaldan war
        was fighting Eleutes and Mohamedans and the
Emperor shot six quail *de suite* with six arrows
and sent the Crown Prince an Eleute horse
saying: I don't know that chinese bean fodder will suit him.
Herewith some Kalkas sheep for prime mutton.
     yr affectionate father KANG HI

Hoang Ho is frozen. In fact the Ortes country seems to be
pretty much as we thought it in Pekin,
small huntin' quite pleasant, a lot of pheasants and hares.
pasturage excellent. Hoang Ho fruz 1/2 a ft. thick.
Ortes very orderly, have lost none of their mongol habits,
their princes in concord, no usury.
Clever especially in lookin' after their animals,
clumsy bowmen, but hit their mark.
And General Feyenkopf wrote him
that the Eleutes had caved in
and KANG HI gave a fur cap to the envoy
and his (KANG HI'S) horse sweat pink
          as in legend the horses of Taouen land, the
Tien ma, or horses of heaven
and this horse in particular had been taken in the battle of
                                        Tchaomed
and they had a grand show in Pekin for next new year's
Mongols, Kaldans and Eleutes.
' It is easy after this to be sure
          that all lamas are traitors.
Keep these prisoners in separate rooms,
sold to the Tipa who is a liar. I have taken
the sun 38° 34'
i.e. one degree 20 less here than in Pekin '
                                        KANG HI
Dogs bark only at strangers. And at Paichen
KANG HI was pleased with the pasture land,
delayed his return to the capital,
stayed stag-hunting outside the great wall
while Kalda had grabbed Samarkand and
          Bokara for the mohammeds
1699 peace year in all Tartary
Grimaldi, Pereira, Tony Thomas and Gerbillon
sent in their *placet* sic:
European litterati

having heard that the Chinese rites honour Kung-fu-tseu
and offer sacrifice to the Heaven etc/
and that their ceremonies are grounded in reason
now beg to know their true meaning and in particular
the meaning of terms for example Material
Heaven and Changti meaning? its ruler?
Does the *manes* of Confucius
accept the grain, fruit, silk, incense offered
　　　　　　and does he enter his cartouche?
The European church wallahs wonder if this can be reconciled.
And the archbish of Antioch spent a year in Canton
mousing round but not coming to Pekin
but was, next year, permitted,
Monseigneur Maillard de Tournon
　　　　　　from Clemens, papa (Number XI) the Kiao Hoang
and the Portagoose king sent an envoy
and they cured KANG HI with wine from the Canaries
　　　　　　w'ich putt 'em up a jot higher
And too much rice went to Batavia
　　　　　　so our lord KANG layed an embargo
　　　　　　(a bit before Tommy Juffusun's)
and a tsong-ping or second class mandarin
putt up a petition:
　　　　　　AGAINST Europes and Xtianity
That there had been nine red boats into Macao
Dutchmen, red-heads or Englanders.
Japan, sez Tching mao, is the only considerable kingdom
　　　　　　to east of us
and Japan kept peace even all through the great Ming rebellion.
Siam and Tonkin pay tribute,
only danger to us is from these Europeans
by Hong-mao I mean any nordic barbarian
there are Yenkeli and Yntsa (meanin' froggies)
　　　　　　　　　　and Holans
all equally barbarous

I have knocked around at sea for some years
and the Dutch are the worst of the lot of them,
                              poifik tigurs,
their vessels stand any wind and carry a hundred cannon
if ten of 'em get into Canton
                  who knows what cd/ happen.
I think we shd/ stop this danger at source
or at least make 'em disarm before coming into our harbours
or have 'em come in one at a time
                  or unlade in a fortress.
They wormed into Japan via Manilla they have been
kicked out but still try to get in again
They spend money, gather the dregs of the people, make maps
I don't know what they are up to
                  and that's not my province
All I know is they refuged in Manilla
And now they are top dog in Manilla
I rest my case in the tribunals of Empire
trusting that this bind-weed will not be permitted
                  to root in and fortify
Humbly to yr MAJESTY
                  Tching Mao, a sea captain
Dug up edict of '69
            PERMIT only Verbiest and his colleagues
We vote to pardon all converts
provided they pull down their churches, and again May eleventh
MISSIONARIES have well served in reforming our
                                          mathematics
and in making us cannon
            and they are therefore permitted to stay
and to practice their own religion but
            no chinese is to get converted
and they are not to build any churches
47 europeans have permits
they may continue their cult, and no others.

Jesuits appealed that they be not
              confounded with Dutchmen
Let stay, if wd/ promise never see Europe again
various churches were levelled and
there came an embassy from PETER of Russia

                                            1720

with cavalcade and drawn sabres
and a new bloke from the Kiao-hoang of Roma.
Tibet was brought under and '22 was a peace year
The Emp'r'r went huntin' as usual
and tiger huntin' in Haitse and died the 20th of this month
at 8 in the evening
              ' no DYNASTY has come in with such justice
as ours has. I have not wasted the treasures of empire
considering them as the blood of the people
              3 million a year on river embankments

I order that YONG TCHING succeed me
                        THOU SHALT NOT
lend money to sojers.
Huntin' keeps manchu fit
              avoid the hot summer in Pekin.'
He began taking trips into Tartary.
History translated to manchu. Set up board of translators
Verbiest, mathematics
Pereira professor of music, a treatise in chinese and manchu
Gerbillon and Bouvet, done in manchu
              revised by the emperor as to questions of style
A digest of philosophy (manchu) and current
Reports on the mémoires des académies
des sciences de Paris.
Quinine, a laboratory set up in the palace.
He ordered 'em to prepare a total anatomy, et
qu'ils veillèrent à la pureté du langage

                        332

et qu'on n'employât que des termes propres
(namely CH'ing ming)

En son Palais divers ateliers
        wanted the best European models
fer paintin' an' scuppchure, his works in one hundred volumes
wuz emperor KANG HI 61 years
from 1662 and came after him

LXI

YONG TCHING
       his fourth son, to honour his forebears
       and spirits of fields
       of earth
heaven
utility public
sought good of the people, active, absolute, loved
No death sentence save a man were thrice tried
and he putt out Xtianity
chinese found it so immoral
his mandarins found this sect so immoral
' The head of a sect ' runs the law ' who deceives folk
' by pretending religion, ought damn well to be strangled.'
No new temples for any hochang, taoists or similars
                              sic in lege
False laws are that stir up revolt by pretense of virtue.
Anyone but impertinent fakers wd have admitted
the truth of the Emperor's answer:
What I say now I say as Emperor
Applied to this daily and all day
Not seeing my children not seeing the Empress
till the time of mourning be ended
Xtians being such sliders and liars.
Public kitchen in famine
Public works for the unemployed, 1725,
a dole, nothing personal against Gerbillon and his
                                        colleagues, but

Xtians are disturbing good customs
seeking to uproot Kung's laws
seeking to break up Kung's teaching.
Officers at Tientsing
          who faked rice distribution

334

and gave bad rice to the needy
can damn well pay up what they have embezzled.
Lieu-yu-y, state examiner said:
              Put magazines in the 4 towns of Chan-si
(that there be set up a fondego)
Look whom you choose to administer
              that these be not the overworked Governors
To keep out graft...if any man have loaned rice in secret...
A 100,000 pund capital
              wd/ mean Thirty thousand great measures
At moderate price we can sell in the spring
to keep the market price decent
And still bring in a small revenue
which should be used for getting more next crop
AMMASSI or sane collection,
to have bigger provision next year,
that is, augment our famine reserve
and thus to keep the rice fresh in store house.
IN time of common scarcity; to sell at the just price
in extraordinary let it be lent to the people
and in great calamities, give it free
                        Lieou-yu-y
                        Approved by the EMPEROR
(Un fontego *)
And in every town once a year
to the most honest citizens: a dinner
                        at expense of the emperor
no favour to men over women
Manchu custom very old, revived now by YONG TCHING
An' woikinmen thought of. If proper in field work
get 8th degree button and
              right to sit at tea with the governor
One, european, a painter, one only admitted
And Pope's envoys got a melon

                    * Canto XXXV.

And they druv out Lon Coto fer graftin'
sent him to confino to watch men breakin' ground
He had boosted the salt price.
And they received the volumes of history
with a pee-rade with portable cases like tabernacles
the dynastic history with solemnity.
    ' I cant ', had said KANG HI
' Resign ' said Victor Emanuel, you Count Cavour can resign
at your convenience.
    ' To comfort the soul of my father
Emperor now defunct and in heaven ', said YONG TCHING;
Don't think that soft talk is wanted
you write down what you take for the facts
call pork pork in your proposals
your briefs shd/ be secret and sealed and our Emperor
    will publish at his discretion.
Eleventh month 23rd day for ceremonial ploughing
    (I take it december)
Out by the Old Worker's Hill
YONG ploughed half an hour
three princes, nine presidents did their stuff
and the peasants in gt/ mass sang the hymns
    befitting this field work
as writ in LI KI in the old days
And they sowed grain and in autumn the grain of that field
was for ceremonial purposes put in sacks of Imperial
yellow as fit for this purpose.
' You Christers wanna have foot on two boats
    and when them boats pulls apart
you will d/n well git a wettin' ' said a court mandarin
tellin' 'em.
    And they set up a yellow pavilion
    with a buffet beneath it
And the dishes and the court silver
and in deep silence sounded suddenly trumpets

and music for the Emperor YONG TCHING
and Dom Metello and the Europeans went to their places
a cushion for Dom Metello
and the Emperor's wine was brought in, which he offered to
Dom Metello
who knelt, drank, and returned to his cushion
whereon they offered him fruit piled high in a pyramid
and the Emperor YONG said: take him somewhere where
                                                    it is cooler.
So they dined him and showed him a comedy
and gave him seven trunks of stuff for himself
and 35 for the Portagoose boss who had sent him
i.e. he wuz honoured but cdn't spill proppergander
and the chink grandees took him down the canal
with a dinner cooked by the chefs of the Palace
and his trappings up-(as they say)-held the honour of Europe
and as to Sounou being Xtian, he wuz probably also a conspiracy
But the population of Yun-nan was growing
and the price of grain kept goin' up.
Lot of land undeveloped
            so they opened it
tax exemption for six years on good rice land
and for ten years on dry
and honours in proportion to
            how much a bloke wd put under culture
button 8th class for enough, and diplomas
for 15 *arpens*. A peasant got two bouquets for his cap
and a cramoisi scarf and a band to walk home wiff.
And a boost for any mandarin
            that wd stake out new settlers
800,000 in doles
a million on canal reparations
Good of the empire of any part of the empire
concerns every mandarin
            no matter where he is located

It is like a family affair
Ghost frightens no honest man. No house is
durable if perched on yr neighbor's ruin
An honest peasant is a prognostic
                    wrote YONG TCHING
passing in silence the other ' prognistics ' of the
                                        Governor's letter
Men are born with a fund of rightness   you will
find good men in any small village
but the bureaucrats take no notice
let Chiyeou be made a 7th class mandarin
give him 100 ounces of silver as incentive to other men
Heaven has scattered riches and poverty
but to profit on other men's loss is no better than banditry
in momentum of avarice, no longer steers his own course.
Chiyeou didn't do it on book readin'
          nor by muggin' up history.
Million in earthquake relief
and a thousand taels to the capital Jesuits
but expelled the rest from Canton
' they go on buying converts '
          Died 1735 at 58
          in the 13th year of his reign
Came KIEN, 40 years before ' our revolution '
YONG TCHING unregretted by canaglia and nitwits
' A man's happiness depends on himself,
               not on his Emperor
If you think that I think that I can make any man happy
     you have misunderstood the FU

(the Happiness ideogram) that I sent you.
Thus Tching whom Coupetai had brought up,

for the number of bye-laws
for his attention to detail
                unregretted by scoundrels
never had death sentences such attention
three trials, publication of details, examination,
to poorest as for the highest
            CAI TSONG HIEN HOANG TI be he credited
so his son Kien Long came to the throne
in the 36th of that century—
and as to the rise of the Adamses—
Extensive Mohamedan treasures
' Question of coin in these conquered towns is very important.
I advise a few of YOUR mintage
and to leave the old pieces current.
Those used here,
            Haskai, yerqui and hotien
are of bronze weighing about 1/5th of one of our ounces
50 of these mahometan discs make a teuke
                about one of our taels.
There are some useless old cannon here
which I suggest we melt up for small cash
to keep commerce moving.'
            Tchao-hou
                to his EMPEROR
            from the camp before Hashan
(or Kasgar, a city in little Boucaria)

This princess entered the palace when YONG TCHING was
                                    emperor
as ' a young lady merely of talents
recited with beautiful voice
            and had other amiable qualities '
concubine, and having a son was made queen
and for forty two years had seen him, this son,
on the first throne of Asia

        in the 86th year of her age
posthumous EMPRESS
        Hiao Ching Hien Hoang Héou
and her son as memorial
        exempted his empire from the land tax
for a year as indeed he had done before on her birthdays
when she was 70 and when she reached her eightieth birthday
and now, in memoriam. And he wrote
        a poem on the Beauties of Mougden
and condensed the Ming histories
        literary kuss, and wuz Emperor
fer at least 40 years.
        Perhaps you will look up his verses.

LXII

'Acquit of evil intention
  or inclination to perseverance in error
  to correct it with cheerfulness
   particularly as to the motives of actions
of the great nations of Europe.'
   for the planting
and ruling and ordering of New England
from latitude 40° to 48°
TO THE GOVERNOR AND THE COMPANIE
   whereon Thomas Adams
   19th March 1628
18th assistant whereof the said Thomas Adams
   (abbreviated)
Merry Mount become Braintree, a plantation near Weston's
Capn Wollanston's became Merrymount.
   ten head 40 acres at 3/ (shillings) per acre
who lasted 6 years, brewing commenced by the first Henry
   continued by Joseph Adams, his son
at decease left a malting establishment.
Born 1735; 19th Oct. old style; 30th new style John Adams
its emolument gave but a bare scanty subsistence.
'Passion of orthodoxy in fear, Calvinism has no other agent
study of theology
   wd/ involve me in endless altercation
to no purpose, of no design and do no good to
    any man whatsoever...
not less of order than liberty...
   Burke, Gibbon, beautifiers of figures...
middle path, resource of second-rate statesmen...
   produced not in Britain:
     tcha
   tax falls on the colonists.

341

Lord North, purblind to the rights of a
continent, eye on a few London merchants...
                         no longer saw redcoat
as brother or as a protector
(Boston about the size of Rapallo)
         scarce 16,000,
                  habits of freedom now formed
even among those who scarcely got so far as analysis
so about 9 o'c in the morning Lard Narf wuz bein' impassible
was a light fall of snow in Bastun, in King St.
and the 29th Styschire in Brattle St
Murray's barracks, and in this case was a
                  barber's boy ragging the sentinel
so Capn Preston etc/
lower order with billets of wood and ' just roving '
force in fact of a right sez Chawles Fwancis
                  at same time, and in Louses of Parleymoot...
so fatal a precision of aim,
                           sojers aiming??
Gent standing in his doorway got 2 balls in the arm
and five deaders ' never Cadmus... ' etc
                  was more pregnant
patriots need legal advisor
                  measures involvin' pro-fessional knowl-edge
BE IT ENACTED / guv-nor council an' house of assembly
         (Blaydon objectin' to form ov these doggymints)
Encourage arts commerce an' farmin'
not suggest anything on my own
         if ever abandoned by administration of England
         and outrage of the soldiery
the bonds of affection be broken
till then let us try cases by law IF by
                  snowballs oystershells cinders
                  was provocation
                  reply was then manslaughter only

in consideration of endocrine human emotions
unuprootable, that is, human emotions—
        merely manslaughter
        brand 'em in hand
but not hang 'em being mere human blighters
        common men like the rest of us
        subjekk to
                passions
law not bent to wanton imagination
              and temper of individuals
mens sine affectu
      that law rules
      that it be
        since affectu in 1770, Bastun.
Bad law is the worst sort of tyranny. Burke
disputed right to seize lands of the heathen
and give it to any king, If we be feudatory
parliament has no control over us
        We are merely
under the monarch
allegiance is to the king's natural person 'The Spensers'
said Coke, hatched treason denying this
allegiance follows natural, not politic person
are we mere slaves of some other people?
        Mercantile temper of Britain
constitution...without appeal to higher powers unwritten
VOTED 92 to 8 against Oliver
      i.e. against king's pay for the judges instead of
        having the wigs paid by the colony
        no jurors wd/ serve
These are the stones of foundation
J. A.'s reply to the Governor
Impeachment of Oliver
These stones we built on

I don't receive a shilling a month, wrote Mr Adams to Abigail
in seventeen 74
June 7th. approve of committee from the several colonies
Bowdoin, Cushing, Sam Adams, John A. and Paine (Robert)
' mope, I muse, I ruminate ' *le*
personnel manque we have not men for the times
Cut the overhead my dear wife and keep yr/ eye on the dairy
non importation, non eating, non export, all bugwash
but until they have proved it
in experiment
no use in telling 'em.
Local legislation / that is basic /
we wd. consent in matters of empire trade, It is
by no means essential to trade with foreign nations at all
as sez Chas Francis, China and Japan have proved it
weekly in Boston Gazette from '74 until Lexington
wrote Novanglus, then shooting started
allus them as putts off taking a side
and lastly in superintending the preparation of
bills of credit, to serve as dollars durin' the struggle
then moved for a navee
which he got, after some ridicule
Guided pubk mind in formation of state constitutions
e.g. N. York and N. Carolina
retain what experience has found good,
central authority, war, trade, and disputes between states
republican jealousy which seeks to cut off all power
from fear of abuses does
quite as much harm as a despotism
9th Feb to end of that year probably very laborious
Birth of a Nation
privateers not independence, what is?
sovereign state
acknowledged of nations and all that
sovreign state and all that

by other nations acknowledged
when his Brit. majesty lords commons have excluded from
crown protection
May 12th, ' as 12 months ago shd/ have been '
regards independency being moved and accepted June 7th
spies and persons counterfeiting—or abetting in same—
                our continental bills of credit
or knowingly passing the same to be punished
no word, orationem, probably not elegantissimam
                Routledge was elegant
' said nothing not hackneyed six months before '
                wrote J. A. to his wife
I said nothing etc/ letter to Chase from John Adams
the people are addicted, as well as the great, to corruption
Providence in which, unfashionable as the faith is, I believe
Schicksal, sagt der Führer
with pomp bells bonfires on the 2nd day of July
than any social community has ever yet carried out
                reasonable act only by its geography
INadequate concession by England,
                always too late (sero)
Britain never in season, reciprocation by trade
                Cavalier, sentiment rather than principle
TO serve liberty at a higher rate than tyrants wd/ pay 'em
                you shd/ have numbered yr/ regiments, you never
                                                send me
accounts e.g. of guns, numbers, their weight of metal
I never know of what size (frigates etc/)
                Impassible moderation of Washington
saved us by stoppin' catfights between officers
                For proportional representation—
                Clearest head in the Congress
                                (John's was)
THUMON
      we want one man of integrity in that embassy

345

Bordeaux, and passed on to Paris
                the ethics, so called, of Franklin
                                IF moral analysis
be not the purpose of historical writing...
Leyden Gazette, Magazine Politique Hollandais, Calkoen,
Amsterdam bankers, directed to Mr A. by Gen. Washington
(Cornwallis' surrender)
                De Ruyter still cherished memories of Dutch freedom
doivent tousjours *crier* la Liberté,—amis de la France shd/
                                remarked Flassans
and especially the consonance of Van Capellen
                personal visits to deputies at der Haag
Leyden, Harlem, Zwol were petitions
                Zeland, Overyssel, Gronye, Utrecht and Guilderland

so on the 19th of April
John got his answer and recognition, categoric
Mr Adams has demanded a categorical answer
for the U.S.N.A. letters of credence / we say that he is
                                to be now
admitted as envoy 1782 Birth of a Nation
                                corps diplomatique
His literary connections sans which was no opening
a stranger to language and manners so in his correspondence
                                                with
Dumas, without money, friends, against intrigue
to pecuniary advances
                in fact from Willink, van Staphorst and Fynje
5,000,000 guilders to maintain our overstrained credit
                                till 1788 relations
His relations with bankers in Amsterdam
in October a treaty of commerce, by no arts or disguises
no flatteries, no corruptions
                who to the age of 40 years
had scarce crossed the edge of his province
346

transferred to Adam Street in the Adelphi
        suspecting the post boy of humour in taking him there
Magazines, daily pamphlets in hands of men of no character
in fact one bookseller said to me: can get 'em at a guinea a day
to write pro or con anything. Hired!
Found archery still being practiced
        Credit till I returned to America
Ice, broken ice, icy water
500 miles on a trotting horse in dead winter
        but never as on that journey to Holland
(England to Holland)
Struck down our men, shattered our mainmast
        never as on that going to Amsterdam,
fundamentals in critical moments
        literature and philosophy are the rage in even
                                fashionable circles
and Frederick's treaty of commerce
toward mitigation of maritime law
        considerably in advance of world standards
philanthropy not wholly free from suspicion that
        the new states cd/ profit
The Duke said that John wd/ be stared at,
        to make gain out of neighbor's troubles
        secondary misfortune of Britain.
AS of a demonstration in Euclid:
        system of government
Immediacy: in order to be of any effect
perceive taste and elegance are the cry
        which I have not
        Libertatem Amicitiam Fidem
a new power arose, that of fund holders
fond of rotation so that to remove
        their abuse from me to the President (Washington)
TO be punctual, to be confined to my seat
        (over the Senate)

to see nothing done (by the senate)
to hear nothing said, to say and DO nothing
borrow for trading very unmercantile
by thought, word, never encourage a war...
      horror they are in lest peace shd/ continue
will accumulate perpetual DEBT
        leading to yet more revolutions
He (Adet) announced to the President the entire
      annihilation of factions in France (18 June '95)
He (Jay) returned yesterday to N. York
      very sociable and in fine spirits
no Chief Justice yet named to succeed him
happily he is elected before the
        treaty was published
as factions
      against him wd/ have quarrelled whether right or
             the contrary
to colour their opposition
elegance of J. Q. A.'s style is admired
properties of serenity in OBservation
but where shall be found (1795) good men and true to fill offices
Washington's cabinet posts go a-begging
to four senators, and to more whom I do not know nominatim
King, Henry, Cotsworth (?) and Pinckney
      all have refused it (similarly for the War Office)
expenses here so far beyond salaries
Integrity rewarded with obloquy
      I believe the President will retire
Dangerous that President and V.P. be in opposite boxes
persons highest class of ability enlisted
habitually in elaborate discussions
      assiduously read by the people
I hate to live in Philadelphy in the summer
      hate speeches messages addresses levees and
             drawingrooms

been 30 years among these rocks whistling
          (Amphion) and none wd/ ever move without money.
Had I eloquence humour or irony, if Mr Jefferson be elected I
believe I must put up for the House
                    believe I
might be of some use in that body, retirement
(Washington's) removed all check upon
                    parties
Mr Jefferson, Mr Hamilton
the latter not enjoying the confidence of the people at large
to oppose Ham to Jeff wd/ be futile
whereon Ham set to undercut Adams
          '96 till 1854 no president chosen against Pennsylvania
' the old man will make a good president ' remarked Mr Giles
' but we shall have to check him occasion'lly '
' manoeuvres that wd/ surprise you ' wrote John to Abigail
a love of science and letters
          a desire to encourage schools and academies
as only means to preserve our Constitution.
Elleswood administered the oath with great energy.
Napoleon's conquest of Italy
          created a paradise for army contractors.
whereon Senor Miranda
          was for making great conquests and Hamilton...
Talleyrand...Mr A. not caught asleep by *his* cabinet
so that on the 18th of Feb. the senate recd/ the nomination
                              of Murray
and a communication of Talleyrand's document
assuming no risk in trusting
          the professions of Talleyrand.
Not vindictive that I can remember
          though I have often been wroth
at any rate staved off a war
          roused the land to be ready
a pardon for all offenders

                    (i.e. poor dutch Fries and companions)
formed own view of Hamilton's game (and his friends')
which wd/ certainly have tangled with Europe
wont to give to his conversation
                    full impetus of vehement will,
charged course of Ham and his satellites
to disappointment that they hadn't
                    got us entangled with Britain
defensive and offensive
                    Snot, Bott, Cott left over from
Washington's cabinet
                    and as for Hamilton
we may take it (my authority, ego scriptor cantilenae)
that he was the Prime snot in ALL American history
                    (11th Jan. 1938, from Rapallo)
But for the clearest head in the congress
                              1774 and thereafter
              pater patriae
the man who at certain points
                    made us
at certain points
                    saved us
by fairness, honesty and straight moving
                                        ARRIBA ADAMS

LXIII

TOWARDS sending of Ellsworth
and the pardon of Fries
25 years in office, treaties put thru and loans raised
and General Pinckney, a man of honour
declined to participate
or even to give suspicion of having colluded
deficiency in early moral foundations (Mr Hamilton's)
they effect here and there simple manners
true religion, morals, here flourish
i.e. Washington 4th March 1801
toward the newly created fount of supply (Mr Jefferson)
in ardour of hostility to Mr Jefferson
to overlook a good deed
If Pickering cd/ mount on
wd/ vote for J. Adams
whose integrity not his enemies had disputed
...rights
diffusing knowledge of principles
maintaining justice, in registering treaty of peace
changed with the times, and not
forgetting what had suffered
by the sedition laws
Obt. svt. Chas Holt
Honoured father
(signed John Quincy Adams (in full)
1825 (when elected)
Scott's fictions and even the vigorous and exaggerated
poetry of Ld/ Byron
when they wd/ not read him anything else
property EQUAL'D land in J. A.'s disposition
From Fancy's dreams to active Virtue turn
The cats thought him (Franklin) almost a catholic

The Church of England laid claim to him as one of 'em
Presbyters thought him half presbyterian
   friends, sectaries,
Eripuit caelo fulmen
and all that to ditch a poor man fresh from the country
Vol Two (as the protagonist saw it:)
    No books, no time, no friends
Not a new idea all this week
    even bagpipe not disagreeable
for amusement reading her (Mrs Savil) the Ars Amandi
1758, around half after three, went to the Court House
With Saml Quincy and Dr Gordon....
And saw the most spacious room and
        finest line
of ladies I ever did see, Gridley
enquired my method of study
and gave me Reeve's advice to his nephew
read a letter he wrote to Judge Leighton: follow the study
   rather than gain of the law, but the gain
enough to keep out of the briars, So that I
believe no lawyer ever did so much business
for so little profit as I during the 17 years that I practised
you must conquer the INSTITUTES
and I began with Coke upon Littleton
   greek mere matter of curiosity (in the law)
to ask Mr Thatcher's concurrence
whole evening on original sin and the
    plan of the universe
and lastly on law, he thinks that the country is full
Van Myden *editio terza* design of the book is
exposition

正

        of technical terms

as of Hawkins' Pleas of the Crown. Bracton,
Britten, Fleta on Glanville, must dig with my fingers
as nobody will lend me or sell me a pick axe.
Exercises my lungs, revives my spirits opens my pores
reading Tully on Cataline quickens my circulation
Ruggles grandeur in boldness of thought honour contempt
                                                   of meanness
was practising law and running a tavern in Sandwich
                 died Novascotia 1788 and a tory.
Read one book an hour
           then dine, smoke, cut wood
                                    in quella parte
dove sta memora, Colonel Chandler not conscious
these crude thoughts and expressions
are catched up and treasured as proof of his character.
Not finding them (Rhine grapes slips) in that city
sends to a village 70 miles away
                 and then sends two packets
one by water and lest that miscarry, the other by post
to Mr Quincy to whom he owes nothing
           and with whom he is but little acquainted
           purely for the purpose of
propagating Rhine wine in these provinces
           (one up to Franklin) I
read Timon of Athens, the manhater
           must be (IRA must be) aroused ere the mind be
                                             at its best

la qual manda fuoco
           dirty and ridiculous litigations been multiplied
proverb; as litigious as Braintree
           fraud and system of bigotry
on which papal usurpations are founded, monument of priestly
                                             ambition
guile wrought into system
' Our constitution ' ' every man his own monarch '
                         353

      all these boasting speeches have heard (1760)
and never failed to raise a hoarse laugh
          An inferior officer in Salem
            whose name was Cockle petitioned
the justices for a Writ of Assistance
to break open ships, shops, cellars and houses
Mr Sewall expressed doubt of legality,
            Oxenbridge Thayer with Otis,
a contest appeared to be opened.

LXIV

To John's bro, the sheriff, we lay a kind word in passing
Cromwell was not prudent
nor honest
nor laudable.
Prayer: hands uplifted
Solitude: a person, a NURSE
plumes: is she angel or bird, is she a bird or an angel?
ruffled, rumpled, rugged...wings
looks down
and pities those who wear a crown
meaning (query) George, Louis or Frederick?
Beautiful spot, am almost wholly surrounded by water
wherein Deacon (later General) Palmer
has surrounded himself with a colony
of glass-blowers from Germany
come to undertake that work in America, 1752,
his lucerne grass
whereof 4 crops a year, seed he had of Gridley of Abingdon
pods an odd thing, a sort of ramshorn of straw
about 70 bushel of 1/4th an acre of land
his potatoes
sub conditione fidelitatis
is it known that Oliver ever advised to lay internal taxes
upon us?
or solicited office of stamps?
to be dragged through the town only in pageantry
to be burnt on a hill, and his house broken open...
but has not the Lieutenant Governor
a near relation etc/
a son etc/
in one family etc/
BY 40 towns, verbatim, their instrument

to their representatives Sam Adams has taken some
                                        paragraphs
Stamp Act spread a spirit from Georgia
to New Hampshire
          with honour, more inquisitive as to their liberties
even the lowest
          Your courts are shut down, justice VOID
I have not drawn a writ since the 1st of November
'if this authority be once recognized
                              ruins America
I must cut down my expenses.
For my ruin as well as America's...
To renounce under tree, nay under the very branch
where they hang'd him in effigy...
          UNANIMOUS for Gridley, Jas Otis, J. Adams
pray that the Courts may be opened
          (original of this is preserved)
If what I wrote last night
          recall what Lord Bacon
wrote about laws...invisible and correspondences...
                              that parliament
hath no authority
          to impose internal taxes upon us.
Common Law. 1st Inst. 142
Coke, to the 3rd Inst. Law is the subject's birthright
Want of right and of remedy are all one.
CONSTRUED that no innocent
          may by literal construction be
damaged actus
          legis nulli facit injuriam
Governor in council as supreme court of probate
...by more ravenous sort of ambition
                              or avarice...
avoid as the plague
tendency of the act to reduce the body of people

to ignorance, dependence and poverty
religious bigots
the worst of men, colonies
becomes a fashionable study...and will probably
stare more and more for some time. Ipswich Instructions
right to tax selves,
rather as allies than as subjects
FIRST settlement not a national act
and not at expense of the nation
nor made on land of the Crown
waddled through snow driving my cattle to water
Shutting courts equals abdication of throne
for entering a vessel at Louisburg
and taking away
10 barrels of
rum
Pitt vs/ Grenville, and for the repeal of the act
Parliament takes as Representative and not Legislative
authority
But Thatcher got him indicted for barratry
And he came near to conviction. Goffe grew warm
and said Eaton's character
was as good as any man's at the bar
punch wine bread cheese apples pipes and tobacco
Thursday oated at Martin's
when we saw five boxes of dollars
going in a horse cart to Salem for Boston
FOR England, said to contain about $18,000
lopping and trimming
walnut trees, and for felling of pines and savins
An irregular misshapen pine will darken
the whole scene in some places
case between negro and owner. At same time a craving man
(Hutchinson)

357

at Dr Tuft's where I found fine wild goose on the spit
                              and cranberries in the skillet
to the White House in Brattle St.
office lucrative in itself but new statutes
                    had been passed in Parliament
J. Q. A. born July eleventh
duty on glass incompatible
                    with my ideas on right, justice and policy
between negro and owner engaged Mr Hawley's attention
100 towns, one week's notice
about 10 o'clock troops began landing under cover of
                                                    the cannon
of the ships, without molestation
                                        Oct. 1st.
Population of Boston retrograde during 25 years
                        that preceded this
was now not above 16,000
                During my absence on circuit
as Byles said ' Our grievances red-dressed '
                under my windows in the square
                drum, fife, and in evening violins, songs
flutes of the serenaders, that is, Sons of Liberty
as well at the extravagance of the populace,
deceptions to which they are liable,
suppression of equity, when thoroughly heated
my drafts will be found in the Boston Gazette for those
                                            years '68, '69
a cargo of wines from Madeira
                belonging to Mr Hancock
without paying customs
                painful drudgery I had in his cause:
as to this statute my client never consented
Mr Hancock never consented, never voted for it himself
nor for any man to make any such law
                                        whenever

358

we leave principles and clear propositions
and wander into construction we wander into a wilderness
a darkness wherein arbitrary power
            set on throne of brass with a sceptre of iron...
Suspended, in fact, only after Battle of Lexington
            which ended all such prosecutions
Mt Wollanston, seat of our ancestors
                                    from
East chamber every ship sloop schooner and brigantine
Three hundred and fifty were under the Liberty Tree,
                                    a young buttonwood,
and preparing the next day's paper, cooking up paragraphs,
articles, working the political engine
            MORNING at Brackett's upon case of a whale...
that I had imported from London the
only complete set of British Statutes
            then in Boston or, I think, in the whole
of the Colonies, and in that work a statute
whose publication they feared, an
express prohibition of empressment
expressly IN America which statute they intended to
            get repealed
and did succeed 1769 toward the end of December so doing.
About 9 o'clock in evening, supposed to be signal of fire
men in front of the barracks and baker's boy afore mentioned
Mr Forest known then as the ' Irish infant '
            tears streaming over his face
' for that very unfortunate man, Captain Preston
                                    in prison
wants council and can get none, Mr Quincy
            will serve if you will
            Mr Auchmuty declines unless you will engage '
' But he must be sensible that this wd/ be as important a case
as was ever tried here or in any country....
not expect me to use art, sophistry, prevarication '

Upon which he offered me a retaining fee of one guinea
which I accepted
            (Re which things was Hutchinson undoubtedly scro-
                        fulous ego scriptor cantilenae
                                    Ez. P)
Bringing it in all to 10 guineas
            for Preston and 8 for the sojers
(But where the devil this brace of Adamses sprung from!
        (Oxenbridge Thatcher...dangers from intemperate
                                                    heats
BUT in Connecticut every family has a little manufactury
                                                    house
and make for themselves things for which they were used
to run into debt to the merchants.)
                        Cited Beccaria
He went out and saddled my horse and bridled him
' as a man of liberty, I respect you
' and from here to Cape Cod you won't find ten men amiss '
                nihil humanum alienum
This landlord, a high son
and has on his sign:
                Sons of Liberty served here...
When he came away he took view of the comet
...to roll and cool themselves and feed on white honeysuckle
our horses had got out of compound.
                        SUBILLAM
Cumis ego occulis meis
sleeping under a window: pray for me,
withered to skin and nerves *tu theleis* respondebat illa
apothanein; pray for me gentlemen
my prayers used to be answered, She prayed for deliverance
110 years of age, and some say she is over that
Anemonie, at Nantasket; non vi sed saepe legendo
Severn Ayres of Virginia, Mr Bull, Mr Trapier of S. Carolina
Chas Second's time was tax voted in Carolina
                        360

Hemp seed cd/ be brought here, mulberry does well in our
                                                    climate
When people of Europe have been insidiously deprived
                                          of their liberties
which wd/ render jurors mere ostentation and pageantry
green tea, from Holland I hope, but dont know,
...recovered at Braintree, pruned by me, grown remarkably
pines better for lopping
STOOD by the people much longer than they wd/ stand
                                          by themselves.
1771 make potash and raise a great number of colts
which they send to the West Indies for rum
Splendours of Hartford and Middletown
just as we got there
              Indian pudding pork greens on the table
One party for wealth and power
                            at expense
                            of the liberty of their country
wars, carnage, confusion
not interested in their servitude
          I am, for all I can see, left quite alone
                              13th, Thursday
landlady great grand daughter of Governor Endicott
new light, continually canting...
said Indian preacher: Adam! Adam when you knew
              it wd/ make good cider!
Mrs Rops, fine woman
              very pretty and very genteel
Tells old stories of witchcraft, paper money and
              Governor Belcher's administration
Always convinced that the liberties of the country
had more to fear from one man (Hutchinson)
              than from all other men whatsoever
              which have always freely and decently uttered
Rich seldom remarkable for modesty, ingenuity or humanity

' Is mere impertinence a contempt? ' asked Mr Otis
I said there was no more justice left in Britain than hell
Hutchinson is etc.
Moore's Reports, for the book was borrowed; its owner
a buyer, not a reader of books
             for it had been Mr Gridley's
N/Y/ state has done partially
22; Monday (this was 1773)
                    Hutchinson's letters received
Oliver, Moffat, Paxton and Rome
             for 1767, '8, '9
avaricious, ambitious, vindictive
these were the letters that Franklin got hold of
Bone of our bone, educated among us,
serpent and deputy serpent
                    that Sir John Temple procured them
                    God knows how or from whom
Gentle rain last night and this morning
                    Hutchinson sucking up to George IIIrd.
falsehood in Rome's letters quite flagrant
Col. Haworth
             attracted no attention until
             he discovered his antipathy to a cat
                         Three cargoes Bohea
were emptied, this is but an attack upon property
I apprehend it was necessary, absolute, indispensable
             irregular recourse to original power
             IMpeachment by House before Council
said shd/ be glad if constitution cd/ carry on
             without recourse to higher powers unwritten...
             Says Gridley: You keep very late hours!

                                        End of this Canto.

LXV

JURORS refuse to take oath
    saying: while Chief Justice of this Court stands
                                    impeached.
    Moses Gill has made many justices by lending money.
        A statue of H.M. (His Majesty)
very large
on horseback
solid lead gilded with gold
on an high marble pedestal
We then walked up Broadway
        magnificent building, cost 20,000 pounds
                                    N.Y. currency
Ship
of 800 tons burden lest leveling spirit of New England
should propagate itself in New York
        whole charge of the Province
between 5 and 6 thousand pounds N. York money
For Massachusetts about 12 thousand lawful
as wd/ equal about 16,000 of N. York
Advised him to publish
from Hakluyt the voyage of J. Cabot,
                                    Hudibras
tavern, Princeton, sing as badly as the presbyterians of
                                    N. York
sez congress shd/ raise money and
        employ men to write in the newspapers (in England)
Washington would raise one thousand men
            at his own expense
and march for release of Boston
            not a Virginian
            but an American Patrick Henry
tenants in capite, Galloway well aware that my arguments

tend to the independency of the colonies
bound by no laws made by Parliament
                    since our ancestors came here
Bill of Rights
                    wished to hear in Congress at large
law of natr/ Brit. constitution
          trade of Empire cd/ be under parliament
Mr Rutledge of S. Carolina said:
                    ' Adams,
We must agree upon   something.'
               Turtle and everything else
a dutchified English prayer
          17th of September:
America will support Massachusetts
          ' that nation
new avows bribery to be part of her system '
Mr Henry, American legislature
               After December 1st no molasses
coffee pimento from Domenica
          fine bowling green and fine turtle, madeira
Congress nibbling and quibbling as usual
               took departure in very great rain from
the happy, the peaceful, the elegant
                    Philadelphy
2 young ladies to sing us the new liberty song
          readiness to be shot / versus / taxes
judgement gives way to fears 1/3rd of humanity
IMbecility of 2nd petition Mr Hancock had ambition
Mr Adams (that is Saml) said nothing, appeared deeply
                                        to consider...
but seconded my motion in Congress
Mr Washington seated near by the door
scuttled into the book room with modesty
                    Dickenson

past meridian, avarice growing on him

                   alum   (p. 432)

Suppose yr/ ladyship has been in the twitters

                            I

oated at the Red Lion

6 sets of works in one building, hemp mill, oil mill, and
a mill to grind bark for tanners, at Bethelehem, a fuller's
mill both for cloth and leather, dye-house, a sharing house
        they raise a great deal of madder
Committee to purchase woollen goods for the Army
              Sept. 1775, to 5000 L/ sterling
delegates of Pennsylvania produced no account of the powder
           100 tons of powder was wanted
Cushing said: I move we take into consideration
        a means of keeping up the army in winter.
Ammunition can not be had unless we open out ports
Can't stand war without trade
tobacco to France and Spain. Rutledge said:

                         Take men from
        agriculture and put 'em in factories
Agriculture and manufacturies
        can not be lost but trade is precarious.
       ' Americans are their own carriers now
Imperative to open out ports,' said Mr Zubly
Provisions to Spain for money
        and cash sent to England for powder
' We are between hawk and buzzard ' said Livingston
pleased that New Jersey raise two battalions
        of eight companies each
68 privates, capn, lieutenant, ensign, 4 sargeants 4 corporals
Who to appoint officers for their artillery
Personal friends have not been suitable
rather Washington's word than any convention's
Trade or no trade
        powder, appointment of officers

How trade? by whose carriage? farms, manufacturies
hitherto as if money
   was province's not of the continent
John Adams as seen by John Adams, squabbles in congress
to shut or not shut customs houses
   ' Everything we want for war is powder and shot '
        said Mr Zubly
2ndly arms and munitions
3rdly that we must have money
We must keep up the notion that this paper is good
     for something (commerciabili?)
Mississippi scheme in France
South Seas in England
   were writ for our learning
    A navy! Can we have one? without trade?
Can we maintain war without it?
Can we get information?
   Spaniards too lazy to come here for goods
   To trade with England or foreigners?
If so, who does the carrying? They to us, we to them?
I speak from principle, it has been said we associate
         in terrorem
Damn well right, Mr Zubly.
Deane wd/ have traders prohibited importing unnecessary...
and export of all livestock save horses
Guadaloupe, Martinique will supply powder against tobacco
each colony shd/ carry this trade, not individuals
       Chase. Oct 20. 1775
Jay says: more from individual enterprise
   than from lukewarmness of assemblies
want french woollens dutch worsteds
     german steel
Wythe says: better open our trade altogether
Why shdn't America have a navy? We abound in firs, iron ore,
         tar

the Romans suddenly built one against Carthage
        RESOLVED that two vessels be fitted.
6th April: to remove all restrictions on trade
oblige Britain to keep up a navy
        that will cost her twice what she takes from us.
        FAECE Romuli non Platonis republica!
' America' (Wythe) will hardly live without trade
        Am for giving letters of marque
and for powder, to make treaties with us, Why
        call ourselves dutiful subjects?
Wd/ France have listened to Bristol or Liverpool?
Resolved: a committee to draft confederation.
To provide flax, hemp, wool and cotton
        in each colony of society for furtherance
of agriculture, arts, manufactures
and correspondence between these societies
        that natural advantages be not neglected
        ducks and sail cloth
Is it in the interest of France to stand neuter?
Resentment a duty, a man's person, property, liberty
        not safe without it
Hooper of North Carolina said: I wish to see a day
        when slaves are not necessary
Lee, Sherman and Gadsden on my side
Rush, Franklin, Bayard and Mifflin putt us wise to
        the rumours against us
' adventurers, bankrupt attourneys
        from Massachusetts
' dependent on popularity.' So prompt fair and explicit.
' Mr Jefferson, you can write ten times better than I can '
Cut about 1/4th and some of the best of it
I have often wondered that J's first draft has not
                    been published
suppose the reason is the vehement philippic against
                    negro slavery '

thus Adams, 40 years later.
To contract for importation of gun powder
or if cannot, then for salt peter and sulphur
        enough to make 500 tons
40 brass field pieces (6 pounders) 10,000 stand arms
June 12th. J. Adams head of the Board of War
        till Nov. eleventh '77
had conversed much with gentlemen
        who conduct our cod and whale fisheries
Our seamen if once let loose on the ocean...
They said: wd/ ruin the character of our seamen etc.
' make 'em mercenary and bent wholly on plundah '
' In any character yr/ Lordship please *except*
        that of a British subject '
        (John to Lord Howe in parley)
88 battalions, September,
dash had already formed lucrative connections in Paris
        by Mr D (Deane's) recommendations
        particularly with Ray de Chaumont
who was shipping stuff to sell on commission
Always have been and still are spies in America (1804)
and I considered the
        fisheries.
To Capn Sam Tucker commanding the Boston:
        (wind high and seas very rough)
You are to afford him every accommodation in yr/ power
and consult him as to what port you shall endeavour to get to.
        W. Vernon
        J. Warren
        Navy Board, Eastern Department
Sunday 15th came under sail before breakfast
        hauled my wind to southward
        found they did chase me
        Log book, Sl. Tucker 19 Feb
after running 3 hours to westward

368

I then hove in the stays
she continued to chase us
all day, but I rather gain on her.
Smoke, smell of sea coal, of stagnant and putrid water
increase the qualminess but do not occasion it
in calm with our guns out
Tucker said his orders were to take me to France
and any prizes that might fall in his way
At night the wind increased to a hurrycane
North, East by North, then North West
ane blasterend bubb gan in the foresail ding
rollings
agonies, the sailors' their countenances language be-haviour
no man upon his legs nothing in place chests casks bottles
etcetera
no place no person dry
by lightning
at mainmast and topmast
wounded 23 men
Log Book of Saml Tucker
continually one thing after another giving way
lay by under main sail
down topgallant yards
4. P.M. carried away slings chains and the mizzen
4 A.M. made sail and began to
repair the rigging
Mr Johnnie's behaviour gave satisfaction (i.e. young
J. Q. Adams
inexpressible inconvenience of having so little
space between decks nothing but
dread of pistol to keep men in quarters in action
ship not properly furnished with glasses
which wd/ save their expense in a thousand ways
INattention in navy as in the army
INattention to health of the sailors

the practice of profane swearing and cursing
1st March: mainmast found sprung in two places
sea, clouds, sea, everything damp, sea,
       clouds, fair sun, 9 knots and no noise
What the state of finances, stocks and their army? So that
the ball passed directly over my head. Tucker in old age said
that J. A. was out with a musket like any damn common
                        marine
       ' Ordered him; but there he wuz out agin
I sez: Me orders, sir, are to git yew to EUrope '
Was a letter of marque, shot through our mizzen yard
we upon this turned our broadside which
the instant she saw, she struck. The Martha, worth 80,000
                    pund sterling
Capn McIntosh much a gentleman
    5 weeks after our embarcation
' Mr McIntosh of North Britain
     very decided against America in the
contest. His passions enkindle '
Numbers of small birds from the shore
instant they light on a ship
     drop asleep from exhaustion
     Oleron, famous for sea laws
at least I take it this is the place
along side with hakes, skates and gurnards
     river very beautiful on both sides
     horses, oxen, great flocks, husbandmen ploughing
     women a half dozen in droves with their hoes
     churches, convents, gentlemen's seats
                 very magnificent.
From perils of the sea, intrigues, business wangles
     rural improvements are brought down to the water's
                   edge
muddy water, grand seats, beautiful groves
a number of vessels in the river land, cattle, horses after

so long a journey
      at Bordeaux, at Blaye
                      de lonh
First dish was a fine french soup then boiled meat
lights of calf one way and liver another
bread very fine and fine salad the
raisins are most delicious
none of us understood french none of them english
on quarter deck I was struck with the hens
           capons cocks in their coops
Saluted a small town called Blaye
          with the INdependent salute
           i.e. 13 for the colonies
All the gentlemen agreed Dr Franklin
        had been rec'd by the King with great pomp
        and a treaty concluded
there are 4 sorts: Château Margaux, Haute Brion, Lafitte
                    and Latour
fish and bean salad, claret, champagne
to see the new comédie and, after, the opera
        dancing very cheerful (our
American theatre not then even in contemplation)
Trompette, work of Vauban
Banished in Louis XVth's time for working with Malesherbes
I concluded there was a form of sincerity in it
        decorated with compliments
        saw ' Les deux avares '.
Tucker tho' not polished
        was an energetic and successful commander
Lights in the garden and an Inscription

GOD SAVE LIBERTY THE CONGRESS AND ADAMS

Their eagerness to sell a knife was as great as that
of some persons I have seen to get offices
fields of grass, vineyards, castles
yet every place swarms with beggars
Rue Richelieu, Hôtel de Valois
then Basse Cour, had been Hôtel Valentinois
Money in Mr Schweighauser's hands
signed; Franklin
Lee
Adams
To J. Williams:
abstain from further expenditure
and close your accounts
Mr Beaumarchais, another of Mr Deane's friends.
Dined that day with Madame Helvetius
to the Long Champ where all carriages of Paris were paraded
As descent modest and regular
a family as ever I saw in France
Among whom was M. Condorcet his face white as a sheet
of paper
Franklin, Deane, Bancroft are friends
never was before I came here
a letter book
a minute book
an account book
Mr Deane lived expensively. Dr Franklin
Great wit, great humourist, great politician, the Lees
are all virtuous men, If
there had been letters, minutes, accounts, Mr Lee
had not seen them
In first box near the celebrated Voltaire
Mme la Duchesse d'Agen a 5 ou 6 enfants
contre la coutume du pays
des Noailles 18 million louis a year from the crown
number of persons with their eyes fixed on our little treasury

You wrote that you wd/ send the invoices *if* we thought
                                                necessary
The King's bed chamber where he was dressing
        one putting on his sword, one his coat
        I accordingly wrote to Sam Adams:
Enormous
sums have been expended, no book of
accounts, no documents wherefrom
able to learn what has been rec'd in America
Wrong in having three commissioners one is enough
in leaving salaries at uncertainty
in mingling public minister and commercial agent
Mr Deane never succeeded in throwing much light on
his mode of doing business in France.
Many other qualities I cd/ not distinguish from virtues
His Majesty ate like a King, solid beef
        and other things in proportion
Offer to make 200 peers (*in* America)
        To the dwelling of Mme du Barry
        who sent to invite us
Turgot, Condillac, Mme Helvetius
M. Genet's son went with me and my son to the menagerie
        Barbier de Séville at the Comédie (Nantes)
        acting indifferent.
        Much conversation
about the electrical eel.
        His voice (P. Jones's)
is still, and soft, and small
Laws of the Visigoths and Justinian still in use in Galicia
13 mules 2 muletiers arriving Corunna at 7
pork of this country excellent and delicious
        also bacon, Chief Justice informs me that much of it
is fattened on chestnuts and upon indian corn
other pork is they say fattened on vipers
        possible imports to Spain:

grain of all sorts pitch turpentine timber,
salt fish, spermaceti and rice.
Tobacco they have from their colonies
                              as also indigo
of the King's tobacco they take 10 millions weight per annum
Saw ladies take chocolate in Spanish fashion
                    dined on board la Belle Poule
Galicia, no floor but ground trodden to mire by
                    men hogs horses and mules
no chimney 1/2 way as you ascend to the chamber
was a stage covered with straw
                    on which lay a fattening hog
above, corn was hung on sticks and on slit work
in one corner a bin full of rape seed or culzar
in the other a bin full of oats
          among which slept better than since my arrival
                                        in Spain
In general the mountains covered with furze
scarce an elm oak or other tree
O'Brien afterward sent me a minced pie and a meat pie
at St James Campostella and 2 bottles of Frontenac wine
nothing rich but the churches, nothing fat but the clergy
NO symptoms of commerce or even of internal traffic
Between Galice and Leon 1780
all of colour made of black sheep's wool undyed
          the river Valcaire between two rows of mountains
          not a decent house since Corunna
4. Tuesday, clean bed, no fleas for the first time in Spain
                              at Astorga
largest turnips I ever saw
Mauregato women, as fine as squaws and a great deal
                                        more nasty
Hoy mismo han llegado
          a esta plaza el Caballero
                    Juan Adams miembro
374

etc/ los Ingleses
                    evacuando Rhode Island
                         los Americanos tomaron...
                         Gazette de Madrid, 24th of December
Great flocks of sheep and cattle
                         Asturias mountains
river runs also down into Portugal
                    a dance they call the fandango
                         Tuesday 11th at Burgos
we go along sneezing and coughing
my patience never nearer exhausted
                         33 religious houses in Burgos
In the last house in Spain we found one chimney
First since that in the French consul's, Corunna.
River Charent runs by it
Vergennes might suppose that I in naiveté
                    wd/ send him my instructions
My determination to insist on the fisheries
(in fact John saved cod to Baastun)
I was not clear that I suspected his motives
U.S. at liberty to negotiate commerce, as peace
they intended to keep us in stew with England
for as long as possible after the peace, as was EFfected
for eleven years until Jay
               sacrificed his popularity and Washington's was
                                        diminished
Those who wish to investigate WHOM in congress
(leaving us no doubt Vergennes was a twister)
with my two sons to Amsterdam
               rye barley oats beans
hemp grain clover lucern and sainfoin
and the pavements are good, vines cattle sheep everything
                                        plentiful
such wheat crops never saw elsewhere
               church music Italian style

a tapestry: number of jews stabbing the wafer
         blood gushing from it
Brussels stone same as Braintree North Common
...excellent character, emperor did not like him
intermixture houses trees ships canals very startling
         neatness remarkable
         Van der Capellen tot de Pol
fears holders of English funds will etc/
tried to end some feudal burdens about here
         and got himself censured
         O.K., as was Van Berckel
Don Joas Tholomeno: Independence of America is assured
                        Sept. 14th '82
Mirabel (Sardegna) only why dont they acknowledge it?
5 copies, English and Dutch side by side,
said wd/ be signed next week.
                    aetat 46
foreign ministers all herd together
Rheingrave, de Salm, Colonel Bentinck
Prussian minister will talk of astronomy natural
history news sieges but very reserved upon politics
              VERJARING
van den veldslag by Lexington
Eerste Memoire dan den Heer Adams
         INDRUK of de Hollandsche Natie
Deputies of Holland and Zeeland
we signed etc/ treaty of commerce
         8 Oct '82
firmness heaven has given you
commerce of Bruge, Ostend grown with our revolution
         vingt à vingtcinq navires dans le bassin
                    (Count Sarsfield)
magazins de la ville sont remplis,
journée d'un homme 15 s/ et nourri.
        Œuvre de M. le Duc de Vauguyon

to sign one's name 16,000 times after dinner
Mr Vischer who was more open than I had known him
said the Stadtholder was *le plus grand t....de ce pays-ci*
entêté comme une she mule
Rode to Valenciennes and found our axletree broken
again, walks, rose gardens, waterspouts, fish ponds
carp will assemble in an huddle before you
sticking their mouths out of water
Mlle de Bourbon her hair uncombed
        came out by the round house
with it hanging over her shoulders, in white
        Thus France taxes Europe
great part of court policy to
        provide national influence over *la mode*
as an occasion of commerce Jay is des Petits Augustins
Franklin intrigues manoeuvres insinuates
        I will make a good peace or no peace
" shall enjoy right to fish unmolested
        on banks and in Gulf of St Lawrence
        or wherever else heretofore to
        dry cure in Nova Scotia
        Cape Sable and on any unsettled bays "
compliments conversation on vapors and exhalations from
                          Tartary
For my part thought that Americans
Had been embroiled in European wars long enough
                easy to see that
France and England wd/ try to embroil us OBvious
that all powers of Europe will be continually at manoeuvre
to work us into their real or imaginary balances
        of power; J. A. 1782 FISHERIES
our natural right, garters stars keys titles ribbons
objects of these men of high life
           France wd/ never
send that money (send any of it) to England

whereas we getting money from Portugal
        must spend it in London, considered
their attack on me an attack on the fisheries.
    ' If I have not ' sez I ' been mistaken
in the policy of France from my first observation
of it to this hour, they have been as averse to
other powers acknowledging our independence
                        as you have been.'
                                        ' GOD! '

sez he (Oswald) ' Now I see it.
I will write home at once on this subject '
            To exempt fishermen husbandmen merchants
            as much as possible from evils of future wars
Dr Franklin (a nice lesson any how)
                        The King
is like Mr Hancock
        Nor where who sows the corn by corn is fed
(Lady Lucan's verses on Ireland)
            The Duke de la Rochefoucauld
made me a visit
(Lady Lucan's verses on Ireland)
made me a visit
            and desired me to explain to him some
passages in the Connecticut constitution
            (at which point Mr Eliot left us)
Mr Vaughn said etc/ that he *saw*
' But ' sez he ' you can not blame us endeavouring
to carry this point to market
            and get something by it '
            (which seems fairly English)
To get Billy (Franklin) made minister here
        and the Doctor to London
Mlle Bourbon is grown very fat, Chatham so dampened the
        zeal of Sardegna
        BLUSH, oh ye records!

congress has double XX'd me
How will they wash it? I
dined with M. Malesherbes uncle of Luzerne
          tiers état contains 30 classes
Dined at Passy; S' il règne un faux savoir
which inflexibility has been called vanity Policy
of frog court to lay stumbling block
                    between England and America
None English have come, apprized, here
                    of where was the danger
Peace is made. Negotiations all passed before I hear
                    of Livingston's letter of Jan '82
such is Doc Franklin (May 3rd 1783)
                    a composed man
plain Englishman Duke and Ambassador Manchester.
I told Hartley their policy with Holland was wrong all wrong
if they backed the Stadtholder the Emperor and French wd/
back the republicans and all Europe enkindle
          England
had now stronger reason to cultivate Holland
and not push up the Bourbon
                    expedient that an intercourse
and commerce be opened, laws of Gt Britain on
plantation trade contrived solely to benefit Britain
          said Dutch vessels had gone to America
          loaded with linens, duck, sailcloth etc
          copper corrodes ships' iron
most agreeable day I ever spent at Versailles
                              (17 May '83)
Sardinian ambassador said it was curious
          to remark on the progress of commerce
          furs from Hudson Bay Company
          sent to London were sent to Siberia

379

LXVI

COULD not let us bring their sugar to Europe
wd/ lessen the number of French and of Spanish
seamen
Generally rode twice a day till made master
of this curious forest (Bois de Boulogne)
view of Issy and the castle of Meudon
game is not very plentiful. Dined at Amiens
put up at Abbeville. Dover view. Mr Johnson
Gt Tower Hill who informs me
that a vessel with one thousand hogshead of tobacco
is passed by in the Channel from Congress
to Messrs Willincks 27 Oct '83
Hague June 22, '84
So there is no drop not American in me
Aye we have noticed that said the Ambassador
Sends to Morocco no marine stores
sends 'em *glaces* and other things of rich value
Said Lord Carmathen wd/ present me
but that I shd/ do business with Mr Pitt very often
Posts not surrendered
are Presq'isle, Sandusky etc/ Detroit Michilimakinac
St Joseph St Mary's.
daughter married less prudently
and they were thinking of sending her to America
Presented
Mr Hamilton to the Queen at the drawing room
Mr Jefferson
and I went in a post chaise
Woburn Farm, Stowe, Stratford
Stourbridge, Woodstock, High Wycombe and back to
Grosvenor Sq
A national debt of
274 million stg/

accumulated by jobs contracts salaries pensions in
the course of a century
                    might easily produce all this magnificence
Pope's pavilion and Thompson's seat made the excursion
                                                            poetic
Shenstone's the most rural of all
19th, Wednesday, anniversary of the battle of Lexington
                    and of my reception in Holland
which latter is considered of no importance
                    to view the seat of the banker Child
three houses, in fact, round a square
blowing roses, ripe strawberries plums cherries etc
deer sheep wood-doves guinea-hens peacocks etc
Dr Grey speaks very lightly of Buffon
                    Mr H. prefers the architecture of this house because it
                    reminds him of Palladio
windows with mahogany columns
there are two stoves but at neither of them
could a student be comfortable in cold weather

July 18th, yesterday, moved all the grass in Stony Hill field
this day my new barn was raised
                    their songs never more various than this morning
Corn by two sorts of worm
                    Hessian fly menaces wheat
Where T. has been trimming red cedars
with team of 5 cattle brought back 22 cedars
Otis full of election: Henry, Jefferson, Burr
T. cutting trees and leaves of white oaks
To barley and black grass at the beach
said one thing wd/ make Rhode Island unanimous
—meaning funding—
                    they wanted Hamilton for vice president
                    I said nothing.
WHERETOWARD THE ARGUMENTS HAD BEEN
as renouncing the transactions of Runing Mede?

381

Prince of Orange, King William by the people
that their rights be inviolable
which drove out James Second...IS still active.
Nothing less than this seems to have been meditated for us
by somebody or other in Britain
              reprinted by Thos. Hollis
              seventeen sixty-five
OB PECUNIAE SCARSITATEM
this act, the Stamp Act, wd/ drain cash out of the country
and is, further, UNconstitutional
              yr/ humanity counterfeit
              yr/ liberty cankered with simulation
Earl Clarendon to Bill Pym in the Baastun Gazette
              Jan 17th 1 7 6 8
Danegeld emptied the land of all coin
what are powers of these new admiralty courts in America
          per pares et legem terrae
          is there any grand jury to bring an indictment
          to find presentments
                    any *petit* for fact
IS this trial *per legem terrae*
or by Institutes Digests Roman?
Become attentive to their liberties
counties, towns, private clubs and sodalities
most accurate judgement
          about the real constitution
which is not of wind and weather
          what is said there
is rather a character
          than a true

 ching
ming

definition. It is a just observation.

Jury answers questions of fact
thus guarding the subject...
pompous rituals theatrical ceremonies
                    so successfully used to
delude to terrify men out of virtue and liberty
Elizabeth tried, James First put out Goodwin
                    and the Commons reversed it
                    (London Chronicle)
By this course, said one member, free election is taken away
common rights our ancestors have left us
By this course, said another, the Chancellor
could call a parliament of only such as he please
                    After repeal of American Stamp Act
we have mortification to see one Act of Parliament after
                                        another,
money collecting from us continually without our consent
by an authority
            in the constitution of which we have no share
and see the little coin that remained among us
transmitted to distance
                    with no hope of return
RESOLUTION to maintain duty and loyalty to our sovreign
and to Parliament as legislative in all cases of necessity
                    to preserve the Empire as a whole
                    17 June, 1768
                    Instructions to Braintree's representatives
We mean by 6th Anne chap. xxxvii section 9
IT IS ENACTED
                    no mariner
be retained on any privateer ship or vessel
in any part of America... be impressed on any ship of
Her Majesty's any time after St Valentine's day 1707
                    on pain of L 20. per man
Small field pieces happened, said Governor Hutchinson,
to point at the door of the Court House

To the Hnbl James Otis and Thos Cushing Esquires
Mr Sam Adams and John Hancock Esquire
; ; ; ; . . . . . demands yr/ fortitude virtue and wisdom
to remove anything that may appear to awe or intimidate
late attack flagrant and formal
on the constitution itself
and the immunities of our charters
Unnecessary to repeat our known sentiments on the revenue
     this 41st section repeals MAGNA
     CHARTA the 29th chapter
as follows the words: NO FREEMAN...to... by his peers
          and the law of the land
Whereon said Lord Coke, speaking of Empson and Dudley,
the end of these two oppressors
shd/ deter others from committing the like
that they bring not in absolute and partial trials by direction
...by every legal measure, sirs, we recommend you...
Natural tendency of the legal profession to side with authority
freeholders and other inhabitants (Cambridge 21 Dec. '72
     Constitutional
means for redress...natural rights...charter right
money extorted from us, appropriated to the augmentation of
burdens upon us
    independent of grants of our commons.
    attest
      Andrew Boardman town clerk
Judges salaries shd/ be independent both of the king
          and of the people
great danger if commission hang upon either
a civil commission gives no new powers
     tyranny in them to assume it
common lay of England, BIRTHRIGHT of every man here
         and at home
' not look on my self as in state of nature

and is pity that other man shd/ '

Wm/ Brattle

It is the wish of almost all good men, replied Adams
that what Brattle states were good law.
But from Edward First's time to the present letters patent
are otherwise worded

        sic: *beneplacitu nostro.*

           Ad regis nutum duratura

                    says Fortescue

                    chancellor

will it be shown that by ' judges ' Genl Brattle
means barons of Exchequer?
custos rotolorum and clerk of the peace
were created by statute not erected by common law
Sir Edward Coke, who being in King's displeasure,
was removed from his place by writ of the King
reciting that whereas etc///...appointed to desist from...
timid jurors and judges who held during pleasure
never failed to second the views of the Crown
he, James Second, was obliged before he brought Hales' case
to displace 4 of his judges
By concerts between King James and Sir Edward...
his coachman was employed to bring action...
Jones had the integrity to tell the King to his face
that he might make 12 judges but wd/ scarce find 12 lawyers
of his opinion.
' Wishing Genl Brattle success in his researches '

J. Adams

By another clause (in our Charter)
that the great and general court or assembly

                    shd/ have power

to erect judicatories courts of record
and other courts

        to determine pleas processes plaints actions etc/
whereby a law (2 William III) have established etc/

and in Edward IV this Beauchamps commission
was, for the uncertainty, VOID
By letters patent and under great seal
in all shires, counties palatine and in Wales
and any other dominions

LXVII

WHEREOF memory of man runneth not to the
contrary
Dome Book, Ina, Offa and Aethelbert, folcright
for a thousand years
and I must add that it appears to me extraordinary that a
gentleman educated under the great Gamaliel, Mr Read, shd/
adduce the single dictum of a counsel at bar uttered *arguendo*,
as an ornament to his discourse, not pertinent to his argument,
as if this settled something
' by the great sages of law formerly and more latterly ';
having behind it no colour or pretence of other authority.
Aula regum, in Norman times split into 4 courts,
the summus justiciarius was laid by, lest he get into
the throne as had Capet. Regalia principis (Saxon)
whence most of the prerogatives of the Crown are derived
in those ages
judiciary a mere deputy of the King
in whose presence his (the judge's) authority ceased
cum delegans revocarit (Bracton)
Baastun Gazette '73

clear
as to definitions
CHING
But he (Brattle) has been extremely unfortunate in having
Bracton, Fortescue, Coke, Foster, Hume, Rapin and Rushworth
directly against him
the materials are at the service of the public
I leave them to jewelers and lapidaries to refine
to fabricate and to polish.
de Burgh in a vain hope of perpetuating his power...
Mr Shirley in 1754 confided to Dr Franklin a secret
that is a scheme for taxing the colonies by act of Parliament

WHERETO Ben said: nuts
            in a very accurate manner.
'Gevernors' sez he 'whose object is in general to make
                                    fortunes'
Shirley a skunk, Pownall a gentleman honest,
Bernard skilled enough in the law to do mischief
and thus the total government was to be rendered wholly
independent of the people
            and the cream to go into their salaries
            (governor's, lieutenant's and judges')
                        (signed) *Novanglus*
This preposterous 'improvement' of Mr Grenville's
            has wellnigh ruin'd the whole
OBSTA PRINCIPIIS
            the army is here merely a publick nuisance
Does the sincere writer really believe that the design
of imposing other taxes has been laid aside by the ministry
            and of the new-modelling of the government?
they had now the governor's salary out of the revenue
and a number of pensions and places   I wish Massachusetts
knew what a democracy is, what a republic
Irritat mulcet et falsis terroribus implet
colonization is at common law a *casus omissus*
no such title is known in that law
no known punishment at common law even for treasons
committed out of the realm
            till Hen. VIIIth
to catch Cardinal Pole i.e. statute.
Most fanatical that ever got into human pericranium
that he had a right to all lands his subjects cd/ find, and
even that infers no right in Parliament...or
feudal, had right of contract (on that tack)
feudal king had no more right to absolute over Englishmen
out of the realm than in Britain
In fact the oily writer now leaps over law
                        388

now over fact now over charters and contracts
there is no fundamental law that makes a king of England
absolute anywhere except it be in conquered countries,
and an attempt forfeits his right even to the limited crown
for 150 years taxed themselves
     and governed their internal concerns
Parliament governed their trade
     Wales was in some things an analogy
held of the crown but not parcel
     Edwardus Deo Gratia Angliae
Dom. Hib. et Dux Aquitaniae terram Walliae cum incolis suis
in nostrae proprietatis dominium
now partly to divert his subjects from the murder of Becket
lays pretence
     that the Irish had sold some English as slaves
Adrian an Englishman by birth being pontiff
very clearly convinced of his own right to dispose of
kingdoms and empires and by power of pence of Peter
to establish an Empire of the World
that Henry's demand upon Ireland proceeded from pious
                     motives
seeds of gospel etcetera fructify for Eire's eternal salvation
and oblige every house to pay yearly one penny to Rome
Macmorral the raper and Rourke of Meath as our junto
and as to how Irish in Henry the Vth's time were let into
                    England
' shall put in surety for their good abearing ',
   contract called Poyning's law,
consent of the Irish Nation and an act in their parliament
(Poyning's) EDGARDUS ANGLORUM BASILEUS
insularum oceani imperator et dominus gratiam ago
Deo omnip. qui meum imperium
sic ampliavit et explicavit super regnum patrum meorum
concessit propitia divinitatis...
Hibernia habet parliamentum (vide Sir J. Pilkington's case)

majesty near the seventy, amiable successor
educated under care of my nearest friends...
militant spirit, and the nation under a very large debt.
How shall we manage it? these noblemen and ignoblemen
words of Lord Mansfield and his admirer (governor
                                          Hutchinson)
AMERICAN governments never were erected by parliament
these *regalia* and jurisdictions not given by parliament
a little knowledge of the subject will do us no harm
Chester a palatine county and had *jure regalia*
Great seal did not run into Chester
for remedy 3 knights of shire
2 burgesses of the city established
Chester in crown and realm exempt from authority
how quickly granted representation when asked it
' In Durham Queen's writ hath not run '
25 Charles II be represented by knights and by burgesses
true our oily opponent
                has here more zeal than knowing
Nation was not polite enough
to have introduced any such phrase or idea into our charter
not one farthing ever was voted
or given by King or his Parliament.
Style royal? as king over France? Ireland? Scotland or
    England?
seals, leagues, coin are prerogative absolute
seals, leagues, coin are prerogative absolute
to the king without parliament
not restrained to any assent of the people
homage, fealty are to the person
                can not be to body politic
the king might have commanded them to return but he did not
                In the Boston Gazette 17th April
Hostilities at Lexington commenced on the 19th of April
several other papers were written and sent to the printer

and probably lost amid that confusion
             (note to the 1819 edition of NOVANGLUS)
PLAN OF GOVERNMENT
             ('76 or '75 from Philadelphy)
to R. H. Lee of Virginia
             on sudden emergency...
legislative, executive and judicial...Printer John **Dunlap**
as likewise to Mr Wythe cf Virginia: some forms are **better**
than others...happiness of society is their aim
KUNG Zoroaster Socrates and Mahomet
' not to mention other authorities really sacred '
fear renders men stupid and miserable...
             honour is a mere fragment of **virtue**, yet sacred...
foundation of every government in some **principle**
or passion of the people
             ma che si sente dicho
Locke Milton Nedham Neville Burnet and Hoadly
empire of laws not of men
...Be in miniature a portrait of the people at large...
             (the representative body)
...of learning and experience of the laws, exemplary morals
great patience calmness attention
             not dependent on any body of men:
judges, Executive....
secrecy and dispatch...whence
a great assembly can not execute, it is too clumsy.
The colonies under such triple government wd/ be
Unconquerable by all the monarchs of Europe
few of the human race have had opportunity like this
to make election of government, more than of air, soil or
                                             climate
When before have 3 million people had option
of the total form of their government?
             (Pat Henry, thus continuing:)
I put up with the Declaration for unanimity's sake

it is not pointed as I wd/ make it
Colonel Nelson is carrying our resolution...
lest the enemy be before us in Paris
confederacy must precede open alliance
the arguments that delegate Bracton favours
        are weak shallow evasive
wd/ to God you and Sam Adams
        were here in Virginia
if all yr/ features can not be kept here
        at least we will keep some family likeness
will you and S. A. now and then write.

Printed by John Taylor of Caroline in 1814
To John Penn '76 from J. Adams:
no more agreeable employment
than the study of the best kind of government
to determine form you must determine the end
        (that is purpose)
single assembly is liable to all the vices follies and frailties
...prerogatives, badges of slavery...
        (similarly to Jonathan Sergeant, he
requiring explicit advice as to taking up powers of government)
Fixed laws of their own making
equitable mode of making the laws
        impartial and of apt execution.
Freeholders of an estate of 3 L/ per annum
or any estate to the value of 60 pounds.
Duty of legislators and magistrates
        to cherish the interest of literature...
and principles of... good humour...
        (Constitution of Massachusetts)
I was apprehensive in particular that
' natural history ' and ' good humour ' wd/ be struck out,
        Wrote John 34 years later
It is significant wrote Chawles Fwancis that persons

who have since been erected have not...etc....
been greatly literate
          and no public man down until 1850
          expressed doubts of the *immaculate*
          nature of govvymint by the
                              majority.
' Either content with the U. S. constitutions
or too timid to speculate on constitutions at large '
representatives of the people...susceptible to improvement
                              (question?)
...read Thucydides without horror?
                    words lost their significance
...Mr Hume has collected massacres from D. Siculus
                    most polished years of Greece
Ephesus three forty killed
Cyrenians 500 nobles
Phaebidas banished 300 Boeotians
in Philiasia they killed 300 people
at Ægesta, 40,000 men women and children
          killed for their money
take away armies, the nobles will overturn every monarch
                              in Europe
          and set up aristocracies
No interviews with the gods by those on this service
                    Grosvenor Sq. 1787
but as architects consulting Vitruvius and Palladio
the young gents of literature in America
          to this kind of enquiry.
...doubted by Tacitus though he admits the theory is a
                              good one
facilius laudari quam invenire
          vel haud diuturna
optime modice confusa, said Cicero.
                    ...
concors tamen efficitur...civitas consensu

393

ubi justitia non est, nec jus potest esse.
San Marino, the founder, a Dalmatian by birth
                    and by trade a mason....
Whole history of Geneva:
                the people have given up all balances
betraying their own rights and those of the magistrates
into the hands of a few prominent families...
                nobles to trade in a general way
to carry on velvet, silk and cloth manufacturies
Venice at first democratical...
Anafeste's real merit. 5 massacred, 5 blinded and exiled
9 deposed, one killed in a foreign war
thus 20 of 50 doges, plus 5 abdications
before they thought of limiting powers
and another 200 years before planning a government
an aristocracy is always more cunning
than an assembly of the people collectively
armies given to kings by the people
                to keep down the nobles
whereon nobles depend from the crown
and the people are still under their domination
2 thousand 5 hundred nobles in Venice
the stadtholder from father to son
who after Lolme need write of regal republics?
recent instance
            the Ukraine insurrection
only in Neuchâtel
                ἄρχειν και ἄρχεσθαι
as in antient Rhodes, probably in three branches
            jura ordo...aequitas leges...
stadtholder, avoyer, alcalde, capitaneo?? if Mons Turgot
            has made any discovery...
orders of officers, not of men in America
no distinct separation of legislative, executive and judicial
            heretofore save in England.

LXVIII

THE philosophers say: one, the few, the many.
  Regis optimatium populique
  as Lycurgus in Spartha, reges, seniores et populus
   both greeks and italians
archons, suffestes or consuls
Athenians, Spartans, Thebans, Achaians
using the people as its mere dupe, as an underworker
   a purchaser in trust for some tyrant
dexterous in pulling down, not in maintaining. Turgot
takes a definition of the commonwealth
   for a definition of liberty.
Where ambition is every man's trade is no ploughing
How shall the plow be kept in hands of owners not hirelings?
   Lycurgus
to the end that no branch by swelling...
to say that some parts of Plato and Sir Thos More
   are as wild as the ravings of Bedlam
(found Milton a dithering idiot, tho' said this with
   more circumspection)
Lowered interest without annulling the debt...
in this transaction....There is nothing like it in the original
Mr Pope has conformed it to the notions
   of Englishmen and Americans
in Tacitus and in Homer, 3 orders, in Greece as in Germany
and mankind dare not yet think upon
   CONSTITUTIONS
' No man in America then believed me '
   J. A. on his Davila, recollecting.
Be bubbled out of their liberties by a few large names,
   Hume, probably not having read them.
Whether the king of the Franks had a negative on that
        assembly

'forward young man' wrote the critic
                on an unsigned J. A. (J. A. being then 53 and vice
                                            president)
Pharamond on the banks of the Sala
                here again the french jargon
                not one clear idea what they mean by
                                    'all authority'
MISERIA servitus, ubi jus vagum
primitive man was gregarious, passions, appetites and
                                            predilections
        to be observed, commended esteemed.

                I take it Mr Hillhouse is sincere
yet wd/ it not be more representative
to say that every colony had a governor,
                a council, senate and house
none of which went by heredity?
Emissaries of Britain and France cd/ speak and hold caucuses
                Commission to France '77
                'chased enemy half a mile'
(Lafayette heading some Morgan's rifles)
                                    Henry Laurens.
' give me leave to present you an introductory letter to
Mons. le Comte de Broglie.'
                        De Klab
' in my entertaining them with the best correspondence '
                                        Lafayette
(' in the noble cause we are fighting for ')
' novelty of the scene, the inexperience of the actors...
        against paying for things we haven't ordered '
                                        J. Adams
' U.S. will doubtless grant some facilities to
                            french privateers '
                                        De Sartine
in much larger sums than in the ordinary course of
                business is needed

Congress having borrowed large sums of this
                          paper money from its possessors
upon interest
              and promised payment of that in Europe
                              B. Fr. A. Lee J. A.
                          to Vergennes
to know how you (Beaumarchais) claim the Theresa
as your proper vessel, because M. Monthieu claims her as his.
Demurrage of her, part of which we have paid...
and John Baptiste
            Lazarus... agent of Caron de Beaumarchais
representative of Roderique Hortalez...
                    ' consecrated my house to Dr Franklin
and associates...was understood I shd/ expect no
                                          compensation
            I beg leave you permit this to remain...
                              Ray de Chaumont
As to Bersolle, charges for repair of the Drake
                          shd/ be Jones's
supplies or slops to the Ranger
                          shd/ be Jones's
(Paul Jones's) as the Chatham belongs 1/2 to the public
                          1/2 to the capturers
charges shd/ be 1/2 to moitie
munitions and repairs to the Ranger
                    to us
                    B.F. A. Lee J.A. commissioners
                    to Schweighauser, banker
Whatever vessels of war are sent to America
shd/ be plentifully supplied with marine woollen cloths
blankets, mittens
difficult without these in cold season
                    the commissioners, Franklin
                    A Lee   J. Adams
                    to de Sartine

It is certain that a loan of money is very much wanted
                    affly/ to Master Johnnie
                    and believe me with gt/ esteem, Sir,
                                        B, Franklin
Leghorn, if Vienna receive an American minister...
also 2 acts of the 4th and 15th ascertaining yr/ salary...
            and making provision for yr/ subsistence in France
                                Huntington, president
My Dear General
            The skill of our enemy (England)
in forging false news...annual custom to
            send out these cargoes of lies it is
            their way of passing the winter
thus by ' appeasing the troubles in Ireland '
                by contracts with German princes
and especially Petersburg: 20,000 russians
                            12 ships of the line
                        also Denmark 45 vessels (line)
(to La Fayette and to Genet)
' the art of political lying in England better than elsewhere)
19th (next day)
                ' no contracts with German princes '
Mr Burke's bill not yet being public
Mr Fox's severe observations on Govr/ Hutchinson
the precise point of the solstice
                                says Bolingbroke
they in sinking scale do not easily cast off habitual
                            prejudice.
' For the calling and cancellation of
                            200 million dollars
has in general been well rec'd '
                        Elbridge Gerry
demands of the treasury generally answered by warrants
                    @ $40 to 1 in specie.
Says Vergennes: for strangers?

' The depreciation of paper, a tax (T, A, X, tax)
        the Americans have laid on themselves...
if french be obliged to submit they will be victims
of zeal or their rashness in supplying the Americans
with arms, clothes and munitions '
                                        De Vergennes
' I thank yr/ Excellency for the confidence,
do you mean that the Chevalier de Luzerne has
already recd/ such instructions or that they are on their
                                        way to him?

Let me quote you some prices in Boston,
foreigners have profited by the difference
between silver and bills of exchange
        that is paper $25 to 1 of silver
but no more than   12 paper for One in bill of exchange
also difference in paper as between Boston and Philadelphia
If any european merchant can show good cause for
exception I doubt not we will do justice to him.'
                                        1780

Mazzei: little hope of success @ so low an interest
more offered by powers of Europe (to T. Jefferson)
Keeps good company, devoted to you, Wythe and the
gentlemen of Virginia, know not how you feel toward him.
' Value differently from yourself, sir, the
union which subsists between France and the U.S.
and that France may deserve some preference
                        over other powers
who have no treaty with America and who have not even
                                        acknowledged
                her independence...'
                                        de Vergennes
Army discipline greatly improved
                        Rush
' If the french fleet shd/ consistently remain on that coast '
                                (to de Vergennes)
' Not able on reflection to see why
                399

I shd/ not have published my powers in February '
                                (To Vergennes, July 17)
that I had intention of going to Amsterdam
no arguments but force respected in Europe...
to show U.S. the importance of an early attention to language
for ascertaining the language.

 Ching
Ming

Mr Bicker:, that I shd/ consider what houses
                were connected with England
and also which had ' other connections '
        equally likely to hinder the loan or defeat it
        (meaning, I found, the French ministry)
and which not of credit sufficient
                (particularly Neufville)
provision for negotiating the capital 2%
for undertakers to furnish the capital 2%
Brokerage 1/2% expenses stamped paper 1/2
amortization 2 1/4
        for 3 million guilders
I answered Mr Calkoen's questions in writing
conversation by interpreters being heavy
                and he then read them to a society
                and thus began to be known...that
wd/ be burdensome for us to go on ten years with the war
but for the English equally so
The taking of Charleston has not strengthened them
                on the contrary...
when England borrows each year a sum equal
                to all her exports
shd/ we be laughed at for
                wanting to borrow up to 1/12th (one twelfth)
                                of our exports?

We shd/ send regular ministers
' Laurens, dont la fâcheuse catastrophe me désole...
              (captured by England)
un parent me témoigne de l'inclination d'y placer
                vingt mille florins d'Hollande '
                          van der Capellen
Ven der Kemp peut être de grand utilité pour le Congrès
' King of Spain so good as to offer his surety
        for interest and the capital '
                                    B. Franklin
P.S. I find the sum he wd/ guarantee is
                          150,000 dollars
            payable in 3 years
No considerable sum here obtainable as Monsieur Necker
is making a loan
          (meaning placing one)
depuis qu'il (Mr Laurens) est enfermé à la Tour
              (i.e. the towYer of London)
America is willing to give a just interest
' Mortier and Meerkemaer act under Mssrs Staphorst
I am sorry Mr Blomberg is ill
I think them (the two Tenkate) are capable
but found them so liable to influence that I never cd/ close
Mr Van Vloten is at Utrecht '
                        H. Bicker
' but have never obtained any money
                      (12 Nov. 1780)
nor the least hope of obtaining '
                    J. A.
Whether Sir Jo. Yorke after 20 years residence
is ignorant of the Dutch constitution
              or is merely insulting
Burgomasters of Amsterdam are *one*
                integral branch of the sovereignty
...and disliking the french they familiarized to call

England the natural ally
King of England demands *punishment* of the regents.
' la persécution contre M. Van Berckel
et ses complices '

Capellen de Pol

de ne pas presser votre départ
les affaires...crise...temps pourrait
but des Anglais outre celui d'amuser la république d'Holland
loss of Charleston
Dutch have joined the neutrality
tout crédit soit d'un peuple soit d'un particulier
...de deux choses
l'opinion de la bonne foi
et de la possibilité
ou il se trouve de faire face...
Affaires (Xmas day, Amsterdam) still suspended
but stockjobbing goes on uninterruptedly
at coffee houses on Sundays and holidays
when it cannot be held upon 'change
' What they cd/ learn from Dutch history
or french of the last 25 years '

J. A. 29 years later

LXIX

IN which case a minister here from Congress wd/ be useful
...if the neutrality, a minister to all neutral courts
might be useful
Dec. 31 Amsterdam 1780
1st Jan. Philadelphia 1781
yr/ commission plenipotentiary sent herewith
Huntington, President
for a secret address you may send under cover
à
Madame la veuve de M. Henry Schorn
op de Agsterburg wal by de Hoogstraat
depreciation of money a TAX on the people
paid in advance and
therefore prevents the public from being found in debt, true
it is an unequal tax and causes perplexity
but by no means disables the people from carrying on the war
Merchants, farmers, tradesmen and labourers gain
they are the moneyed men,
The capitalists those who have money at interest
or those on fixed salaries
lose.
England has increased her debt 60 million
ours is not over   6 million
who can hold out the longer?
the depreciation has not tended to make the people
submit to Britain
American exports 1774,   12 million
English debt   200 million
the American debt only   six
a british minister and stock-jobber
Vergennes is fixedly resolved to commit himself to nothing
not even his treaty with the U.S. now existing

For the purpose of chicaning the U.S. out of their liberty
this congress proposed at Vienna with the two Emperors
                    part of England's palaver
La Cour de Londres éludera autant et aussi long qu'elle peut
l'aveu direct
            ou indirect de l'indépendence des Etats Unis
Cornwallis' fate has emboldened the Hollanders
                                                    4 Dec. '81
Crops in U.S. finest known
' 12,000 florins, J'ai honte d'être Hollandais '
                                            6 Jan. Capellen
' 2 burgomasters, 2 schepens and a pensionary.'
                    ' I believe this set receive ample salaries
                        to resist American loan
British ministers, Dutch court, and the holders of
                                            English stocks '
                            (to Franklin. Jan 25)
that the province of Friesland and M. Berdsma be remembered
that Mr Adams be admitted minister from
                    the congress of the U.S.N.A.
resolved in the Province House (Friesland)
                to treat with the hanseatic
I found the old gentleman perfectly sound in his
                    system of politics
very poor opinion of the new ministry
                    and of the preceding, insincerity
duplicity Shelbourne still flatters the
                King with ideas of CONciliation
                all to raise the price of stocks
                                        Amsterdam 26 April
if the houses Fiseaux, Hodshon, Crommelins, van Staphorst
            5 million by August
        Le corps des négociants de cette ville
souhaitant joindre leurs acclamations à ceux de toute la nation
        J. Nollet, Schiedam

' On m'a dit que ces Messieurs de Schiedam
                donnent ce repas de cent couverts
et qu'il y aura beaucoup de personnes de Rotterdam '
                                                    Dumas
It is true I may *open* a loan for 5 million
                cash is not infinite in this country
WE THEREFORE (May 11th 1780)
accept the terms you propose 4 1/4th% for remedium
                                            Willinck
                                            Staphorst
                                            Fynje
the words piddling etc/ once cost me very dear
If you wd/ open for 3 million at first
                ...Van Vloten and I have agreed
                3000 bonds @ 1000 francs each
                                            Willinck
                                                etc.
the minister of the Emperor is 90 years of age and
                                            never appears
                        Oswald's credentials
to treat with the ' U.S.A. (named specificly)
                        after this statuum quorum
My Dear General (Lafayette)
                million and a half, of the 3 million, in cash
                                            Amsterdam Sept. 29
Treaty ready by monday (J. A. to Jefferson)
                                            7 Oct '82
that France will not
                be in necessity of purchasing from Russia
after the war as she can then get some from America?
                The King's loans do not fill
                                    Paris, 7th November
Vergennes certainly knows this or is not even
                an European statesman

405

/...avoid too great dependence
            on any one power in Europe
            Nous sommes en attendant charmés de voir
que les états des autres provinces et conséquemment la
république entière ont, à l'exemple des Etats de Frise
                                        reconnu...
            signed Les membres de la Société Bourgeoise
                                        de Leeuwarde
                                        W. Wopkins
                                        V. Cats

S.P.Q. Amst. faustissimo foedere juncta
                            (on a medal)
factions, cabals, and slanders
many things said to me, false, more I suspect
            and yet others wd/ do no good if repeated

                                London May 27. 1785
to his Majesty in his closet
To T. J/... of ruining our carrying trade if they can
                    (remaining page ciphered)
Between St James and Versailles
                    ACT of navigation 12 Car. II, c 18
navigation by an American master
            three fourths of the seamen American
bubbles of our own philosophical liberality
                            (to Jay, 19 Aug. '85
and of the U.S. which wd/ find market in Barbary
if both governments are possessed of the contents of my letter
by opening it in the post office...
                Mr Pitt said that wd/ surprise
people here for that wars never interrupted
            the interest of DEBTS
Fat of the spermaceti whale
            gives the clearest
and most beautiful light of any substance known in nature
406

Consequence...that Portugal has, for four score years,
clothed herself in British woolens like any British colony
and has never been able to introduce woollen manufacturies
                                        at home
AND the British Islands have drunk no other than
                Port, Lisbon and Madeira
although the wines of France are much better.
                His Lordship wished so too.
                Million guilders new loan from Holland
Paris 1787
        ' This country will within the next 12 or 15 years
        come to a pretty good constitution '
                        Yrs/ Lafayette
To T. Jefferson:
        ' You fear the one, I the few.'
In this matter of redeeming certificates
        that were used payin' the sojers
                vignette *in margine*
                King, Sam Johnson of N. Carolina
                Smith (W.) S. Carolina, Wadsworth (Jeremiah
                J. Lawrence, Bingham, Carrol of Carrolton
                gone piss-rotten for Hamilton
                Cabot, Fisher Ames, Thomas Willing
                Robt Morris, Sedgwick
                                natural burella
                squad of the pink-haired snot
                traitors blacker than Arnold
                        blacker than Bancroft
                per l'argine sinistra dienno volta
                behind that mask Mr Schuyler (Filippo)
                these the betrayers, these the sifilides
                advance guard of hell's oiliness
                in their progeny no repentence
quindi Cocito, Cassio membruto
                        407

Mr Madison proposed that the original holders
                    shd/ get face value,
but not speculators who had bought in the paper for nothing.
ov the 64 members ov the House ov reppyzentativs
            29 were security holders.
                    lappin cream that is, and takin it
off of the veterans.
                    an' Mr Madison's move wuz DEE-feated.
Maclay and Jim Jackson stood out against dirtiness'
            smelled this stink before Madison
smelt it or before he told Tom about it.

LXX

'MY situation almost the only one in the world
where firmness and patience are useless '
J. A. vice president and president of the senate
1791
Will the french refuse to receive Mr Pinckney?
idea of leading Mr Adams...
Blount (senator) has been speculating with the English...
surrounded by projecters and swindlers, you will be, Gerry,
Friendship, Marshall a plain man and the frogs
countenance only enemies of our constitution.
set our seamen ashore at St Jago de Cuba
till our ships arm...office of Secretary as rival of president
in aim to have quintuple directory....Vervennes' friends
dislike the facts laid to his charge.
Hamilton no command,
too much intrigue. McHenry was secretary for war, in 98
We shd/ have frigates, no European peace can be lasting.
expedient to recommend war against France?
(presupposing they shall not have declared war against us
(thus to Pickering.) ' Talleyrand
affects utter ignorance, Mr Gerry has communicated, although
knowing that Talleyrand had much greater acquaintance
with the
said X, Y, Z than has Mr Gerry.
(Signed Gerry)
Hague 1st July '98
peculators, cd/ they be aroused to drive out the French...
Vans M/ exhausted all things in enormous bribes ' (ciphered)
Talleyrand, leaving however reserves for chicanery,
and Murray not yet removed from the Hague
about ' peace '

shortly ago were howling for war with Britain,
peace, war
aimed at elections. My appointment of Murray
   has at least laid open characters to me
' you are hereby discharged '
     John Adams, President of the United States
    to Tim Pickering
to execute office so far as to affix seal to enclosed commission
John Marshal of Virginia, to be Chief Justice
    and certify your own name *pro hac vice*
Hamilton's total ignorance (or whatever)
    of practice and usage of nations.
eternal neutrality in all wars of Europe.
     I leave the state with its coffers full
     Dec 28th 1800
73 for Jefferson
73 for Burr
a few foreign liars, no Americans in America
our federalists no more American than were the antis
And in the mirror of memory, *formato loco*
My compliments to Mrs Warren
    as to the sea nymphs
Hyson, Congo, Bohea, and a few lesser divinities
Sirens shd/ be got into it somehow.
    Tories were never so affable
    Tories were never so affable.
We shall oscillate like a pendulum.
slow starvation, a conclave, a divan,
    what shall we do when we get there
(first congress of Philadelphy) a nursery
    for American statesmen
treasons, felonies, new praemunires
Virginia has sown wheat instead of tobacco
    never happy in large and promiscuous companies

410

Quincy's knowledge of Boston harbour, 2 million issued in bills
old to bind young unconsenting, what right?
why exclude women from franchise?
                    power follows balance of land
been months here, and never on horseback.
                    fountain head of Justinian,
deep, Bracton, Domat, Ayliffe and Taylor
            from '61 here in Braintree
was aversion to paper, they preferred to do business by barter
you are right, Rush, our trouble is iggurunce
                    of money especially
are still stockjobbers to believe English reports
        ' No extravagance is too great
Ten thousand of General Washington's army
gone over to Clinton. Count D'Estaing making procession
                                        through
Boston with the Host, and seizing a meeting house
for a chapel and the devil knows what.'
            40,000 Russians about to go through
more solicitation as to means of obtaining it, than as to
                                        amount of
                    my salary
At any rate send me the *news*.
            quails, partridges, squirrels
God willing, I will not go to Vermont
I must be
            (whole of french policy)
within scent of
            (merely to string us along to keep us from)
the sea
            (sinking entirely, to have us strong enough for their
purpose, but not strong enough for our own, to prevent us
from obtaining consideration in Europe. Hence my pleasure
            in having set up a standard in Holland.

411

populariser, dépopulariser
>   to popularize Mr Jefferson
and *dépopulariser* General Washington, all on system.
>   were our interest the same as theirs
we might better trust them, yet not entirely
for they do not understand even their own.
>   I have hitherto paid the Dutch interest out of capital
>   (London '85 to Art Lee)
Court as putrid as Amsterdam, divine science of politics.
sale of six million acres to diminish the national debt—
and the society of a few men of letters.
left at New England Coffee House, London
will be brought me by some Boston sea captain
>   I shall call my brook, Hollis Brook
After generous contest for liberty, Americans forgot
>   what it consists of
after 20 years of the struggle *meminisse juvebit*
' seeks information from all quarters and judges more
independently than any man I ever met '
>   J. A. on G. Washington
that there were Americans indifferent to fisheries
>   and even some inclined to give them away
>   this was my strongest motive
>   for twice going to Europe.
fish boxes were rec'd in my absence.
' Their constitution, experiment, I KNOW
that France can not be long governed by it.'
>   To Price, 19 April 1790
aim of my life has been to be useful, how small in
any nation the number who comprehend ANY
system of constitution or administration
>   and these few do not unite.
Americans more rapidly disposed to corruption in elections
>   than I thought in '74
fraudulent use of words monarchy and republic

I am for balance

and know not how it is but mankind have an aversion
        to any study of government
Thames a mere rivulet in comparison to the Hudson river
73 to Jefferson, to Mr Burr 73
       DUM SPIRO
nec lupo committere agnum
      so they are against any rational theory.
       DUM SPIRO AMO

LXXI

A GERMAN ambassador once told me he cdn't bear
$\hspace{6cm}$ St Paul
he was, he said, so hard on fornication.
$\hspace{2cm}$ Dismissed to the joy of both parties, I do not
curse the day I entered public affairs.
$\hspace{3cm}$ Now in the first year before congress
$\hspace{3cm}$ (that is before '74)
I was drying my saddlebags and four yeomen in the bar room
were talking politics: ' If ' says one ' they can take
Mr Hancock's wharf and Mr Rowe's wharf
They can take my house and your barn.' Rebel!
I was disgusted at their saying rebel. I wd/ *meet* rebellion
when British governors and generals should begin it,
that is, their rebellion against principles of the constitution.
$\hspace{2cm}$ ' and in the mean time build frigates '
$\hspace{3cm}$ (1808 he wrote this as in the beginning)
in every principal sea port...not to fight squadrons at sea
but to have fast sailing frigates.
$\hspace{3cm}$ From England greater injuries
than from France,
I am for fighting whichever forces us first into a war.
depreciated by the swindling banks, a multitude
$\hspace{3cm}$ of such swindling banks have ruin'd our medium
Their issues are against gold or on nothing.
$\hspace{3cm}$ In '45 as a boy
I heard of the Cape Breton campaign and of
$\hspace{5cm}$ British ingratitude
Injustice of Shirley, of Braddock, of Abercrombie
and of Webb and Lord Loudon especially.
In '59 Pitt, Wolf, Amherst enthused me, but it was short
in '61 came writs of assistance.

No history of the past 20 years without documents
especially the circular letters to
members of congress, without these libels
no history of these decades '89 to '09
I am *totis viribus*
against any division. By the North River
or by the Delaware or by the Potomac I am against
any division of the Union by any river
or by any chain of mountains. Independence against
British policy? Independence against french interference,
federal papers hired by England.
When public opinion is rightly informed, as it now is not,
Vergennes said to me: Mr Adams, newspapers govern the world.

Took Matlock, Cannon and Young's constitutions
believing them Franklin's, they,
Beaumarchais and Condorcet, have paid. They did not like mine.
I have said the English Constitution *for*
a great nation *in*
Europe.
An alliance with France *or* England
wd/ put an end to our system of liberty.
Their inexperience, so superficial their reading...
Merchants wd/ say: the merchants are to do as they please.
without Louisiana no hold on the Mississippi river
westerners wd/ do any thing to obtain free use of that river
they wd/ have united with England or France
to elucidate the meaning of words *at that time*
and then determine intentions
oligarchy, insatiable gulf, irresistible.
I am a church-going animal
but if I inculcate fidelity to the marriage bed
they will say it is from resentment against General Hamilton.
and I had forgot the story
of the four English girls General Pinckney was to hire

in England, two for me and two for himself.
            The number of licensed houses
was soon reinstated, you may as well preach against rum to
                                                    Indians
Little Turtle petitioned me
to prohibit it ' because I had lost 3000 of my children
in his tribe alone in one year.'
                        Funds and Banks I
never approved I abhorred ever our whole banking system
but an attempt to abolish all funding in the
present state of the world wd/ be as romantic
as any adventure in Oberon or Don Quixote.
Every bank of discount is downright corruption
taxing the public for private individuals' gain.
            and if I say this in my will
the American people wd/ pronounce I died crazy.
                        their wigwams
where I never failed to be treated with whortle berries
black berries strawberries apples plums peaches etc
for they had planted a number of fruit trees about them
but the girls went out to service and the boys to sea
till none were left there...
                and so will be, believe me, whilever we feel like
                                                    colonists
dependent on France or England.
            With wood hemp iron, said the Chef d'Escadre
a nation may do what it please.
Taxes laid, war supported. This must be.
                Adams writing in Quincy in 1813
Histories are annihilated or interpolated or prohibited...
            our ' pure uncorrupted uncontaminated unadulterated
                                                    etc '

Sir Wm. Keith in 1739 proposed such an assembly to the
                                                    ministry

aiming at stamp tax—he being then, I believe, in Fleet prison
            His hint was taken in '54 and in '64
No gentlemen of talents has undertaken this history.
            Thos McKean
can remember *no* British friendship
            during the years that you indicate
            (1600 to 1813)
                THEMIS CONDITOR
In the Congress of '74 only Pat Henry
            had sense of the precipice whereon
            ...and courage to face it
French, english, mongrels
            we were divided a third to a third
Persons who saw that with our independence
            their salaries (from the Gospel Society of London)
                wd/ necessarily cease.
Laws of Charondas, destroyed I presume by spirit of party.
Civic polity ecclesiastical bigotry
destroy everything that cd/ give true light or clear insight
into antiquity...
            aristocratical and democratical fury...
adopted by Moses, by no means account for the facts
            ...entitled acta Sanctorum
whether the prepuce shown at Antwerp be authentic...
many a kept mistress has dared for her lover
hazards and sufferings as you find in the mission records
or tales of militant glory.
            ' Will his son save 'em (the fishing rights)
                        for a second time? '
No confidence in Clay, Gallatin, Russell...
            lake!! we should have command of the ocean!
J. Bull still bellows (July 1814)
            I wish France may not still regret Bonaparte
Bull greater tyrant, our treaty of 1783 has not lapsed.
Little intercourse between the separate states. No part of

my administration so unpopular, even in Marblehead,
          as was my fight for the navy
That is to GET a navy.

> JOHN ADAMS
> FOR PEACE
> 1800

I believe no printer in Boston wd/ print 'em.
                    Adams to L. Lloyd, in 1815)
I do not believe they cd/ get printed even today
in any newspaper in Boston. Circular letters, the lot of 'em
are full of as many lies as the Acta Sanctorum.
Mihites in Pennsylvania. And they believed firmly that
                                        Bonaparte
was the ' instrument ' to bring in Milennium
chosen of Providence to put an end to the pope
Jefferson knew them... all courting him 15 years
My answer was: Col. Lyman
it will be as you say but ruin honester men than the lot of 'em.
Burr folded it with great gravity, saying:
          Now I have him all hollow.
(re/ list of Hamilton's delegates)
                Walcott persisted for 8%
Did they believe South Americans
          were capable of free government?
lucid interval. The Directory had one for that moment
          No people in Europe cares anything
about constitutions, 1815, whatsoever
not one of 'em understands or is capable of understanding
          any consti-damn-tution whatever
God forbid that our navy
          ever be as England's has been a scourge.
No indian's hatchet raised while I was president

Nor has nature nor has art partitioned the sea into empires
                or into counties or knight's fees
on it be no farms ornate or unornate, no parks and no gardens
Fish to us, fisheries, Britain still has navigation rights on
                the Mississippi
money or no money, she can never conquer this country.
                'They will print anything that will sell.
'Our correspondence is considered a curiosity by both parties'
                Adams to Jefferson 1815
but I do not think that it is tampered with
                Your letters seem to get here unopened.
Price found 'gloomy predictions' most unwelcome
when Adams said the french revolution wd/ flop
'Give more for Jefferson's letters
                than for all the rest in his (Morgan's) volume.'
speeches, restarted inquisition in Spain...
                black white and pied British allies.
fleet to protect Paxton, Birch, Temple.
                Credit Otis with a great part of my argument
he showed illegality; toward destroying the charters
Poor soldiers knew not what sent 'em
North called 'em Sam Adams two regiments
                enormous wigs that Hutchinson brought here
like fleeces. Believe I had only set
                of 'State Trials' in America
...at State House with my musket and bayonet
                under Paddock
even Jesuits popes sorbonnists must have some conscience
so had Sylla, so Marius, and if Hancock had vanity
so had I also, if he riled me, I him
                4 large ships between Boston and London
in '55 his uncle left him the business
                and this made no change in John Hancock
thousand families in his dependence

419

The people elected him and Sam Adams approved their
                                                  intelligence
Joseph Hawley, Otis, Sam Adams, Hancock
add Jay, without knowing their actions
you know not what made us our revolution
                    magis decora poeticis fabulis
Otis wrote on greek prosody
            I published what he wrote on the latin
His daughter told me he had burnt all his papers
                    in melancholia
may be from that swat on the pow
                    From '74 dates neutrality
I begged Otis to print it (the greek prosody)
He said there were no greek types in America
and if there were, were no typesetters cd/ use 'em.
Otis resigned his post (Advocate General)
                and was beaten up by coffee house bandits
                                          in good looking clothes.
Otis against the writs, J. A. versus judiciary,
Defended Preston, defended the soldiers;
Fisheries, peace, nomination of Washington, kept peace with
France 1800. Gold, silver are but commodities
Pity, says Tracy, they ever were stamped save by weight
They are commodities as is wheat or is lumber.
            Keep out of Europe
And thus before Charlie Mordecai:
            ' not free 'em to something worse ' and quoted
' consider what substance allow to; what labour extract from
them (slaves) in my interest which will work out to this
If you work 'em up in six years on an average
            that most profits the planter '
with comment:
            ' and is surely very humane IF we estimate
the coalheaver's expectation: two years on an average
and the 50,000 girls on the streets, at three years' of life

' for the better securing of the plantations ' trade
whereas divers acts 7th and 8th William Third
in preamble for Chapter the twenty second
Don't it remind you of alderman Bekford
instructing his overseers
                    (treat 'em rough) in the West Indies
                    Adams to William Tudor
                    1818
                    24 years before Hobhouse.
' Ignorance of coin, credit and circulation! '
                    Κύδιστ' ἀθανάτων, πολυώνυμε,
                              πανκρατὲς
                                   αἰεὶ
                    Ζεῦ, φύσεως ἀρχηγέ,
                         νόμου μέτα πάντα
                              κυβερνῶν.

THE PISAN CANTOS
LXXIV-LXXXIV

LXXIV

THE enormous tragedy of the dream in the peasant's bent
        shoulders
    Manes! Manes was tanned and stuffed,
    Thus Ben and la Clara *a Milano*
            by the heels at Milano
That maggots shd/ eat the dead bullock
DIGONOS, Δίγονος, but the twice crucified
                    where in history will you find it?
yet say this to the Possum: a bang, not a whimper,
        with a bang not with a whimper,
To build the city of Dioce whose terraces are the colour of stars.
The suave eyes, quiet, not scornful,
                        rain also is of the process.
What you depart from is not the way
and olive tree blown white in the wind
washed in the Kiang and Han
what whiteness will you add to this whiteness,
                            what candor?
" the great periplum brings in the stars to our shore."
You who have passed the pillars and outward from Herakles
when Lucifer fell in N. Carolina.
if the suave air give way to scirocco
ΟΫ ΤΙΣ, ΟΫ ΤΙΣ? Odysseus
                    the name of my family.
the wind also is of the process,
                        sorella la luna
Fear god and the stupidity of the populace,
but a precise definition
        transmitted thus Sigismundo
        thus Duccio, thus Zuan Bellin, or trastevere with La Sposa
Sponsa Cristi in mosaic till our time / deification of emperors

425

but a snotty barbarian ignorant of T'ang history need not deceive
                                                              one
        nor Charlie Sung's money on loan from anonimo
that is, we suppose Charlie had some
and in India the rate down to 18 per hundred
but the local loan lice provided from imported bankers
so the total interest sweated out of the Indian farmers
        rose in Churchillian grandeur
as when, and plus when, he returned to the putrid gold standard
as was about 1925   Oh my England
that free speech without free radio speech is as zero
        and but one point needed for Stalin
you need not, i.e. need not take over the means of production;
money to signify work done, inside a system
        and measured and wanted
" I have not done unnecessary manual labour "
says the R. C. chaplain's field book
                        (preparation before confession)
squawky as larks over the death cells
                        militarism progressing westward
im Westen nichts neues
and the Constitution in jeopardy
and that state of things not very new either

" of sapphire, for this stone giveth sleep "
not words whereto to be faithful
        nor deeds that they be resolute
                only that bird-hearted equity make timber
                and lay hold of the earth
and Rouse found they spoke of Elias
in telling the tales of Odysseus   ΟΥ ΤΙΣ
                        ΟΥ ΤΙΣ
" I am noman, my name is noman "
but Wanjina is, shall we say, Ouan Jin
or the man with an education

426

and whose mouth was removed by his father
               because he made too many *things*
whereby cluttered the bushman's baggage
vide the expedition of Frobenius' pupils about 1938
                              to Auss 'ralia
Ouan Jin spoke and thereby created the named
                         thereby making clutter
the bane of men moving
and so his mouth was removed
as you will find it removed in his pictures
                    in principio verbum
          paraclete or the verbum perfectum: sinceritas
from the death cells in sight of Mt. Taishan @ Pisa
as Fujiyama at Gardone
when the cat walked the top bar of the railing
and the water was still on the West side
flowing toward the Villa Catullo
where with sound ever moving
                  in diminutive poluphloisboios
in the stillness outlasting all wars
" La Donna " said Nicoletti
                    " la donna,
                         la donna! "
" Cosa deve continuare? "
" Se casco " said Bianca Capello
" non casco in ginnocchion "
and with one day's reading a man may have the key in his hands
Lute of Gassir. Hooo Fasa
came a lion-coloured pup bringing fleas
and a bird with white markings, a stepper
                    under *les six potences*
Absouldre, que tous nous vueil absoudre
lay there Barabbas and two thieves lay beside him
infantile synthesis in Barabbas
minus Hemingway, minus Antheil, ebullient

and by name Thos. Wilson
Mr K. said nothing foolish, the whole month nothing foolish:
" if we weren't dumb, we wouldn't be here "
                                                 and the Lane gang.
Butterflies, mint and Lesbia's sparrows,
the voiceless with bumm drum and banners,
                                    and the ideogram of the guard roosts
el triste pensier si volge
        ad Ussel. A Ventadour
                va il consire, el tempo rivolge
and at Limoges the young salesman
bowed with such french politeness " No that is impossible."
I have forgotten which city
But the caverns are less enchanting to the unskilled explorer
        than the Urochs as shown on the postals,
we will see those old roads again, question,
                                                 possibly
but nothing appears much less likely,
                                        Mme Pujol,
and there was a smell of mint under the tent flaps
especially after the rain
                and a white ox on the road toward Pisa
                        as if facing the tower,
dark sheep in the drill field and on wet days were clouds
in the mountain as if under the guard roosts.
                A lizard upheld me
                the wild birds wd not eat the white bread
                from Mt Taishan to the sunset
From Carrara stone to the tower
        and this day the air was made open
                for Kuanon of all delights,
                Linus, Cletus, Clement
                                        whose prayers,
the great scarab is bowed at the altar
the green light gleams in his shell

428

plowed in the sacred field and unwound the silk worms early
                                        in tensile
in the light of light is the *virtù*
            " sunt lumina " said Erigena Scotus 顯
            as of Shun on Mt Taishan
and in the hall of the forebears
                        as from the beginning of wonders
the paraclete that was present in Yao, the precision
in Shun the compassionate
in Yu the guider of waters

4 giants at the 4 corners
        three young men at the door
and they digged a ditch round about me
        lest the damp gnaw thru my bones
            to redeem Zion with justice
sd/ Isaiah. Not out on interest said David rex
                        the prime s.o.b.
Light tensile immaculata
            the sun's cord unspotted
" sunt lumina " said the Oirishman to King Carolus,
            " OMNIA,
all things that are are lights "
and they dug him up out of sepulture
soi disantly looking for Manichaeans.
Les Albigeois, a problem of history,
and the fleet at Salamis made with money lent by the state to the
                                    shipwrights
            Tempus tacendi, tempus loquendi.
Never inside the country to raise the standard of living
but always abroad to increase the profits of usurers,
            dixit Lenin,
and gun sales lead to more gun sales
        they do not clutter the market for gunnery
            there is no saturation

                        429

Pisa, in the 23rd year of the effort in sight of the tower
and Till was hung yesterday
for murder and rape with trimmings   plus Cholkis
        plus mythology, thought he was Zeus ram or another one
                Hey Snag wots in the bibl'?
                wot are the books ov the bible?
                Name 'em, don't bullshit ME.

莫   ΟΫ ΤΙΣ

a man on whom the sun has gone down

the ewe, he said had such a pretty look in her eyes;
and the nymph of the Hagoromo came to me,
                                as a corona of angels
one day were clouds banked on Taishan
        or in glory of sunset
                and tovarish blessed without aim
wept in the rainditch at evening
                        Sunt lumina
that the drama is wholly subjective
stone knowing the form which the carver imparts it
the stone knows the form
sia Cythera, sia Ixotta, sia in Santa Maria dei Miracoli
        where Pietro Romano has fashioned the bases
ΟΫ ΤΙΣ
a man on whom the sun has gone down
nor shall diamond die in the avalanche
                be it torn from its setting
first must destroy himself ere others destroy him.
4 times was the city rebuilded, Hooo Fasa
                Gassir, Hooo Fasa   dell' Italia tradita
now in the mind indestructible, Gassir, Hoooo Fasa,
With the four giants at the four corners
and four gates mid-wall Hooo Fasa
and a terrace the colour of stars
pale as the dawn cloud, la luna

                    thin as Demeter's hair
Hooo Fasa, and in a dance the renewal
        with two larks in contrappunto
                at sunset
                        ch'intenerisce
a sinistra la Torre
            seen thru a pair of breeches.
Che sublia es laissa cader
between NEKUIA where are Alcmene and Tyro
            and the Charybdis of action
                to the solitude of Mt. Taishan
femina, femina, that wd/ not be dragged into paradise by the hair,
under the gray cliff in periplum
        the sun dragging her stars
            a man on whom the sun has gone down
and the wind came as hamadryas under the sun-beat
                        Vai soli
                            are never alone
amid the slaves learning slavery
        and the dull driven back toward the jungle
        are never alone 'ΗΛΙΟΝ ΠΕΡΙ 'ΗΛΙΟΝ
            as the light sucks up vapor
                and the tides follow Lucina
        that had been a hard man in some ways
            a day as a thousand years
as the leopard sat by his water dish;
        hast killed the urochs and the bison sd/ Bunting
            doing six months after that war was over
as pacifist tempted with chicken but declined to approve
of war " Redimiculum Metellorum "
                                privately printed
            to the shame of various critics
nevertheless the state can lend money
            and the fleet that went out to Salamis
            was built by state loan to the builders

                    hence the attack on classical studies
and in this war were Joe Gould, Bunting and cummings
as against thickness and fatness

black that die in captivity
        night green of his pupil, as grape flesh and sea wave
undying luminous and translucent

                Est consummatum, Ite;

            surrounded by herds and by cohorts looked on Mt Taishan

but in Tangier I saw from dead straw ignition
                From a snake bite
        fire came to the straw
        from the fakir blowing
        foul straw and an arm-long snake
        that bit the tongue of the fakir making small holes
                and from the blood of the holes
                    came fire when he stuffed the straw into his mouth
dirty straw that he took from the roadway
                        first smoke and then the dull flame
        that wd/ have been in the time of Rais Uli
            when I rode out to Elson's
            near the villa of Perdicaris
            or four years before that
        elemental he thought the souls of the children, if any,
but had rented a shelter for travelers
        by foot from Siria, some of them
nor is it for nothing that the chrysalids mate in the air
                            color di luce
green splendour and as the sun thru pale fingers
Lordly men are to earth o'ergiven
            these the companions:
Fordie that wrote of giants

and William who dreamed of nobility
                and Jim the comedian singing:
                    " Blarrney castle me darlin'
                    you're nothing now but a StOWne "
and Plarr talking of mathematics
                or Jepson lover of jade
Maurie who wrote historical novels
                and Newbolt who looked twice bathed
                                are to earth o'ergiven.
                And this day the sun was clouded
—" You sit stiller " said Kokka
" if whenever you move something jangles."
and the old Marchesa remembered a reception in Petersburg
and Kokka thought there might be some society (good) left in
                            Spain, wd. he care to frequent it, my god, no!
        opinion in 1924
Sirdar, Bouiller and Les Lilas,
                or Dieudonné London, or Voisin's,
Uncle George stood like a statesman 'PEI ΠΑΝΤΑ
fills up every hollow
        the cake shops in the Nevsky, and Schöners
not to mention der Greif at Bolsano   la patronne getting older
Mouquin's or Robert's 40 years after
        and La Marquise de Pierre had never before met an American
        " and all their generation "
                no it is not in that chorus
        Huddy going out and taller than anyone present
                                où sont les heurs of that year
Mr James shielding himself with Mrs Hawkesby
as it were a bowl shielding itself with a walking stick
as he maneuvered his way toward the door
Said Mr Adams, of the education,
                Teach? at Harvard?
                Teach? It cannot be done.
and this I had from the monument

Haec sunt fastae
                Under Taishan quatorze Juillet
with the hill ablaze north of Taishan
and Amber Rives is dead, the end of that chapter
                        see Time for June 25th,
Mr Graham himself unmistakeably,
                on a horse, an ear and the beard's point showing
        and the Farben works still intact
        to the tune of Lilibullero
and they have bitched the Adelphi
niggers scaling the obstacle fence
                in the middle distance
and Mr Edwards superb green and brown
                in ward No 4 a jacent benignity,
of the Baluba mask: " doan you tell no one
        I made you that table "
                methenamine eases the urine
and the greatest is charity
to be found among those who have not observed
                        regulations
        not of course that we advocate—
        and yet petty larceny
        in a regime based on grand larceny
        might rank as conformity nient' altro
        with justice shall be redeemed
who putteth not out his money on interest
        " in meteyard in weight or in measure "
                XIX Leviticus or
First Thessalonians 4, 11
300 years culture at the mercy of a tack hammer
                thrown thru the roof
Cloud over mountain, mountain over the cloud
I surrender neither the empire nor the temples
                                plural
nor the constitution nor yet the city of Dioce

each one in his god's name
as by Terracina rose from the sea Zephyr behind her
　　　　　and from her manner of walking
　　　　　　　　　　　as had Anchises
　　till the shrine be again white with marble
　　till the stone eyes look again seaward
　　　　　　　　　　　　The wind is part of the process
　　　　　　　　　　　　The rain is part of the process
and the Pleiades set in her mirror
Kuanon, this stone bringeth sleep;
　　　　offered the wine bowl
　　　　　　　　　　　grass nowhere out of place
χθόνια γέα, Μήτηρ,
　　　by thy herbs menthe thyme and basilicum,
　　　　　　from whom and to whom,
　　　　　　will never be more now than at present
being given a new green katydid of a Sunday
emerald, paler than emerald,
　　　　　　minus its right propeller
　　　this tent is to me and ΤΙΘΩΝΩΙ
eater of grape pulp
　　　in coitu inluminatio
Manet painted the bar at La Cigale or at Les Folies in that year
　　　she did her hair in small ringlets, à la 1880 it might have been,
red, and the dress she wore Drecol or Lanvin
　　　　　a great goddess, Aeneas knew her forthwith
by paint immortal as no other age is immortal
　　　　　la France dixneuvième
Degas Manet Guys unforgettable
a great brute sweating paint said Vanderpyl 40 years later
　　　　　　　　　　　　of Vlaminck
　　　　for this stone giveth sleep
　　　　　　　staria senza più scosse
　　　and eucalyptus that is for memory
　　　under the olives, by cypress, mare Tirreno,

435

Past Malmaison in field by the river the tables
   Sirdar, Armenonville
Or at Ventadour the keys of the chateau;
   rain, Ussel,
To the left of la bella Torre the tower of Ugolino
in the tower to the left of the tower
   chewed his son's head
and the only people who did anything of any interest were H., M.
                             and

   Frobenius der Geheimrat
der im Baluba das Gewitter gemacht hat
   and Monsieur Jean wrote a play now and then or the
                        Possum

   pouvrette et ancienne   oncques lettre ne lus
I don't know how humanity stands it
   with a painted paradise at the end of it
   without a painted paradise at the end of it
the dwarf morning-glory twines round the grass blade
magna NUX animae   with Barabbas and 2 thieves beside me,
   the wards like a slave ship,
       Mr Edwards, Hudson, Henry   *comes miseriae*
       Comites Kernes, Green and Tom Wilson
   God's messenger Whiteside
and the guards op/ of the . . .
   was lower than that of the prisoners
  " all them g.d. m.f. generals c.s. all of 'em fascists "
" fer a bag o' Dukes "
         " the things I saye an' dooo "
  ac ego in harum
so lay men in Circe's swine-sty;
   ivi in harum *ego* ac vidi cadaveres animae
    " c'mon small fry " sd/ the little coon to the big black;
of the slaver as seen between decks
   and all the presidents
Washington Adams Monroe Polk Tyler

plus Carrol (of Carrolton) Crawford
Robbing the public for private individual's gain ΘΕΛΓΕΙΝ
every bank of discount is downright iniquity
 robbing the public for private individual's gain
 nec benecomata Kirkê, mah! κακὰ φάργακ' ἔδωκεν
neither with lions nor leopards attended
  but poison, veleno
in all the veins of the commonweal
if on high, will flow downward all thru them
  if on the forge at Predappio? sd/ old Upward:
  " not the priest but the victim "
   his seal Sitalkas, sd/ the old combattant: " victim,
withstood them by Thames and by Niger with pistol by Niger
 with a printing press by the Thomas bank "
  until I end my song
    and shot himself;
      for praise of intaglios
Matteo and Pisanello out of Babylon
   they are left us
for roll or plain impact
 or cut square in the jade block

nox animae magna from the tent under Taishan
amid what was termed the a.h. of the army
the guards holding opinion. As it were to dream of
morticians' daughters raddled but amorous
To study with the white wings of time passing
   is not that our delight
to have friends come from far countries
   is not that pleasure
nor to care that we are untrumpeted?
    filial, fraternal affection is the root of humaneness
    the root of the process
nor are elaborate speeches and slick alacrity.
   employ men in proper season

not when they are at harvest
E al Triedro, Cunizza
e l'altra: " Io son' la Luna."
dry friable earth going from dust to more dust
grass worn from its root-hold
is it blacker? was it blacker? Νύξ animae?
is there a blacker or was it merely San Juan with a belly ache
writing ad posteros
in short shall we look for a deeper or is this the bottom?
Ugolino, the tower there on the tree line
Berlin   dysentery   phosphorus
la vieille de Candide
(Hullo Corporal Casey) double X or burocracy?
Le Paradis n'est pas artificiel
but spezzato apparently
it exists only in fragments unexpected excellent sausage,
the smell of mint, for example,
Ladro the night cat;
at Nemi waited on the slope above the lake sunken in the pocket
of hills
awaiting decision from the old lunch cabin built out over the
shingle,
Zarathustra, now desuete
to Jupiter and to Hermes where now is the castellaro
no vestige save in the air
in stone is no imprint and the grey walls of no era
under the olives
saeculorum Athenae
γλαύξ, γλαυκῶπις,

olivi
that which gleams and then does not gleam
as the leaf turns in the air
Boreas Apeliota libeccio
" C'è il babao," said the young mother
and the bathers like small birds under hawk's eye

438

shrank back under the cliff's edge at il Pozzetto
al Tigullio
" wd." said the guard " *take* everyone of them g.d.m.f. generals
c.s. all of 'em fascists "
Oedipus, nepotes Remi magnanimi
so Mr Bullington lay on his back like an ape
singing: O sweet and lovely
o Lady be good "
in harum ac ego ivi
Criminals have no intellectual interests?
and for three months did not know the taste of his food
in Chi heard Shun's music
the sharp song with sun under its radiance
λιγύρ'
one tanka entitled the shadow
babao, or the hawk's wing
of no fortune and with a name to come
Is downright iniquity said J. Adams
at 35 instead of 21.65
doubtless conditioned by what his father heard in
Byzantium
doubtless conditioned by the spawn of the gt. Meyer Anselm
That old H. had heard from the ass eared militarist in Byzantium:
" Why stop? " " To begin again when we are stronger."
and young H/ the tip from the augean stables in Paris
with Sieff in attendance, or not
as the case may have been,
thus conditioning.
Meyer Anselm, a rrromance, yes, yes certainly
but more fool you if you fall for it two centuries later
. . .
from their seats the blond bastards, and cast 'em.
the yidd is a stimulant, and the goyim are cattle
in gt/ proportion and go to saleable slaughter
with the maximum of docility.   but if

439

a place be versalzen,,,?
With justice,
by the law, from the law or it is not in the contract
    Yu has nothing pinned on Jehoveh
        sent and named Shun who to the
autumnal heavens *sha-o*
with the sun under its melody
    to the compassionate heavens
    and there is also the XIXth Leviticus.
    " Thou shalt purchase the field with money."
      signed Jeremiah
from the tower of Hananel unto Goah
unto the horse gate $8.50 in Anatoth
which is in Benjamin, $8.67
      For the purity of the air on Chocorua
        in a land of maple
From the law, by the law, so build yr/ temple
    with justice in meteyard and measure
a black delicate hand
a white's hand like a ham
      pass by, seen under the tent-flap
        on sick call : comman'
        comman', sick call comman'
    and the two largest rackets are the alternation
    of the value of money
(of the unit of money METATHEMENON TE TON
                          KRUMENON
and usury @ 60   or lending
    that which is made out of nothing
and the state *can* lend money   as was done
by Athens for the building of the Salamis fleet
    and if the packet gets lost in transit
        ask Churchill's backers
    where it has got to   the state need not borrow
    nor do the veterans need state guarantees

for private usurious lending
in fact that is the cat in the woodshed
    the state need not borrow
    as was shown by the mayor of Wörgl
    who had a milk route
    and whose wife sold shirts and short breeches
and on whose book-shelf was the Life of Henry Ford
and also a copy of the Divina Commedia
    and of the Gedichte of Heine
    a nice little town in the Tyrol in a wide flat-lying valley
near Innsbruck and when a note of the
            small town of Wörgl went over
a counter in Innsbruck
    and the banker saw it go over
    all the slobs in Europe were terrified
    " no one " said the Frau Burgomeister
    " in this village who cd/ write a newspaper article.
    Knew it was money but pretended it was not
    in order to be on the safe side of the law."
But in Russia they bungled and did not apparently
grasp the idea of work-certificate
and started the N.E.P. with disaster
and the immolation of men to machinery
        and the canal work and gt/ mortality
            (which is as may be)
and went in for dumping in order to trouble the waters
                    in the usurers' hell-a-dice
all of which leads to the death-cells
each in the name of its god
or longevity because as says Aristotle
philosophy is not for young men
their *Katholou* can not be sufficiently derived from
    their *hekasta*
their generalities cannot be born from a sufficient phalanx
                        of particulars

441

lord of his work and master of utterance
          who turneth his word in its season and shapes it
          Yaou chose Shun to longevity
who seized the extremities and the opposites
holding true course between them
shielding men from their errors
cleaving to the good they had found
holding empire as if not in a mortar with it
          nor dazzled thereby
wd/ have put the old man, *son père* on his shoulders
          and gone off to some barren seacoast
Says the Japanese sentry : Paaak yu djeep over there,
some of the best soldiers we have says the captain
          Dai Nippon Banzai from the Philippines
remembering Kagekiyo : " how stiff the shaft of your neck is."
          and they went off each his own way
" a better fencer than I was," said Kumasaka, a shade,
" I believe in the resurrection of Italy   quia impossibile est
          4 times to the song of Gassir
          now in the mind indestructible

                    .   .   .   .

               ΚΟΡΗ, ᾽ΑΓΛΑΟΣ ᾽ΑΛΑΟΥ
Glass-eye Wemyss treading water
          and addressing the carpenter from the seawaves
because of an unpinned section of taff-rail
          we are not so ignorant as you think in the navy
Gesell entered the Lindhauer government
which lasted rather less than 5 days
          but was acquitted as an innocent stranger
Oh yes, the money is there,
          il danaro c'è, said Pellegrini
                    (very peculiar under the circs)
          musketeers rather more than 20 years later
an old man (or oldish) still active

                         442

serving small stones from a lath racquet

Περσεφόνεια under Taishan

     in sight of the tower che pende

on such a litter rode Pontius

     under such canvass

in the a.h. of the army

     in sight of two red cans labeled " FIRE "

Said Von Tirpitz to his daughter : beware of their charm

ΣΕΙΡΗΝΕΣ this cross turns with the sun

and the goyim are undoubtedly in great numbers cattle

whereas a jew will receive information

        he will gather up information

     faute de...something more solid

        but not in all cases

ΣΕΙΡΗΝΕΣ   had appreciated his conversation

  ΧΑΡΙΤΕΣ possibly in the soft air

  with the mast held by the left hand

  in this air as of Kuanon

enigma forgetting the times and seasons

but this air brought her ashore a la marina

with the great shell borne on the seawaves

        nautilis biancastra

  By no means an orderly Dantescan rising

but as the winds veer

          tira libeccio

now Genji at Suma   , tira libeccio

    as the winds veer and the raft is driven

    and the voices   , Tiro, Alcmene

    with you is Europa nec casta Pasiphaë

       Eurus, Apeliota as the winds veer in periplum

Io son la luna " . Cunizza

       as the winds veer in periplum

  and from under the Rupe Tarpeia

  drunk with wine of the Castelli

   " in the name of its god " " Spiritus veni "

adveni / not to a schema
        " is not for the young " said Arry, stagirite
but as grass under Zephyrus
      as the green blade under Apeliota
Time is not, Time is the evil, beloved
Beloved the hours βροδοδάκτυλος
      as against the half-light of the window
      with the sea beyond making horizon
le contre-jour the line of the cameo
profile " to carve Achaia "
      a dream passing over the face in the half-light
      Venere, Cytherea " aut Rhodon "
      vento ligure, veni
" beauty is difficult " sd/ Mr Beardsley
      and sd/ Mr Kettlewell looking up from a
pseudo-Beardsley of his freshman composition
  and speaking to W. Lawrence:
                       Pity you didn't finish the job
while you were at it "
      W.L. having run into the future non-sovereign Edvardus
on a bicycle equally freshman
            a.d. 1910 or about that
beauty is difficult
in the days of the Berlin to Bagdad project
      and of Tom L's photos of rock temples in Arabia Petra
but he wd/ not talk of
      LL.G. and the frogbassador, he wanted to
      talk modern art (T.L. did)
      but of second rate, not the first rate
      beauty is difficult.
He said I protested too much   he wanted to start a press
and print the greek classics....periplum
      and the very *very* aged Snow created considerable
hilarity quoting the φαίνε-τ-τ-τ-τττ-αί μοι
in reply to *l'aer tremare*

                    beauty is difficult
But on the other hand the President of Magdalen
(rhyming dawdlin') said there were
too many words in " The Hound of Heaven "
                    a moddddun opohem he had read
and there was no doubt that the dons lived well
                                        in the kawledg
it was if I remember rightly the burn and freeze that the fresh-
                                                        men
had failed to follow
or else a mere desire to titter etc.
and it is (in parenthesis) doubtless
            easier to teach them to roar like gorillas
than to scan φαίνεταί μοι
                    inferior gorillas
of course, lacking the wind sack
        and although Siki was quite observable
            we have not yet calculated the sum   gorilla + bayonet
and there was a good man named Burr
            descendant of Aaron during the other war
who was amused by the British
            but he didn't last long AND
Corporal Casey tells me that Stalin
        le bonhomme Staline
        has no sense of humour (dear Koba!)
and old Rhys, Ernest, was a lover of beauty
        and when he was still engineer in a coal mine
        a man passed him at high speed radiant in the mine gallery
his face shining with ecstasy
        " A'hv joost........Tommy Luff."
        and as Luff was twice the fellow's size, Rhys was puzzled
The Muses are daughters of memory
        Clio, Terpsichore
and Granville was a lover of beauty
and the three ladies all waited

                    445

" and with a name to come "
εσσομένοισι

aram vult nemus

Came Madame Lucrezia
and on the back of the door in Cesena
are, or were, still the initials
joli quart d'heure, (nella Malatestiana)
                    Torquato where art thou?
to the click of hooves on the cobbles by Tevere
and " my fondest knight lie dead ".. or la Stuarda
" ghosts move about me "   " patched with histories "
                    but as Mead said: if they were,
what have they done in the interval,
                    eh, to arrive by metempsychosis at....?
and there are also the conjectures of the Fortean Society
Beauty is difficult....the plain ground
                              precedes the colours
and this grass or whatever here under the tentflaps
        is, indubitably, bambooiform
representative brush strokes wd/ be similar
....cheek bone, by verbal manifestation,
        her eyes as in " La Nascita "
        whereas the child's face
is at Capoquadri in the fresco square over the doorway
        centre background
the form beached under Helios
                    funge la purezza,
and that certain images be formed in the mind
        to remain there
                    formato locho
    Arachne mi porta fortuna
to remain there, resurgent ΕΙΚΟΝΕΣ
and still in Trastevere

446

for the deification of emperors
and the medallions
            to forge Achaia
and as for playing checquers with black Jim
    on a barrel top where now is the Ritz-Carlton
and the voice of Monsieur Fouquet or the Napoleon 3rd
barbiche of Mr Quackenbos, or Quackenbush
as I supposed it,
and Mrs Chittenden's lofty air
        and the remains of the old South
           tidewashed to Manhattan and brown-stone
           or (later) the outer front stair
leading to Mouquin's
    or old Train (Francis) on the pavement in his plain wooden
                                      chair
or a fellow throwing a knife in the market
past baskets and bushels of peaches
                  at $1. the bushel
and the cool of the 42nd St. tunnel   (periplum)
white-wash and horse cars, the Lexington Avenue cable
refinement, pride of tradition, alabaster
                      Towers of Pisa
                      (alabaster, not ivory)
coloured photographs of Europa
carved wood from Venice venetian glass and the samovar
and the fire bucket, 1806 Barre Mass'chusetts
        and the Charter Oak in Connecticut
        or to begin with Cologne Cathedral
        the Torwaldsen lion and Paolo Uccello
        and thence to Al Hambra, the lion court and el
        mirador de la reina Lindaraja
orient reaching to Tangier, the cliffs the villa of Perdicaris
Rais Uli, periplum
Mr Joyce also preoccupied with Gibraltar
                     and the Pillars of Hercules

not with my *patio* and the wistaria and the tennis courts
or the bugs in Mrs Jevons' hotel
    or the quality of the beer served to sailors
veder Nap'oiiiii or Pavia the romanesque
                being preferable
and by analogy the form of San Zeno the
        columns signed by their maker
            the frescoes in S. Pietro and the madonna in Ortolo
e " fa di clarità l'aer tremare "
as in the manuscript of the Capitolare
Trattoria degli Apostoli (dodici)
" Ecco il tè " said the head waiter
in 1912 explaining its mysteries to the piccolo
with a teapot from another hotel
but coffee came to Assisi much later
                that is, so one cd/ drink it
when it was lost in Orleans and France semi-ruin'd
thus the coffee-house facts of Vienna
        whereas Mr Carver merits mention for the
cultivation of peanuts,
arachidi, and the soja has yet to save Europe
                and the wops do not use maple syrup
the useful operations of commerce
        stone after stone of beauty cast down
and authenticities disputed by parasites
                (made in Ragusa) and : what art do you handle?
" The best " And the moderns? " Oh, nothing modern
we couldn't sell anything modern."
But Herr Bacher's father made madonnas still in the tradition
carved wood as you might have found in any cathedral
        and another Bacher still cut intaglios
            such as Salustio's in the time of Ixotta,
where the masks come from, in the Tirol,
        in the winter season
            searching every house to drive out the demons.

448

Serenely in the crystal jet
            as the bright ball that the fountain tosses
(Verlaine) as diamond clearness
            How soft the wind under Taishan
                        where the sea is remembered
            out of hell, the pit
            out of the dust and glare evil
             Zephyrus / Apeliota
This liquid is certainly a
            property of the mind
nec accidens est   but an element
                        in the mind's make-up
est agens and functions   dust to a fountain pan otherwise
            Hast 'ou seen the rose in the steel dust
                        (or swansdown ever?)
so light is the urging, so ordered the dark petals of iron
we who have passed over Lethe.

LXXV

Out of Phlegethon!
  out of Phlegethon,
    Gerhart
      art thou come forth out of Phlegethon?
with Buxtehude and Klages in your satchel, with the
Ständebuch of Sachs in yr/ luggage
      —not of one bird but of many

LXXVI

ᴀɴᴅ the sun high over horizon hidden in cloud bank
    lit saffron the cloud ridge
        dove sta memora

" Will " said the Signora Agresti, " break his political
but not economic system "

But on the high cliff Alcmene,
    Dryas, Hamadryas ac Heliades
    flowered branch and sleeve moving
    Dirce et Ixotta e che fu chiamata Primavera
      in the timeless air

that they suddenly stand in my room here
between me and the olive tree
    or nel clivo ed al triedro?
    and answered : the sun in his great periplum
leads in his fleet here
      sotto le nostre scogli
under our craggy cliffs
      alevel their mast-tops
      Sigismundo by the Aurelia to Genova
        by la vecchia sotto S. Pantaleone
Cunizza qua al triedro,
e la scalza, and she who said: I still have the mould,
and the rain fell all the night long at Ussel
cette mauvaiseh venggg blew over Tolosa
and in Mt Segur there is wind space and rain space
    no more an altar to Mithras

from il triedro to the Castellaro

the olives grey over grey holding walls
and their leaves turn under Scirocco

la scalza : Io son' la luna
and they have broken my house

the huntress in broken plaster keeps watch no longer

tempora, tempora and as to mores

by Babylonian wall (memorat Cheever)
out of his bas relief, for that line
we recall him
and who's dead, and who isn't
and will the world ever take up its course again?

very confidentially I ask you: Will it?
with Dieudonné dead and buried
not even a wall, or Mouquin, or Voisin or the cake shops
in the Nevsky

The Greif, yes, I suppose, and Schöners and perhaps
the Taverna and Robert's
but La Rupe no longer la Rupe, finito
Pré Catalan, Armenonville, Bullier
extinct as Willy and there are I suppose
no reprints

Teofile's bricabrac Cocteau's bricabrac
seadrift snowin' 'em under
every man to his junk-shop
houses shd/have been built in the '80's
(or '60's) for a' that
but Eileen's trick sunlight softens London's November
progress, b . . . . h yr/progress

la pigrizia   to know the ground and the dew

    but to keep 'em three weeks   Chung
                we doubt it

and in government not to lie down on it

                                the word is made

perfect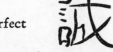

better gift can no man make to a nation
    than the sense of Kung fu Tseu
        who was called Chung Ni
    nor in historiography nor in making anthologies

    (b . . . . h yr/progress)
    each one in the name of his god

So that in the synagogue in Gibraltar
    the sense of humour seemed to prevail
    during the preliminary parts of the whatever
but they respected at least the scrolls of the law
        from it, by it, redemption
    @ $8.50, @ $8.67 buy the field with good money
no unrighteousness in meteyard or in measure (of prices)

and there is no need for the Xtns to pretend that
    they wrote Leviticus
    chapter XIX in particular
        with justice Zion
not by cheating the eye-teeth out of Don Fulano
        or of Caio e Tizio;
Why not rebuild it?

Criminals have no intellectual interests?
" Hey, Snag, wot are the books ov th' bibl' "

" name 'em, etc.
" Latin? I studied latin."
            said the nigger murderer to his cage-mate
(cdn't be sure which of the two was speaking)
" c'mon, small fry," sd/the smaller black lad
                to the larger.
" Just playin' " ante mortem no scortum
(that's progress, me yr' ' ' se/call it progress/)

in the timeless air over the sea-cliffs
" the pride of all our D.T.C. was pistol-packin' Burnes "
But to set here the roads of France,
            of Cahors, of Chalus,
        the inn low by the river's edge,
the poplars; to set here the roads of France
Aubeterre, the quarried stone beyond Poitiers—
        —as seen against Sergeant Beaucher's elegant profile—
and the tower on an almost triangular base
            as seen from Santa Marta's in Tarascon

" in heaven have I to make? "

        but all the vair and fair women
        and there is also the more northern (not nordic)
tradition from Memling to Elskamp, extending
                to the ship models in Danzig...
if they have not destroyed them
            with Galla's rest, and...

is measured by the *to whom* it happens
        and to what, and if to a work of art
        then to all who have seen and who will not

Washington, Adams, Tyler, Polk
        (with Crawford to bring in a few Colonial
                families) the unruly

455

Tout dit que pas ne dure la fortune

In fact a small rain storm...
                    as it were a mouse, out of cloud's mountain
recalling the arrival of Joyce et fils
                    at the haunt of Catullus
with Jim's veneration of thunder and the
          Gardasee in magnificence
But Miss Norton's memory for the conversation
          (or " go on ") of idiots
was such as even the eminent Irish writer
          has, if equalled at moments (? sintheticly)
          certainly never surpassed

          Tout dit que pas ne dure la fortune

and the Canal Grande has lasted at least until our time
          even if Florian's has been refurbished
and shops in the Piazza kept up by
                    artificial respiration
and for La Figlia di Jorio they got out a
                    special edition
                    (entitled the Oedipus of the Lagunes)
of caricatures of D'Annunzio

                    l'ara sul rostro
20 years of the dream
          and the clouds near to Pisa
               are as good as any in Italy
said the young Mozart: if you will take a *prise*
               or following Ponce (" Ponthe ")
                    to the fountain in Florida
de Leon alla fuente florida
          or Anchises that laid hold of her flanks of air
drawing her to him
                    Cythera potens, Κύθηρα δεινά

456

no cloud, but the crystal body
       the tangent formed in the hand's cup
   as live wind in the beech grove
      as strong air amid cypress

Κόρη, Δελιά δεινά/et libidinis expers
the sphere moving crystal, fluid,
   none therein carrying rancour
Death, insanity/suicide degeneration
that is, just getting stupider as they get older
πολλά παθεῖν,

        nothing matters but the quality
of the affection—
in the end—that has carved the trace in the mind
dove sta memoria

and if theft be the main principle in government
   (every bank of discount J. Adams remarked)
there will be larceny on a minor pattern
a few camions, a stray packet of sugar
    and the effect of the movies
     the guard did not think that the Führer had started it
Sergeant XL thought that excess population
      demanded slaughter at intervals
       (as to the by whom...) Known as ' The ripper.'

   Lay in soft grass by the cliff's edge
with the sea 30 metres below this
     and at hand's span, at cubit's reach moving,
the crystalline, as inverse of water,
    clear over rock-bed

    ac ferae familiares
the gemmed field *a destra* with fawn, with panther,

corn flower, thistle and sword-flower
        to a half metre grass growth,
lay on the cliff's edge
                ...nor is this yet *atasal*
        nor are here souls, nec personae
        neither here in hypostasis, this land is of **Dione**
and under her planet
        to Helia the long meadow with poplars
to   Κύπρις
        the mountain and shut garden of pear trees in flower
here rested.

                    •   •   •   •

" both eyes, (the loss of) and to find someone
        who talked his own dialect. We
        talked of every boy and girl in the valley
        but when he came back from leave
he was sad because he had been able to feel
        all the ribs of his cow...."
this wind out of Carrara
is soft as *un terzo cielo*
                    said the Prefetto
as the cat walked the porch rail at Gardone
        the lake flowing away from that side
was still as is never in Sirmio
        with Fujiyama above it: " La donna..."
                said the Prefect, in the silence

        and the spring of their squeak-doll is broken
and Bracken is out and the B.B.C. can lie
        but at least a different bilge will come out of it
                at least for a little, as is its nature
can continue, that is, to lie.

            As a lone ant from a broken ant-hill
from the wreckage of Europe, ego scriptor.

The rain has fallen, the wind coming down
    out of the mountain
    Lucca, Forti dei Marmi, Berchthold after the other one...
parts reassembled.
    ...and within the crystal, went up swift as Thetis
in colour rose-blue before sunset
and carmine and amber,

spiriti questi? personae?
            tangibility by no means *atasal*
            but the crystal can be weighed in the hand
formal and passing within the sphere: Thetis,
Maya, Ἀφροδίτη,

                no overstroke
        no dolphin faster in moving
                nor the flying azure of the wing'd fish under Zoagli
        when he comes out into the air, living arrow.
and the clouds over the Pisan meadows
        are indubitably as fine as any to be seen
from the peninsula
        οἱ βάρβαροι have not destroyed them
            as they have Sigismundo's Temple
        Divae Ixottae (and as to her effigy that was in Pisa?)
        Ladder at swing jump as for a descent from the cross
O white-chested martin, God damn it,
        as no one else will carry a message,
        say to La Cara: amo.

Her bed-posts are of sapphire
        for this stone giveth sleep.

        and in spite of hoi barbaroi
        pervenche and a sort of dwarf morning-glory
        that knots in the grass, and a sort of buttercup

et sequelae

Le Paradis n'est pas artificiel
    States of mind are inexplicable to us.
        δακρύων   δακρύων   δακρύων
L.   P.   gli onesti
                J'ai eu pitié des autres
probablement pas assez, and at moments that suited my own con-
                                                            venience
            Le paradis n'est pas artificiel,
                    l'enfer non plus.

Came Eurus as comforter
and at sunset la pastorella dei suini
    driving the pigs home, benecomata dea

            under the two-winged cloud
            as of less and more than a day
by the soap-smooth stone posts where San Vio
meets with il Canal Grande
between Salviati and the house that was of Don Carlos
shd/I chuck the lot into the tide-water?
        le bozze " A Lume Spento "/
                and by the column of Todero
    shd/I shift to the other side
            or wait 24 hours,

            free then, therein the difference
            in the great ghetto, left standing
with the new bridge of the Era where was the old eyesore
            Vendramin, Contrarini, Fonda, Fondecho
        and Tullio Romano carved the sirenes
            as the old custode says: so that since
then no one has been able to carve them
    for the jewel box, Santa Maria Dei Miracoli,

460

Dei Greci, San Giorgio, the place of skulls
                in the Carpaccio
and in the font to the right as you enter
                are all the gold domes of San Marco

Arachne, che mi porta fortuna, go spin on that tent rope

Unkle George in Brassitalo's abbazia
                voi che passate per questa via:
Does D'Annunzio live here?
said the american lady, K. H.
        " I do not know " said the aged Veneziana,
                " this lamp is for the virgin."
            " Non combaattere " said Giovanna,
                meaning: don't work so hard,

Arachne che mi porta fortuna;
                        Athene, who wrongs thee?
                    τίς ἀδικεῖ
That butterfly has gone out thru my smoke hole

Unkle George observing Ct/Volpe's neck at the Lido
        and deducing his energy. Unkle G. stood like a statue
            " Rutherford Hayes on a monument "
                as the princess approached him
            " You from New England? " barked the 10th District,

and it came over me as he talked:
                this is Dafne's Sandro—
        How? after 30 years,

Trovaso, Gregorio, Vio

" Dawnt let 'em git you " burred the bearded Dottore
when was the Scottch Kirrrk in Venice

to warn one against Babylonian intrigue
      and there have been since then
very high episcopal vagaries

      well, my window
    looked out on the Squero where Ogni Santi
meets San Trovaso
      things have ends and beginnings

and the gilded cassoni neither then nor up to the present
the hidden nest, Tami's dream, the great Ovid
      bound in thick boards, the bas relief of Ixotta
      and the care in contriving
Olim de Malatestis
         the long hall over the arches at Fano
olim de Malatestis
         " 64 countries and down a boilin' volcano "
           says the sargent
ex rum-runner (the rum being vino rosso)
      " runnin whisky " sez he; mountain oysters?

      lisciate con lagrime
      politis lachrymis ΔΑΚΡΥΩΝ

      bricks thought into being ex nihil
      suave in the cavity of the rock la concha
        ΠΟΙΚΙΛΟΘΡΟΝ', 'ΑΘΑΝΑΤΑ
         that butterfly has gone out thru my smoke hole
'ΑΘΑΝΑΤΑ,   saeva. Against buff the rose for the
background to Leonello, Petrus Pisani pinxit
      that a cameo should remain

in Arezzo an altar fragment (Cortona, Angelico)
         po'eri di'aoli
po'eri di'aoli sent to the slaughter

Knecht gegen Knecht
to the sound of the bumm drum, to eat remnants
for a usurer's holiday to change the
price of a currency
ΜΕΤΑΘΕΜΕΝΩΝ....
ΝΗΣΟΝ 'ΑΜΥΜΟΝΑ
woe to them that conquer with armies
and whose only right is their power.

LXXVII

AND this day Abner lifted a shovel. . . . .
            instead of watchin' it to see if it would
      take action

Von Tirpitz said to his daughter..as we have elsewhere
recorded / he said: beware of their charm
            But on the other hand Maukch thought he
would do me a favour by getting me onto the commission
to inspect the mass graves at Katin,
            le beau monde gouverne
      if not toujours at any rate it is a level of
some sort whereto things tend to return
            Chung

            in the middle

whether upright or horizontal
      " and having got 'em (advantages, privilege)
there is nothing, italics *nothing*, they will not do
to retain 'em "
                  yrs truly   Kungfutseu
Entered the Bros Watson's store in Clinton N. Y.
            preceded by a crash, i.e. by a
      huge gripsack or satchel
      which fell and skidded along the 20 foot aisle-way
      and ceased with a rumpus of glassware
            (unbreakable as it proved)
            and with the enquiry: WOT IZZA COMIN'?

" I'll tell you wot izza comin'
            Sochy-lism is a-comin'

(a.d. 1904, somewhat previous but effective
for immediate scope
    things have ends (or scopes) and beginnings.　　**To**
know what precedes 先　　　　and what follows 後

　　　　will assist yr/ comprehension of process
　　　　vide also Epictetus and Syrus

As Arcturus passes over my smoke-hole
　　　the excess electric illumination
　　　is now focussed
on the bloke who stole a safe he cdn't open
　　　　(interlude entitled: periplum by camion)
　　　and Awoi's *hennia*　　　plays hob in the tent flaps
　　　　　　k-lakk.....thuuuuuu
　　　　　　　making rain
　　　　　　　　　　uuuh
2,　　7,　　hooo
　　　　　　der im Baluba

　　　Faasa　!　　4 times was the city remade,
now in the heart indestructible
　　　　　　4 gates, the 4 towers
(Il Scirocco è geloso)
　　　　　　　　men rose out of χθόνος
　　　　　　　　　Agada, Ganna, Silla,
　　　and Mt Taishan is faint as the wraith of my first friend
　　　who comes talking ceramics;
　　　　　　　　mist glaze over mountain 何

　　" How is it far, if you think of it? "

Came Boreas and his kylin
to brreak the corporal's heart 遠

465

Bright dawn 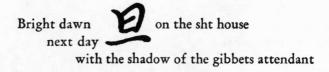 on the sht house
        next day
                with the shadow of the gibbets attendant

The Pisan clouds are undoubtedly various
            and splendid as any I have seen since
at Scudder's Falls on the Schuylkill
        by which stream I seem to recall a feller
settin' in a rudimentary shack doin' nawthin'
            not fishin', just watchin' the water,
        a man of about forty-five

        nothing counts save the quality of the affection

        mouth, is the sun that is god's mouth
or in another connection   (periplum)
        the studio on the Regent's canal
        Theodora asleep on the sofa, the young
        Daimio's " tailor's bill "
        or Grishkin's photo refound years after
            with the feeling that Mr Eliot may have
missed something, after all, in composing his vignette
                            periplum

(the dance is a medium)
        " To his native mountain "
        ψυχάριον ὰι βάσταζον νεκρὸν

a little flame for a little
conserved in the Imperial ballet, never danced in a theatre
Kept as Justinian left it
        Padre José had understood something or other
            before the deluxe car carried him over the precipice

sumne fugol othbaer

learned what the Mass meant,
        how one shd/ perform it

the dancing at Corpus   the toys in the
        service at Auxerre

top, whip, and the rest of them.

[I heard it in the s.h.   a suitable place

to hear that the war was over]

the scollop of the sky shut down on its pearl

    καλλιπλόκαμα   Ida.
With drawn sword as at Nemi
        day comes after day

and the liars on the quai at Siracusa
                still vie with Odysseus
seven words to a bomb

dum capitolium scandet
    the rest is explodable
Very potent, can they again put one together
as the two halves of a seal, or a tally stick?

                Shun's will and
                King Wan's will

were as the two halves of a seal
        ½s
    in the Middle Kingdom

Their aims as one
directio voluntatis, as lord over the heart
        the two sages united

467

and Lord Byron lamented that he (Kung)
had not left it in metric
          " halves of a seal,"

Voltaire choosing almost as I had
          to finish his " Louis Quatorze "

and as to the distributive function
                    1766 ante Christum
it is recorded, and the state *can* lend money
as proved at Salamis
          and for notes on monopoly
          Thales;   and credit, Siena;
          both for the trust and the mistrust;
          " the earth belongs to the living "
          interest on all it creates out of nothing
the buggering bank has;   pure iniquity
          and to change the value of money, of the unit of money
money
          METATHEMENON
          we are not yet out of *that* chapter
          Le Paradis n'est pas artificiel
Κύθηρα,   Κύθηρα,
Moving ὑπὸ   χθονὸς   enters the hall of the records
          the forms of men rose out of γέα
          Le Paradis n'est pas artificiel
                    nor does the martin against the tempest
fly as in the calm air
" like an arrow, and under bad government
                    like an arrow "
" Missing the bull's eye seeks the cause in himself "
" only the total sincerity, the precise definition "
and no sow's ear from silk purse
                    even in that case...

the clouds over Pisa, over the two teats of Tellus, γέα

" He won't " said Pirandello " fall for Freud,
  he (Cocteau) is too good a poet."

Well, Campari is gone since that day
   with Dieudonné and with Voisin
and Gaudier's eye on the telluric mass of Miss Lowell

" the mind of Plato... or that of Bacon "   said Upward
   seeking parallel for his own
" Haff you gno bolidigal basshunts?....
Demokritoos, Heragleitos " exclaimed Doktor Slonimsky 1912

So Miscio sat in the dark lacking the gasometer penny
  but then said: " Do you speak German? "

  to Asquith, in 1914

" How Ainley face work all the time
      back of that mask "
But Mrs Tinkey never believed he wanted her cat
for mouse-chasing
   and not for oriental cuisine

" Jap'nese dance all time overcoat " he remarked
with perfect precision

" Just like Jack Dempsey's mitts " sang Mr Wilson

 . so that you cd/ crack a flea on eider wan
   ov her breasts
sd/ the old Dublin pilot
   or the precise definition

  bel seno (in rimas escarsas, vide sopra)

2 mountains with the Arno, I suppose, flowing between them
so kissed the earth after sleeping on concrete

bel seno   Δημήτηρ copulatrix
                    thy furrow

in limbo no victories, there, are no victories—
that is limbo; between decks of the slaver
          10 years, 5 years

" If he wd/ *only* get rid of Ciano " groaned the admiral
" people who are used to take orders " he said
          when the fleet surrendered
" I would do it " (finish off Ciano) " with a pinch of
          insecticide."
          said Chilanti's 12 year old daughter.
Sold the school-house at Gais,
cut down the woods whose leaves served for bedding cattle
                    so there was a lack of manure...

for losing the law of Chung Ni,
               hence the valise set by the alpino's statue in Brunik
               and the long lazy float of the banners
and similar things occurred in Dalmatia
               lacking that treasure of honesty
which is the treasure of states
          and the dog-damn wop is not, save by exception,
honest in administration any more than the briton is truthful

Jactancy, vanity, peculation to the ruin of 20 years' labour

bells over Petano   ...are softer than other bells
remembering Alice and Edmée
          till the dog Arlechino makes his round
               blanket holding the hills' form in cloudy aurora

E la Miranda was the only one who changed personality
              changing her roles

Which fact, it wd/ seem, escaped most, if not all, of the critics

" If you had a f....n' brain you'd be dangerous "
                remarks Romano Ramona
      to a by him designated c.s. in the scabies ward
            the army vocabulary contains almost 48 words
one verb and participle one substantive   ὕλη
            one adjective and one phrase sexless that is
used as a sort of pronoun
from a watchman's club to a vamp or fair lady

And Margherita's voice was clear as the notes of a clavichord
tending her rabbit hutch,
                          O Margaret of the seven griefs
who hast entered the lotus

      " Trade, trade, trade.." sang Lanier
      and they say the gold her grandmother carried under her
skirts for Jeff Davis
      drowned her when she slipped from the landing boat;
doom of Atreus

      (O Mercury god of thieves, your caduceus
      is now used by the american army
                        as witness this packing case)

Born with Buddha's eye south of Mason and Dixon
as against:
                Ils n'existent pas, leur ambience leur confert
                      une existence...and in the case of

Emanuel Swedenborg...." do not argue "
            in the 3rd sphere do not argue

above which, the lotus, white nenuphar
Kuanon, the mythologies

we who have passed over Lethe

            there are in fact several coarse expressions used in the
army and Monsieur Barzun had, indubitably, an idea, about anno

domini 1910 but I do not know what he has done with it
            for I wd/ steal no man's raison
                        and old André
preached vers libre with Isaiaic fury, and sent me to old Rousselot
who fished for sound in the Seine
                        and led to detectors
" an animal " he said " which seeks to conceal the
            sound of its foot-steps "
                        L'Abbé Rousselot
who wrapped up De Sousa's poems (fin oreille)
and besought me to do likewise returning them
            lest his housekeeper know that he had them.

" Un curé déguisé " sd/ Cocteau's of Maritain
            " Me parait un curé déguisé " A la porte
" Sais pas, Monsieur, il me parait un curé déguisé.

" Thought " said M. Cocteau   " that I was among men of letters
            and then perceived a group of mechanics and garage assistants."
" As long as Daudet is alive they will never have him

            in the Académie Goncourt "
                        sd/ La Comtesse de Rohan, and Mr Martin
we believe did a similar wrong to his party

472

"   30,000, they thought they were clever,
why, Hell / they cd/ have had it for 6000 dollars,
and after Landon they picked Wendell Willkie

                    Roi je ne suis, prince je ne daigne
Citizen of Florence, cd/ not receive noble titles
                    but carry the arms to this day
who resisted at Arbia when the fools wd/ have burnt down
Florence " in gran dispitto "   " men used to obeying orders "
          " there was also the King who signed those decrees "
              se casco, non casco in ginocchion'

—niggers comin' over the obstacle fence
                    as in the insets at the Schifanoja
(del Cossa) to scale, 10,000 gibbet-iform posts supporting
                    barbed wire
" St. Louis Till " as Green called him. Latin !
    " I studied latin " said perhaps his smaller companion.
" Hey Snag, what's in the bibl' ?
              what are the books of the bibl' ?
Name 'em! don't bullshit me! "
          " Hobo Williams, the queen of them all "
" Hey / Crawford, come over here / "

                    Roma profugens Sabinorum in terras
" Sligo in heaven " murmured uncle William
          when the mist finally settled down on Tigullio

But Mr Joyce requested sample menus from the leading hotels
and Kitson had tinkered with lights on the Vetta

Mist covers the breasts of Tellus-Helena and drifts up the Arno
came night and with night the tempest
              " How is it far, if you think of it? "

                    473

If Basil sing of Shah Nameh, and wrote

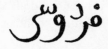

Firdush' on his door

Thus saith Kabir: " Politically " said Rabindranath
            " they are inactive. They think, but then there is
climate, they think but it is warm or there are flies or
some insects "

" And with the return of the gold standard " wrote Sir Montagu
" every peasant had to pay twice as much grain
            to cover his taxes and interest "

It is true that the interest is now legally lower
but the banks lend to the bunya
who can thus lend more to his victims
and the snot press and periodical tosh does not notice this
thus saith Kabir, by hypostasis
if they can take Hancock's wharf they can take your cow
                                    or my barn
and the Kohinoor and the rajah's emerald etc.

and Tom wore a tin disc, a circular can-lid
            with his name on it, solely:
for Wanjina has lost his mouth,

            For nowt so much as a just peace
That wd/ obstruct future wars
as witness the bombardment at Frascati after the armistice
            had been signed

who live by debt and war profiteering
            Das Bankgeschäft
                        "....of the Wabash cannon ball "

in flat Ferrarese country seemed the same as here under Taishan

men move to scale   as in Del Cossa's insets
          at Schifanoja under the Ram and Bull

in the house-boats bargaining half a day for ten bob's worth
          of turquoise

mind come to plenum when nothing more will go into it

the wind mad as Cassandra
          who was as sane as the lot of 'em

Sorella, mia sorella,
          che ballava sobr' un zecchin'

成   bringest to focus   成

ch'êng   Zagreus   *ch'êng*

          Zagreus

中先後何遠旦口符節

非其鬼而祭之諂也志成

1 - middle

2 - precede

3 - follow

4 - how (is it)

far

5 - dawn

6 - mouth

7 - not

one's own

spirit

and

sacrifice

is

flattery

bi gosh

To sacrifice to a spirit not one's own is flattery (sycophancy).

8 - halves of a
tally stick

9 - direction
of one's will

10 - perfect or
focus

LXXVIII

BY THE square elm of Ida
    40 geese are assembled
    (little sister who could dance on a sax-pence)
    to arrange a pax mundi
        Sobr' un zecchin'!
Cassandra, your eyes are like tigers,
    with no word written in them
You also have I carried to nowhere
    to an ill house and there is
        no end to the journey.
        The chess board too lucid
the squares are too even...theatre of war...
" theatre " is good. There are those who did not want
    it to come to an end

and those negroes by the clothes-line are extraordinarily like the
        figures del Cossa
Their green does not swear at the landscape
2 months' life in 4 colours
    ter flebiliter: Ityn
to close the temple of Janus bifronte
    the two-faced bastard
" and the economic war has begun "
    Napoleon wath a goodth man, it took uth
    20 yearth to crwuth him
it will not take uth 20 years to crwuth Mussolini "
    as was remarked in via Balbo by the Imperial Chemicals
its brother.
    Firms failed as far off as Avignon...
...my red leather note-book

                              pax Medicea
        by his own talk in Naples, Lorenzo
            who left lyrics inoltre
            that men sing to this day
        " alla terra abbandonata "
                                followed him Metastasio;
    " alla " non " della " in il Programma di Verona
            the old hand as stylist still holding its cunning
    and the water flowing away from that side of the lake
    is silent as never at Sirmio
                    under the arches
    Foresteria, Salò, Gardone
                to dream the Republic. San Sepolchro
                the four bishops in metal
    lapped by the flame, amid ruin, la fede—
            reliquaries seen on the altar.
    " Someone to take the blame if we slip up on it "
    Goedel's sleek head in the midst of it,
                the man out of Naxos past Fara Sabina
    " if you will stay for the night "
    " it is true there is only one room for the lot of us "
    " money is nothing "
    " no, there is nothing to pay for that bread "
                        " nor for the minestra "
    " Nothing left here but women "
                    " Have lugged it this far, will keep it " (il zaino)
                No, they will do nothing to you.
    " Who *says* he is an American "
            a still form on the branda, Bologna
    " Gruss Gott," " Der Herr! " "Tatile ist gekommen! "
            Slow lift of long banners
                    Roma profugens Sabinorum in terras
    and belt the citye quahr of nobil fame
        the lateyn peopil taken has their name
    bringing his gods into Latium

                            478

                    saving the bricabrac
" Ere he his goddis brocht in Latio "
              " each one in the name "
in whom are the voices, keeping hand on the reins
Gaudier's word not blacked out
                    nor old Hulme's, nor Wyndham's,
Mana aboda.
The touch of sadism in the back of his neck
tinting justice, " Steele that is one awful name."
    sd/ the cheerful reflective nigger
Blood and Slaughter to help him
                dialog repartee at the drain hole
Straight as the bar of a ducking stool " got his pride "
get to the states you can buy it
                    Don't try that here
the bearded owl making catcalls
                    Pallas Δίκη sustain me
" definition can not be shut down under a box lid "
but if the gelatine be effaced whereon is the record?
" wherein is no responsible person
            having a front name, a hind name and an address "
" not a right but a duty "
                those words still stand uncancelled,
    " Presente! "
                and merrda for the monopolists
                    the bastardly lot of 'em
Put down the slave trade, made the desert to yield
and menaced the loan swine
                Sitalkas, double Sitalkas
                " not the priest but the victim "
            said Allen Upward
knew something was phoney, when he (Pellegrini)
    sd/ : the money is there.
Knowledge lost with Justinian, and with Titus and Antoninus
    (" law rules the sea " meaning lex Rhodi)

479

that the state have vantage from private misfortune
No! Or the story of property
           to Rostovseff (is it Rostovseff?)
nothing worse than fixed charge
                    several years' average
Mencius III, 1. T'ang Wan Kung
                         Chapter 3 and verse 7
Be welcome, O cricket my grillo, but you must not
                         sing after taps.
Guard's cap quattrocento
           o-hon dit que'ke fois au vi'age
                    qu'une casque ne sert pour rien
                    'hien de tout
           Cela ne sert que pour donner courage
                    a ceux qui n'en ont pas de tout
So Salzburg reopens
           Qui suona Wolfgang grillo
           P° viola da gamba
one might do worse than open a pub on Lake Garda
           so one thinks of
Tailhade and " Willy " (Gauthier-Villars)
           and of Mockel and La Wallonie...en casque
de crystal rose les baladines

                    with the cakeshops in the Nevsky
and Sirdar, Armenonville or the Kashmiri house-boats
en casque de crystal rose les baladines
messed up Monsieur Mozart's house
           but left the door of the new concert hall
So he said, looking at the signed columns in San Zeno
" how the hell can we get any architecture
                    when we order our columns by the gross? "
red marble with a stone loop cast round it, four shafts,
and Farinata, kneeling in the cortile,
           built like Ubaldo, that's race,

Can Grande's grin like Tommy Cochran's
                "E fa di clarità l'aer tremare"
            thus writ, and conserved (or was) in Verona
So we sat there by the arena,
                    outside, Thiy and il decaduto
the lace cuff fallen over his knuckles
    considering Rochefoucauld
but the program (Cafe Dante) a literary program 1920 or
                thereabouts was neither published nor followed
    Griffith said, years before that, : " Can't move 'em with
a cold thing like economics   I am pledged not to
come here (London) to Parliament "
            Aram vult nemus
as under the rain altars
asking how to discover delusions (confusions)
            " Chose Kao-yao and the crooks disappeared."
            " Chose I Yin and the crooks toddled off."
            2 hours of living, knew when they left
that there wd/ be one hell of a fight in the senate
        Lodge, Knox against world entanglement
Two with him in the whole house against the constriction of
                                        Bacchus
moved to repeal that god-damned amendment
        Number XVIII
                    Mr Tinkham
Geneva the usurers' dunghill
        Frogs, brits, with a few dutch pimps
as top dressing to preface extortions
        and the usual filthiness
for detail see Odon's neat little volume
            , that is, for a few of the more obvious details,
the root stench being usura and METATHEMENON
and Churchill's return to Midas broadcast by his liary.
            " No longer necessary," taxes are no longer necessary
in the old way if it (money) be based on work done

inside a system and measured and gauged to human
requirements
inside the nation or system

道、

and cancelled in proportion
to what is used and worn out
à la Wörgl.   Sd/ one wd/ have to think about that
but was hang'd dead by the heels before his thought in proposito
came into action efficiently
" For a pig," Jepson said, " for a woman." For the infamies of
usura,
The Stealing of the Mare,   casûs bellorum,   " mits "
sang Mr Wilson, Thomas not Woodrow, Harriet's spirited heir
(the honours twice with his boots on,
that was Wellington)
and if theft be the main motive in government
in a large way
there will certainly be minor purloinments
As long as the socialists use their accessories as red herring
to keep man's mind off the creation of money
many men's mannirs   videt et urbes πολύμητις
ce rusé personnage, Otis,   so Nausikaa
took down the washing or at least went to see that the
maids didn't slack
or sat by the window
at Bagni Romagna   knowing that nothing could happen
and looking ironicly at the traveler
Cassandra your eyes are like tigers'
no light reaches through them
eating lotus, or if not exactly the lotus, the asphodel
To be gentildonna in a lost town in the mountains
on a balcony with an iron railing
with a servant behind her
as it might be in a play by Lope de Vega

482

and one goes by, not alone,
                    No hay amor sin celos
Sin segreto no hay amor
                    eyes of Doña Juana la loca,
Cunizza's shade al triedro and that presage
                    in the air
which means that nothing will happen that will
     be visible to the sargeants
Tre donne intorno alla mia mente
but as of conversation to follow,
boredom of that roman on Olivia's stairs
                    in her vision
that stone angle all of his scenery
                    with the balustrade, an antipodes
and as for the solidity of the white oxen in all this
     perhaps only Dr Williams (Bill Carlos)
                    will understand its importance,
          its benediction. He wd/ have put in the cart.
The shadow of the tent's peak treads on its corner peg
marking the hour. The moon split, no cloud nearer than Lucca.
In the spring and autumn
     In "The Spring and Autumn"
                              there
                              are
                              no
                              righteous
                              wars

LXXIX

Moon,   cloud,   tower,   a patch of the battistero
                                all of a whiteness,
    dirt pile as per the Del Cossa inset
    think not that you wd/ gain if their least caress
were faded from my mind
I had not loved thee half so well
Loved I not womankind "
                   So Salzburg reopens
        lit a flame in my thought that the years
               Amari—li   Am——ar—i—li!
and her hair gone white   from the loss of him
          and she not yet thirty.
On her wedding day and then thus, for the next time,
           at the Spielhaus,
        ...might have been two years later.
Or Astafieva inside the street doors of the Wigmore
               and wd/ not have known her
         undoubtedly wd/ have put in the cart)
present Mr G. Scott whistling Lili Marlene
        with positively less musical talent
        than that of any other man of colour
          whom I have ever encountered
but with bonhomie and good humour
          (to Goedel in memoriam)
Sleek head that saved me out of one chaos
and I hear that G. P. has salmoned thru all of it.
Où sont? and who will come to the surface?
And Pétain not to be murdered   14 to 13
        after six hours' discussion
Indubitably, indubitably re/ Scott
          I like a certain number of shades in my landscape

as per / " doan' tell no one I made you that table "
or Whiteside:
                    " ah certainly dew lak dawgs,
                    ah goin' tuh wash you "
(no, not to the author, to the canine unwilling in question)
                    with 8 birds on a wire
or rather on 3 wires, Mr Allingham
The new Bechstein is electric
and the lark squawk has passed out of season
whereas the sight of a good nigger is cheering
        the bad'uns wont look you straight
Guard's cap quattrocento passes *a cavallo*
        on horseback thru landscape Cosimo Tura
            or, as some think, Del Cossa;
up stream to delouse and down stream for the same purpose
seaward
different lice live in different waters
some minds take pleasure in counterpoint
        pleasure in counterpoint
and the later Beethoven on the new Bechstein,
or in the Piazza S. Marco for example
finds a certain concordance of size
                not in the concert hall;
can that be the papal major sweatin' it out to the bumm drum?
what castrum romanum, what
            " went into winter quarters "
is under us?
as the young horse whinnies against the tubas
            in contending for certain values
(Janequin per esempio, and Orazio Vechii or Bronzino)
Greek rascality against Hagoromo
        Kumasaka vs/ vulgarity
            no sooner out of Troas
than the damn fools attacked Ismarus of the Cicones
        4 birds on 3 wires, one bird on one

the imprint of the intaglio depends
        in part on what is pressed under it
the mould must hold what is poured into it
             in
                discourse

                     what matters is
to get it across e poi basta
        5 of 'em now on 2;
          on 3; 7 on 4
              thus what's his name
     and the change in writing the song books
        5 on 3   aulentissima rosa fresca
so they have left the upper church at Assisi
        but the Goncourt shed certain light on the
french revolution
        " paak you djeep oveh there "
the bacon-rind banner alias the Washington arms
        floats over against Ugolino
in San Stefano dei Cavalieri
        God bless the Constitution
and *save* it
        " the value thereof "
        that is the crux of the matter
and god damn the perverters
        and if Attlee attempts a Ramsey
" Leave the Duke, go for the gold "
        " in less than a geological epoch "
and the Fleet that triumphed at Salamis
        and Wilkes's fixed the price per loaf
ἦθος
     Athene cd/ have done with more sex appeal
caesia oculi
" Pardon me, γλαύξ "
              (" Leave it, I'm not a fool.")
mah?

"The price is three altars, multa."
    "paak you djeep oveh there."
                     2 on 2
what's the name of that bastard? D'Arezzo, Gui d'Arezzo
notation

            3 on 3
         chiacchierona   the yellow bird
   to rest   3 months in bottle
                         (auctor)
by the two breasts of Tellus
   Bless my buttons, a staff car/
si come avesse l'inferno in gran dispitto
Capanaeus
     with 6 on 3, swallow-tails
as from the breasts of Helen, a cup of white gold
2 cups for three altars. Tellus γέα feconda
   " each one in the name of its god "
   mint, thyme and basilicum,
the young horse whinnies against the sound of the bumm band;
to that ' gadgett,' and to the production and the slaughter
(on both sides) in memoriam
" Hell! don't they get a break for the whistle? "
   and if the court be not the centre of learning...
in short the snot of pejorocracy...
                tinsel gilded
of fat fussy old woman
   and fat snorty old stallions
   " half dead at the top "
My dear William B. Y. your ½ was too moderate
" pragmatic pig " (if goyim) will serve for 2 thirds of it
to say nothing of the investment of funds in the Yu-en-mi
and similar ventures
   small arms 'n' chemicals
whereas Mr Keith comes nearest to Donatello's
     O Lynx, my love, my lovely lynx,

Keep watch over my wine pot,
Guard close my mountain still
Till the god come into this whiskey.
Manitou, god of lynxes, remember our corn.
Khardas, god of camels
                    what the deuce are you doing here?
I beg your pardon...
" Prepare to go on a journey."
    " I..."

    " Prepare to go on a journey."
or to count sheep in Phoenician,
            How is it far if you think of it?
So they said to Lidya: no, your body-guard is not the
                    town executioner
the executioner is not here for the moment
the fellow who rides beside your coachman
        is just a cossak who executes...
Which being the case, her holding dear H. J.
        (Mr. James, Henry) literally by the button-hole...
in those so consecrated surroundings
                    (a garden in the Temple, no less)
                    and saying, *for once*, the right thing
namely: " Cher maître "
to his checqued waistcoat, the Princess Bariatinsky,
as the fish-tails said to Odysseus, ἐνὶ Τροίῃ,

    The moon has a swollen cheek
and when the morning sun lit up the shelves and battalions
of the West, cloud over cloud
                    Old Ez folded his blankets
Neither Eos nor Hesperus has suffered wrong at my hands

            O Lynx, wake Silenus and Casey
            shake the castagnettes of the bassarids,

the mountain forest is full of light
      the tree-comb red-gilded
Who sleeps in the field of lynxes
      in the orchard of Maelids?
(with great blue marble eyes
      " because he likes to," the cossak)
Salazar, Scott, Dawley on sick call
      Polk, Tyler, half the presidents and Calhoun
" Retaliate on the capitalists " sd/ Calhoun " of the North "
ah yes, when the ideas were clearer
      debts to people in N. Y. city
      and on the hill of the Maelids
in the close garden of Venus
      asleep amid serried lynxes
set wreathes on Priapus Ἴακχος, Io! Κύθηρα, Io!
      having root in the equities
Io!
    and you can make 5000 dollars a year
all you have to do is to make one trip up country
then come back to Shanghai
      and send in an annual report
as to the number of converts
      Sweetland on sick call
     ἐλέησον   Kyrie eleison
    each under his fig tree
    or with the smell of fig leaves burning
so shd/ be fire in winter
with fig wood, with cedar, and pine burrs

    O Lynx keep watch on my fire.

So Astafieva had conserved the tradition
From Byzance and before then
    Manitou remember this fire
O lynx, keep the phylloxera from my grape vines

Ἴακχε, Ἴακχε, Χαῖρε, AOI
    " Eat of it not in the under world "
    See that the sun or the moon bless thy eating
Κόρη, Κόρη, for the six seeds of an error
or that the stars bless thy eating

    O Lynx, guard this orchard,
    Keep from Demeter's furrow

This fruit has a fire within it,
    Pomona, Pomona
No glass is clearer than are the globes of this flame
what sea is clearer than the pomegranate body
    holding the flame?
    Pomona, Pomona,

    Lynx, keep watch on this orchard
    That is named Melagrana
or the Pomegranate field
    The sea is not clearer in azure
    Nor the Heliads bringing light

Here are lynxes   Here are lynxes,
Is there a sound in the forest
    of pard or of bassarid
or crotale   or of leaves moving?

    Cythera, here are lynxes
Will the scrub-oak burst into flower?
    There is a rose vine in this underbrush
Red? white? No, but a colour between them
    When the pomegranate is open and the light falls
half thru it

    Lynx, beware of these vine-thorns
    O Lynx, γλαυκῶπις coming up from the olive yards,

Kuthera, here are Lynxes and the clicking of crotales
There is a stir of dust from old leaves
    Will you trade roses for acorns
    Will lynxes eat thorn leaves?
    What have you in that wine jar?
            ἰχώρ, for lynxes?

Maelid and bassarid among lynxes;
       how many? There are more under the oak trees,
We are here waiting the sun-rise
    and the next sunrise
for three nights amid lynxes. For three nights
    of the oak-wood
and the vines are thick in their branches
    no vine lacking flower,
no lynx lacking a flower rope
    no Maelid minus a wine jar
this forest is named Melagrana

        O lynx, keep the edge on my cider
        Keep it clear without cloud

We have lain here amid kalicanthus and sword-flower
    The heliads are caught in wild rose vine
The smell of pine mingles with rose leaves
       O lynx, be many
       of spotted fur and sharp ears.
       O lynx, have your eyes gone yellow,
       with spotted fur and sharp ears?

Therein is the dance of the bassarids
    Therein are centaurs
And now Priapus with Faunus
    The Graces have brought Ἀφροδίτην
    Her cell is drawn by ten leopards

O lynx, guard my vineyard
As the grape swells under vine leaf
Ἥλιος is come to our mountain
there is a red glow in the carpet of pine spikes

O lynx, guard my vineyard
As the grape swells under vine leaf

This Goddess was born of sea-foam
She is lighter than air under Hesperus
δεινὰ εἶ, Κύθηρα
terrible in resistance
Κόρη καὶ Δήλια καὶ Μαῖα
trine as praeludio
Κύπρις Ἀφρόδιτη
a petal lighter than sea-foam
Κύθηρα
aram
nemus
vult

O puma, sacred to Hermes, Cimbica servant of Helios.

LXXX

A IN' committed no federal crime,
     jes a slaight misdemeanor "
   Thus Mr A. Little or perhaps Mr Nelson, or Washington
   reflecting on the vagaries of our rising θέμις

Amo ergo sum, and in just that proportion
    And Margot's death will be counted the end of an era
and dear Walter was sitting amid the spoils of Finlandia
a good deal of polar white
     but the gas cut off.
Debussy preferred his playing
     that also was an era (Mr. W. Rummel)
an era of croissants
    then an era of *pains au lait*
and the eucalyptus bobble is missing
     " Come pan, niño! "
that was an era also, and Spanish bread
     was made out of grain in that era
     senesco
       sed amo
Madri', Sevilla, Córdoba,
    there was grain equally in the bread of that era
     senesco sed amo
Gervais must have put milk in his cheese
(and the mortal fatigue of action postponed)
and Las Meniñas hung in a room by themselves
and Philip horsed and not horsed and the dwarfs
      and Don Juan of Austria
Breda, the Virgin, Los Boracchos
     are they all now in the Prado?
y Las Hilanderas?

Do they sell such old brass still in " Las Américas "
　　　with the wind coming hot off the marsh land
　　　　　or with death-chill from the mountains?
and with Symons remembering Verlaine at the Tabarin
　　　　　or Hennique, Flaubert
Nothing but death, said Turgenev (Tiresias)
　　　　　is irreparable
ἀγλαὸς ἀλάου πόρνη Περσεφόνεια
　　　Still hath his mind entire
But to lose faith in a possible collaboration
To raise up the ivory wall
or to stand as the coral rises,
as the pilot-fish nears it
　　　　　　　　(will they shoot X——y)
or the whale-mouth　　　　　for wanting a northern league
for demanding a Scandinavian Norse coalition
　　　　　　　inexorable
　　　　　　　　　this is from heaven
　　　the warp
　　　and the woof
with a sky wet as ocean
flowing with liquid slate
Pétain defended Verdun while Blum
　　　　　was defending a bidet
the red and white stripes
　　　　　cut clearer against the slate
　　　than against any other distance
the blue field melts with the cloud-flow
To communicate and then stop, that is the
　　　law of discourse
　　　To go far and come to an end
simplex munditiis, as the hair of Circe
perhaps without the munditiis
as the difference between the title page in old Legge
and some of the elegant fancy work

494

I wonder what Tsu Tsze's calligraphy looked like
they say she could draw down birds from the trees,
     that indeed was imperial; but made hell in
the palace
               as some say : a dark forest
                         the warp and the woof
                              that is of heaven
" and I be damned " said Confucius:
This affair of a southern Nancy
          and as for the vagaries of our friend
                         Mr Hartmann,
Sadakichi a few more of him,
were that conceivable, would have enriched
     the life of Manhattan
     or any other town or metropolis
the texts of his early stuff are probably lost
with the loss of fly-by-night periodicals
          and our knowledge of Hovey,
                    Stickney, Loring,
the lost legion or as Santayana has said:
They just died   They died because they
     just couldn't stand it
and Carman " looked like a withered berry "
          20 years after
Whitman liked oysters
at least I think it was oysters
          and the clouds have made a pseudo-Vesuvius
                    this side of Taishan
Nenni, Nenni, who will have the succession?
To this whiteness, Tseng said
     " What shall add to this whiteness? "
and as to poor old Benito
               one had a safety-pin
one had a bit of string, one had a button
     all of them so far beneath him

half-baked and amateur
   or mere scoundrels
To sell their country for half a million
     hoping to cheat more out of the people
bought the place from the concierge
    who could not deliver
but on the other hand emphasis
  an error or excess of
      emphasis
the problem after any revolution is what to do with
your gunmen
as old Billyum found out in Oireland
   in the Senate, Bedad! or before then
    Your gunmen thread on moi drreams
    O woman shapely as a swan,
Your gunmen tread on my dreams
Whoi didn't he (Padraic Colum)
   keep on writing poetry at that voltage
" Whenever you get hold of one of their banknotes
(i.e. an Ulster note) burn it "
     said one of the senators
     planning the conquest of Ulster
This he said in the Oirish Senate
   showing a fine grasp of...
    of possibly nothing,
If a man don't occasionally sit in a senate
   how can he pierce the darrk mind of a
       senator?

and down there they have been having their Palio
" Torre! Torre! Civetta! "
  and I trust they have not destroyed the
old theatre
    by restaurations, and by late renaissance giribizzi,
    dove è Barilli?

this calvario " we will not descend from," sd/ the *prete*
on the damn'd hard bench waiting the horses
         and the parade and the carrocchio and the flag-play
and the tossing of the flags of the contrade
      " for another four hours "
" non è una hontrada è un homplesso "
explained an expert to an inexpert
re/ the remains of the guilds or *arti*
where they say: hamomila de hampo
      and the Osservanza is broken
         and the best de la Robbia busted to flinders
         and near what? Li Saou
and the front of the Tempio, Rimini
It will not take uth twenty yearth
                    to cwuth Mutholini
and the economic war has begun

                                        35 via Balbo
(Napoleon etc.) Since Waterloo
nothing etc.   Leave the Duke, go for the gold!
action somewhat sporadic
      " Will never be used at home
                    but abroad to increase the
etc. of the lenders," the eh...investors
      and is buried in the Red Square in Mosqu
      along with Andy Jackson, Napoleon and others
there is according to some authors a partial resurrection
      of corpses
on all souls day in Cairo
      or perhaps all over Egypt
      in identity but not atom for atom
but the Sadducees hardly give credence
to Mr Eliot's version
Partial resurrection in Cairo.
Beddoes, I think, omits it.
         The bone *luz,* I think was his take off

Curious, is it not, that Mr Eliot
has not given more time to Mr Beddoes
            (T. L.) prince of morticians
        where none can speak his language
centuries hoarded
to pull up a mass of algae
                    (and pearls)
or the odour of eucalyptus or sea wrack
        cat-faced, croce di Malta, figura del sol
        to each tree its own mouth and savour
        " Hot   hole   hep   cat "
or words of similar volume
        to be recognized by the god-damned
                    or man-damned trainee
Prowling night-puss leave my hard squares alone
        they are in no case cat food
                    if you had sense
you wd/ come here at meal time
            when meat is superabundant
you can neither eat manuscript nor Confucius
        nor even the hebrew scriptures
        get out of that bacon box
        contract W, 11   oh   oh   9   oh
now used as a wardrobe
                ex 53 pounds gross weight
the cat-faced eucalyptus nib
            is where you cannot get at it
        Tune: kitten on the keys
            radio steam Calliope
following the Battle Hymn of the Republic
        where the honey-wagon cease from stinking
                        and the nose be at peace
" mi-hine eyes hev "
                    well yes they *have*
seen a good deal of it

there is a good deal to be seen
fairly tough and unblastable
and the hymn...
well in contrast to the *god*-damned crooning
put me down for temporis acti
ΟΥ ΤΙΣ
ἄχρονος
now there are no more days
οὔ τις
ἄχρονος
the water seeps in under the bottle's seal
Till finally the moon rose like a blue p.c.
of Bingen on the Rhine
round as Perkeo's tub
then glaring Eos stared the moon in the face
(Pistol packin' Jones with an olive branch) *ch'üan*[3]
man and dog

on the S. E. horizon
and we note that dog precedes man in the occident
as of course in the orient if the bloke in the
is proceeding to rightwards
" Why war? " sd/ the sergeant rum-runner
" too many people! when there git to be too many
you got to kill some of 'em off."
" But for Kuan Chung," sd/ Confucius
" we shd / still be buttoning our coats tother way on."
the level of political education in our
eminent armies
is, perhaps, not yet established   ma
così discesi per l'aer maligno
on doit le temps ainsi prendre qu'il vient
or to write dialog because there is
no one to converse with
to take the sheep out to pasture
to bring your g.r. to the nutriment

            gentle reader   to the gist of the discourse
                   to sort out the animals

so that leaving America I brought with me $80
        and England a letter of Thomas Hardy's
        and Italy one eucalyptus pip
from the salita that goes up from Rapallo
                            (if I go)
" a S. Bartolomeo mi vidi col pargoletto,
Chiodato a terra colle braccie aperte
                            in forma di croce gemisti.
                    disse: Io son' la luna."
Coi piedi sulla falce d'argento
        mi parve di pietosa sembianza
The young Dumas weeps because the young Dumas
has tears
        Death's seeds move in the year
                                semina motuum
            falling back into the trough of the sea
            the moon's arse been chewed off by this time
semina motuum
        " With us there is no deceit "
                    said the moon nymph   immacolata
                    Give back my cloak, *hagoromo*.
                    had I the clouds of heaven
                        as the nautile borne ashore
                    in their holocaust
                        as wistaria floating shoreward
with the sea gone the colour of copper
        and emerald dark in the offing
the young Dumas has tears thus far from the year's end
At Ephesus she had compassion on silversmiths

revealing the paraclete
standing in the cusp
    of the moon et in Monte Gioiosa
    as the larks rise at Allegre
                  Cythera egoista
    But for Actaeon
    of the eternal moods has fallen away
in Fano Caesaris for the long room over the arches
olim de Malatestis

      wan   caritas   ΧΑΡΙΤΕΣ

and when bad government prevailed, like an arrow,
fog rose from the marshland
        bringing claustrophobia of the mist
beyond the stockade there is chaos and nothingness
            Ade du Piccadilly
            Ade du Lesterplatz
Their works like cobwebs when the spider is gone
    encrust them with sun-shot crystals
and in 40 years no one save old Bellotti
      " There is no darkness but ignorance "
    had read the words on the pedestal
The things I cd/ tell you, he sd/ of Lady de X
and of how he caught the Caressor's about to be
        Imperial coat tails
and only twice had rec'd 3 penny bits
      one from Rothschild and one from DeLara
and brought in about 2 ounces of saffron
for a risotto during that first so enormous war
      Jah, the Bard's pedestal ist am Lesterplatz
in the city of London
but the trope is, as the accurate reader will have observed,
not to be found in Sam Johnson's edition
The evil that men do lives after them "

501

well, that is from Julius Caesar
            unless memory trick me
who crossed the Rubicon up near Rimini
Where is, or was, an arch of Augustus
            " Wanted to borrow it back " said H. Cole
    " I sd/ why? he thought he wd/
make another one like it " so Horace C. started
buying someone else's paintings
            whose name, be it not Innes, escapes me
But impersonated a sultan
of was it Zanzibar and took up the paving in Bond St.
    to compensate for a partial deafness
which, he felt, lost him part of life's fun
and persuaded an Aussie or Zealander or S. African
to kneel with him in prayer
            outside the Kardomah tea rooms
and also roused a street demonstration
            in Soho for Italy's entry into combat in
                19 was it 15?
pass Napper, Bottom (correct that to Bottomly)
                Gaddy on sick call
will be wanted for gunstocks or need belladonna
                and as for sulking
I knew but one Achilles in my time
and he ended up in the Vatican
                Hannibals, Hamilcars
in profusion nearly all humble persons
" Jolly woman " said the resplendent head waiter
20 years after i.e. after old Kait'
had puffed in, stewing with rage
concerning the landlady's *doings*
                with a lodger unnamed
az waz near Gt Tichfield St. next door to the pub
" married wumman, you couldn't fool *her* "
Torn from the *sacerdos*

                    hurled into unstillness, Ixion
          Trinacrian manxman
                    So old Sauter
front hall full of large photos of Bismark
          and Von Moltke
so that during the Boer war Whistler used to come
and talk strategy
                    but that he, Sauter, never cd/ see
the portrait of Sarasate
          " like a black fly hanging stuck to that canvas "
till one day after Whistler's death
          I think it was Ysaÿe was with him
                    who saw the Whistler
for the first time and burst out:
                              What a fiddle!

It is said also that Homer was a medic
who followed the greek armies to Troas
so in Holland Park they rolled out to beat up Mr Leber
(restaurantier) to Monsieur Dulac's disgust
and a navvy rolls up to me in Church St. (Kensington End) with:
                    Yurra Jurrmun!
To which I replied: I am *not*.
" Well yurr szum kind ov a furriner."
                    ne povans desraciner
But Tosch the great ex-greyhound
          used to get wildly excited
                    at being given large beefsteaks
in Tolosa
                    and leapt one day finally
right into the centre of the large dining table
and lay there as a centre piece
                    near the cupboard piled half full
with novels of " Willy " etc
                    in the old one franc editions

and you cd/ hear papa Dulac's voice
	clear in the choir that wd/ ring ping on the high altar
in the Bach chorals
		true as a pistol shot
and he dumped all his old stock
	of calicos plumb bang on the germans
after two or more years of stagnation
	it was at Leber's that old Colonel Jackson
had said to Gaudier:
			" mes compliments "
when Gaudier had said he wd/ fight for la Patrie if war came
but that anarchy was the true form of government
(meaning, so far as I cd/ make out, some form of
		sindical organization
Jackson at 80 proposed to cook for the armies of Ulster
	" la bonne soupe fait le bon soldat ")
	and he said to Yeats at a vorticist picture show:
		" You also of the brotherhood? "
But Dolmetsch died without ever knowing that Dulac
	had broken and mended the support to the lid
of one of his clavichords, Dolmetsch' own clavichords
		painted and toned with that special sacred vermilion,
" Il est bon comme le pain "
				sd/ Mockel of " Willy "
(Gauthier Villars) but I cdn't explain to him (Willy)
what the Dial wanted and Gluck's " Iphigénie "
		was played in the Mockel's garden
	Les mœurs passent et la douleur reste.
" En casque de crystal rose les baladines "
	Mallarmé, Whistler, Charles Condor, Degas
and the bar of the Follies
			as Manet saw it, Degas, those two gents crossing ' La
					Concorde ' or for that matter
Judith's junk shop
			with Théophile's arm chair

one cd/ live in such an apartment
      seeing the roofs of Paris
                      Ça s'appelle une mansarde
The old trees near the Rue Jacob
           were propped up to keep them from falling
à l'Amitié
and M. Jean wanted to save that building
what do you call it,
can it have been the old École Militaire?
   " Il me paraît," said his housekeeper
                  " un curé déguisé "
(that was Maritain)
   and Natalie said to the apache:
         vous êtes très mal élevé
and his companion said: Tiens, elle te le dit...
    so they left her her hand bag
and the jambe-de-bois stuck it up
      at an angle, say about 140 degrees
and pretended it was a fiddle
     while the 60 year old bat did a hoolah
to the great applause of that bistro
      " Entrez donc, mais entrez,
c'est la maison de tout le monde "
(This to me and H. Liveright vers le Noël)
And three small boys on three bicycles
     smacked her young fanny in passing
before she recovered from the surprise of the first swat
ce sont les mœurs de Lutèce
    where there are also the scant remains of an arena
and Le Musée de Cluny.
     Arena or is it a teatro romano?
and there was also Uncle William
          labouring a sonnet of Ronsard
and the ink's heir painting high lights
     and Monsieur C. who paid, I think, bills for La Falange

and M. Arnold Bennett etc
" Ah Monsieur " said old Carolus (Durand)
" vous allez raser une toile? "
and after Puvis had come Carrière
                         (o-hon dit quelque fois au vi'age)
when they elected old Brisset Prince des Penseurs,
            Romains, Vildrac and Chennevière and the rest of them
            before the world was given over to wars
            Quand vous serez bien vieille
                  remember that I have remembered,
mia pargoletta,
            and pass on the tradition
there can be honesty of mind
                  without overwhelming talent
I have perhaps seen a waning of that tradition
(young nigger at rest in his wheelbarrow
      in the shade back of the jo-house
      addresses me: Got it *made*, kid, you got it made.
White boy says: do you speak Jugoslavian?)
And also near the museum they served it mit Schlag
      in those days (pre 1914)
      the loss of that café
            meant the end of a B. M. era
                  (British Museum era)
Mr Lewis had been to Spain
      Mr Binyon's young prodigies
pronounced the word: Penthesilea
            There were mysterious figures
that emerged from recondite recesses
            and ate at the WIENER CAFÉ
which died into banking, Jozefff may have followed
his emperor.
" It is the sons pent up within a man "
mumbled old Neptune
                  " Laomedon, Ahi, Laomedon "

or rather three " ahis " before the " Laomedon "
　　" He stood " wrote Mr Newbolt, later Sir Henry,
" the door behind " and now they complain of cummings.
So it is to Mr Binyon that I owe, initially,
Mr Lewis, Mr P. Wyndham Lewis. His bull-dog, me,
　　as it were against old Sturge M's bull-dog, Mr T. Sturge Moore's
　　　　bull-dog, et
　　meum est propositum, it is my intention
in tabernam, or was, to the Wiener café
you cannot yet buy one dish of Chinese food in all Italy
hence the débacle
" forloyn " said Mr Bridges (Robert)
" we'll get 'em all back "
meaning archaic words and there had been a fine old fellow
named Furnivall and Dr. Weir Mitchell collected

And the Franklin Inn club...
　　and young fellows go out to the colonies
but go on paying their dues
but old William was right in contending
　　that the crumbling of a fine house
profits no one
　　(Celtic or otherwise)
nor under Gesell would it happen

As Mabel's red head was a fine sight
worthy his minstrelsy
a tongue to the sea-cliffs or " Sligo in Heaven "
or his, William's, old " da " at Coney Island perched on an elephant
beaming like the prophet Isaiah
　　and J. Q. as it were aged 8 (Mr John Quinn)
at the target.

　　　　" Liquids and fluids! "
　　　　said the palmist. " A painter?

well ain't that liquids and fluids? " [To the venerable J. B.
    bearded Yeats]

    " a friend," sd/ mr cummings, " I knew it 'cause he
never tried to sell *me* any insurance "

(with memorial to Warren Dahler the Chris Columbus of
    Patchin)

Hier wohnt the tradition, as per Whitman in Camden
and an engraving 596 Lexington Ave.,
                        24 E. 47th,
with Jim at the checquer board by the banana cage

" Funny looking wood, James," said Aunt F.
" it looks as if it had already been burnt "
                                        [Windsor fire]
        " Part o deh roof ma'am."
    does any museum
contain one of the folding beds of that era?
And now, why?   Regents Park
        where was the maison Alma-Tadema
        (with a fountain) or Leighton House
                        for that matter?
and the mass of preraphaelite reliques
        in a trunk in a walled-up cellar in Selsey
" Tyke 'im up ter the bawth " (meaning Swinburne)
" Even Tennyson tried to go out
    through the fire-place."

which is what I suppose he, Fordie, wanted me to be able to picture
when he took me to Miss Braddon's
    (I mean the setting) at Richmond
But that New York I have found at Périgueux
            si com' ad Arli

508

in wake of the sarascen
               As the " Surrender of Breda " (Velásquez)
was preceded in fresco at Avignon
      y cavals armatz with the perpendicular lances
and the red-bearded fellow was mending his
          young daughter's shoe
" Me Hercule!   c'est nôtre comune "
(" Borr," not precisely Altaforte)
          with such dignity
and at Ventadour and at Aubeterre
or where they set tables down by small rivers,
and the stream's edge is lost in grass
          (Unkle George cd/ not identify the place on that road
because the road had been blown off the side of the mountain
but he climbed about 200 steps of the tower
to see what he had seen thru the roof
      of a barn no longer standing
                    sul Piave
where he had fired that howitzer
and the large eye that found him
at its level was a giraffe's eye
          at dawn, in his nest, hunting leopards.

" The pose " he said " is a taxidermist's fake
          the cobra is not a constrictor
and would not wrap itself round the mongoose "
But on the subject of terrapin
      would not believe they cd/ fly
          and the bishop brought action for libel
(I think half a million but did not, finally,
                    take the case into court)

by which time Uncle George was computing
      Volpe's kilowatt energy
from the back of his neck as seen at the Lido Excelsior

and in that year at Florian's Sir Ronald
had said: the Negus is not a bad fellowe.
         In fact the milk-white doe for his cousin
      reminding me of the Bank of Egypt
                     and the gold bars
in old Menelik's palace and the mahogany counters
and desk work in the branch in, was it, Alessandria
put there by Pea (Enrico)

and wd/ Whitcomb Riley be still found in a highbrow anthology

      Nancy where art thou?
Whither go all the vair and the cisclatons
and the wave pattern runs in the stone
on the high parapet (Excideuil)
Mt Segur and the city of Dioce
Que tous les mois avons nouvelle lune
What the deuce has Herbiet (Christian)
      done with his painting?
Fritz still roaring at treize rue Gay de Lussac
with his stone head still on the balcony?
Orage, Fordie, Crevel too quickly taken

      de mis soledades vengan

lay there till Rossetti found it remaindered
      at about two pence
(Cythera, in the moon's barge whither?
      how hast thou the crescent for car?

or did they fall because of their loose taste in music
      " Here! none of that mathematical music! "
Said the Kommandant when Münch offered Bach to the regiment
or Spewcini the all too human
      beloved in the eyetalian peninsula

for quite explicable reasons
    so that even I can now tolerate
    man seht but with the loss of criteria
and the wandering almost-tenor explained to me:
        well, the operas in the usual repertoire
have been sifted out, there's a reason

Les hommes ont je ne sais quelle peur étrange,
        said Monsieur Whoosis, de la beauté

La beauté, " Beauty is difficult, Yeats " said Aubrey Beardsley
    when Yeats asked why he drew horrors
    or at least not Burne-Jones
    and Beardsley knew he was dying and had to
    make his hit quickly

hence no more B-J in his product.

    So very difficult, Yeats, beauty so difficult.

    " I am the torch " wrote Arthur " she saith "
in the moon barge βροδοδάκτυλος Ἠώς

with the veil of faint cloud before her
        Κύθηρα δεινὰ as a leaf borne in the current
pale eyes as if without fire

all that Sandro knew, and Jacopo
        and that Velásquez never suspected
lost in the brown meat of Rembrandt
        and the raw meat of Rubens and Jordaens

" This alone, leather and bones between you and τὸ πᾶν,"
                    [*toh pan,* the all]
        (Chu Hsi's comment)

                    or the bone *luz*
        as the grain seed and the biceps
            books, arms, men, as with Sigismundo

and of portraits in our time Cocteau by Marie Laurencin
and Whistler's Miss Alexander
                (and the three fat ladies by Sargent, adversely)
                and somebody's portrait of Rodenbach
                    with a background
as it might be L'Ile St Louis for serenity, under Abélard's bridges
for those trees are Elysium
        for serenity
                under Abélard's bridges   πάντα 'ρεῖ
for those trees are serenity

as he had walked under the rain altars
                or under the trees of their grove
                or would it be under their parapets
in his moving was stillness
as grey stone in the Aliscans
        or had been at Mt Segur
and it was old Spencer (, H.) who first declaimed me the Odyssey
with a head built like Bill Shepard's
on the quais of what Siracusa?
        or what tennis court
near what pine trees?

care and craft in forming leagues and alliances
        that avail nothing against the decree
the folly of attacking that island
        and of the force ὑπὲρ μόρον

with a mind like that he is one of us
        Favonus, vento benigno
        Je suis au bout de mes forces/

                            512

That from the gates of death,
　　　that from the gates of death: Whitman or Lovelace
　　　　　found on the jo-house seat at that
in a cheap edition! [and thanks to Professor Speare]
hast'ou swum in a sea of air strip
　　　through an aeon of nothingness,
when the raft broke and the waters went over me,

Immaculata, Introibo
　　　for those who drink of the bitterness
Perpetua, Agatha, Anastasia
　　　　　　　　saeculorum

repos donnez à cils
　　　senza termine funge　Immaculata Regina
　　　　　Les larmes que j'ai creées m'inondent
Tard, très tard je t'ai connue, la Tristesse,
I have been hard as youth sixty years

　　　if calm be after tempest
that the ants seem to wobble
　　　as the morning sun catches their shadows
　　　(Nadasky, Duett, McAllister,
　　　also Comfort K.P. special mention
　　　on sick call Penrieth, Turner, Toth hieri
　　　(no fortune and with a name to come)
Bankers, Seitz, Hildebrand and Cornelison
　　　Armstrong special mention K.P.
　　　White gratia Bedell gratia
　　　Wiseman (not William) africanus.
with a smoky torch thru the unending
　　　　　labyrinth of the souterrain
or remembering Carleton let him celebrate Christ in the grain
and if the corn cat be beaten
　　　Demeter has lain in my furrow

This wind is lighter than swansdown
the day moves not at all
(Zupp, Bufford, and Bohon)

men of no fortune and with a name to come

his helmet is used for a pisspot
this helmet is used for my footbath
    Elpenor can count the shingle under Zoagli
Pepitone was wasting toothwash
    as I lay by the drain hole
the guard's opinion is lower than that of the
    prisoners

        o.   t.   a.

Oh to be in England now that Winston's out
    Now that there's room for doubt
        And the bank may be the nation's
        And the long years of patience
        And labour's vacillations
May have let the bacon come home,
        To watch how they'll slip and slide
        watch how they'll try to hide
        the real portent
        To watch a while from the tower
        where dead flies lie thick over the old charter
        forgotten, oh quite forgotten
        but confirming John's first one,
    and still there if you climb over attic rafters;
to look at the fields; are they tilled?
is the old terrace alive as it might be
with a whole colony
        if money be free again?

Chesterton's England of has-been and why-not,
or is it all rust, ruin, death duties and mortgages
and the great carriage yard empty
                    and more pictures gone to pay taxes

        When a dog is tall but
        not so tall as all that
        that dog is a Talbot
                (a bit long in the pasterns?)
When a butt is ½ as tall as a whole butt
That butt is a small butt
            Let backe and side go bare
and the old kitchen left as the monks had left it
and the rest as time has cleft it.

[Only shadows enter my tent
                as men pass between me and the sunset,]
beyond the eastern barbed wire
        a sow with nine boneen
matronly as any duchess at Claridge's

and for that Christmas at Maurie Hewlett's
Going out from Southampton
they passed the car by the dozen
        who would not have shown weight on a scale
                    riding, riding
                        for Noel the green holly
        Noel, Noel, the green holly
        A dark night for the holly

That would have been Salisbury plain, and I have not thought of
        the Lady Anne for this twelve years
                Nor of Le Portel
How tiny the panelled room where they stabbed him
            In her lap, almost, La Stuarda

Si tuit li dolh ehl planh el marrimen
for the leopards and broom plants

Tudor indeed is gone and every rose,
Blood-red, blanch-white that in the sunset glows
Cries: " Blood,   Blood,   Blood! " against the gothic stone
Of England, as the Howard or Boleyn knows.

Nor seeks the carmine petal to infer;
Nor is the white bud Time's inquisitor
Probing to know if its new-gnarled root
Twists from York's head or belly of Lancaster;

Or if a rational soul should stir, perchance,
Within the stem or summer shoot to advance
Contrition's utmost throw, seeking in thee
But oblivion, not thy forgiveness, FRANCE.

as the young lizard extends his leopard spots
          along the grass-blade seeking the green midge half an ant-size
and the Serpentine will look just the same
and the gulls be as neat on the pond
and the sunken garden unchanged
and God knows what else is left of our London
          my London, your London
and if her green elegance
          remains on this side of my rain ditch
          puss lizard will lunch on some other T-bone

sunset grand couturier.

LXXXI

Zeus lies in Ceres' bosom
          Taishan is attended of loves
                    under Cythera, before sunrise
          and he said: " Hay aquí mucho catolicismo—(sounded
                                        catoli*th*ismo)
               y muy poco reliHion "
and he said: " Yo creo que los reyes desaparecen "
(Kings will, I think, disappear)
That was Padre José Elizondo
                    in 1906 and in 1917
or about 1917
               and Dolores said: " Come pan, niño,"   eat bread, me lad
Sargent had painted her
                    before he descended
(i.e. if he descended
          but in those days he did thumb sketches,
impressions of the Velázquez in the Museo del Prado
and books cost a peseta,
               brass candlesticks in proportion,
hot wind came from the marshes
          and death-chill from the mountains.
And later Bowers wrote: " but such hatred,
     I had never conceived such "
and the London reds wouldn't show up his friends
               (i.e. friends of Franco
working in London) and in Alcázar
forty years gone, they said: go back to the station to eat
you can sleep here for a peseta "
               goat bells tinkled all night
               and the hostess grinned: Eso es luto, *haw!*
mi marido es muerto
               (it is mourning, my husband is dead)

when she gave me paper to write on
with a black border half an inch or more deep,
	say 5/8ths, of the locanda
" We call *all* foreigners frenchies "
and the egg broke in Cabranez' pocket,
		thus making history. Basil says
they beat drums for three days
till all the drumheads were busted
		(simple village fiesta)
and as for his life in the Canaries...
Possum observed that the local portagoose folk dance
was danced by the same dancers in divers localities
		in political welcome...
the technique of demonstration
		Cole studied that (not G.D.H., Horace)
" You will find " said old André Spire,
that every man on that board (Crédit Agricole)
has a brother-in-law
		" You the one, I the few "
		said John Adams
speaking of fears in the abstract
	to his volatile friend Mr Jefferson.
(To break the pentameter, that was the first heave)
or as Jo Bard says:	they never speak to each other,
if it is baker and concierge visibly
		it is La Rouchefoucauld and de Maintenon audibly.
" Te cavero le budella "
			" La corata a te "
In less than a geological epoch
			said Henry Mencken
" Some cook, some do not cook
	some things cannot be altered"
Ἴυγξ. . . . . . 'ἐμὸν ποτί δῶμα τὸν ἄνδρα
What counts is the cultural level,
	thank Benin for this table ex packing box

518

              " doan yu tell no one I made it "
                       from a mask fine as any in Frankfurt
" It'll get you offn th' groun "
                       Light as the branch of Kuanon
And at first disappointed with shoddy
the bare ram-shackle quais, but then saw the
high buggy wheels
                   and was reconciled,
George Santayana arriving in the port of Boston
and kept to the end of his life that faint *thethear*
of the Spaniard
                  as a grace quasi imperceptible
as did Muss the *v* for *u* of Romagna
and said the grief was a full act
              repeated for each new condoleress
working up to a climax.
and George Horace said he wd/ " get Beveridge " (Senator)
Beveridge wouldn't talk and he wouldn't write for the **papers**
but George got him by campin' in his hotel
and assailin' him at lunch breakfast an' dinner
                three articles
and my ole man went on hoein' corn
        while George was a-tellin' him,
come across a vacant lot
         where you'd occasionally see a wild rabbit
or mebbe only a loose one
        AOI!
        a leaf in the current
                     at my grates no Althea

Yet
Ere the season died a-cold
Borne upon a zephyr's shoulder
I rose through the aureate sky
                Lawes and Jenkyns guard thy rest
                Dolmetsch ever be thy guest,

ibretto

Has he tempered the viol's wood
To enforce   both the grave   and the acute?
Has he curved us the bowl of the lute?

> Lawes and Jenkyns guard thy rest
> Dolmetsch ever be thy guest

Hast 'ou fashioned so airy a mood
To draw up leaf from the root?
Hast 'ou found   a cloud   so light
As seemed neither mist nor shade?

> Then resolve me, tell me aright
> If Waller sang or Dowland played.

> Your eyen two wol sleye me sodenly
> I may the beauté of hem nat susteyne

And for 180 years almost nothing.

Ed ascoltando al leggier mormorio
     there came new subtlety of eyes into my tent,
whether of spirit or hypostasis,
     but what the blindfold hides
or at carneval
                    nor any pair showed anger
     Saw but the eyes and stance between the eyes,
colour, diastasis,
     careless or unaware it had not the
     whole tent's room
nor was place for the full Εἰδώς
interpass, penetrate
     casting but shade beyond the other lights
          sky's clear
          night's sea
          green of the mountain pool
          shone from the unmasked eyes in half-mask's space.
What thou lovest well remains,

                              the rest is dross
What thou lov'st well shall not be reft from thee
What thou lov'st well is thy true heritage
Whose world, or mine or theirs
                              or is it of none?
First came the seen, then thus the palpable
      Elysium, though it were in the halls of hell,
What thou lovest well is thy true heritage
What thou lov'st well shall not be reft from thee

The ant's a centaur in his dragon world.
Pull down thy vanity, it is not man
Made courage, or made order, or made grace,
      Pull down thy vanity, I say pull down.
Learn of the green world what can be thy place
In scaled invention or true artistry,
Pull down thy vanity,
                              Paquin pull down!
The green casque has outdone your elegance.

" Master thyself, then others shall thee beare "
      Pull down thy vanity
Thou art a beaten dog beneath the hail,
A swollen magpie in a fitful sun,
Half black half white
Nor knowst'ou wing from tail
Pull down thy vanity
                  How mean thy hates
Fostered in falsity,
                  Pull down thy vanity,
Rathe to destroy, niggard in charity,
Pull down thy vanity,
                  I say pull down.

But to have done instead of not doing
                  this is not vanity

To have, with decency, knocked
That a Blunt should open
            To have gathered from the air a live tradition
or from a fine old eye the unconquered flame
This is not vanity.
            Here error is all in the not done,
all in the diffidence that faltered . . .

LXXXII

WHEN with his hunting dog I see a cloud
" Guten Morgen, Mein Herr " yells the black boy
from the jo-cart

(Jeffers, Lovell and Harley
also Mr Walls who has lent me a razor
Persha, Nadasky and Harbell)

Swinburne my only miss
and I didn't know he'd been to see Landor
and they told me this that an' tother
and when old Mathews went he saw the three teacups
two for Watts Dunton who liked to let his tea cool,
So old Elkin had only one glory
He did carry Algernon's suit case *once*
when he, Elkin, first came to London.
But given what I know now I'd have
got thru it somehow...Dirce's shade
or a blackjack.
When the french fishermen hauled him out he
recited 'em
might have been Aeschylus
till they got into Le Portel, or wherever
in the original

" On the Atreides' roof "
" like a dog...and a good job
ΕΜΟΣ ΠΟΣΙΣ...ΧΕΡΟΣ
hac dextera mortus
dead by this hand
believe Lytton first saw Blunt in the bull ring

as it might have been brother Packard
and " our brother Percy "
                    Basinio's manuscript with the
greek moulds in the margin
                    Otis, Soncino,
the " marble men " shall pass into nothingness,
Three birds on the wire
            so requested Mr Clowes to sleep on the same
and as to who wd/ pay for the composition
if same were not used
                        (Elkin Mathews, my bantam)
        After all " said Mr Birrell, " it is only the old story
of Tom Moore and Rogers "

                    Her Ladyship arose in the night
and moved all the furniture
            (that is her Ladyship YX)
her Ladyship Z disliked dining alone and
        The proud shall not lie by the proud
                amid dim green lighted with candles
Mabel Beardsley's red head for a glory
Mr Masefield murmuring: Death
        and Old Neptune meaning something unseizable
        in a discussion of Flaubert
Miss Tomczyk, the medium
baffling the society for metaphysical research
                and the idea that CONversation......
            should not utterly wither
even I can remember
        at 18 Woburn Buildings
Said Mr Tancred
        of the Jerusalem and Sicily Tancreds, to Yeats,
" If you would read us one of your own choice
            and
                    perfect

lyrics "
and more's the pity that Dickens died twice
with the disappearance of Tancred
        and for all that old Ford's conversation was better,
consisting in *res* non *verba,*
        despite William's anecdotes, in that Fordie
        never dented an idea for a phrase's sake

and had more humanitas 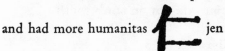 jen

        (Cythera   Cythera)
        With Dirce in one bark convey'd
Be glad poor beaste, love follows after thee
Till the cricket hops
                but does not chirrp in the drill field
        8th day of September
            f   f
                d
                    g
                        write the birds in their treble scale
Terreus!   Terreus!

        there are no righteous wars in " The Spring and Au-
                                                    tumn "
that is, perfectly right on one side or the other
total right on either side of the battle line
        and the news is a long time moving
    a long time in arriving
                thru the impenetrable
crystalline, indestructible
        ignorance of locality
The news was quicker in Troy's time
a match on Cnidos, a glow worm on Mitylene,
        Till forty years since, Reithmuller indignant:

" Fvy! in Tdaenmarck efen dh' beasantz gnow him,"
    meaning Whitman, exotic, still suspect
    four miles from Camden
        " O troubled reflection
        " O Throat, O throbbing heart "
How drawn, O GEA TERRA,
        what draws as thou drawest
            till one sink into thee by an arm's width
    embracing thee. Drawest,
            truly thou drawest.
    Wisdom lies next thee,
            simply, past metaphor.
Where I lie let the thyme rise
                        and basilicum
        let the herbs rise in April abundant
By Ferrara was buried naked, fu Nicolo
        e di qua di la del Po,
wind: ᾽εμὸν τὸν ἄνδρα
lie into earth to the breast bone, to the left shoulder
        Kipling suspected it
    to the height of ten inches or over
man, earth : two halves of the tally
but I will come out of this knowing no one
neither they me
                    connubium terrae   ἔφατα πόσις ἐμός
                                    ΧΘΟΝΙΟΣ, mysterium
fluid ΧΘΟΝΟΣ o'erflowed me
        lay in the fluid ΧΘΟΝΟΣ;
                    that lie
under the air's solidity
        drunk with ᾽ΙΧΩΡ of ΧΘΟΝΙΟΣ
                fluid ΧΘΟΝΟΣ, strong as the undertow
        of the wave receding
but that a man should live in that further terror, and live

the loneliness of death came upon me
    (at 3 P. M., for an instant)   δακρύων

                                ἐντεῦθεν

three solemn half notes
                 their white downy chests black-rimmed
on the middle wire
                periplum

LXXXIII

ύδωρ
HUDOR et Pax
Gemisto stemmed all from Neptune
     hence the Rimini bas reliefs
Sd Mr Yeats (W. B.) " Nothing affects these people
      Except our conversation "
lux enim
     ignis est accidens   and,
wrote the prete in his edition of Scotus:
Hilaritas   the virtue *hilaritas*

the queen stitched King Carolus' shirts or whatever
while Erigena put greek tags in his excellent verses
     in fact an excellent poet, Paris
       toujours Pari'
          (Charles le Chauve)

     and you might find a bit of enamel
     a bit of true blue enamel
      on a metal pyx or whatever
    omnia, quae sunt, lumina sunt, or whatever

so they dug up his bones in the time of De Montfort
    (Simon)

       Le Paradis n'est pas artificiel
and Uncle William dawdling around Notre Dame
in search of whatever
        paused to admire the symbol
with Notre Dame standing inside it
Whereas in St Etienne

or why not Dei Miracoli:
mermaids, that carving,

      in the drenched tent there is quiet
           sered eyes are at rest

      the rain beat as with colour of feldspar
      blue as the flying fish off Zoagli
pax, ὕδωρ   ΥΔΩΡ
        the sage
delighteth in water
      the humane man has amity with the hills

as the grass grows by the weirs
        thought Uncle William   *consiros*
as the grass on the roof of St What's his name
      near " Cane e Gatto "
        soll deine Liebe sein
it would be about a-level the windows
      the grass would, or I dare say above that
      when they bless the wax for the Palio

Olim de Malatestis
        with Maria's face there in the fresco
      painted two centuries sooner,
      at least that
before she wore it
      As Montino's
in that family group of about 1820
      not wholly Hardy's material

      or πάντα 'ρει

as he was standing below the altars
      of the spirits of rain

" When every hollow is full
         it moves forward "
to the phantom mountain above the cloud
But in the caged panther's eyes:

                    " Nothing. Nothing that you can do..."

green pool, under green of the jungle,
caged: " Nothing, nothing that you can do."

Δρυάς, your eyes are like clouds

Nor can who has passed a month in the death cells
         believe in capital punishment
No man who has passed a month in the death cells
         believes in cages for beasts

Δρυάς, your eyes are like the clouds over Taishan
         When some of the rain has fallen
         and half remains yet to fall

The roots go down to the river's edge
         and the hidden city moves upward
               white ivory under the bark

With clouds over Taishan-Chocorua
         when the blackberry ripens
and now the new moon faces Taishan
one must count by the dawn star
         Dryad, thy peace is like water
There is September sun on the pools

Plura diafana
         Heliads lift the mist from the young willows
there is no base seen under Taishan

but the brightness of *'udor*   ὕδωρ
the poplar tips float in brightness
only the stockade posts stand

And now the ants seem to stagger
            as the dawn sun has trapped their shadows,
this breath wholly covers the mountains
            it shines and divides
it nourishes by its rectitude
does no injury
overstanding the earth it fills the nine fields
            to heaven

Boon companion to equity
      it joins with the process
            lacking it, there is inanition

When the equities are gathered together
as birds alighting
it springeth up vital

If deeds be not ensheaved and garnered in the heart
there is inanition

        (have I perchance a debt to a man named Clower)

that he eat of the barley corn
and move with the seed's breath

the sun as a golden eye
        between dark cloud and the mountain

" Non combaattere " said Giovanna
        meaning, as before stated, don't work so hard

531

don't

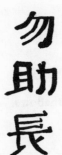

     as it stands in the Kung-Sun Chow.
San Gregorio, San Trovaso
Old Ziovan raced at seventy after his glories
          and came in long last
and the family eyes stayed the same Adriatic
         for three generations (San Vio)
and was, I suppose, last month the Redentore as usual

Will I ever see the Giudecca again?
     or the lights against it, Ca' Foscari, Ca' Giustinian
or the Ca', as they say, of Desdemona
or the two towers where are the cypress no more
       or the boats moored off le Zattere
or the north quai of the Sensaria DAKRUŌN   ΔΑΚΡΥΩΝ

     and Brother Wasp is building a very neat house
     of four rooms, one shaped like a squat indian bottle
     La vespa, *la* vespa, mud, swallow system
so that dreaming of Bracelonde and of Perugia
and the great fountain in the Piazza
or of old Bulagaio's cat that with a well timed leap
     could turn the lever-shaped door handle
It comes over me that Mr. Walls must be a ten-strike
with the signorinas
and in the warmth after chill sunrise
an infant, green as new grass,

has stuck its head or tip
out of Madame La Vespa's bottle

mint springs up again
        in spite of Jones' rodents
as had the clover by the gorilla cage
        with a four-leaf

When the mind swings by a grass-blade
        an ant's forefoot shall save you
the clover leaf smells and tastes as its flower

        The infant has descended,
        from mud on the tent roof to Tellus,
like to like colour he goes amid grass-blades
        greeting them that dwell under XTHONOS   ΧΘΟΝΟΣ
ΟΙ ΧΘΟΝΙΟΙ;   to carry our news
        εἰς χθονίους   to them that dwell under the earth,
begotten of air, that shall sing in the bower
        of Kore,   Περσεφόνεια
and have speech with Tiresias, Thebae

        Cristo Re, Dio Sole

in about ½ a day she has made her adobe
(la vespa) the tiny mud-flask

        and that day I wrote no further

There is fatigue deep as the grave.
The Kakemono grows in flat land out of mist
        sun rises lop-sided over the mountain
                so that I recalled the noise in the chimney
as it were the wind in the chimney
                but was in reality Uncle William

533

downstairs composing
that had made a great Peeeeacock
    in the proide ov his oiye
        had made a great peeeeeeecock in the...
made a great peacock
    in the proide of his oyyee

proide ov his oy-ee
as indeed he had, and perdurable

a great peacock aere perennius
    or as in the advice to the young man to
breed and get married (or not)
        as you choose to regard it

at Stone Cottage in Sussex by the waste moor
(or whatever) and the holly bush
    who would not eat ham for dinner
because peasants eat ham for dinner
    despite the excellent quality
and the pleasure of having it hot

well those days are gone forever
       and the traveling rug with the coon-skin tabs
and his hearing nearly all Wordsworth
    for the sake of his conscience but
preferring Ennemosor on Witches

did we ever get to the end of Doughty:
      The Dawn in Britain?
                 perhaps not
   Summons withdrawn, sir.)
(bein' aliens in prohibited area)

clouds lift their small mountains
        before the elder hills

A fat moon rises lop-sided over the mountain
The eyes, this time my world,
        But pass and look *from* mine
            between my lids
                sea, sky, and pool
                alternate
                pool, sky, sea,

morning moon against sunrise
like a bit of the best antient greek coinage

            und

Mir sagen
Die Damen
Du bist Greis,
        Anacreon

And that a Madonna novecento

cd/ be as a Madonna quattrocento
This I learned in the Tirol
            and as perfect
where they paint the houses outside with figures
and the deep inner courts run back triple

    " Das heis' Walterplatz "
        heard in Bozen (Bolzano)
and in my mother's time it was respectable,
it was social, apparently,
                    to sit in the Senate gallery

or even in that of the House
        to hear the fire-works of the senators
(and possibly representatives)
as was still done in Westminster in my time
and a very poor show from the once I saw it)

but if Senator Edwards cd/ speak
and have his tropes stay in the memory 40 years, 60 years?
in short / the descent
has not been of advantage either
        to the Senate or to " society "
                                or to the people
        The States have passed thru a
                        dam'd supercilious era
Down, Derry-down /
        Oh let an old man rest.

LXXXIV

8th October:
> Si tuit li dolh elh plor
> > Angold τέθνηκε
>
> tuit lo pro, tuit lo bes
> > Angold τέθνηκε

" an' doan you think he chop an' change all the time
stubborn az a mule, sah, stubborn as a MULE,
got th' eastern idea about money "
> > Thus Senator Bankhead
" am sure I don't know what a man like you
> would find to *do* here "
> > said Senator Borah
Thus the solons, in Washington,
on the executive, and on the country, a.d. 1939

ye spotted lambe
> that is both blacke and white
is yeven to us for the eyes' delight

and now Richardson, Roy Richardson,
> says he is different
will I mention his name?

and Demattia is checking out.
> White, Fazzio, Bedell, *benedicti*
Sarnone, two Washingtons (dark) J and M
> Bassier, Starcher, H. Crowder and
no soldier he although his name is Slaughter

this day October the whateverth   Mr. Coxey
aged 91 has mentioned bonds and their
> > > interest

537

apparently as a basis of issue
and Mr Sinc Lewis has not
          and Bartók has left us
and Mr Beard in his admirable condensation
(Mr Chas. Beard) has given one line to the currency
at about page 426 " The Young Republic "
We will be about as popular as Mr John Adams
and less widely perused
and the he leopard lay on his back playing with straw
in sheer boredom,
          (Memoirs of the Roman zoo)
                    in sheer boredom
Incense to Apollo
          Carrara
                    snow on the marble
snow-white
          against stone-white
on the mountain
and as who passed the gorges between sheer cliffs
as it might be by, is it the Garonne?
          where one walks into Spagna
that T'ao Ch'ien heard the old Dynasty's music
          as it might be at the Peach-blossom Fountain
where are smooth lawns with the clear stream
between them, silver, dividing,

and at Ho Ci'u destroyed the whole town
for hiding a woman, Κύθηρα δεινά
and as Carson the desert rat said
" when we came out we had
          80 thousand dollars' worth "
                    (" of experience ")
that was from mining
          having spent their capital on equipment
but not cal'lated the time for return

and my old great aunt did likewise
with that too large hotel
but at least she saw damn all Europe
  and rode on that mule in Tangiers
   and in general had a run for her money

like Natalie
   " perhaps more than was in it "

  Under white clouds, cielo di Pisa
out of all this beauty something must come,

O moon my pin-up,
     chronometer
Wei, Chi and Pi-kan
Yin had these three men full of humanitas (**manhood**)
    or jên^2
Xaire Alessandro
    Xaire Fernando, e il Capo,
Pierre, Vidkun,
    Henriot
and as to gradations
who went out of industrials into Government
  when the slump was in the offing
as against whom, prepense, got OUT of Imperial Chemicals
in 1938
so as not to be nourished by blood-bath?

quand vos venetz al som de l'escalina
     ἦθος gradations
These are distinctions in clarity

ming^2 明   these are distinctions

John Adams, the Brothers Adam
        there is our norm of spirit

our   中   chung[1]

        whereto we may pay our
                        homage
                Saith Micah:
                        Each in the name of...
So that looking at the sputtering tank of nicotine and
        stale whiskey
                        (on its way out)
Kumrad Koba remarked:
                I will believe the American.
                                Berlin 1945
the last appearance of Winston P.M. in that connection
        e poi io dissi alla sorella
della pastorella dei suini:
e questi americani?
                si conducono bene?
ed ella: poco.
        Poco, poco.
ed io: peggio dei tedeschi?
                ed ella: uguale, thru the barbed wire
                        you can, said Stef (Lincoln Steffens)
do nothing with revolutionaries
        until they are at the end of their tether
and that Vandenberg has read Stalin, or Stalin, John Adams
is, at the mildest, unproven.

If the hoar frost grip thy tent
Thou wilt give thanks when night is spent.

SECTION: ROCK-DRILL
DE LOS CANTARES
LXXXV-XCV

LXXXV

LING[2]

Our dynasty came in because of a great sensibility.

All there by the time of I Yin

All roots by the time of I Yin.

Galileo index'd 1616,

Wellington's peace after Vaterloo

chih[3]

          a gnomon,

Our science is from the watching of shadows;

That Queen Bess translated Ovid,

          Cleopatra wrote of the currency,

Versus who scatter old records

          ignoring the hsien[2] form

and jump to the winning side

(turbae)

II. 9. have scopes and beginnings

tchōung

仁　　智

chèu

jen²　　　　　chih⁴　　　i-li

are called chung¹⁻⁴

衷

仁　好　　(*1508, Mathews*)

甲

no mere epitome without organization.

The sun under it all:

Justice, d'urbanité, de prudence

wei heou,　　　Σοφία

the sheltered grass hopes, chueh, cohere.

(No, that is *not* philological)

Not led of lusting, not of contriving

but is as the grass and tree

eccellenza

not led of lusting,

not of the worm, contriving

544

THE FOUR TUAN[1]

端

or foundations.

Hulled rice and silk at easter
  (with the *bachi* held under their aprons
From T'ang's time until now)
That you lean 'gainst the tree of heaven,
  and know Ygdrasail

poi   時   shih[2]

        忱   ch'ên[2]

恣

"Birds and terrapin lived under Hia,
   beast and fish held their order,
Neither flood nor flame falling in excess"

        i
        moua
        pou
        gning

Perspicax qui excolit se ipsum,
Their writings wither because they have no curiosity,
This "leader", gouged pumpkin
   that they hoist on a pole,

But if you will follow this process

not a lot of signs, but the one sign
            etcetera
        plus always Τέχνη
and from Τέχνη back to σεαυτόν
Neither by chinks, nor by sophists,
        nor by hindoo immaturities;
Dante, out of St Victor (Richardus),
        Erigena with greek tags in his verses.
Y Yin sent the young king into seclusion
by T'ang Tomb to think things over,
        that they make total war on CONTEMPLATIO.
Not to pamper this squirrel-headedness
        "in T'oung loco palatium"
and not to bitch this whole generation in fish-traps
        k'o
        tchoung
        ìun
        te
put some elbow-grease into it
        the third séu

                szu'   Mat. 5592

Nor by vain disputations

nor sitting down on a job that is done
i jênn iuên

whereby, in the long run,

貞　　chên

reddidit gubernium imperatori

陳　　ch'ên

戒　　chiai

As the pivot perceived by Y Yin
　　quam simplex animus Imperatoris
that the different clans say: Bigob! He *said* it.
III. 6. xi, Right here is the Bill of Rights

獲
夫　自
匹　盡
婦　匹

Three hundred years until P'an

盤 P'an Keng

各
長
于
厥
居

Baros metetz en gatge!
    Alexander paid the debts of his troops.
Not serendipity
    but to spread

tê   thru the people.
The pusillanimous
    wanting all men cut down to worm-size.
Mr. Roosevelt chose Dexter White.
As against culture as quick-sand
    after "'48"   (1848)

philology subdivided,
Nap III had the composition divided,
    to each compositor in the print shop
    a very few lines,
        none seeing the whole Proclamation.
Keep 'em off the market four years
        and leave 'em without understanding,
No classics,
    no American history,
        no centre, no general root,
No *prezzo giusto* as core.
                UBI JUS VAGUM.
Alexander paid the debts of his soldiery.
Wishing to bring back T'ang's state of awareness

 KAO

 TSOUNG 1324
              1265 a.c.
              ——
              59

Whetstone whirling to grind,   jòu
                       tso
                       li

    cymba et remis
Trees prop up clouds,
Praecognita bonum ut te moveas
    and then consider the time

   liú

cheu

"Fatigare in sacris

dicitur non revereri"

Fou iue

III. viii, 11.

tchoung

in rites not flame-headed.

"Up to then, I just hadn't caught on."

chung

wang

hsien

顯   said KAO TSOUNG

Imperator. Sicut vinum ac mustum

brew up this directio, tchéu,

fermentum et germina,

study with the mind of a grandson

and watch the time like a hawk

taó   tsi

½ research   and ½   Τέχνη

½ observation,   ½   Τέχνη

½ training,   ½   Τέχνη

Tch'eng T'ang for guide.

You will go a long way without slipping,

without slopping over.
Nisi cum sapientibus non regit,
      nor sage feed from poisoned trough.
      200 years after:
        "Best you retire.
but as for me, nunquam ego

罔   wang.

僕   pou.

Not after this dynasty."
              Ki went into Corea,
"abire decere", lest the line be no more.

                       IV.

And in spring time
      assembled at Meng-ford
      tá houéi Méng tsin,
that had from Heou Tsi under Shun
by the three streams, the three rivers,
      Ping, Foung were their cities,
and North-East to Mount Ki.
      Tàn Fóu, to King Wan.
"Our dynasty came in because of a great sensibility."
Les mœurs furent réformées,
              la vertu fleurit 靈

Ad Meng vadum,
      south bank of the Yellow River,
Huang Ho.

Heaven and Earth begat the perceiver,
　　　　　"ch' e' ditta dentro"
& Cheóu demittit aerumnas.
Ling²

靈

　　　　　was basis of rule.

　　Ts'oung

聰

　　tàn

　　ming　　　　　　　　　　　　tso

亶

　　　　　　　　　　　　　　　iuên

明　　　　　　　　　　　　heóu

Cheóu demittit aerumnas:
"Gentlemen from the West,
　　　　　Heaven's process is quite coherent
and its main points perfectly clear.

顯　　　hsien.

Wu 武 leant on the yellow halbard

　　　　　in his right, the white signal tail:
"e canta la gallina,
"　　　　　he is ganged up with racketeers
" 6 steps or 7, reform.
" 4, 5, 7 strokes, reassemble

止 chèu

齊 t'sì

nài tcheù t'sì

and do not chase fugitives."

Cheóu's host was like a forest in Mu plain,

林 quasi silvam convenit
jo lin.

"Liking some, disliking others, doing injustice to no man."

極

血

偏

The 4th part: marginalia.

Liu dogs, serendipity? No.

恫 t'oung

瘝 kouan 9.6

T'oung kouan nài chenn

乃

not water, ôu iu chouèi

身

戾 min

監 kién　　10.12

There be thy mirror in men.

土

中 Tán

旦 iue

曰 p'ei

配 houâng

XIII, 9　　k'i p'eng

皇

其

朋 Odysseus "to no man"

火

tcho

敬

and you can know the sincere
That Tch'eng T'ang

戈
成
湯
甸

overthrew Hia

Praestantissimos regere

tien[4]

from Tch'eng T'ang to Ti I
    nullus non splendidas fecit,
    nullus non se sociavit   (tien[4])
k'i tche, ut benefaceret.
Tcheou neither watching his
own insides, nor respecting the workings.
Our Dynasty came in because of great Ling[2]

sensibility

丕　　　　　p'i

The arrow has not two points

貳　　　　pou éul cheu
　　　　　pu erh[4]

"O nombreux officiers

邑

Imperator ait.

Iterum dico

太　　T'AI MEOU　1637
戊　　　　　　　1562

武　　OU TING　1324
丁　　　　　　　1265

cognovit aerumnas

TSOU KIA reigned 33 years

惟　　　　wei

tcheng

tcheu

XV: 11   koung

naught above just contribution

invicem docentes   siu   M.2835

hsü, in the first tone

kiaó. chiao,[1-4]

that is Sagetrieb

chêu

ngò

We flop if we cannot maintain the awareness   XVI.4
Diuturna cogites   10
respect the awareness and
    train the fit men.

明 mîng ngò tsiun 俊   XVI.20

chün[4]   1727. Mat.

Cdn't see it (ming) could

 extend to the people's subsidia,

that it was in some fine way tied up with the people
"And don't pester your officers"   XIX.18
"Don't get into small dog-fights
        Hio kòu jou kouàn   XX.16
"Get the mot juste before action."

        touán cf. The Ta Seu

Awareness restful & fake is fatiguing.   18
XXI. 7. nor laws as a means of oppression.
        Not all things from one man

備   (pei⁴)

容   yung²

That is, in some cases, charity
        iou ioung te nai ta

                        awareness extended

生   chong   XXI, 14

厚   heóu

The 5 laws have root in an awareness
                        che funge.

"One of those days", said Brancusi,
          "when I would not have given
"15 minutes of my time
          for anything under heaven."
Dead in the Piazzale Loreto,
In Holohan's case, murder protected.
          Jury trial was in Athens.
Tyrants resisted
          οὐ ταῦτα . . . κακοῖσι δειλίαν
King Owen had men about him:
          Prince of Kouo,
          Houng Ieo, San I Cheng

Sagetrieb

as the hand grips the wheat,

Risked the smoke to go forward

aperiens tibi animum:

NOTE. Kung said he had added nothing. Canto 85 is a somewhat detailed con-
firmation of Kung's view that the basic principles of government are found in the
Shu, the History Classic. The numerical references are to Couvreur's Chou King.
Meaning of the ideograms is usually given in the English text; transliterations as
in Couvreur and Mathews.

LXXXVI

WITH   solicitude

IV. xvi. 18

that mirroured turbationem,
Bismarck forgotten, fantasia without balance-wheel,
"No more wars after '70" (Bismarck.)
"Dummheit, nicht Bosheit," said old Margherita
    (or Elenor? dowager)
"Sono tutti eretici, Santo Padre,
    ma non sono cattivi."
Mind (the Kaiser's) like loose dice in a box.
Ballin said: "If I had known,
    wd/ indeed have stuffed all Hamburg with grain."
Bülow believed him. But Talleyrand set up Belgium,
Two dynasties, two buffer states,
    wd/ have set Poland.
So that Belgium saved Frogland; Svizzera neutral.
xvi.20: only two of us who will roll up our sleeves.
And Brancusi repeating: je peux commencer
    une chose tous les jours, mais

                fiiniiiir

  hsiang²   xvii, 7

Lost the feel of the people   xviii, 5
xviii, 19

教
簡

way repeatedly not clean, noisy, & your hearts loveless.　　22
Get men, it will grow
Milites instar ursorum, xxiii, 5, men strong as bears
Not in two minds

端　　jóung
　　　touan

Edictorum

體　　t'i

要　　iao

ta seu　　tá hiún　　　　　　　　　　(xxiv, 11)
te í　tá hiún

Quis erudiet without documenta?
even barbarians who button their coats t'other way on　　13
Non periturum

既　　kiue sin　　(xxiv, 15)

心

　　　leading to

Mencius, chi⁴ (453, Mathews)

MOU WANG

穆
王

King Mou   1001-946

repeating the

篤

tou

忠

tchoung

貞

tchen

to Kiun Ia,
      3rd of his line in office:
"Their names are banner'd,
      year'd on the T'ai Tch'ang

the   常   tch'âng.

Now my turn for thin ice and tigers.
      Live up to your line

and the constitution

憲
呂

etiam habitus inspiciendus

貌　mao⁴
亦
尚
一
人

It may depend on one man
      ... as in the case of Edwardus
and von Hoesch on the telephone:
      to good for three years,
         or to evil
Eva's pa heard that on the telephone,
      but forgetful of Bismarck;

lost to all i⁴　　　　義

"No wars after '70."
      "Nicht Bosheit, Dummheit!"
"Sono tutti eretici, Santo Padre,
      ma non sono cattivi."
It can't be all in one language"
      "They are all prots YR HOLINESS,
      but not bad.

Yes yr/ Holiness, they are all of them prots."
"Wd/ have filled Hamburg with grain."
"No, Miss Wi'let, on account of bischniz relations."
20 years to crush Bonaparte,
          gold through France into Spain
The purchase and sale of
          Geschäft,
and Buchanan's remark about monarchies
          (1850 to Pierce)
mentioning only those on the Continent
question? England not yet sold for the Suez —
That would have been 20 years later,
          or was it '74?
At any rate, sold down the river,
          passed over Parliament,
     "whatever else he believed in,
it was not representative government"
     Nor visible responsibilities.
All, that has been, is as it should have been,
     but what will they trust in

                    now?

"Alla non della", in the Verona statement
          οὐ ταῦτα ... κακοῖσι
     Section Rock Drill.
Alexander paid the debts of his soldiery.   They
thought there was a catch in it somewhere, but he set up
   the tables
at camp's edge; "Any note will be paid."
OBIT apud Babylonios

(date . . . out of Arrian).
And in the great Hamurabi Inscription:
                    THEY LIED.
That is the Regius Professorships
                    (apud Chris. Hollis)
to falsify history
      and impose the Whig point of view.
"Such hatred"
            wrote Bowers,
                  and La Spagnuola saying:
"We are perfectly useless, on top,
      but they killed the baker and cobbler."
"Don't write me any more things to tell him
            (scripsit Woodward, W. E.)
"on these occasions

HE

            talks." (End quote)
"What" (Cato speaking) "do you think of
                              murder?"
But some Habsburg or other
            ploughed his Imperial furrow,
And old Theresa's road is still there in Belgium.
Tree-shadowed
            and her thalers
            were current in Africa,
standard in our time,
                  "characters by their coinage";
Cleopatra wrote of her coinage.
      (Joseph two, verify? ploughed his furrow)

Up out of Tuscany, Leopoldine.
"We don't hate anybody."

                       Quoted Konody,
"We fight when our Emperor says so."
                    (Austrians 1914)
"Decent chaps" (Schwartz '43)
           "a shame that we have to fight 'em."
"Mais le prussien!
          Le prussien
                c'est un chic homme."
Said the aged femme de ménage with four teeth out.
     "Vous voullez me rouler,
         mais 'ous ne me
                 roulerez pas,
"paaasque je suis trop rosse."

litigantium dona   féi

                  寶   pào

non coelum non in medio
      but man is under Fortuna
? that is a forced translation?
      La donna che volgo
Man under Fortune,
           CHÊN

Iou Wang, 770

King Jou

    killed by barbarians

"I

                    Houo

      in angustiis me defendisti,
"Millet wine, fragrant,
    and a red bow
        with a hundred arrows
    and a black bow
        and a hundred arrows.
    ne inutile quiescas."   end quote.
"Will not rustle cattle,
will not take oxen and horses,
will close all traps and pitfalls
      that they have set for wild game"

    Pe

    K'in

    order for mobilization against insurrection
by tribes from t'other side of the Houai river

in time of

TCH'ENG 成

WANG 王 1115-1078

"will not traipse into peoples' fields
chasing fugitives, real or . . .
"in eleven days we will go into Sui,
prepare your provisions."

end quote.

"On these occasions

HE

talks."

end quote, Woodward '36
Eleven literates
and I suppose Dwight L. Morrow"
re Senate enrollment

Br . . . C . . . . g
question? about '32
"hysteric presiding over it all" '39
House, Foreign Relations.
Bellum cano perenne . . .

LXXXVII

       . . . between the usurer and any man who
     wants to do a good job
       (perenne)
without regard to production —
                a charge
for the use of money or credit.
       "Why do you want to
"— perché si vuol mettere —
      your ideas in order?"
                 Date '32
Or Grock: Où ça?
   (J'ai une idée.)
           Grock: Où ça?
  Berchtold as if been blown up by dynamite,
Calm on the surface.
   If I had known more then,
      cd/ have asked him,
as Varchi — one wanting the facts.
Of Roanoke, EIGHTEEN 31:
     "Nation silly to borrow its own."
Polk, Tyler, an honour roll.
     paideuma fading,
               Buchanan still fairly clean,
Infantilism increasing till our time,
   attention to outlet, no attention to source,
     That is: the problem of issue.

Who issues it? How?
And after the year 1600 Nakae Toji
    carried Wai' Ya'
        (name worn out in some dialects)
           Min's lamp to Nippon.
The total dirt that was Roosevelt,
and the farce that was Churchill
    (vide Grenfell re/ phoney war)
"But", said Antoninus,
          "Law rules the sea".
"And that the state shd/ have benefit
    from private misfortune,
        not in my time, not under me."
Until Salmasius, wanting precision:
          Want, χρεία,
"Common practice!" sd/Ari re business;
    "Cogitatio, meditatio, contemplatio."
      Wrote Richardus, and Dante read him.
Centrum circuli.
Remove the mythologies before they establish clean values.
"Europe" said Picabia
    "exhausted by the conquest of Alsace-Lorraine."
Vlaminck: "... is local." "Art is."
The pusillanimous wanting all men cut down to worm size.
Wops, maggots, crumbled from simple dishonesty.
διάβορον ... ἐδεστὸν ἐξ αὐτοῦ φθίνει πρὸς κακοῖσι ...
      quia impossibile est.
Ver novum
    are protected of course,
    hic est medium

止 chih in the 3rd/ tone
and a radical.

Was not unanimous
        'Αθάνα broke tie,
That is 6 jurors against 6 jurors
        needed 'Αθάνα.
Right, all of it, was under Shang
        save what came in Athens.
Y Yin, Ocellus, Erigena:
        "All things are lights."
Greek tags in Erigena's verses.
    And when they bumped off Alexander in Babylon
that wrecked, said Gollievski "a good deal".
    Greece had no Quattrocento.
Justinian's codes inefficient
        "abbiamo fatto un mucchio . . .
(a haystack of laws on paper)
                Mus. viva voce:
"We ask 'em to settle between 'em.
    If they can't, the State intervenes."
They deny, of course, but it percolates,
Ocellus:

    jih   日

    hsin   新

the faint green in spring time.
The play shaped from φλογιζόμενον
      gospoda Δηάνειρα, λαμπρὰ συμβαίνει

From the dawn blaze to sunset
"What has been, should have
    "All metal as barter"
        Destutt or whomso,
"Pity to stamp save by weight."
Always the undertow,
    gold-bugs against ANY order,
Seeking the common (as Ari says)
          practice

for squeeze.   chih[4]

    directio voluntatis.
"An instrument of policy
    even more than a measure." Said Douglas (C. H.)
and the squirmers plunder men's mind,
    wanting all men cut down to worm-size.
"A few" said Jean C.
       "gros légumes."
in pochi,
   causa motuum,
      pine seed splitting cliff's edge.
Only sequoias are slow enough.
    BinBin "is beauty".
"Slowness is beauty.":
    from the

         San

         Ku
          to Poictiers.

The tower wherein, at one point, is no shadow,
            and Jacques de Molay, is where?
and the "Section", the proportions,
            lending, perhaps, not at interest, but resisting.
Then false fronts, barocco.
            "We have", said Mencius, "but phenomena."
monumenta. In nature are signatures
            needing no verbal tradition,
oak leaf never plane leaf. John Heydon.
            Σελλοί sleep there on the ground
And old Jarge held there was a tradition,
            that was not mere epistemology.
Mohamedans will remain, — naturally — unconverted
If you remove houris from Paradise

            as to hsin

In short, the cosmos continues
            and there is an observation somewhere in Morrison.
leading to Remy?
            Bombs fell, but not quite on Sant'Ambrogio.
Baccin said: I planted that
                        tree, and *that* tree (ulivi)
Monsieur F. saw his mentor
            composed almost wholly of light.
(Windeler's vision: his letter file
            the size of 2 lumps of sugar,
but the sheet legible. Santa Teresa . . .
Butchers of lesser cattle, their villain the grain god.
Fell between horns, but up . . .
            and the murmur: "salta sin barra,"

There is no such play for a goat.
Tho' Mr Paige has described Ligurian butchery,
And the hunting tribes require some preparation.
Mont Ségur, sacred to Helios,
    and for what had been, San Bertrand de Comminges.
        "Wherever"
said Frobenius "we find these drawings, we
    find water at not more than 6 feet,
And the headless clay lions leave place for the head."
Squirrils white, perhaps before a hard winter, oak cats,
Indians say: when high weeds.
As the water-bug casts a flower on stone
        nel botro,

One interaction. Tê interaction. A shadow?

"Bomb him down. He comes up again" said
    the sergeant detailed perhaps to impress me.
"Und tey vere dhere, shentlemenn,
        mit tearsz hrolling tdown dhere vaces
"Gentlemennn, shinn bones!!"
    ecstacy at a mathematical congress, ottocento.
The bone is in fact constructed,
    according to trigonometrical whichwhat. Shinbones!
Which illustrated Speech as a medium,
    the problem of order.
But an economic idea will not (Mencken auctor) go into them
    in less than a geological epoch.
"Nowt better than share (Mencius)
    nor worse than a fixed charge."
That is the great chapter, Mencius III, 1, III, 6

T'ang Wan Kung　　　上

pu erh. "Why must say profit

　　利　　　　　(the grain cut).

No dichotomy.
　　Who leave the sun out of

　　chih　　　智

Religion? with no dancing girls at the altar?
　　　　　　　REligion?
Cytharistriae.
　　　　　　Vide Neruda's comment,
but focus, can they even animadvert on focus?
or true editions?
　　　　　　　"or even the use of process?
That fine old word"
　　sd/ "Stink" Saunders,
　　　　　　　"An independence".
The nomignolo not reflecting on character
but at that time, 1900 or thereabouts,
applied to all professors of chemistry.
And they count on the amount of coherence,
the amount of endurance,
　　　　　　　　　durations,
Henry's remarks on "dissolving view"
Should be registered.
　　　　　　　Chiefs' names on a monument,

Seepage,
the élan, the block,
                    dissolution.

                    止

Or as Henry again: "we have, in a manner of speaking,
                    arrived.
Got to, I think he says "got to, all got to."
The ubicity, ascertaining.
Was De Molay making loans without interest?
Church councils bumbling. Fanatics do not understand
                    interest.
Justice, directio voluntatis,
    or contemplatio as Richardus defined it in Benjamin Major.
Old crocks to die in a bug-house:
Gallagher (Patrick) mentioned London loans to Tibet,
an old colonel turned against masonry.
And as to what old T. F. saw in the Treasury . . .
                    probably nothing.
Tigers mourn Sikandar.

LXXXVIII

It was Saturday the 1st day of April, toward noon,
the Senate not being that day in session . . .
        came to my room at Brown's asking was I
Mrs Clay's blood-relation?
Prompt in agreeing to meet . . . exact in protesting Clay's
        right to call him. "Col. Tatnall, the bearer,
        is authorized . . .
Was defiance of Adams, not Clay,
        in the senate speech, but to Jessup had said
He would waive privilege,
        which constitutes a very palpable difference.
Vague report that he had said that Salazar's letter
        bore earmarks
           ("blackleg")
Which led to absolute challenge absolutely accepted,
By which time it had become "forgery"
           (Jessup to Tatnall)
"Forged or manufactured"
(Tatnall quoting his principle: Charlotte jury
Wd/ find presumptive strong likeness
        "in points of style" to other papers,
Not proof but suspicion, for which he declined to offer
        explanation.
Adams and Clay were for entanglement.
Right bank, which is in Virginia *
        above bridge of the Little Falls
ten paces

     * where there was a law
       against duelling.
I alone knew how he meant to avoid that.
I went to Clay's on the Friday, the youngest child
      went to sleep on the sofa.
Mrs Clay, as always since the death of her daughter,
      the picture of desolation
But calm and conversable.
      Clay and I parted at midnight.
Saturday, Randolph's, Georgetown,
Could not ask him
      but mentioned the child asleep on the sofa.
He said:
      "I shall do nothing to disturb its sleep
      or the repose of its mother",
and went on making codicils for things of slight value;
To Macon, some english shillings to
      keep game when he played whist;
 Young Bryan sent back to school to
      save him shock if . . . and so forth.
Wanted gold, coins not then in circulation,
     sent Johnny to Branch bank to get a few pieces,
who returned, saying they had none.
     "They are liars from the begining. My HORSE!"
which was brought him, for he never rode Johnny's . . .
Down Penn. Avenue to what is now Corcoran, Riggs,
      Johnny behind him at 40 paces.
Asked for the state of his account. The teller
     took up packages of bills and
     asked in what size notes he wd/ have it.

"I want money."
      said Mr Randolph.
The teller, beginning to understand him, said: Silver?
      "My MONEY!" said Mr Randolph.
"Have you a cart, Mr Randolph?"
        By that time the cashier
told him there was a mistake in the answer to Johnny
and that he shd/ have what he wanted.
        He got it, and closed the account,
Returned and gave me an envelope
      to open if he were killed,
And a slip to read before I got to the ground:
to feel in his breeches pocket:
      nine pieces, I think it was,
3 for me, Tatnall, Hamilton, each
      to make seals of, as mementos.
We were all three then at his lodgings.
      He and the seconds took carriage,
        I followed on horseback.
His (R's) stepfather
      brought out a "Blackstone"   (a. D. 1804)
The place was a thick forest in which a little
      depression or basis.
Bellum perenne:
1694: on what it creates out of nothing
1750: shut down on colonial paper.
Lexington;
      '64 "greatest blessing" said Lincoln.
1878: in circulation as currency.
     · *sangue, fatica,* in our time.

And there is, undoubtedly, blood on their silver,
Without honour men sink into servitude.
Responsible, or irresponsible government?
                Minimum of land without surveillance.
And as to peerage:
I. Edward vi, c. 12

lords of parliament and peers of the realm, having place
and voys in parliament may have benefit of their peerage,
equiv/ that of clergy, for first offence, though they cannot
read, and without being burned in the hand, for all offences
then clergyable and also for housebreaking for robbery on the
high-ways, horse stealing and robbing of churches.

                                        Hal. P. C. 377

The books of a scholar, his countenance (wainagium)
                that of a villein.
        That these are the Histories

                        OR

Thus recapitulate:
        That T'ang opened the copper mine
(distributive function of money).
Nothing on which he leans, the *chuntze*, under heaven
        should have nothing on which he leans,
Or monopoly, Thales, common practice, but dirty,
Antoninus lent money at four percent
        that being the summit of Empire

                        (Roman)
"Trying", he said, "to keep some of the
non-

        interest-bearing national debt in circulation as currency.
                one, eight, seven, eight,
Mencius on tithing,

PERENNE.

Cano perenne,
        I believe the Dai Gaku.
Belascio or Topaze, and not have it sqush,
    a "throne", something God can sit on
        without having it sqush;
With greek tags in his excellent verses,
                   Erigena,
In reign of Carolus Calvus.
       "Captans annonam
maledictus in plebe sit!"
       that was Ambrose:
"Hoggers of harvest!" Delcroix (properly):
      "always the same."
Get the meaning across and then quit.
      Said Baccin: "That tree, and that tree,
    "Yes, I planted that tree ... "
                Under the olives
Some saecular, some half-saecular
    trees, conduits, cisterns, ad majorem
Dum ad Ambrosiam scandet,
           sacro nemori.
             altro che tacita

ἀφρήτωρ, ἀθέμιστος, ἀνέστιος
To the all-men as to the Emperor.
Antoninus as apex, but on slavery and on bhoogery ...
Not un-man, my Estlin, but all-men

                   ching
      as   敬   in the 4th
                   tone

To respect the vegetal powers
　　Or "life however small" (Hindoustani).
Make him of wood with steel springs".

　　　　尸　　to act that, training the child as

　　　　尸　　shih, in the 1st tone.

Père Henri Jacques still
　　　　speaks with the sennin on Rokku,
"These people" said Mr Tcheou "should
be like brothers. They read the same books."
　　　　meaning chinese and japanese.
Marse Adams done tol' 'em.
The Major done told 'em
　　having a First Folio (Shx) in his lock-box
could afford waiting to see it.
　　　　　　"Every . . . etc . . .
downright corruption". "To the consumer".
　　　　Waal, they bust the abundance
and had to pay Europe,
　　　　an' Anatole tol' 'em:
　　　　"no export? No need to make war."
　　　　　　Ile des Pinqouins,
So that Perry "opened" Japan.
Use of foreign coin until 1819.
　　　　Exception Spanish milled dollars,
every dealer occupied in exporting them,　　　　page 446
their exclusion an unconstitutional fraud . . .
A currency of intrinsic value FOR WHICH

They paid interest to NOBODY

page 446
column two

("Thirty Years", Benton)
Is suppressed in favour of fluctuation,
        this country a thoroughfare.
        OBEUNT 1826, July 4.
Not battlements, but that the land go to the settlers,
Tariff! Monsieur de Tocqueville
        may pass *in Europe* for American history.
Macon, Guilford. "Renewal has failed to achieve that end.
In England, salt tax overthrown.
        Andy vetoed the Maysville Road bill . . .
        unconvertable paper . . .
                mines now yielding . . .
Prospects, as Peru, now ½ million per annum
and what is still better, have exports.
        Geryon's prize pup, Nicholas Biddle.
Mr Benton then proposed an amendment:
        on imported indigo 25 cents toward
producing a home supply in a valuable staple,
First planted in Carolinas, in or about 1740
                encouraged by George, Number 2,
at outbreak of revolution over one million pounds,
Britain then turned to India and the Carolinas' product
                declined.
1814: 40 thousand.
        Our manufacturers seek it, now seek it, abroad
and pay ready money at
                two fifty per pound.

583

You cannot carry cloth without indigo,
Cotton, woolen, importation already 2 million a year.
And yet the South HAD four staples
          (Sardegna 1954, queery)
Rice, cotton, indigo and tobacco,
Has exported for 800 million,
     in value to ½ the gold coined in Mexico
        from Cortez' time until now.
The tariff of 1816 murdered indigo.
Freemen do not look upward for bounties.
Freeholds, Mirza Mohammed on the persian Abbas' authority
"for production of barley, rice, cotton
     free of tax or of any contribution whatsodam."
             July 8, 1823.
Jackson 183. to 83 for Mr Adams
     no jealousy in the North at that time.
Stay laws, stop laws, replevin.
     And he has abolished the national debt.
Did not care for relieving one part of the country
     by taxing another,
And New Orleans occurred in 1815, Monsieur de Tocqueville
may pass in Europe for American history
     in a foreign tongue. Guilford
Made Yorktown possible. In 1828 Macon retired.
Used plough and hoe until he was sixty
Γᾶν ἄφθιτον ἀκαμάταν ἀποτρύεται
And to receive all guests in his house,
     Drew a knife to defend Mr. Randolph.
Unnecessary duration of which (i. e. DEBT)
     is incompatible with real independence,

Counteract profligacy public and private which
		profuse outpouring is apt to engender.
Confirmed Martin Van Buren, Jas Hamilton son of
		the late General Hamilton, Ingham, Berrien, Barry.
For defence, not for conquest,
		direct trade with the West Indies
						(124)
And at the foundation of the northwestern states
		Nathan Dane drew it, excluding servitude
Save it were by the will of the serving.
		ORDINANCE
						passed not by the North alone.
Repeal of the salt tax
And has already been shown by A. J's first message . . .
		then vetoed the Maysville Road.
To pull down, insufficient.
		Willing to see a currency of hard money
(under circumstance AT that time)
		as France since the time of mandats and assignats.
Filled France with metals,
		having neither mines in her land, nor yet exports
Which command others' specie.
		Ours yield half a million per annum,
Our mines do,
		and above mines we have exports.
His reference to
		Parnells, Humes, Ellices, Wm. Pultneys
Was laid on the table
		but printed.
"Was now acting as pawn-broker

on system entirely contrary to institution's intention".

    Said Mr Hume (Joseph)

"Privileges" sd/ Ellice

    "which belonged to no other contraption".

Mr Benton proceeding: American

    part of the stockholders, I would not reply to foreign
                 complaints.

Must have known this. They

    have laid up real estate of three million . . .

peculiar privileges enabled them to make profits

stock-holders ought to be grateful

    at 46 in the hundred.

SCIRE FACIAS

            institution too great and too powerful,

The Vice President directed that Mr Benton proceed.

    Direct power prodigious . . . boundless emissions,

To whom is this power granted?

    in a remote corner, a company.

By whom directed?

    By seven, by four, none by the people elected

Nor responsible to them.

    Encroaching on power of States,

        monopoly absolute.

Gt Britain in '95, had been noted:

    "Wish of the Court of Directors"

Political as well as pecuniary. Such

    a bank tends to subjugate government;

It tends to collusions,

    to borrow 50 and pay back one hundred,

    it tends to create public DEBT.

1694: Loan One Million 200,000.

        Interest 80,000, Expenses 4.

GERM, nucleus, and is now 900 Million.

It tends to beget and prolong useless wars;

        aggravate inequalities; make and break fortunes.

"To carry on trade of banking

        upon the revenues,

           and in the name of the

United States;

           to pay revenues to the

Government

        in its own (the bank's own) notes of promise. To

Hold United States moneys

        in deposit, without making compensation;

To discredit other banks and disparage 'em; to

        hold real estate, and retain a

        body of tenantry; To

set branches in States without their consent or approval;

to be exempt from liability if they fail;

        To have the U. S. for a partner, and to have partners

        outside this country;

To be exempt from the regular administration of Justice,

        and to have all this in

           Monopoly.

             Yeas:

             Barnard, Benton, to 20.

             Nays: 23 Webster, Wil-

                    ley

That it failed to produce a uniform currency,

Issued illegal and vicious paper

        "payable at Philadelphy"

tho' usually issued by remote and inaccessible branches
and so made into a local currency pro
tected by distance
AND, being of small denominations,
lingered in the hands of labouring people
until through "wear and tear" it
became a large item of gain
(for the Bank).
It was invented by a scotch banker in Aberdeen
who issued his notes on London in England
and always of small denominations
So that no one wd- take them there for redemption.
Mr Benton asked leave . . .

joint in character
against these orders as
currency...

"Are they signed by the president?
They are not.
Are they under corporate seal?
Are they drawn in the name of the body?
Are they subject, as credit, to time and amount?
They may exceed 60 days.
And no Treasury supervision.
Has the holder the right to sue?
No Sir, but he is allowed to go,
at his own charge to Philadelphia, at his own cost
And as for the charter?
Seven violations,
15 abuses."
These Mr Clayton read to the house, not Polk,

Mr Clayton,
from a narrow strip of paper, rolled round his finger
so that the writing shd not be seen,
He not having had leisure to copy and amplify.

And

fifty

2

weeks

in

4

seasons

LXXXIX

To know the histories

                      to know good from evil

And know whom to trust.

                      Ching Hao.

Chi crescerà
       (Paradiso)
             "of societies" said Emanuel Swedenborg.
Mr Jefferson lining up for Louis Philippe,
     a fact which shd have been known to
                  M. de Tocqueville.
Privilege to serve with King and Macon
         & John Taylor of Caroline.
Entangling alliance with none,
         would be from their cultivation,
That is to say: revenue from the waste lands would be.
Freedom not favoured by tenantry,
       compare as above Abbas Mirza
         "wheat, cotton, barley" July 1823.
As to whether law cd/ be abolished by Indian treaty . . .
    to which the "enlightened classes" had sunk.
Macon mentioned hillsides for grave yards.
      Mr Webster erroneous.
               Obit Picabia 2. Dec. '53

And paper cd/ be left to the states.
Filled France with precious metals
      when England with her overgrown bank . . .
and France had no mines for these metals.   (187)
Public debt increased (England) 400 million.
        Debt born of the Bank of England.
by paper, when the Bank, on its own declaration,
        had not a shilling.
Profuse issues,
   Sudden contractions.
     By power of "construction"

               CONstrued.
Branch forced on Alabama,
     trade in bills Ersatz for products   (199)
Hence WAR, 30 years later.
     Prototype in Threadneedle St. failed . . . overtrading.
Our OWN money lent 'em and WE
        paid one and one half million interest.
and more serious: the POlitical aspect.
     As against its hug as well as its blow,
I speak of Sir William Pulteney.
     Name for name, king for king

          王   wang

          王   wang

Foreigners own 7 million
   usury at 46 in violation,
if beneficial, why not several?

Adams match for ½ the House till the last,
>Randolph scourge of corruption.
"An advantage, Mr Van Buren".

>>>>(Aukland at Talleyrand's)
2 buffer states and 3 dynasties.
>>>>*Ca'our, tessitore.*
Auctor: Good God you don't mean they're worse than the
>>>>>>other gang?
Borah: "Eh ... e ... No,
>>I ... eh ... can't say that e ... exactly."
"Borrowing its own
>>(the Nation's own)
>>>>money".
>>>Said Randolph of Roanoke,
"And paying interest."
>>>Tariff promoted sectional feeling.
Excessive issues, all on public deposits.
>Treasury wd/ pay one hundred Cents on the $
>for what cd/ be had for odd 60.
As Indian silver in our time
>21 but the suckers paid 75.
Catron (I think it was) had shown horse-sense.
If our government must

>>>>>>sell monopolies!
>>>>>>sd/ Andy Jackson

70 million,
>>>mehercule ventum!
with bowie knives
>>>pre- not ex-officio.
Do our cottons sold in Canton & Calcutty

       need such protection at home?

And do not tax salt, said Aurelian.

Mr Taney.

             Burr did his job 20 years late.

Monsieur Vebbstair voulait lézarder.

Ut moveat, ut doceat, ut dilectet

& J. Q. A. objecting to slavery

      Roman law 2/3rds hogswoggled by same

Old John on funding, old John, vide infra, quite a way,

     on depreciation,

        or on being mercantile,

"And if the bills be bottomed . . . " sd/ Mr Jefferson

          loc. cit to Crawford 1816

From our own mines, metal

1824: 5,000 N. Carolina

1833: 868,000 (six states)

and in '34 presumably will be 2 millyum

     and a greater source is our foreign commerce.

From Napoleon Consul "to this day '34"

       have been specie payments.

Mr Hamilton set 15 to one, 15 silver one gold,

when in Spain, Portugal it was sixteen,

     From Natchez and N'Yoleans: doubloons

and to suppose metal will stay with us when the exporter

      can gain one buck on every 15 carried out . . .

doubloons, guineas, half-Joes

      and, to depart from the great senator's most

           courteous language,

6 suspensions till 1819,

     exclusion of foreign coin part of the system:

a currency (foreign coin was) for which they paid tribute to
no one."

OU TIS

Nothing in course of exchanges to
carry specie from Atlantic States to the West
Page refs/ to "Thirty Years View"
and as for the Adamses, Brooks and Henry,
they went back to their grandfather, dratt 'em,
and not back to old John.
Under heading DOMESTIC MANUFACTURES EXPORTED $
TWO MILLION oh five eight four seven four
... the highest and most delicate sovreignty ...
tho charter forbade 'em dealin in coin ...
POWER vested not in one, but in 3 parts of government.
Every city protect its own commerce
Gold: pontifex; silver wangled;
Bronze was to certain cities,
vid Mommsen
And sovreignty in the power to issue.
Benton's when? when there was metal.
Benton's why: no interest to be paid.
The Government ceases to be independent
when currency is at will of a company.
page 450.1
All property is at their mercy.
"I have a friend" said Voltaire.
Drove out not gods, but the Emperor, Imperator.
remarked Del Mar:
"ratios in Rome and in the Orient."
Government wanted "of deposit, not circulation".

義　i⁴

Without historic black-out
　　　　they cannot maintain perpetual wars.
Taney ('34) showed an increase
　　　　in all branches of revenue
Benton b. 1782, d. 1858.
"How often had they been told trade was paralyzed
　　　　& ships idle?
"Hid the books but cd/ not hide weekly statements."
"In specie and without interest.
Against which such a bank is a nuisance."
16 to 1 for above 300 years in the Spanish dominions.
Against Biddle one million and some chicken feed
　　　　for which no vouchers are found.
Levari facias. Louis Philippe suggested that
　　　　Jackson stand firm
and not sugar his language.
　　　　Public debt was extinguished.　　　1834.

何　ho²

必　pi⁴⁻⁵

曰　yüeh⁴⁻⁵

利　li⁴

This quotation is not from Mr Webster.
Clay opposed mints in New Orleans and North Carolina.
The Civil War rooted in tariff.
Philadelphia did not diffuse,

  France had ten mints, and in Mexico there are 8,
Every citizen now more or less cheated.

  Mr B. said he had but two bank-notes
    both of them counterfeit.
French currency had stood two revolutions, one conquest,

  20 millions entered that country,
    no interest was paid for its use.
Land not safe against "issue"

  Crops not safe against "issue"
    Sovreignty is in the right over coinage.
"All that it (the Bank) creates out of nothing."

  600 banks to be broken,
    Fictitious woe, and the Senate's organized sorrow.
"My fellow slave-holder"

    sd/ Mr Randolph
    (masnatosque liberavit)
"Ef my bull-dog" said Mr Bishop

  to a co-detenuto "had a face like yours, hang'd if
I wouldn't shave his arse and make him walk backwards."
And in the time of Mr Randolph, Mr Benton, Mr Van Buren

  he, Andy Jackson
    POPULUM AEDIFICAVIT
which might end this canto, and rhyme with

    Sigismundo.
Commander Rogers observed that the sea was sprinkled with

  fragments of West India fruit

and followed that vestige.

      Giles talked and listened,
more listened, and did not read.

      Young Jessie did not forward dispatches
so Frémont proceeded toward the North West and
      we ultimately embraced Californy
The Collingwood manned 80 guns.

      "Those who wish to talk
May leave now" said Rossini,
      "Madame Bileau is going to play."
"Trade,

    trade,

        trade!"
      Sang Lanier.
Van Buren already in '37 unsmearing Talleyrand.
And the elderly Aida, then a girl of 16, in the '90 s,
    visiting some very stiff friends in New England
giggled (and thereby provoked sour expressions)
      when some children crossed the front lawn with
a bottle of water strung on a string between them
      and chanting:
          "Martin
Van Buren, a bottle of urine".

          Sagetrieb, or the
oral tradition.
"Ten men", said Ubaldo, "who will charge a nest of machine
                    guns
    for one who will put his name on chit."
"No dog, no goat."
      said Pumpelly.

Said Bonaparte: Imagination.
220 riflemen and one piece of artillery
"To environ us" said Mr Dix.

        "The irish are devout, moral, industrious"
he even said: sober.

                Kit Carson sea-sick.

                Ciudad de los Angeles.

                That g sounded as h.
3 days with no food but rosebuds,
Che tolgo lo stato.

            Don Jesus broke his parole.

            Guadalupe ('48) Hidalgo.
Out of von Humboldt: Agassiz, Del Mar and Frobenius
            The wrong way about it: despair.

                (I think that is in Benton)
Randolph of Roanoke: Charlotte Court House, '32,
Henry's passion: fiddling, dancing and pleasantry

                (Patrick Henry)
"We ought not to have turned you out."

            said some old crump to Van Buren
"Great blackguard from Tennessee, by name of Jackson."
"No auction of slaves here in the Capital."

            Τὴν τῶν ὅλων ἀρχήν
Slave labour is very expensive.
But for Price, Sloat might damn well have lost it.

            Quam parva sapientia regitur

Macauley somewhat extravagant in conclusions,
        Palmerston never expressing what he did not believe

"was pleased 25 years later to find him
            at the head of the government."
Jury from the vicinage.

            And Disraeli sold the brit fools down the river.
It was a Tory not a Liberal who gave up the right of search.

    Galileo from Mang   tzu
                                    caliginem vespertinam
πύρωσιν καὶ τῆς θαλάττης
"And here are Caleb Johnson and two others
as demure" (said T.H.B.) "as three whores at a christening."
That Calhoun called him a quadruped.
Firm taste for good company
            evinced by both Benton and Mr Van Buren,
and men even in our time (survivals)
            as Domvile and degli Uberti
"His agreeable niece, la Duchesse de Dino."
Betrayed Mihailovitch, assassinated Henriot and Gentile
    "China, the longest, and with the lowest per cent
            of burocracy.
"200 years" said the Emperor "and no trouble."
            Benton: no trouble, no treaty.
"And mark me," wrote Cambreling,
            "if S/ don't default in four years
"I'll swallow the Treasury."
Tazewell
            wd/ see more fun pitching quoits than
            standing round the Court of St James.
"Of great suavity and gentleness of deportment,
            Mr Van Buren"

An experiment on his nerves was resolved on,
Had Crab such crystal, winter were as a day.
    You cannot make mariners out of slaves
        and the mud, mud, said Guinicelli
Mr Tyler

            i   一

        jin   人

"even if an independent press cd/ be found to
            attempt it"
    M. Hottinguer à Paris
Vicountess Barrington. Lady Bloomfield
    defended by Thesiger and other eminent counsel
        and they got 14 years transportation,
The sub-treasury was revived.
Louis Philippe wd/ not let them cut down their notes to 200.
From '34 to '41 our specie rose to 100 million,
"ad valorem" involving a horde of appraisers.
Wright spoke to mind not to passions and
        he it was brought in Polk.
            Quiditas, remarked D. Alighieri.
Under head of "medicine": whiskey, coal, harness,
        hay, corn, stoves, beef & mutton.
            δ' ἀνθρώπων ἴδεν
Frémont, with small arms and one howitzer,
So that after two hours entered der Schwiegersohn,
    considered the family's low in intelligence:
        "Was sagt er?"
Herr Marcher: Der Jud will Geld.

"Neither by force nor by fraud, that there be
no coercion, either by force or by fraud,
That is law's purpose, or should be.
'Αθήνη swung the hung jury

 tuan, there are four of them.

貞 chen, beyond ataraxia

From Charlemagne's grain price, Venice, Hansa,
    to the forged Donation "of Constantine"
"Perchè in ordine?" (vuol metter le sue idee)
                said Mussolini.
Thalers from Maria Teresa,
        a road still there in Belgium.
The Emperor's furrow,
        Antoninus: Law rules the sea,
            meaning Lex Rhodi,
    they mixed in money rent, and insurance,
This section is labled: Rock Drill.
Wd/ have packed Hamburg with grain. Bülow believed him
    And to young Windsor we owe three years' peace.
"What he meant to *us* in those days"
        said old Image (Selwyn) referring to Ruskin.
Tasso, Kidd, Raleigh, all jailed.
My father (General Frémont) said that if anyone shot Napoleon
    it ought not to be from his (Frémont's) window.
My grandfather boosted Morse' telegraph.

"Pige-moi le type" said old Gustav
   qui vous peindra un fauteuil carthaginois.
Henry J. had Coburn take photographs.
I need add nothing, wrote Van Buren, to the description
  by Col. Benton.
"Good-bye Tazewell, good-by Van Buren!"
   (that was Randolph)
"on borrowed capital, very unmercantile,"
    said John Adams.
Judge Marshall, father of war.
   Agamemnon killed that stag, against hunting rites.
"Leave the Duke, go for gold."
  And they forged those thalers, in our time,
      quest'oggi.
Brits did, nacherly Brits did.
  "Benton has begun understanding me"
       (Randolph)
In Venice the bread price was stable,
  ship models still there in Danzig.
Alex said: set up the tables,
  any soldier's note will be paid.
Gold was under the Pontifex,
  Caesar usurped that.
Bezants were stable till Dandolo broke into Stamboul,
  there had been some arab uneasiness.
The forgery was from ignorance,
  Valla found it.
12 to one, Roma, and about half that in Karachi.
  And the Portagoose, as we cease not to mention,
   uprooted spice trees

Orage remarked on the "recession of power"
    Uncle George said he knew when he came out
(Lodge, Knox) that there wd/ be one hell of a row in the Se-
                                                   nate.
"offensive, defensive"
                    and there was one.
"50 mocking birds, 40 robins," wrote Randolph.
    and "construe all our liberties from us"
Mazzini: Doveri
                "κατὰ σφαγάς"
N' Yoleanz syrop proof 8
        West Indies is at 16 . . .
            Not that I object to morality.
Yes, it was Catron, had already told Jackson.
"Shd/have shot Clay and hung John Calhoun."
        A. J's sole repentence.
And of Antoninus very little record remains.

    semina motuum

Deluged the old hawk at Rip Raps,
    Mr Biddle pinching the baby,
"You damn sadist!" said mr cummings,
        "you try to make people think."
"Yes, Mr Van Buren, the Bank IS
        trying to kill me."
Mr Taney's statement was never refuted.   Aug. '33
And as to expunging?
    that is perhaps prose,
        you can find it in Benton.
Securing his (A. J's) admiration by the majesty

of his (Dante's) in'elect.
"No civilization" said Knittl,
            "they got no stone". (Hrooshia)
Make distress, on system, in order to use it.
"The angrier, the cooler he (Benton) became."
      We have had one "assumption".
English debt could have been paid by the time of George
                                        Second.

      they prefer to send it down to posterity.
And when "EXPUNGED", A. J. sent back the bullet,
      which is, I suppose, part of parliamentary history
dull or not, as you choose to regard it.
      I want Frémont looking at mountains
            or, if you like, Reck, at Lake Biwa,

XC

Animus humanus amor non est,
sed ab ipso amor procedit, et
ideo seipso non diligit, sed amore
qui seipso procedit.

"From the colour the nature
      & by the nature the sign!"
Beatific spirits welding together
      as in one ash-tree in Ygdrasail.
      Baucis, Philemon.
Castalia is the name of that fount in the hill's fold,
      the sea below,
            narrow beach.
Templum aedificans, not yet marble,
      "Amphion!"

And from the San Ku

to the room in Poitiers where one can stand
      casting no shadow,
That is Sagetrieb,
      that is tradition.
Builders had kept the proportion,
      did Jacques de Molay
         know these porportions?
and was Erigena ours?
      Moon's barge over milk-blue water

Kuthera δεινά
Kuthera sempiterna
              Ubi amor, ibi oculus.
Vae qui cogitatis inutile.
          quam in nobis similitudine divinae
                    reperetur imago.
"Mother Earth in thy lap"
                    said Randolph
          ἠγάπησεν πολύ
liberavit masnatos.
Castalia like the moonlight
          and the waves rise and fall,
Evita, beer-halls, semina motuum,
          to parched grass, now is rain
not arrogant from habit,
          but furious from perception,
                    Sibylla,
from under the rubble heap
                    m'elevasti
from the dulled edge beyond pain,
                    m'elevasti
out of Erebus, the deep-lying
          from the wind under the earth,
                    m'elevasti
from the dulled air and the dust,
                    m'elevasti
by the great flight,
                    m'elevasti,
                         Isis Kuanon
          from the cusp of the moon,
                    m'elevasti

606

the viper stirs in the dust,
                              the blue serpent
glides from the rock pool
     And they take lights now down to the water
the lamps float from the rowers
          the sea's claw drawing them outward.
"De fondo" said Juan Ramon,
          like a mermaid, upward,
but the light perpendicular, upward
and to Castalia,
                    water jets from the rock
and in the flat pool as Arethusa's
               a hush in papyri.
Grove hath its altar
          under elms, in that temple, in silence
a lone nymph by the pool.
          Wei and Han rushing together
two rivers together
          bright fish and flotsam
torn bough in the flood
          and the waters clear with the flowing
Out of heaviness where no mind moves at all
          "birds for the mind" said Richardus,
"beasts as to body, for know-how"
Gaio! Gaio!
               To Zeus with the six seraphs before him
The architect from the painter,
          the stone under elm
Taking form now,
          the rilievi,
          the curled stone at the marge

Faunus, sirenes,
        the stone taking form in the air
        ac ferae,
            cervi,
                the great cats approaching.
Pardus, leopardi, Bagheera
        drawn hither from woodland,
woodland ἐπὶ χθονί
        the trees rise
        and there is a wide sward between them
οἱ χθόνιοι myrrh and olibanum on the altar stone
giving perfume,
        and where was nothing
now is furry assemblage
        and in the boughs now are voices
grey wing, black wing, black wing shot with crimson
and the umbrella pines
            as in Palatine,
as in pineta. χελιδών, χελιδών
For the procession of Corpus
        come now banners
comes flute tone
        οἱ χθόνιοι
to new forest,
        thick smoke, purple, rising
bright flame now on the altar
        the crystal funnel of air
out of Erebus, the delivered,
        Tyro, Alcmene, free now, ascending
e i cavalieri,
        ascending,
no shades more,

                lights among them, enkindled,
and the dark shade of courage
                         ’Ηλέκτρα
            bowed still with the wrongs of Aegisthus.
Trees die & the dream remains
                    Not love but that love flows from it
                    ex animo
                    & cannot ergo delight in itself
                    but only in the love flowing from it.
        UBI AMOR IBI OCULUS EST.

XCI

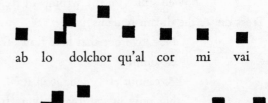

ab lo dolchor qu'al cor mi vai

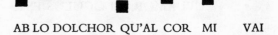

AB LO DOLCHOR QU'AL COR   MI   VAI

that the body of light come forth
           from the body of fire
And that your eyes come to the surface
           from the deep wherein they were sunken,
Reina — for 300 years,
           and now sunken
That your eyes come forth from their caves
           & light then
                     as the holly-leaf
           qui laborat, orat
Thus Undine came to the rock,
                     by Circeo
and the stone eyes again looking seaward
           Thus Apollonius
                     (if it was Apollonius)
& Helen of Tyre
           by Pithagoras
           by Ocellus
(pilot-fish, et libidinis expers, of Tyre;

Justinian, Theodora
            from brown leaf and twig
The GREAT CRYSTAL
                        doubling the pine, and to cloud.
        pensar di lieis m'es ripaus
Miss Tudor moved them with galleons
from deep eye, versus armada
from the green deep
                he saw it,
in the green deep of an eye:
        Crystal waves weaving together toward the gt/
                                        healing
Light *compenetrans* of the spirits
The Princess Ra-Set has climbed
            to the great knees of stone,
She enters protection,
            the great cloud is about her,
She has entered the protection of crystal
                        convien che si mova
                        la mente, amando
                                XXVI, 34
Light & the flowing crystal
        never gin in cut glass had such clarity
That Drake saw the splendour and wreckage
        in that clarity
Gods moving in crystal
                ichor, amor
Secretary of Nature, J. Heydon.
            Here Apollonius, Heydon
            hither Ocellus
                "to this khan"

The golden sun boat
                    by oar, not by sail
Love moving the stars παρὰ βώμιον
by the altar slope
                    "Tamuz!   Tamuz!"
They set lights now in the sea
    and the sea's claw gathers them outward.
The peasant wives hide cocoons now
                                under their aprons
                                    for Tamuz
That the sun's silk

            hsien   tensile

                                be clear
'Ελέναυς That Drake saw the armada
                & sea caves
Ra-Set over crystal

                            moving

in the Queen's eye the reflection
& sea-wrack—
                green deep of the sea-cave
ne quaesaris.
            He asked not
nor wavered, seeing, nor had fear of the wood-queen, Artemis
                        that is Diana
nor had killed save by the hunting rite,
                                sanctus.
Thus sang it:
        Leafdi Diana, leove Diana

Heye Diana, help me to neode
Witte me thurh crafte
whuder ich maei lidhan
to wonsom londe.

                    Rome th'ilke tyme was noght.
So that he spread a deer-hide near the altar,
Now Lear in Janus' temple is laid

     timing the thunder

Nor Constance   hath his hood again,
    Merlin's fader may no man know
    Merlin's moder is made a nun.
Lord, thaet scop the dayes lihte,
        all that she knew was a spirit bright,
A movement that moved in cloth of gold
        into her chamber.
"By the white dragon, under a stone
    Merlin's fader is known to none."
Lay me by Aurelie, at the east end of Stonehenge
    where lie my kindred
Over harm
Over hate
            overflooding, light over light
And yilden he gon rere
                (Athelstan before a. D. 940)
the light flowing, whelming the stars.
        In the barge of Ra-Set
On river of crystal
So hath Sibile a boken isette.
Democracies electing their sewage

613

till there is no clear thought about holiness
a dung flow from 1913
and, in this, their kikery functioned, Marx, Freud
    and the american beaneries
Filth under filth,
                Maritain, Hutchins,
or as Benda remarked: "La trahison"
                and damn all
                I wd/ like to see Verona again
"ecco il tè"
                said the head waiter —
en calcaire, quarante quattre gradins,
        "Dodici Apostoli" (trattoria)
and the affable putana wanting to adjust the spelling of Guido
as it is *not* in the "Capitolare".
        "Come rassembra al martire! sd/ the piccolo
"there were french here,
        but they found some dead in the street one morning,
they did not come back again"
            (That was that war. Battista martire)
in Ortolo, San Zeno, San Pietro
                        and the hell-cats,
"quel naszhong" said the gamin to Ed
        re/ the bronze doors of San Zeno
"buy columns now by the gross"
        as for the four porphery
        with the stone-loop.
Nanni (Torquato) did 3 years with Battista
and wasn't shot till after Salò.
Threw himself in front of a friend (Arpinati)
        but cd/ not save him.

Farinata pudg'd still there in the cloister,
Can Grande's grin like Tommy Cochran's, pleno d'alegreça.
                    Rapunzel did not.
And as donors: Adah Lee, Ida
                    (for an altar piece)
narrow lace at her collar in mourning.
            "A spirit in cloth of gold"
                    so Merlin's moder said,
or did not say,
                    left the quidity
                            but remembered
& from fire to crystal
                    via the body of light,
                            the gold wings assemble
That Rhea's lions protect her
(to the tough guy Musonius: honour)
Rose, azure,
                    the lights slow moving round her,
Zephyrus, turning,
            the petals light on the air.
Bright hawk whom no hood shall chain,
They who are skilled in fire

        shall read   tan₄the dawn.

Waiving no jot of the arcanum
            (having his own mind to stand by him)
As the sea-gull Κάδμου θυγάτηρ said to Odysseus
KADMOU THUGATER
                    "get rid of parapernalia"
                            TLEMOUSUNE

615

And that even in the time of Domitian
        one young man declined to be buggar'd.
"Is this a bath-house?"
ἄλλοτε δ'αὖτ' Εὖρος Ζεφύρῳ εἴξασκε διώκειν
        "Or a Court House?"
Asked Apollonius
            who spoke to the lion
                charitas insuperabilis
to ascend those high places
            wrote Heydon
stirring and changeable
            "light fighting for speed"
and if honour and pleasure will not be ruled
    yet the mind come to that High City . . .
        who with Pythagoras at Taormina
Souls be the water-nymphs of Porphyrius
    Νυκτὸς δ'αὖτ'αἴθηρ τε καὶ ἡμέρα Ζηνὸς πυρός
Formality. Heydon polluted. Apollonius unpolluted
    and the whole creation concerned with "FOUR"
            "my bikini is worth your raft"
And there be who say there is no road to felicity
        tho' swallows eat celandine
        "before my eyes into the aether of Nature"
The water-bug's mittens
                petal the rock beneath,
The natrix glides sapphire into the rock-pool.
            NUTT overarching
"mand'io a la Pinella"
            sd/ Guido
                "a river",

616

"Ghosts dip in the crystal,
                    adorned"
That the tone change from elegy
                        "Et Jehanne"
            (the Lorraine girl)
A lost kind of experience?
                    scarcely,
O Queen Cytherea,
            che 'l terzo ciel movete.

XCII

And from this Mount were blown
                              seed
and that every plant hath its seed
        so will the weasel eat rue,
        and the swallows nip celandine
and as engraven on gold, to be unity
but duality, brass
        and trine to mercurial
shall a tetrad be silver
        with the smoke of nutmeg and frankincense
and from this a sea-change?
And honour?
                Fitzgerald: " I was."
When he freed a man
        who had not been at the Post Office
(Oireland 1916) or "Signori,
        Io facevo la sentinella?
        O non facevo la sentinella?"
accused of not taking cover during bombardment.
                                "Gran dispitto."
"A chi stima . . . "
        (Guicciardini)
        . . . l'onore assai"
& from pool of the silver circlet
    is calm as the sapphire
Ra-Set in her barge now
                    over deep sapphire

but the child played under wave . . .
   e piove d'amor
   in nui
   a great river, the ghosts dipping in crystal
& to Pinella . . .
But "Her love" sd/ Hewlett
    "like a cage hath bars
that break my head, seeking to touch the stars."
To another the rain fell as of silver.
      La Luna Regina.
Not gold as in Ecbatan
O Anubis, guard this portal
   as the cellula, Mont Ségur.
Sanctus
   that no blood sully this altar
ex aquis nata
   τά ἐκ τῶν ὑδάτων γενόμενα
"in questa lumera appresso"
      Folquet, nel terzo cielo.
"And if I see her not,
   no sight is worth the beauty of my thought."
Then knelt with the sphere of crystal
That she should touch with her hands,
     Coeli Regina,
The four altars at the four coigns of that place,
But in the great love, bewildered
   farfalla in tempesta
under rain in the dark:
      many wings fragile
Nymphalidae, basilarch, and lycaena,
Ausonides, euchloe, and erynnis

And from far
               il tremolar della marina
chh   chh
    the pebbles turn with the wave
chh   ch'u
               "fui chiamat'
                          e qui refulgo"
Le Paradis n'est pas artificiel
                          but is jagged,
For a flash,
          for an hour.
Then agony,
          then an hour,
                    then agony,
Hilary stumbles, but the Divine Mind is abundant
                    unceasing
                    improvisatore
Omniformis
          unstill
and that the lice turned from the manifest;
               overlooking the detail
and their filth now observes mere dynamic;
That the Pontifex ceased to be holy
          — that was in Caesar's time —
               who was buggar'd
and the coin ceased to be holy,
          and, of course,
                    they worshiped the emperor.
Margarethe von Taufers
          and Uncle Carlo
both tried a clean-up,

hence, in a way, the Rimini bas-reliefs
   and Semele's personality shot to atoms.
Even you were happy last Wednesday.
    "Io porto"
sd/ Delcroix
   "la cecità" for I forget how many
    ten thousand Italians.
"Two evils:
    usury in the bank rot
& theft in les soc/ anonymes".
   Grabbed his phone and called un ministro.
Bottai also phoned Torino
   instanter, to dig out Vivaldi,
And ministri went to the fighting line
as did old Marinetti
"Hans Sachs"
    sd/ Schnitz Brandt
     "war ein Schuh-
macher und poet dazu."
   Yet, having seen the armada
    turn back?
That wd/ scarcely . . . from sea-caves
300 years.
   Nein! aber in Wolken.
And against usury
   and the degradation of sacraments,
For 40 years I have seen this,
   now flood as the Yang tse
also desensitization
   25 hundred years desensitization

2 thousand years, desensitization
After Apollonius, desensitization
    & a little light from the borders:
    Erigena,
    Avicenna, Richardus.
Hilary looked at an oak leaf
    or holly, or rowan
as against the brown oil and corpse sweat
& then cannon to take the chinks opium
& the Portagoose uprooting spice-trees "a common"
    sez Ari "custom in trade"

XCIII

"A man's paradise is his good nature"

                                    sd/ Kati.

"panis angelicus" Antef
          two ½s of a seal
having his own mind to stand by him
                    Κάδμου θυγάτηρ
Apollonius made his peace with the animals,
     so the arcivescovo fumbled round under his
          ample overcloaks as to what might have been
a left-hand back pocket of civil clothing
and produced a cornucopia from "La Tour"
or as Augustine said, or as the Pope wrote to Augustine
     "easier to convert after you feed 'em"
but this was before St Peter's
          in move toward a carrozza
from the internal horrors (mosaic)
     en route to Santa Sabina
               & San Domenico
where the spirit is clear in the stone
          as against
Filth of the Hyksos, butchers of lesser cattle.
     Narrow alabaster in sunlight
          in Classe, in San Domenico
(Yes, my Ondine, it is so god-damned dry on these rocks)

"The waves rise, and the waves fall
But you are like the moon-light:
                              Always there!"
            Old Grinell had remembered that.
By olibanum, the polite salutation, the smoke sign;
                  Do not pester the spirits.
"non fosse cive"
                  Dant' had it,
Some sense of civility
                  & from Avon (whence they do not suspect it)
As in "dragons' spleens",
            or "a pelting farm",
Liquidity from the alum at Tolfa
            — Papal, that was.
                  And the Medici failed
From accepting excess deposits.
            "Te voilà, mon Bourienne."
corrent' attrattiva,
                        with the ureus, azure
                        that is from turquoise and gold,
                        Iside, out of turquoise and gold.
Peitz trai pena d'amor   Que Tristans l'amador
            Qu'a suffri mainta dolor
                        per Iseutz la bionda
First petals   and then cool rain
            sward Castalia again
                        Peitz trai pena d'amor
                        Que Tristans l'amador
                        Qu'a suffri mainta dolor
                        Per Iseutz la bionda

      First petals

and then cool rain
By sward Castalia again
The suicide is not serious   from conviction
    One should first bump off some nuisance.
From sheer physical depression, c'est autre chose.
San Cristoforo provided transport
        with a little Christo gripping his hair
the mist domed over Gardasee
        the east lobe bluer from sulphur
            dove siede Peschiera
no such blue north of Sorrento
        Cortesia, onestade
            out of the Ureus
Nine knowledges about

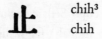   chih³
                                       chih

Avicenna and Algazel
The 8th being natural science, 9th moral
8th the concrete, 9th the agenda,
Agassiz with the fixed stars, Kung to the crystaline,
To Queen Nephertari this incense
    To Isis this incense
                    "quest' unire
"quale è dentro l'anima
        veggendo di fuori quelli che ama"
                                    Risplende
From the sea-caves
            degli occhi
Manifest and not abstract

In the time of Numa Pompilius
    che Pitagora si chiamò.
"non sempre" (in the 3rd of Convivio)
or as above stated "jagged"
   l'amor che ti fa bella
("ut facias" — Goddeschalk — "pulchram")
    That love is the "form" of philosophy,
is its shape (è forma di Filosofia)
and that men are naturally friendly
  at any rate from his (Dant's) point of view
tho' he puts knowledge higher than I should
and, elsewhere: "her" beltà,
        cioè moralitade,
rains flakes of fire",
    but is not speaking of knowledge.
Though Jacopo Sellaio included it
  "e solo in lealtà far si diletta"
e "d'udir . . . prode" both of antient times and our own,
and on another point
      600 years before Beaumarchais
   38 hundred years after KATI

"compagnevole animale" 

   or "Perché" said the Boss
"vuol mettere le sue idee in ordine?"
    "Pel mio poema."
bellezza (outside Perugia,
    seated on three sacks of laundry,
     pargoletta
"onestade risplende". Dio, la prima bontade

626

which can be written 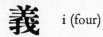 i (four)

whence saith Augustine.

　　Alessandro & Saladin & Galasso di Montefeltro
and mentions distributive justice, Dante does, in Convivio
　　　　　　　　Four, eleven
"cui adorna esta bontade". Know agenda,
　　　　to the utmost of its virtu,
of its own.

　　　　　　All ov which may be a little slow for the reader
or seem platitudinous
　　　　　　　　　und kein Weekend-Spass
Mr Hoepli sent a small brochure to Svitzerland
　　　　and his banker friend replied "*urgente*":
"destroy it e farlo sparire."
　　　　　　Shivers has received (again) nomination
and "Alfalfa" is no longer in Who's Who,
　　　　current issue.
Grenfell's death was (like some others)
　　　　　　suspiciously sudden.
The Bard of Avon mentioned the subject,
Dante mentioned the subject,
　　　and the lit profs discuss other passages
　　　　　　in abuleia
or in total unconsciousness
　　　Four thousand years after KATI

Taffy went putty-colour when I mentioned Zaharoff (1914)
And general Whoosis, when he read the name, Aquarone,
　　　　30 years later

or as Ub said: "ten to charge a nest of machine guns
for one who will put his name on a chit.
The autumn leaves blow from my hand,
agitante calescemus . . .
and the wind cools toward autumn.
Lux in diafana,
Creatrix,
oro.
Ursula benedetta,
oro
By the hours of passion,
per dilettevole ore,
guide your successor,
Ysolt, Ydone,
have compassion,
Picarda,
compassion
By the wing'd head,
by the caduceus,
compassion;
By the horns of Isis-Luna,
compassion.
The black panther lies under his rose-tree.
J'ai eu pitié des autres.
Pas assez! Pas assez!
For me nothing. But that the child
walk in peace in her basilica,
The light there almost solid.

力   li⁴

行　hsing²

近　chin⁴

乎　hu¹ 2154

仁　jên²

holding that energy is near to benevolence.
Au bois dormant,

　　　　　not yet...! Not yet!

　　　　do not awaken.

The trees sleep, and the stags, and the grass;
The boughs sleep unmoving.
"Krr! Krr!" from the starling:

　　　　　"mai tardi...

"per l'ignoto"

　　　　and the soul's job? (Ocellus)

　　　　　"Renew"

as on the T'ang tub:

　　　　　Renew

　jih

　hsin　日新見

　renew

Plus the luminous eye

　　　　　chien⁴

the terror of all four-flushers
& there is no doubt that D'Annunzio
                    could move the crowd in a theatre
or that the stone rose in Brescia,

                                        Amphion!
And yet for Venus and Roma
                    a wraith moved in air
And Rapicavoli lost for a horse-jump.
                    Quarta Sponda
                            transient as air
Waste after Carthage.
                    not yet! not yet!
                            Do not awaken.
Came then Flora Castalia
            "Air hath no petals now,
                where shall come leaf on bough
                        naught is but air.
                        "pone metum, Cerinthe,
Nec deus laedit
and the Lorraine girl heard in the fields.
Tho' the skater move fast or slow
                    the ice must be solid
                        Pone metum, Cerinthe
        volucres delphinasque ad auditum
                tone, tide, tide
                if the tone draw the dolphin

                                hsien

                    nuova vita
        e ti fiammeggio.

                            630

Such light is in sea-caves
e la bella Ciprigna
         where copper throws back the flame
from pinned eyes, the flames rise to fade
                       in green air.
A foot-print? alcun vestigio?
         thus was it for 5 thousand years

         thus saith (Kati).

and as for the trigger-happy mind
            amid stars
            amid dangers; abysses
going six ways a Sunday,
                       how shall philologers?
A butcher's block for biographers,
         quidity!
                       Have they heard of it?
"Oh you," as Dante says
         "in the dinghy astern there"
There must be incognita
            and in sea-caves
            un lume pien' di spiriti
            and of memories,
Shall two know the same in their knowing?
         You who dare Persephone's threshold,
         Beloved, do not fall apart in my hands.
E "chi crescerà" they would be individuals.
         Swedenborg said "of societies"
                       by attraction.
"Blind eyes and shadows"

to enter the presence at sunrise
up out of hell, from the labyrinth
the path wide as a hair
& as to mental velocities:
Yeats on Ian Hamilton: "So stupid he
couldn't think unless there were a cannonade going on."
The duration
in re/ mental velocity
as to antennae
as to malevolence.
Six ways to once
of a Sunday. Velocity.
Without guides, having nothing but courage
Shall audacity last into fortitude?
You are tender as a marshmallow, my Love,
I cannot use you as a fulcrum.
You have stirred my mind out of dust.
Flora Castalia, your petals drift thru the air,
the wind is ½ lighted with pollen
diafana,
e Monna Vanna . . . tu mi fai rimembrar.

XCIV

"Brederode"
        (to Rush, Ap 4. 1790)
. . . treaties of commerce only,
    Blue jay, my blue jay
that she should take wing in the night
by the Kingdom of

      T'ai   太

      Wu   武

      Tzu   子

      as mentioned in Rollin,
re/ Lincoln, 14th May. 1810
"or whose depreciations are to the favour of the whole people"
    Mr Adams saw thru the bank hoax
& Suvitch a century plus 20 years later:
      "d- d- d- dina- mite!
    sssi si
        d-d-
           dinamite!
& the Medici failed from accepting too many deposits.
Alex . . . , a respectable
    or at least meritorious Biddle,
               alive 1890

"& consequently the corruption of history"
              J. A. to Rush
                  18 'leven.
Beyond civic order:
                  l'AMOR.
Was it Frate Egidio — "per la mente"
     looking down and reproving
"who shd/ mistake the eye for the mind".
Above prana, the light,
                  past light, the crystal.
Above crystal, the jade!
The clover enduring,
                  basalt crumbled with time.
"Are they the same leaves?"
          that was an intelligent question.
And that all gates are holy.
          (Pandects 1. 8 out of Gaius)
divini et humani juris communicatio
          and to the highest integrity.
Ius Italicum (Digest Fifty, xv)
     Antoninus gave this to Tyre (Paulus, two)
Consul for the fourth time, 7th December & Paulus
               in Constantinople
& then the fun starts
               with the "Code"
     I. 3, Title:
          "feed 'um"
The Bulgar was trying to hold onto horse sense
     & an impression
perhaps in too general language, that
          Constantine was a louse
"BUT by the new law,"

                  634

127
"from affection alone"
CODE. V. 27, the paragraph preceding 2.
Code V. iv, 23,5. called also "fuss-cat"
To Kung, to avoid their encirclement,
To the Odes to escape abstract yatter,
to Mencius, Dante, and Agassiz
for Gestalt seed,
pity, yes, for the infected,
but maintain antisepsis,
let the light pour.
Apollonius made peace with the animals
Was no blood on the Cyprian's altars
Justinian inserted that sentence:
"from affection" the novel, 127
From the hawk-king
Goth, Agdu
Prabbu of Kopt, Queen Ash
may Isis preserve thee
Manis paid for the land
1 bur: 60 measures, lo staio, 1 mana of silver
as is said on the black obelisk
somewhere about 27 o 4
in the long boats east of Abydos.

darkness, do you want
darkness, caligine?
½ the year to get tin –
Agada, Gana . . .

635

½ the year to get tin.

             Swans came to the meadow

πολλοὺς τιμῶν πιστεύων δὲ ὀλίγοις

For styrax to Pamphilia,

                    leopards

and Apollonius said to King Huey

梁 Leang

惠 Hwuy

以 i

財 ts'ai²

發 fa

wu² 無

i³ 以

pao³ 寶 rhymed in Taxila

Phraotes' tigers worship the sun.

νυμφόληπτοι... βάκχοι τοῦ νήφειν

ὕμνον ἡμέραν
ξῶον... τὸν κόσμον... γὰρ ζωογονεῖ πάντα
                                    III 34
ἔρωτά ἴσχει... καὶ ξυνίστησιν
                                    III 34 F. P.
no full trans/ till 1811,
        remarks F. C. Conybeare, the prelector,
who says it is (sic:) "lightly written"
although no theologian touches it... well?
        NO! not even Richardus
        Ἰάρχας
        Apollonius & Richardus
or, as Swedenborg says: "of societies"
& that griffins dig rocks spotted with gold
and the phoenix
προπεμπτηρίους ὕμνους αὐτῷ ἄδειν
as do swans for those having ear.
By the nymphs... and have ecstasy, sober
and that the universe is alive
        ἔρωτά ἴσχει
& keeping the Ganges on his right hand
went down ten days toward the sea
& the "red" sea named after Erythras
        not from its colour, the cyanine
ὑμᾶς δεδώκατε τὴν θάλατταν ἔρρωσθε
Balàra full of myrtles and date palms
        a place well watered by springs
παρὰ τοῖς τὴν σοφίαν τιμῶσιν
and they bell the boat to keep off the seals
Grant, O Muses,
        καὶ ἐρασθῆναι ἀλλήλων

that was Smyrna,
> but found Ephesus full of pipers, buggars & noise.
"We are the plant." said Hugo Rennert
or
as Homer says:
> πολλαῖς ἰδέαις
not merely set stone
πράττειν ἕκαστον... οἵ τι δύναται
ἐπὶ τὴν ναῦν ἑσπέρας ἤδη
> embarking at sunset.
That he passed the night on the mound of Achilles
"master of tempest and fire"
> & he set up Palamedes
an image that I, Philostratus, saw
> and a shrine that will hold ten people drinking.
"It was not by ditch-digging and sheep's-guts ...
> "in Aeolis close to Methymna"
in the summer lightning, close upon cock-crow.
So that walking here under the larches of Paradise
the stream was exceedingly clear
> & almost level its margin
"was thrown in my way a touch-stone
γὰρ βάσανος καθαρὸν καὶ ἀπ' οὐδενὸς θνητοῦ
"Hic sunt leones",
> Calpis,
> on the North side "as gold from the Heliads' poplar"
and at Gadara (Cadiz) sumerian capitals to their pillars
> δὲ τοῖς ὅσια πράττουσι
> for the doers of holiness
> γῆν μὲν πᾶσαν ἀσφαλῆ
they may ship or swim, being secure.   v. 17

638

We have already raised our stele to Musonius,
　　　the man with the spade

Five, twenty two 發 fa¹⁻⁵

　　　　　　　　財 ts'ai²

29- 中 chung
　　　　　　　　　as yung chung

VESPASIAN a. D. 69
　　　formó nuevos archivos
　　　　　BUT did not show good sense in Greece.

Said ANTONINUS:
　　　"Law rules the sea"
　　　　　meaning lex Rhodi
Daughter of a sun priest in Babylon
　　　told Philostratus to set down this record
　　　　　of TYana
τῶν ἑαυτοῦ παίδων ὑπὸ τοῖς θεοῖς
not particular about theoretical organizations

V. 35 worth attention
ἐπὶ νοῦν ἐλθὸν εἰρήσεται
εἰ τὴν ψυχὴν τὴν ἐμὴν ᾤκεις

& do not mow the high stalks
ANTONINUS reigned 138 to 161
SEVERUS and Julia Domna about 198

王

王

ἑλληνίξοντας μὲν Ἑλληνικῶν
as against that schnorrer Euphrates
and he said to Dion:
                    Set it to music
and sent the lion up country
            after sacrifice to Amasis
            ἐπ᾽ αὐτῷ ἄδοντες
& keeping the Nile on their right hand
about ten of them went with Apollonius
"μὴ ὀβολὸς ὀβολὸν τέκη"
        "Which is all nuts" said Apollonius,
        "The Africans have more sense than the greeks".
            book Six, chap. 2
Ἠῴῳ Μέμνονι Memnon of the Dawn
the one word meaning to burn and be warm
ψυχὴ ἀθάνατος ἢ τὶ μετὰ ξῳοῖσιν ἐὼν τιμητέον

That it is of thrones,
                    and above them: Justice
Acre, again,

       with an Eleanor
who sucked the venom out of his wound,
      and came up via Padua,
for a balance of wine & wool,
      distraint and tolls not unbridled
and in 1288 a thunderbolt passed between them
    this wd/ be in the time of Federico Secondo,
Alfonso, St Louis, and Magnus of Norway
and two years later she died and his luck went out,
Edwardus, who played Baliol against the Bruce
    and brought the stone down to London
      where it is seen to this day.
         PACTUM SERVA
           Be Traist
As against anyone who takes his blessings into a corner,
    and after that we will go up to the Cataracts
καὶ κελαδοῦνος ἀκοῦσαι
    Φαντασία σοφωτέρα μιμήσεως
not baffled by terror,
    and wanted to keep Sparta, Sparta,

      that the king   **王**   shd/ be king

             王

   μὴ ἐνομιλούντων
      not a melting pot
& when Athens exceeded the tributes set by Aristides,
Coke, after he got into Parliament,
The boat of Ra-Set moves with the sun.

"To build light

日　　　　　　　jih

新　　　　　　　hsin

　　　　　　　　said Ocellus.

XCV

LOVE, gone as lightning,
   enduring 5000 years.
Shall the comet cease moving
   or the great stars be tied in one place!
  "Consonantium demonstratrix"
       ἔφατ' Beda
Deus est anima mundi,
   animal optimum
     et sempiternum.
Tempus est ubique,
    non motus
      in vesperibus orbis.
Expergesci thalamis, gravat serpella nimbus
Mist weighs down the wild thyme plants.
  "In favour of the whole people". "They repeat"
    said Delcroix
Van Buren unsmearing Talleyrand,
    Adams to Rush before that, in 1811
And there were guilds in Byzantium.
  "Not political", Dante says, a
    "compagnevole animale"
Even if some do coagulate into cities
    πόλις, πολιτική
reproducteur,
    contribuable. Paradis peint
but πολεύω meaning to plough
  πολύγλωσσος

There were many sounds in that oak-wood.
Benton: when there was plenty of metal,
Van Buren already desmearing Talleyrand
J. A. "the whole people (devaluation)."
Alexander paid the debts of his soldiery
    And over an arch in Vicenza, the stemma,
the coat of arms, stone: "Lapo, ghibbeline exile".
    "Who knows but I also from some vento di siepe?"
six centuries later "de gli Uberti".
        Queen of Heaven bring her repose
        Κάδμου θυγάτηρ
        bringing light *per diafana*
λευκὸς Λευκόθοε
          white foam, a sea-gull
And damn it there were men even in my time
    Nicoletti, Ramperti, Desmond Fitzgerald
      (the one alive in 1919)
That the crystal wave mount to flood surge

近   chin⁴

平   hu¹

仁   jên²

    The light there almost solid.
YAO'S worry: to find a successor

& the three years peace we owe Windsor
'36 - '39
As from the terrace, Saint Bertrand
to southward from Montrejeau
Elder Lightfoot is not downhearted,
Elder Lightfoot is cert'nly

not

downhearted,
He observes a design in the Process.
Miss Ida by the bars in the jail house
"de Nantes
il y a un prisonnier", periplum
from Madrid more than 40 years earlier,
Carrière show in Paris,
"Bret" in la rue Grande Chaumière.
the jap girl: "Mais Rembrandt"
in ecstasy
And the *russe*
bringing all the "Smoke" of Turgenev.
"Are" as Uncle William said "the daughters of Memory"
"Pirandello,
because that is the sort of thing that . . .
that does go on in one's mind."

Whose mind?
Among all these twerps and Pulitzer sponges
no voice for the Constitution,
No objection to the historic blackout.
"My bikini is worth yr/ raft". Said Leucothae
And if I see her not
No sight is worth the beauty of my thought.

645

The immense cowardice of advertised litterati
      & Elsa Kassandra, "the Baroness"
von Freitag etc. sd/ several true things
in the old days /
                driven nuts,
Well, of course, there was a certain strain
      on the gal in them days in Manhattan
the principle of non-acquiescence
                      laid a burden.
Dinklage, where art thou,
      with, or without, your *von*?
You said the teeth of the black troops
      reminded you of the boar-hunt,
I think yr/ first boar hunt, but
The black prisoners had such a nice way with children,
Also what's his name who spent the night in the air
caught in the mooring-ropes.
            Lone rock for sea-gull
who can, in any case, rest on water!
Do not Hindoos
                lust after vacuity?
With the Gardasee at our disposition.
"O World!"
            said Mr Beddoes.
"Something *there*."
                sd/ Santayana.
Responsus:
        Not stasis/
            at least not in our immediate vicinage.
a hand without face cards,

the enormous organized cowardice.
And there is something decent in the universe
    if I can feel all this, *dicto millesimo*
At the age of whatever.
I suppose St. Hilary looked at an oak-leaf.
(vine-leaf? San Denys,
    (spelled Dionisio)
Dionisio et Eleutherio.
Dionisio et Eleutherio
    "the brace of 'em
that Calvin never blacked out
                  en l'Isle.)
That the wave crashed, whirling the raft, then
Tearing the oar from his hand,
                  broke mast and yard-arm
And he was drawn down under wave,
        The wind tossing,
Notus, Boreas,
        as it were thistle-down.
Then Leucothea had pity,
            "mortal once
Who now is a sea-god:
         νόστου
γαίης Φαιήκων,..."

THRONES DE LOS CANTARES
XCVI-CIX

XCVI

Κρήδεμνον . . .
κρήδεμνον . . .
and the wave concealed her,
        dark mass of great water.
Aestheticisme comme politique d'église, hardly religion.
& on the hearth burned cedar and juniper . . .
        that should bear him thru these diafana
Aether pluit numismata
Tellus vomit cadavera,
        Thusca quae a thure,
from the name of the incense, in this province is
        ROMA *quae olim* . . .
In the province of Tuscany is Rome, a city which formerly . . .
And Sabines with a crow on their flag.
Brennus came for the wine, liking its quality,
Bergamo, Brescia, Ticino,
& inviting his wife to drink from her father's skull
(Cunimundus) a cup which I, Paulus, saw . . .
that Tiberius Constantine was distributist,
Justinian, Chosroes, Augustae Sophiae,
lumina mundi, ἐπικόμβια . . . τὸν λαόν
or a hand out. 586 chronologically
        (more or less)
Authar, marvelous reign, no violence and no passports,
        Vitalis beati
More water about San Zeno than had flowed since the days of
                    Noah

on the 16th of November
15th of Childibert, a.D. 589
                    water and snakes over the granaries.
Theodolinda, Theoderic from Brunhilda,
Roma caput Ecclesiae, the persians into Jerusalem
and my grand-dad got out of what is now Jugoslavia
with a bow, arrows and a wolf acting as guide
till it thought gramp looked too hungry,
                    comes itineris
Rothar touched with the Arian heresy
put father, son, ghost in that order
whereas we catholics stand for equality,

        And here, 77 years, lombards had been in Ticino,
and Rothar got some laws written down
        and a prolog, dope already used,
even the snake cult,   585
concubines, bacchatur, and a murder in
            San Giovanni's basilica.
Constans Augustus stripped the brass tiles from the Pantheon,
shipped 'em toward Constantinople,
and got bumped off in his bath
            in Siracusa.   620
Reyna says the lombards struck gold for St. Michael
            (Migne 95, 620)
Cedwald, Architriclin
From the golden font, kings lie in order of generation
            Cuningpert elegant, and a warrior . . .
de partibus Liguriae . . . lubricus
Aripert sank, auro gravatus, because he was carrying gold.
Who shall know throstle's note from banded thrush

by the wind in the holly bush
Floods came in the Via Lata
and from St. Peter's down to the bridge, Ponte Milvio
et quia Karolus followed Pippin,
not Plectrude's son but Alpaide's
Wait, wait, Martel father of Pippin,
Pippin of Charlemagne,
Alpaide's son, one of 'em, not Plectrude's
empty grave outside San Zeno, to the right as you face it,
another bloke in Milano, "seven Cardinals attended his funeral,"
apud Pictavium, Aquitaine, Narbonne and Proença.
Martel, that would be in the "thirties,"
Lombards pro Carolus:
ACTUM TICINI IN PALATIO,
et Arimnium, a stone in Modena by the ambon...
sent his son to Luitprand for a hair cut,
kept peace with franks and avars
verbo et actu corruscans
Wang's middle name not in Mathews
in the second year of Eirene sent Constans to Carolus Magnus
sardonix pario, lilia mixta rosis,
at Tyana some idea they disapproved of.
DIOCLETIAN, 37th after Augustus, thought: more if we
tax 'em
and don't annihilate. Haud procul Salonis
not far from Salo otio senuit, quietly aging,
and alleged Saturn started brass currency
"changing bowers for travertine"
Vespasiano serenitas... urbes renovatae
Under Antoninus, 23 years without war... apud Eboricum,

Severus' wife spoke to Philostratus about the biography
and about 1165 of the City (A.U. ab urbe)
             Galla Placidia,
Pictorum,
Vandali,
             "called Bosphorus from the bull tax"
treaty with lombards under Justinian,
             goths out of Verona et Brixia,
all italian "reip." under law.
             A memorial to archivists and librarians:
Bernicoli in Ravenna, and that stuffed-shirt who
             wrote such an elegant postcard.
Some sort of embargo, Theodora died in the 19th Justinian.
And the money sellers Ablavius and Marcellus
thought they would bump off Justinian.
A flood of fads swilled over all Europe.
             But there could have been two Abduls
and it would not have annoyed one.
             That is something to note. I mean as
personality, when one says "oriental." The third bahai
said nothing remarkable. Edgar Wallace had his kind of
                                      modesty.
Caedual went to Roma, baptised 689 by some counting.
And the Eparch's book was down somewhere under all of this,
ΕΠΑΡΧΙΚΟΝ ΒΙΒΛΙΟΝ.
After 500 years, still sacrificed to that sea gull,
a colony of Phaeacians θῖνα θαλάσσης
ALDFRID, King of Northumbria, Nordanhymbrorum
             defunctus 7 oh 5,
Aldhelm, against errors of Britons,

pro virginity in hexameters,
de Metaplasmo, De Sinalimpha, &
fads for some hundred years,
        a comet with its face toward Aquilo,
fussed about hair-cuts,
        an appeal to reason is about a 13%
            appeal to reality,
job-hunting in our time, and in the 3rd/ year of Justin
        Sophia Augusta
        made the money-sellers cough up something or other,
pecuniarium venditoribus, and in the 12th
            took over the synagog,
heaped fads on Eleusis, flame under the rubble
        TIBERIUS 5, 7, 3
            by his spending
Thrax, Cappadox,
            Lombards, Avars.
(Theophanem sequitur.)
        Lombards in Exarchate, MAURICIUS Imperator
Barbarians enjoyed Roman calamities,
            calamitatibus delectabantur,
equestribus speculationibus and by dealings
        urbem splendidam reddidit,
            this is MAURICIUS, five seventy seven,
and of course there is no local freedom
            without local control of local purchasing power.
Del Mar spotted "bronze to the cities,"
        sanguinibus gaudium, homicidiis amorem,
            infidelitatem, jactantiam et violentiam (Hormisdae).
Priscus copped the king drunk

(Musacius) at his brother's wake,
aerumnae non defuerunt variae,
        plenty of shindies, assorted,
With eyes pervanche,
        all under the Moon is under Fortuna

 CHEN,

e che permutasse.
        With castled ships and images Dei Matris,
HERACLIUS, six, oh, two
imperator simul et sponsus,
        found the "reip's" business unstuck,
that is, Avars made Europe a desert,
        Persians exterminated all Asia

Chosroes (Second) pro sun   日

& melted down the church vessels & coined them
        νομίσματα καὶ μιλιαρίσια
(which is not in Liddell D. D.),
        The Deacon, col. 1026, thinks it "argenteos,"
nummos aureos et argenteos, HERACLIUS versus Chosroes
coined candle-sticks to keep off Chosroes
εἰκόνος
Justinian 527
Tiberius Justin
Mauricius 577
Phocas

Heraclius, six oh two, all dates approximate.
          Deutschland unter Dulles, U.S.A., slightly nostalgic
by the boat-bridge over Euphrates.
          Wintered then in Sebastia,
Laws aim? is against coercion.
          And called them the Golden Spears, Χρυσολόχας,
Avars, Bulgars, Gepidae,
                    quatenus Hunnos,
                              against the City, Fu Lin.
Turcos quos Cazaros vocant. Six eighteen, that is.
God's Mother superlaudabilis
                    populus epulantes
                    Deum glorificantes,
pepper & zinziber, tigrides mirae magnitudinis
                    live ones, and antelopes,
and in sky a great phantom
                    from Mesembra to Arcturus
                              preannouncing Arabian power
and in the 11th of Constans ashes from heaven,
                    in the 12th Muhavis broke the Colossus
that had stood thirteen sixty years,
                    mille tre centos sexaginta, and
sold 900 camel-loads, aere oneravit, of its brass
          to a jew
(all this chronology seven years less than the accepted).
Habdimelich made peace with the 2nd Justinian
. . . contra Zubir and burnt his home and his idols
with their idolator, sed susciperent, we are getting to
the crux of one matter

Anno sexto imperii sui Justinianus (the second)
pacem, quam ad Habdimelich habuit, ex amentia
dissolvit, et omnem Cypriorum insulam, et populum
irrationabiliter voluit transmigrare, et characterem
qui missus fuerat ab Habdimelich, eum noviter visus
esset . . . et his auditis Habdimelich satanice stimu-
latus rogabat ne pax solveretur, sed susciperent mo-
netam suam, cum Arabes non susciperent Roma-
norum incisionem in suis nummis. Verum dato
pondere auri ait: Nullum Romanis damnum effici-
tur, ex eo quod Arabes nova cuderent . . .
Quod et factum est, et misit Habdimelich ad aedifi-
candum templum Muchan, et voluit auferre co-
lumnas . . .

— col. 1060, The Deacon, Migne's Patrologia.

In fact this item, with that bit from the Eparch's edict
which was still there for Kemal in our time,
        PANTA'REI, said DuBellay translating,
the base shall we say, and the slide of Byzantium,
bags, baskets full of, presumably, coinage,
and lured twenty thousand sclavons.
And in the 7th Absimarus Habdimelich died
        and Justinian came back thru the aqueduct.
Franks out of Thrace in periplum,
Blood in Watling St, ruin'd by vicarious government.
        Hyacinthinis,
μεγαλοζήλων why not fake purple,
vocabulary not Dr. Liddell's,
chastised and brought into the house (coom ben)

verberator et bonis mulcator

παιδευέσθω καὶ εἰσκομιζέσθω

register all silk purchases over ten aurei

δέκα νομισμάτων (Nicole: purpureas vestes) τὰ βλαττία

but the ἀναιδῶς is rather nice, Dr. Nicole,

before the μὴ αὐξάνοντες ἢ ἐλαττοῦντες τὴν τιμήν

and the idea of just price is somewhere,

        the haggling, somewhere,

also

     ἀλογίστους quite beautifully used   tzu³

         tho' utopian

καπηλεύων   or   chih¹

στομύλος   that is "mouthy"

ἀγοραῖος   forensic   to²⁻⁵

λάλος   babbler   chu¹

ταραχώδης   as on the East bank from Beaucaire

μὴ τῇ τοῦ ἐπάρχου ἐσφραγισμένον

not stamped with the prefect's seal βούλλη

καμπανὸν νενοθευμένον

Ducange: στατήρ

Here, surely, is a refinement of language

> *If we never write anything save what is already*
> *understood, the field of undertanding will never be*
> *extended. One demands the right, now and again,*
> *to write for a few people with special interests*
> *and whose curiosity reaches into greater detail.*

ἢ καὶ νομίσματα ξέει
Wd / appear to be tetarteron tokens
  not affecting the aureus
vel pactum pretium augens
  and a few words about hoarding
καιρὸν ἐνδέιας ἀποθησαυρίζῃ
ἐνοίκιον house rent
αὔξων ἐνοίκιον
"Sire, dist Hues..."
  that was de Bosschère,
leather for carriages, not for footwear,
Xoirempers do not buy sheep
  or hide pigs in the house of an arkhon
   οἶκον ἀρχοντικόν
Who useth an unstamped stater
  ad pretium empti
κατὰ τὴν ἐξώνεσιν νομίσματος ἑνὸς
that's how Nicole slanted it, grave on the omicron,
meaning one aureus, bankers
  to profit one keration 2 miliarisia
μηδεμιᾷ λειτουργίᾳ
  and no liturgy (as above)
  nor their beasts,
  but that baking be uninterrupted
and that they take due care against fire.
TAVERNERS are to inform the prefect of wine's arrival
  that he arrange the modus of sale
ὀικονομία... ὅπως... πιπράσκεσθαι
constraining 'em to analogous ezonesis.
Stathmos, usually weight & aggaîa, vessels

660

fitting in, working together.
The stathmon shd / hold 30 litras
          and the mina, as it is called, shd / be 3,
And on great holidays and the Lord's day κυριακαῖς
not to open before 2 o'clock
by whatever 2 that was reckoned
          δευτέρας ὥρας
and at the second hour of night
          ἀσφαλίζειν
lock up & σβεννύειν τὰ λεβήτια
put out their cook-fires
          λέβης, a cauldron
& those who have been loafing all day there
          not to come back at night and raise ructions
τοῦ οἴνου ἐμφορούμενοι
"Constantinople" said Wyndham "our star,"
Mr. Yeats called it Byzantium,
emphorio, to be borne about, to be filled with
oinos, the fermented
katakremnízo, to throw down or headlong
diaphora, variance
bias, vigors
and if wine-seller be found with false measures
          & not bearing the proper seals
shall be smacked, cropped and
          put out of the sunthema ἐκδιωκέσθωσαν
ΠΕΡΙ ΛΕΓΑΤΑΡΙΟΥ
seem to be foreign importers,
          are to stay 3 months only,
the name ΒΟΘΡΩΝ ought to explain what it means

διασημαίνεται but doesn't exactly
dealin' with animals βοτόν, βοτήρ in the Foro Amastriani
τῶν ζώων τὰς αἰτίας
some animals are imperfect.
RE all contractors for fine work, plaster,
      marble, askothurariōn, paint & the rest of 'em
ΛΕΠΤΟΥΡΓΩΝ
an askós is a leather bag,
      with inane loquacity hoisting the wages
αὔξει τοὺς μισθοὺς σκαιότητι τῶν λόγων
      lubberly, westerly στομυλία
the stench of the profit motive has covered their names
and that louse G. burnt the Palatine
      and messed up the music
      to speak clearly
ἀπληστία, insatiate κακουργία
This is not a mere stunt to lay fines
      as is found in the hodge-podge.
θόλος a round building
καμάρα arched over
all ἀσφάλειαν to be unlikely to fall
ἐμπειρίαν & experienced
θεμέλιος the foundation, not wobbly σαθρός
After all Justinian's boy *had* built Santa Sophia
      "vurry," says Pearson, N.H. "in'erestin'."
out of odd hollows and solids
μὴ τὸ κτιζόμενον λοξὸν, slanty
There is an ideogram somewhere in Morrison,
de Saumase, de Reitz
      πυρὸς, ἀέρος, ὕδατος, γῆς

after Julien d'Askalon: fire, air, water, earth,
the old men on the swaying τραπέζιον
βυρσοδέψαι, raw leather
μαλακατάριοι, softeners, second process
βυρσοποιοί
μάγκιπες the baker from his *four*,
governors, oveners
No yugo-slav to propose to a girl
          until he has planted trees, 50 olives
(Ronnie, this year)
ἐγκύκλιος παίδευσις
          and the chaplains of cabarets
& that Nicephoras
          kolobozed the tetarteron
need not have applied to the aureus
or caused Nicole to understand token coinage
in the long war between episkeptiks
and any andrárion agorîan kai bánauson
          (currently rendered as s.o.b.)
12% says Nicole, illegal
κατὰ τὴν ποιότητα
     (τῶν ζώων)
          acc. the quality.
Good-bye to the sun, Autumn is dying
Χαῖρε ὁ "Ηλιος
whom the ooze cannot blacken
Χαῖρε clarore.

          And in the sixth year of this Justinian the devil got
          into Habdimelich, satanice stimulatus, who said if

663

we put the same amount of gold into our coinage it
will do no harm to the Romans. Ut supra, as before
stated in latin. And he wanted some columns for
Muchan.

iustitiae ... nihil   antiquius
"Honest feathers" says Dante, or: "What about murder?"
          De Officiis, TWO, 89: "Quid occidere?"
Pascere satis, or in the '20s (our time)
          driving latin out of the schools
               (France or whereso)
humiles non omnes improbi. Cicero
               mousing round the edge of the paddock.
"An ater, an albus" Catullus in interrogative.
"Queer cuss with a sense of humour," Tully observing:
Nihil ... antiquius
and no such blue north of Capri
          as on the side toward Peschiera,
Ocelle Veronensis.
          Under Leo ΕΠΑΡΧΙΚΟΝ ΒΙΒΛΙΟΝ
"Following God's example Our Serenity
          (γαληνότης, as of the sea)
to stop trampling by one on another
          have codified πολιτικῶν σωματείων
(To Professor Nicole's annoyance) Leo 886-911
: may buy linen to line bombazine
          "les arrhes du marché" re/ the drapers
               βασιλεῦσι Λέων
And the notary
          must have some general culture or he will

            make a mess of the contracts.
: may buy gold, silver, pearls,
                but not copper
                ni cuivre ni tissus de lin
that is, not for resale.
Not hoard 'em and hold for a rise,
                any perfumer
who wangles to get another's rent hoisted
                κατὰ δόλον ἐπαύξων
shall be shaved, whipped and chucked out.
And not hold up coin either;
                foreigners to sell in three months and leave,
Perfumers not to buy groceries,
        but nard, aloe-wood, cinnamon,
                stick to what's sold on a two pan balance, not a "romaine"
                a stadera, one of those things with a yard-arm.
Let him be either perfumer or grocer,
        Candle-makers to work in their own ergastorios;
and that
        grocers may open shops anywhere
        so that one can get groceries anywhere /
And if his weights aren't stamped with the prefect's seal
        profits at 16 and ³/₄ ths (two miliarisia)
No baker or mill beast shall be subject to other service,
        bread must go on,
No ovens in anyone's cellar
and that they go to the Prefect when the grain price
                rises or falls
                to find the right bread price,
Whoso tries any monkey-shines

shall be put on a jackass and led through the streets quite
slowly,
flogged, shaved, and put out. Wine shops
    will close at 8 in the evening.
Anybody wanting to put up a cupola must prove experience.
If a wall falls inside of ten years the builder,
    unless he can prove god's wrath must
      put it up again at his own cost.
To be tabulary, must know the Manuale
    to recite it, and the Basiliks, 60 books
and draw up an act in the presence, and be sponsored
by the primicier and his colleagues
    and have a clear Handschrift
and be neither babbler nor insolent, nor sloppy in habits
and have a style. Without perfect style
    might not notice punctuation and phrases
      that alter the sense,
    and if he writes down a variant
      his sponsors will be responsible.
Give him time to show what he's got.
And the smoke at his consecration,
    incense θυμίαμα ἐνώπιον Κυρίου
shows how his thought shd/ go. Upward, videlicet.
And be fined if he miss procession
    and the college shall go to his funeral.
SILVERSMITHS may buy what pertains to their trade,
    not copper,
    οὐ μὴν χαλκὸν
nor linen save for their personal use.
If ladies (ʔεἴ τις) want to sell jewelry

let the goldsmith report to the Prefect &
Be sure it is not for export.
                        If they adulterate
Shall cost 'em a hand χειροκοπείσθω
'Ο δόλον ποιῶν εἰσ ἀσήμιον
If foreigners try to sell the two metals,
                        report it.
If a silversmith buy sacred vessels, intact or otherwise,
            let him report this to the Eparch
and a goldsmith report purchase of any unmarked
            gold over one pound;
Work to be done ἐν . . . τῆς Μέσης on Main St.
            Not in the goldsmith's home
And no one to be brought into the guild without notice
        (aveu du prefet) What was the greek for aveu
in this instance? εἰδήσεως τοῦ ἐπάρχου
            rather nice use of *aveu*, Professor,
                though you were looking at ἄνευ.
From the Palace, half-circle that street is,
            ending near the seven-towered castello.
Bankers not to file coins
                nor make false ones
Nor put a slave (δοῦλον) in charge of their business
        Καταλλάκτης <   > κεκομμένον (double m)
If they do not notify counterfeits that come in
            and from whom
shall be flogged, shaved and exiled
And in this there can have been few innovations
And before this was that affair of Habdimelich
Anno sexto imperii, of the Second Justinian
            "pacem".

667

XCVII

Melik & Edward struck coins-with-a-sword,
"Emir el Moumenin" (Systems p. 134)
            six and ½ to one, or the sword of the Prophet,
SILVER being in the hands of the people
            "and for the first time in my life
"I had thousand $ bills in my hand-bag"
                        (Princess A.)
after the 27/75 Spew Deal wangle
one billion and whatso in dinars, Gothic 8,
barleycorn, habbeh, tussuj, danik, one mithcal,
Shafy and Hanbal both say 12 to 1,
Roman Christers
            "and by devlish ingenuity Abd-el-Melik"
                says, ut supra Paulus the Deacon, out of Theophanus,
& went decimal,
                    and the Prophet
                            set tax on metal
(i. e. as distinct from) & the fat 'uns pay for the lean 'uns,
                            said Imran,
& a king's head and "NOUCH KHOR" persian,
optative, not dogmatic,
                in fact as sign of
                    cordiality and Royal benevolence.
AND in 1859 a dirhem "A.H. 40" was
                paid into the post-office, Stamboul.
Struck at Bassora
            36.13 English grains.

"I have left Irak its dinar",
                    & one fifth to God.
Percussum forma publica corium. JANUS ACE.
Said Lear: "not for coining." "Can't get me on *that*, I am Royal."
"This leather" (Seneca)
                    Charisius, cited by Scaliger,
                              Andoleon of Paeonia,
          Gold scrupulum: 20 aces. A.U. 437
but now they play with 12 draughtsmen,
          the scrupulum one 9th of an aureus
                                        B. C. 316
"Outre la livre pondérable,"
          2000 aces: one double eagle,
Monsieur Gibbon nearer than Mommsen at this point
or than Lenormant
          "Qu'on décrie"
               that was after Caligula
And that the Senate coined after Nero
June 9th, 68,
          LIBERTATI
               to July of the next year
LIBERTAS RESTITUTA.
               £. s. d. as from Caracalla,
Venice, Florence, Amalfi maintained 12 to 1 ratio,
          one gold against that in silver,
leather stamped at the siege of Faenza &
in Mathew Paris for 1250 anno Domini (Aug.).
In Avignon wrote of transmutation, that is, Papa Johannes
          wrote there of the transmutation of metals,
Darius, and Targitaus, nowt new in monopoly.

Cicero tried to keep gold in the country Senatus Consulto,
"gravissime me consule judicavit".

        Theodosian Code thirteen, eleven, eleven,
    £. s. d. from Caracalla
first fish & vadmal or cloth money, then "baug" rings
pseudo roman, and then, later, moslem
        dinars, maravedis,
kelt coin & norse "herring", 8 stycas: one scat
"That most powerful engine" says Del Mar.
King Offa at 6 and ½
                 Alfred, finally, Athelstan 12;
Canute opposing Byzantium, 20 scads to the dinar,
       100 scads to the mark (of accountancy)
Edgar's leather (?) came after Athelstan
      "thon yilden he gon rere"
         that is, guilds into England,
"And he, the president, is true to his caste
      "and that caste," said old Lampman, "the underworld."
                          1948

Mencken joked inopportunely. "I am sorry,"
said the London judge, "that this has been brought as a civil
        and not as a criminal action."
Missenden, Dunmore for coining, not me, said Lear,
       a canon of Sempingham, clandestine export.
Offa's gold, then an hiatus, then Henry,
Crimen majestatis, the Third, & the plebs
        not then in public affairs
AT all, utterly, and in 1914 british sovreigns
poured into the Philadelphia mint in great quantity
      and were promptly restamped with eagles.

Coins struck by Coeur de Lion in Poitou,
Caxton or Polydore, Villon: "blanc",
     a gold Bacchus on your abacus,
Henry Third's second massacre, wheat 12 pence a quarter
that 6 4/5ths pund of bread be a farden
Act 51, Henry Three. If a penny of land be a perch
      that is grammar
nummulary moving toward prosody
πρόσοδος φόρων ἡ ἐπέτειος..
μεταθεμένων after Dandolo got into Byzance
& worsened AND . . .
     and the Third Edward
        (not to mention the VIIth)
Thus Dante: "Senna"; and Villon: "décrie".
& in 1311 the barons wanted a voice in the chapter
"coignagio stagminis"
      "that religious men as well as all other
        shall forfeit."
Almoravedis' gold was in Britain
     with bezants
         & after
           40 to 43 grains of true gold.
Old standard of Araby, 9, 7, 9?
And out of Scanda in Colchis,
     Getes had been in Cythera
     (vide Pausanias, the Laconics)
2 doits to a boodle, 3 ⅓ bawbee: 160 doits.
Will they get rid of the Rooseveltian dung-hill
And put Capn. Wadsworth back in the school books?
ED. Three, dei gratia, "old standard"

& there was a good deal of sand-paper ordered,
a staple which seems to move without great publicity.
Mons of Jute should have his name in the record,
   thrones, courage, Mons should have his name in the
              record.
Vasa klipped for the people, Lycurgus, nomisma,
and "limitation is the essence of good nomisma"
but Goertz von Schlitz had not thought of this,
   Sweden, Pultawa, and was in any case,
    executed for something
1745 Copjenhaven, the nine year old bank relieved of conver-
              sion.
When kings quit, the bankers began again.
15.08 Denmark and Scandinavs (ratio) in '73
    18, that is 1873
on which Mr Benton would have reflected, as per:
the CONtinuous effort to have it different somewhere or other.
And if these were quarter dirhems in Friesland
   they should be of ratio 6 & one half
to the quarter (talis est) dinars of Spain.
   "The olde double-ducat,
   The olde turkish grouch."
And then Amsterdam (1609) busted the Wisselbank
and said who shd/ deal in exchange,
But Mr Del Mar does not, at this point,
   connect issue with backing,
though he is all for a proper total proportion
   between total issue and buyables,
Ike, '55, had got that far.
   And Baffico had papers, daily papers, giornali.

"And as to Thomas, *legat de Leicestre*:
　　　　that our coin be raised
　　　　as is that of the Emperor."　　　　　　　1526
"As ours is being conveyed out of the Realm". "Ad perpetuam
liberationis divinae memoriam", said the Dutch on white
　　pasteboard.
"Rien de ce monde", said Villon, inclusively
　　　　　　"Godt behoede."
　　　　　　Pugno pro patria. And
degradations, depradations, degradations whatsodam
of emperors, kings and whatsodam,
Dukes et cetera have since been exceeded,
　　　　　Kitson, Fenton & Tolstoi had observed this.
And by curious segregation Brooks Adams ignores him, Del
　　　　　　　　　　　　　　　　　　　　　　Mar,
and he, Adams, so far as I have yet met them,
　　　　　despite stylistic resemblance.
"Salzburg alone struck full weight."
The 1806 Prussian notes
　　　　　　ran 90 years,
Octonary sun-worshiping Baltic.
371 ¼ grains silver in Del's time
as I have seen them by shovels full
　　　　　　lit by gas flares.
　　　　　One wd/ suppose Theresa's 390,
　　　　　but were, apparently, 353 and a fraction,
at Salzburg 5 more, or supposedly 361, or
"Window-dressing" as Bryan admitted to Kitson.
"Legal in all states (1841) of the Zollverein
and in 1873 was a crisis

673

in vain did Hume, in vain von Humboldt!"
Such suckers, or at any rate sophists as
            Cobden and Liverpool.
A disc of light over von Humboldt.
Von Schultz and Sir William Harcourt
            both wished to retain some national independence,
"so long as a state resigns . . .
            "something" sd/ Frank Harris
            "the value of which is unknown".
Albuquerque made discs in Goa.
            18, CHARLES SECOND c. 5
In 1816 gave up power over the ratio
            and 1870 gave up the remains of prerogative.
"Victoria, Victoriaa, w'ere 'ave I 'eard that nyme?"

Goldsmiths not aiming at i

            not ruled by Sophia (σοφία)
                  πίστις, σοφία
Del Mar examined Gansl,
            that would have been in the time of Centennial
50 years after Mr Jefferson's death.
            "Duped into double indebtedness",
"Portcullis" struck by the Crown, but Charles
            let the East Indias do it
"with the Company's own devices".
Assyria, Babylon, Macedonia,
            always more somewhere than somewhere,
but the (abbreviare) the great gap declining.
            Steed asked Douglas about the rupee.
1858: End of the Company.

Sylla 9 (ratio 9), Caesar 12
      and stayed there till the fall of Byzantium.
"The signal was given by Mr Marble"
      (a modest name from some angles)
"Not read except by title". Mr Carlyle:
"This coil of Geryon" (Djerion) said Mr Carlyle,
        in Congress,
          who later went to the Treasury,
New fronds,

novelle piante 新

       what ax for clearing?

親 ch'in¹   旦 tan⁴   親 ch'in¹
   οἶνος αἰθίοψ the gloss, probably,
not the colour. So hath Sibilla a boken ysette
as the lacquer in sunlight ἀλιπόρφυρος
& shall we say: russet-gold.
            That this colour exists in the air
not flame, not carmine, orixalxo, les xaladines
lit by the torch-flare,

     & from the nature the sign,
as the small lions beside San Marco. Out of ling
the benevolence

靈

     Kuanon, by the golden rail,
       Nile διιπετέος the flames gleam in the air
and in the air ἀίσσουσιν
Bernice, late for a constellation, mythopoeia persisting,

(now called folc-loristica)
reserpine clearing fungus,
      Uncle William frantically denying his
most intelligent statements (re/every individual soul, per esem-
                                          pio)

δολιχηρέτμοισι

仁　爲　親
親　寶　以

"Ten men" said degli Uberti "who will charge a
                nest of machine guns
"for one who will put his name on a chit."
All neath the moon, under Fortuna,
        splendor' mondan',
beata gode, hidden as eel in sedge,
        all neath the moon, under Fortuna

hoc signo   貞   chen (*four*), hoc signo
with eyes pervanche,
        three generations, San Vio
darker than pervanche?
        Pale sea-green, I saw eyes once,
and Raleigh remarked, on Genova's loans non-productive,
        that they had only their usury left,
and there was that Führer of Macedon, dead aetat 38,

        The temple 山 is holy,
        because it is not for sale.

"No, George, don't you be with that fellow for president,
    "We don't know what he'll do next."
Some faint connection
          between criminality and calamity,
              lo jorn, Der Tag

that at least a few should perceive this   旦   tan

Arnaut spoke his own language, 26th Purgatorio,
above the Moon there is order,
          beneath the Moon, forsitan.
And if, say, we had a pope, like Pisani?
          abbreviare
faster than it distributes the power to buy,
          but the interval, 15, 16, (vide Benton)
as from 12 to 6 and one half,
          but by that time they found some other wangle,
by '78, T.C.P. said "non-interest-bearing"
          as from Adams to Rush, as from Vasa (Gustavus)
Since when they have had several wars.
          Pieire Cardinal mentioned *that* subject.
Earth under Fortuna,
                    each sphere hath its Lord,
with ever-shifting change, sempre biasmata,
          gode,
                "Not difficult to make"
                              said Brancusi
"mais *nous*, de nous mettre en état DE les faire."
"Je peux commencer une chose tous les jours,
              mais fi- - -nir!"

"All true," said Griffith

        "but I can't move 'em with it."

Ownership? Use? there is a difference.

The temple ⊔⊔ is not for sale.

"Always" said Del Croix, "the same things".

"By the conquest," said Picabia, "of Alsace-Lorraine".

        Art is local,

Ike driven to the edge, almost, of a thought.

Started with a limited (if not by dogma, but in practice)

        suffrage of the qualified,

πανουργία now at the top.

Tried to get Essad out,

               but he died at the gate-post,

and you will certainly not convert them

        if you remove the houris from Paradise.

Even Aquinas could not demote her, Fortuna,

        violet, pervanche, deep iris,

          beat' è, e gode,

the dry pod could not demote her, plenilune,

        phase over phase.

Dante had read that Canzone.

        Birds, said Hudson, are not automata.

Even Jonathan Edwards is said to have noticed trees,

and as for who have a code and no principles . . .

The Twelve Tables penalized satire,

        and some one has wiped out most of Lucilius

and there is, of course, very little about Antoninus
        left in their records,
Luigi, *gobbo*, makes his communion with wheat grain
        in the hill paths
                        at sunrise

ONE, ten, eleven, *chi con me* tan?

And the dogmatic have to lie now and again
        to maintain their conformity,
the chun tze, never.
And as for the original-sin racket . . . the hex-hoax,
Aswins drawing the rain-cloud,
        Fou-Hi by wood.
In a buck-board with a keg of money: Damn you, I
        said I would get it (the wages).

   The temple is holy  because it is not for
                                                    sale

From Sargon of Agade

                a thousand years before T'ang,
gothic arch out of India,
        from Multan 700 *li*,
        torchlight, at Multan, offer perfume,

Son of Herakles, Napat son of Waters,
　　　Panch, that is Phoenician, Tyanu

 lion head

Came then autumn in April and
　　　"By Knoch Many now King Minos lies",
From Sargon to Tyana
　　　　　　no blood on the altar stone.
"As THAT!" said Ungaro,
　　　　　　　"It is just as hard as that"
(jabbing a steel cube with his pencil butt
　　　and speaking of mind as resistant).
Ville d'Avray, Pré Catalan, permanence,
an interest in equity
　　　　　　not in mere terminology
μετά τά φυσικά
　　　metah, not so extraneous, possibly not so extraneous
most "*metas*" seem to be in with.
"Had not *thought* about government", Adams;
　　　"or civilization" said Monsieur Bonaparte,
at least I think it was Bonaparte.
　　　The artigianato bumbles into technology,
"Buckie" has gone in for structure (quite rightly)
　　　but consumption is still done by animals.
"Luce benigna, negli occhi tuoi,
　　　Quel che voglio io, tu vuoi?
　　　　　　Tu vuoi."
May 4th. Interruption
　　　mid dope-dolls an' duchesses

tho' orften I roam,
some gals is better,
some wusser
than some.
But that the free-born run wode into slavery
this is not good;
run wode in job hunting,
this is NOT good.

"Got no stone" said Knittl.

Flowers, incense, in the temple enclosure,
no blood in that TEMENOS
when crocus is over and the rose is beginning.
PAUL, the Deacon, Migne 95.
Upsala, was the golden fane,
ministrat virtutem, Fricco, pacem. Voluptatem,
ingenti Priapo.
Dea libertatis, Venus.
Agelmund son of Ayon, reigned 33 years.
PUER APULIUS
"Fresca rosa" sang Alcamo.

Of Antoninus very little record remains

That he wrote the book of the Falcon.
Mirabile brevitate correxit, says Landulph
        of Justinian's Code
and built Sta Sophia, Sapientiae Dei

正
名

As from Verrius Flaccus to Festus (S.P.)
        that the greeks say ἀρσενικά,
ἀνδρικά being less elegant.
All this came down to Leto (Pomponio)
        wanting the right word θηλυκά.
Deorum Manium, Flamen Dialis & Pomona
        (seeking the god's name)
"that remain in all aethera terrenaeque"
Manes Di, the augurs invoke them
per aethera terrenaeque
        are believed to stay on
              manare credantur
ἐν νέμει σκιερῷ
        ἐπὶ τε λῖν ἔμβαλε δαίμων
& Spartans in Mount Taygeto
        sacrifice a horse to the winds,

as in Campo Martio, in October,
in Lacedaemon, dust to the uttermost
and at Rhodos, the sun's car is thrown into the sea,
rubbing their weapons with parsley,
Flamen Portualis
"inter mortua jam et verba sepulta"

伯
馬
祖

And that Athelstan set up guilds there
kadzu, arachidi, acero,
not lie down

無
倦

XCVIII

The boat of Ra-Set moves with the sun
"but our job to build light" said Ocellus:
Agada, Ganna, Faasa　　新　　hsin[1]

Make it new
Τὰ ἐξ Αἰγύπτου φάρμακα
Leucothea gave her veil to Odysseus
Χρόνος
πνεῦμα θεῶν
καὶ ἔρως σοφίας
The Temple (hieron) is not for sale.
Getting the feel of it, of his soul,
while they were making a fuss about Helen
No man in Greece will sell a slave out of his country
　　　　　　ne quaesaris
Mines, quarries, salt-pans, of the state,
　　　a guild system in Constantinople
ius Italicum, *more Sabello*,
　　　　no more black shawls in the Piazza
more Sabello, for Demeter.
　　　　"Ut facias pulchram"
there is no sight without fire.
　　　　Thinning their oar-blades
　　　　θῖνα θαλάσσης
　　　　nothing there but an awareness
In Byzantium 12% for a millennium

The Manchu at 36 legal, their Edict
the next pass.
Anselm: that some is incarnate awareness,
thus trinitas; some remains spiritus.
"The body is inside". Thus Plotinus,
But Gemisto: "Are Gods by hilaritas";
and their speed in communication.
et in nebulas simiglianza,
καθ' ὁμοίωσιν Deorum
a fanned flame in their moving
must fight for law as for walls
— Herakleitos' parenthesis —
And that Leucothoe rose as an incense bush
— Orchamus, Babylon —
resisting Apollo.
Patience, I will come to the Commissioner of the Salt Works
in due course.
Est deus in nobis.   and
They still offer sacrifice to that sea-gull
est deus in nobis
Χρήδεμνον
She being of Cadmus line,
the snow's lace is spread there like sea foam
But the lot of 'em, Yeats, Possum and Wyndham
had no ground beneath 'em.

Orage had.
Per ragione vale
Black shawls for Demeter.
"Eleven literates" wrote Senator Cutting,

"and, I suppose, Dwight L. Morrow".
Black shawls for Demeter.
The cat talks – μάω – with a greek inflection,
    Mohammed in sympathy: "is part of religion"
    Sister to Phoebus;
And some with the tone of bird talk
"Noi altri borghesi
        could not speak efficiently to the crowd
        in piazza,"
said the Consigliere, "we thought we could control Mussolini."

Uncle William two months on ten lines of Ronsard
        But the salt works . . .
        ψεῦδος δ' οὐκ ἐρέει
            . . . γάρ πεπνύμενος
Patience, ich bin am Zuge . . .
            ἀρχή
            an awareness
Until in Shensi, Ouang, the Commissioner Iu-p'uh

volgar' eloquio

The King's job, vast as the swan-flight:
thought built on Sagetrieb:
        civil, the soldier's
suns rise, the sun goes into shadow

Hsuan, in the first tone 示 proclaim

a filiality that binds things together.

First the pen yeh 本

686

then τέχνη 業

and to philosophise in old age (Ari's καθόλου)
"and that Buddha abandoned such splendours,
　　　　is it likely!" said Yong Tching ...
"Who has seen Taoist priests fly up in broad daylight?
They destroy the 5 human relations,
mules saddled with trappings,
　　　　　　deeper in debt every day
and next they are selling their farmsteads.

佛

And as for these Bhud-foés,
　　　　they provide no mental means for
Running an empire, nor do taoists
with their internal and external pills
– is it external? the gold pill? –
to preserve them from physical death?
　　　　　and as for those who deform thought with iambics...
ten billion wordings
　　　　and destroy the five human relations,
Is the Bhud likely to return for these harridans?
　　　　having had his palace with court yards
and a dragon verandah, plus a feng-ko
presumably furnished with phoenix
and he *ch'i'd* 'em or *shed* 'em

棄　捨

Will you now bait him with nunneries?"

嗎

that sign is a horse and mouth.
Sitting in heaven he needs you to build him a roof?
"To unscrew φύσιν τοῦ θεοῦ
(Procopius and old Peabody) the inscrutable."
Antoninus and Leo got down the percentage
and, as Stock says, "the historians missed it".
Does god need a clay model? gilded?
hua⁴ t'ou,²   these tongue words!
The maker of words ascending,
          whiteness of bones beneath.
The celestial wants your small change?
          or bears grudge when he does not get it,

(Cf/ Gemisto) a *hsiao jên?*

And the language in all their "classics"
          fan¹ hua⁴
If you don't swallow their buncombe
          you won't have to drive 'em out.

Ouang -iu- p'uh
          on the edict of K'ang -hsi
in volgar' eloquio taking the sense down to the people.
"Who display no constructive imagination;

who use no connection, grits in the mortar,
impediments.
        You, I mean *you* should know why,
and start new after an inadvertence

義 i⁴ shên¹ 深 that is the root of it

li³⁻⁴ 裏 on the inside

yüan² 原 the spring

small ... white ... under cover.
and that the equilibrium

太 t'ai⁴

平 p'ing²

of the Empire grips the earth in good manners
Earth and water dye the wind in your valley

        tso feng 風 tso feng suh

that his feelings have the colour of nature

        en¹ 恩 ch'ing² 情

And as Ford said: get a dictionary
        and learn the meaning of words.
        "De tribus ...", and a book on falcons, from Federico
in Sicily. "Aulentissima" sang Alcamo
        "ver l'estate"
More solid than pearls or than cassia

i⁴
ch'i⁴ 義氣康熙

From Kati to Kang Hi

two ½s of a seal

"De libro Chi-king", wrote his father: "Ostendit, incitatque,
            that you may reap in the sunlight
A soul, said Plotinus, the body inside it.
"By Hilaritas", said Gemisto, "by hilaritas: gods;
            and by speed in communication.
Anselm cut some of the cackle, and relapsed for sake of
                                    tranquillity.
Thus the gods appointed john barleycorn Je tzu,
And Byzance lasted longer than Manchu
            because of an (%) interest-rate.
Thought is built out of Sagetrieb,
            and our debt here is to Baller
and to *volgar' eloquio*.

            Despite Mathews this Wang was a stylist.
Uen-li will not help you talk to them,
            Iong-ching republished the edict
But the salt-commisioner took it down to the people
            who, in Baller's view, speak in quotations;
            think in quotations:
"Don't send someone else to pay it."
Delcroix was for repetition.
            Baller thought one needed religion.

Without ²muan ¹bpo . . . but I anticipate.

  There is no substitute for a lifetime.

The meaning of the Emperor,

    ten thousand years heart's-tone-think-say,

he had reigned for 61 years

敬 reverence

and τὸ χαλόν

    order 孝

"Parents naturally hope their sons will be gentlemen."

正 cheng

經 king

The text is somewhat exigeant, perhaps you will consider the

            meaning of

    cheng 正

    king 經

From Kung's porch 門 mên,³

    and not cheat the Administration.

Filial piety is very inclusive: it does not include

Family squabbles over

田 land 錢 money, etcetera

Or pretendings.

II. Ten thousand years say men have clans and descendents.

III. There are districts. Avoid litigation.

IV. Without grain you will not eat or tend silkworms,
   Imperial paradigm was by ploughing.
V. and then waste not,
   Nor scrape iron off the point of a needle.
VI. Ten thousand years: to improve the habits of scholars
   "as an ox with trappings"
   or as a mule with a fancy saddle;
That the books you read shall be

      cheng

      king

       ut supra

And your pals fit to read 'em.
   Sixteen bitched by an (%) interest rate
Byzantium rather more durable.
   "from rib to cheek whose palate cost so dear"
Miss Mitford (or one-ov'um) thought this was "gothic"
   Paradiso, XIV: this light does not dis-unify.
VII. No need of contraptions.
VIII. State the laws in clear language.
IX. Iu-an tied the stray cow and fed it.
The Xth clause is for

   pen

   yeh

      ne ultra crepidam,
But establish it. What do children know about evil?
And XVth. Not a fixed charge.
   This is from Mang Tzu 孟
XVI. Yield not to anger.

XIIth. "As for those who lie in a law-court!"
            (In 1670 Kang Hsi) whereto Iong Ching:
"That you should hear it unblurred"
Deliberate converse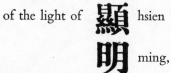

            and with the colour of Nature
Iong Ching, Canto 61

        of the light of 顯 hsien
                       明 ming,

by the silk cords of the sunlight,
Chords of the sunlight (*Pitagora*)
            non si disuna (xiii)
Splendor
        2nd year
        2nd month

        2nd day   as to the *Sheng* 聖
                                        諭
            The Edict.

"Each year in the Elder Spring, that is the first month of it,
The herald shall invite your compliance.
There are six rites for the festival
            and that all should converge!
And not to lose life for bad temper.

XCIX

Till the blue grass turn yellow
        and the yellow leaves float in air
And Iong Cheng (Canto 61)
            of the line of Kang Hi
by the silk cords of the sunlight
        non disunia,
2nd year
2nd month
2nd day
        SHENG U, the Edict
Each year in the elder spring, that is the first month
        of the spring time,
The herald shall incite yr/ compliance
There are six rites for festival
        and 7 instructions
that all converge as the root tun^1 pen^3
the root veneration (from Mohamed no popery)
To discriminate things
        $shih^{2-5}$ solid
mu^2 a pattern
fa^1 laws
$kung^1$ public
szu^1 private
great and small
        (That Odysseus' old ma missed his conversation)
To see the light pour,
        that is, toward sinceritas

of the word, comprehensive
                KOINE ENNOIA
all astute men can see it encircling.
Chou saw it, my SIRE also,
With splendour,
                Catholicity,
Woven in order,
                as on cords in the loom
cognome, indirizzo (pien¹ hu⁴
sincerity, simplicity, red: South, and naïveté
meng², the people, the many, the menée,
                                the perishing.
Sage men have plans,
simplicity a thousand generations, no man can change.
The Sage Emperor's heart is our heart,
His government is our government
                        yao² high, hsiao³ dawn
The Venerated Emperor
                        watched things grow with affection,
His thought was not dry on a shelf
Not exhaustible, on sale in a (kuei⁴) shop.
That job was the swan's flight (hung² yeh⁴⁻⁵)
To trace out and to bind together
From sonship this goes to clan
and to avoid litigations
                out of the field, from the trees,
Food is the root.
                Feed the people.
This much I, Chên, have heard. *Yo el rey.*
Yang³ nourish

chih²⁻⁵ ma   set out hemp
chung³ mi'en² cotton
                   t'ung² all together.

IV. There are functions.
Rats' gnaws, and bird's pecks: litigations,
pine rat and oak cat, squirrel to you,
sparrow, hemp-bird, rats' gnaws and tit-horns
                         rush to law without cause;
tie knots into ruin of property
fei (four), waste time, flounder in business,
The organization is functional
and to maintain a liquidity . . .
            begin at the precinct level . . .
Dripping with sympathy to fan up contentions,
       good luck as a door that is sealed,
Nor scrape iron off the point of a needle.

There can be equity in plowing and weeding
         when men of war know the Odes.
Esteem sanity in curricula.
       You cannot leave out the classics . . .
Prey on the people because they have no solid principles

And of Taosers, Chu says:
         concerned neither with heaven, earth
         or with anything on the square
but wholly subjective, for the Dragon moaning,
the screaming tiger, mercury, pills, pharmacopia,

And the Bhud rot: that floaters eat
                without maintaining their homesteads
        Hence the learned Redson's remarks.
And don't believe papists merely because they
                helped with the calendar.
                Odysseus' old ma missed his conversation.
Nestor "too intelligent to prevaricate."

Unsifted hot words, at first merely to flatter
as an animal his eye eating light
                or run to rat holes
Laws must be for the general good,
                for the people's uprightness,
                their moral uprightness.
Ch'ung² venerate
Black out the eroders, hsieh²
                venerate honest men
The great balance is not made in a day
                nor for one holiday only.
The business of relatives is filiality,
        a gentleman's job is his sincerity.
Build pen yeh
                the family profession
It will bring luck out of the air
If you mind your own business they (the phonies)
                will fade out before they have to be druv.
Wang: that man's phallic heart is from heaven
        a clear spring of rightness,
Greed turns it awry,
Bright gleaming, ming

697

kuang[1] in traverse

need you go so far to burn incense?

VIII. Let the laws be made clear,

   Illumine the words of procedure,

Peace comes of good manners

     feng[1] su[2-5] li feng su

INTENZIONE li feng su jang[4].

The sages of Han had a saying:

    Manners are from earth and from water

    They arise out of hills and streams

    The spirit of air is of the country

      Men's manners cannot be one

       (same, identical)

Kung said: are classic of heaven,

They bind thru the earth

      and flow

With recurrence,

    action, humanitas, equity

ne ultra crepidam,

    for greater exactness

The Tenth is PEN YEH

"a developed skill from persistence"

        Thus Mang Tzu

(Crysippus, Simbabwe: "the un-good merely dissolve")

        se non fosse cive

"a share, not a fixed charge"

don't pester scholars,

nor lose life for bad temper.

Heaven, man, earth, our law as written

    not outside their natural colour,

water, earth and biceps,   fa³⁻⁵ lu 法
Crusaders' bows gnawed by gold-lice,
                    Normandy pawned,
"some of the non-interest-bearing"
                              (T. C. P. '78)
A man's paradise is his good nature
                         (Khati)
          doubled kuang¹ ming²
Synesius thought myth expedient. Al Kindi: The classics
          if our intentions were serious.
Mencken said: No longer *fromm*.
Han (IX, i. e. nine) believed in the peoples,
Different each, different customs
              but one root in the equities,
One in acumen,
                    with the sun (chih)
                              under it all
                    & faith with the word
Hills and streams colour the air,
              vigour, tranquility, not one set of rules.
Vigour, quietude, are of place
Uen Ogn of Han-time built schools,
              rode circuit,
                         selected
And even now you can't *buy* office in Fourstreams
          tuan¹
                    cheng⁴
                         the teacher's job is not
just filling paper with detours
nor in dull float (fou³ po²⁻⁵)

Four tuan, and verity.   VII

And still men lust after; try to build on
                              lopsidedness.
Phoenix to *t'ung* tree
a mirrour to flowers, as water is to the moon
"Bother," said Chu Wan Kung of Sung court,
"neither with a man's politics nor his religion"
"neither with a man's politics nor with heaven"
And Plotinus, his bellyache
A great perversion
                from Plotinus his bellyache,
Though he still thought: God of all men.
                        The body is inside.

"This clean out and that's all."
                        Sd/ Chu, the accomplished
                                re Tao talk
"e basta."
            Thazz all there is to it; prolong the animal spirits,
But you folk (V.) will go and believe 'em.
SEVEN: Get rid of flimsy foundations.
            Our ancestors thought that closed minds
                    do no good to the Empire, nor
ut supra "scraping iron off the point of a needle."
Let a man do a good job at his trade,
                whence is honesty;
                whence are good manners,
                        good custom
            this is tuan[1]   cheng[4]
                                good living

e basta
There are five relativities: state, family and friendship,
amicitia.
Dolt, clear musician; the precise man and the clumsy.
There are Four Books and the 5 relations.
Fools fall for weapons and poison,
You are not all of you idiots,
There are a lot of you who will not
fall for this hokum.
But your females like to burn incense
and buzz round in crowds and processions
(Mr Baller animadverts on the similarities
in all priestcraft
(vide subject: "Missions" in Canto whatever)

Buddha ipse is said to have been annoyed with such hoakum
And as for their argot . . .
for the dialect of their incantations . . .
& the Taozers turn out to chase devils
(The Papist did help with the calendar
pu
k'o
hsin)
Of heaven, earth and of things without shadows,
Cut the cackle and do not believe 'em.
Better physical poison than brain wash
hsin^1 shu$^{4\text{-}5}$
hai^4
The mind at the start had
cheng^4

Greed defrauds it
Some want more than they can get in a lifetime.

2 incarnations in every home
huo⁴⁻⁵ fu²⁻⁵ 佛

and you go up hill to seek wooden ones.
Kuang
Kuang
Ming   Saith Khaty
Ming
                          tien
                          t'ang²
                          hsin¹
                          li³⁻⁵
Confucians observe the weather,
                  hear thunder,
                        seek to include.
Bhud: Man by negation.
But their First Classic: that the heart shd / be straight,
The phallos perceive its aim.

Tinkle, tinkle, two tongues? No.
But down on the word with exactness,
        against gnashing of teeth (upper incisors)
                              chih, chih!
                  wo chih³ chih³
                    wo⁴ wo ch'o ch'o, paltry yatter
                    wo⁴⁻⁵ wo⁴⁻⁵ ch'o⁴⁻⁵ ch'o⁴⁻⁵
                              paltry yatter.
But as Chu said, nowt to do with taking hold of anything

in the four coigns of the universe,
        heaven, earth or whatsodam,
No handle,
      no clear kuan^3
           chao^4 kuan^3
                care for control,
But to live as flowers reflected,
         as moonlight,
free from all possessiveness in affections
        but, as Chu says, egoistical.
As to building temples for the benefit of contractors
        or images for the benefit of the gilders,
The incense market will benefit
        from your wives' red and green dresses
As they run about mid riff-raff
         acquiring merit by comedy
         or by tragedy after fool vows.
To release souls with burnt paper?
Bhudda? divine?
        to be bought with a few bits of silver?
And enraged if his priests do not get it?
     But if the scholar wants by one sniff to force up
             his reputation
or has eye on grain-cut in exchange
        agiotage, profit motive,
in and out of the yamen, horning in on officials
mediate hand-outs and hand-overs
        raise fire-word swish-swash
& not one dot of decency in his conduct
a mere dribble with an ex-mortar-board label

che yang ti jen
> a low-flow and a liu² flow

a rice dog-head pai lui for ruin
An Ting made rules and observed them:
2 schools for government preparation:
> > Classic and Govt. Business,

And they were neat as a bird's beak, his students
and in Han time was Wen² Weng¹
> > held office in Fourstreams

> > > > pen

> > ne ultra crepidam   yeh

As Dolmetsch or Big Top
& that scholars read Odes
> and turn conversation toward justice

hsiu⁴ ts'an² in the home
kuan¹ ch'ang² in office
talk modus,
> keep mind on the root;

Ability as grain in the wheat-ear
Establish the homestead
XI Teach kids to keep out of mischief,
> Sow to the very corner,

Most people have sons or brothers,
Study the ancient King Sages
> as compass and T-square

To have masters in village schools
To teach 'em classics not hog-wash
&
that the Kiang Sheng is to be read once a month
> to start 'em

(like the ceremonial furrow)
Generation being linked to posterity
                    excellence is from learning
                    hao hsin²
                        an abbreviation for
O⁴⁻⁵ from ignorance, foulness.
Completeness, focus,
                    or ruin, huai, tone four.
And if your kids don't study, that's your fault.
Tell 'em. Don't kid yourself,.and don't lie.
In statement, answer; in conversation
                    not with sissified fussiness (chiao¹)
                    always want your own way.
Let 'em ask before taking action;
That there be no slovenly sloppiness
                    between goodman & wife.
Gt. is gt. . Little is little;
With friends one is one
                    2 is 2
Not to lie out of heedlessness
                    let alone out of trickery
Fitting the tone to their words
                    as water goes over the mill-wheel.
Dress 'em in folderols
                    and feed 'em with dainties,
In the end they will sell out the homestead.
Taxes, for public utility,
                    a share of a product,
People have bodies
                    ergo they sow and reap,

Soldiers also have bodies,
                take care of the body as implement,
It is useful,
To shield you from floods and rascality.

Born of the blue sky and a wild cat
                Cloud in thunder and rain,
Basalt, the stone gong
      "if," as Yao said: "you can keep these two lovelies
      in order!"
You forget the timing of budgets
            that is to say you probably don't even know that
Officials exist in time. You are fairly unconscious
          Hsiang i hsiang
but in muddle and incomprehension   14.5
        the contemplation of outlay
           hsiao^4
tsou (four) memorial
the k'ao ch'eng is according to harvest,
the tax as a share of something produced.

You can waste more on tips and wangles
         (Thiers a progress from Talleyrand,
less brain and more morals)
      PANURGIA? SOPHIA:
         what will *not* do,
Are distinguished by what they will not—
Cannibals wd/ resist canneries, Ersatz
   a given state of enlightenment, scienza
       XIV

Thru the ten voices of the tradition
                    the land has been ploughed
                              t'ien² ti⁴
& there have been taxes in kind, and by (liang²) measure
This is important
          as to the scope of such taxes
all Courts have levied them
                    the right pattern of levy is yang⁴ cheng¹
                              id est: for use
not a fountain of folderols
for top poppinjays.
                              Wranglings won't get you out of it
High & low, top & under
                    INCORPORATE
& one body.
The ups are not malevolent,
                    you might consider their complications;
Dykes for flood-water,
                    someone must build 'em;
                    must plan 'em,
By the ten mouths of the tradition:
                              have peace
Meaning get rid of criminality. Catch 'em!

Ancestral spring making breed, a pattern
Yong (2. 2. 3)
"12 inches, guinea an inch!" said Elkin Mathews
                    in regard to Courtney's review.
The State is corporate
                    as with pulse in its body

& with Chou rite at the root of it
The root is thru all of it,
                    a tone in all public teaching:
This is not a work of fiction
                    nor yet of one man:
The six kinds of action, filial, reciprocal,
Sincerity from of old until now,
                    holding together
Not shallow in verbal usage
                    nor in dissociations;
Shallow prides, feeble dissociations,
And spend their time slanting rumours;
            keep things off center slander and blabber-mouth;
Rail; scold and ructions; *manesco*
        and the whole family suffers.
The whole tribe is from one man's body,
        what other way can you think of it?
The surname, and the 9 arts.
            The father's word is compassion;
            The son's, filiality.
            The brother's word: mutuality;
            The younger's word: deference.
Small birds sing in chorus,
Harmony is in the proportion of branches
            as clarity (chao¹).
Compassion, tree's root and water-spring;
            The state: order, inside a boundary;
            Law: reciprocity.
What is statute save reciprocity?

One village in order,
        one valley will reach the four seas.

CHÊN, *yo el Rey*, wish you to think of this EDICT.
        4.
Having heard that provisions are the root of the people
                (logistica)
        nung
           sang
To sprout in season
        and have trees for your silk-worms,
One big chap not plow,
        one female not weave
Can mean shortage,
From of old the sovereign likes plowing
& the Empress tends trees with reverence;
    Nor shrink from the heat of labour

兆   an omen

The plan is in nature
        rooted
Coming from earth, times (ch'ang^2) respected
Their powers converging
        (chu four assemble
There is a must at the root of it
        not one man's mere power,
Thru high-low, parch and dampness
High, dry for panicled millet
Damp, low for rice (non-glutinous) and paddy
    wu^2 mu ch'i^2 ying^2 pei^4 li^4

                         (interest)
not for a quick buck at high interest
the legal rate does not exhaust things
                (Byzance did better)
Don't burn to abandon production and go into trading,
        Dig up root to chase branches
vide Michelet & Ambrose "De Tobia"
                The rate in Byzance was lower,
as can continuous far
                        (*que ça doure*)
Established that everybody got some education
AND you had literate Confucians
                                in the burocracy,
Focus of men of ability solidified our good customs.
Shut out graceful bigots
                        and moderate thundering phalloi
                            (this is a mistranslation)
Strong, weak, to one coöperation,
                our SAGE FOREBEAR examined to
                                stimulate anagogico
and more especially magnified schools—
everything that wd/ bring up esprit de corps

                    en¹ 恩

trained his officers not to slant government
                and to be ready for anything.
1 st/ the basic in his own practice,
                then village usage
                to see what style for the casting
Filiality and fraternity are the root,

                    710

Talents to be considered as branches.
Precise terminology is the first implement,
                    dish and container,
After that the 9 arts.
AND study the classic books,
                the straight history
                        all of it candid.
Be friends with straight officers
                    chiao¹ communicate,
They *are* your communications,
            a hasty chirrp may raise ruin.
You, soldiers, civilians,
            are not headed to be professors.
The basis is man,
            and the rectification of officers
But the four TUAN
                are from nature
        jen, i, li, chih
Not from descriptions in the school house;
They are the scholar's job,
            the gentleman's and the officer's.

There is worship in plowing
            and equity in the weeding hoe,
A field marshal can be literate.
        Might we see it again in our day!

7
All I want is a generous spirit in customs
        1st/ honest man's heart demands sane curricula

(no, that is not textual)
Let him analyze the trick programs
                and fake foundations
The fu jen receives heaven, earth, middle
                and grows.

C

"Has packed the Supreme Court
    so they will declare anything he does constitutional."
                         Senator Wheeler, 1939.
— and some Habsburg ploughed his imperial furrow
                      Eu ZoOn —
Not that never should, but if exceeding and
        no one protest,
               will lose all of your liberties.
"Would have thought of something"
              said Joffre of Napoleon.
And Lenin: "Aesopian language (under censorship)
      where I wrote 'Japan' you may read 'Russia'",
And small bank accounts are now guaranteed.

      By increase of debt? strengthen??
     with . . . posing as Moslem?
"not a trial but a measure" committed Danton.
     And which Henry committed Jo Skelton?
Wiseman to Isaacs, Aug 18, 1918
        "try to shift power to the Executive"
         i.e. out of Congress.
No french public debt before Francis
           (at 8½ to the hundred)
— S . . . W . . . fished out of a duck-pond —
     After Mazarin over 400 million,
       I think four hundred and thirty
                 PERENNE

BELLUM "not constructif"
                    but the Code out of Corsica
                    Civilization from Peloponesus
Maison Quarrée, by greek workmen.

                         Gave up to England (1708)
The monopoly
Of the slave trade,
                    at this time Gibraltar
and the old bitch de Medicis died in miseria,
          '29, John Law obit
as you may read in San Moisé, in the pavement,
                              SUMBAINAI
Grevitch, bug-house, in anagram: "Out of vast
a really sense of proportion
                    and instantly."
wanted me to type-write his name on an handkerchief.
In 1766 was beheaded, in the charming small town of Abbeville,
          Young Labarre, for reading Arouet de Voltaire,
where the stream runs close between houses.
1810-'61, Cavour; 1819 to nineteen one Hohenlohe, Clodovic
                    Carlos Victor,
Peace from '70 until 1914
          Chez nous la presse est encore très peu civilizée
this to Napoleon Third, '67.
'69: southern Slavs against union with Russia
                    Feb. 24: Zollverein
"the peculiarities of french character"
                         wrote Prince Napoleon,.
Ionides did not like him.
          Count Usedom: Bismarck, like all germans, fanatic,

714

A fanatic for peace. 1868 in December.
(cf/ no more wars after '70)
Clodovic against capital punishment
  ˋand for representation, of some sort, by trades.
                                Ultramontaines
bitched France
          and then Austria, aristos are ignorant
plus illiteracy of the ploots.
                    "JESUS!!"
quoth the Queen, 1584 anno Domini, "sterling,
pund sterling how much? 13,000. It is not to be looked for."
From ploughing of fields is justice,
            and if words be not solid
Von Moltke, Fontainebleau, 1867, "a stag hunt"
              "In locis desertis
"laetamur, silvis in mediis.
              "tondentur, occiditis, mulgentur
"quibus agrum colitis.
          "Cruorem funditis,
          "carnes intrinsecus vos onerant
          "Corporum sepulcra mortuorum viventia."
                  Ambrose "De Brachmanorum".
"That Virginia be sovreign," said Andy Jackson
          "never parted with . . ."
                  Oh GAWD!!! that tenth section . . .
"any portion of . . ."
      DAMN IT.
George Second encouraged,
          the tariff of 1816 murdered indigo.
          Freemen do not look upward for bounty.

Barley, rice, cotton, tax-free
                           with hilaritas.
Letizia, Dante, Canto 18   a religion
Virtù enters.
                 Buona da sè volontà.
Lume non è, se non dal sereno
                 stone to stone, as a river descending
the sound a gemmed light,
                           form is from the lute's neck.
Jackson 83; 83 Adams,
                           no jealousy in the North at that time.
"further errors of Monsieur de Tocqueville" . . .
                 "Taney in place of Duane"
                           Out of Erebus
Where no mind moves at all.
                           In crystal funnel of air
                           Out of heaviness
And that all gates (bab, gate) are holy
                 Pandects I. 8 out of Gaius.
Consul for 4th time, December 7th.
                           To Windsor we owe three years PEACE.
Agassiz, Kung, to avoid the encirclement,
                 La France, maison close.
                 "an' moh religions",
said Lightfoot
                 "thanna dawg is got hairs on its back".
So that the mist was quite white on that part of the sea-coast
                 Le Portel, Phaecia
                           and he dropped the scarf in the tide-rips
KREDEMNON

that it should float back to the sea,
and that quickly
                    DEXATO XERSI
          with a fond hand
                    AGERTHE
But their technique is two lies at once
          so there be no profit in conflict,
CODE functioned in all Latin countries
          till even Bulgars had their Gesetzbuch
                    in Justin's village
"Non della" (Verona)
          and J. Austin, an Englander,
               attempted to separate law from moral philosophy.
Of which the value . . .
               said Frank Harris, they deal in things,
always, the value of which is unknown.
               No greek sells a slave out of Hellas
Silk news came up, by monks, out of India,
Shingled flakes on a moth's wing.   monetary (218 a. D.)
commission. Belisarius
forbade cavalry to damage any man's standing grain.
          "NO, not THAT boat"
     shouted his captain at Ratto, when the latter had
nicely aimed his torpedo
                    at a Lloyd Triestino
in which wops held certain shares.
                    Wanted her (%) interest, De Stael did.
"More" said Santayana "for Rome than three Napoleons".
               I suppose he meant than Nap had done for Paris.

                    717

Nel mezzo 中 the crystal,

a green yellow flash after sunset

the fu$^{2-5}$ provide no mental means for running an

empire

nor has one seen taozers ascending in   pai 白

jih 日

in the white light 白

the pai jih 日

with ten billion wordings.
Alighieri, a rag over his eyes, and
"They miss Tyler"
            (Stock wrote)
"   as well as Polk and VanBuren."
"With the horned moon for his tea-pot,
"   does he need a clay model
"   or tongue words adorned with gilding?
"Floating hands for a horse deal,
"   respectable Han folk
"   and these bright specimens huddled together—
"Bright, Celestial,
"   wants your small change

"   and bears grudge if he does not get it
"(Wang on the Sheng Edict,
"   and a blaze of light over Shensi)
"You will not be misled by damn foolishness,
"   If you don't swallow their buncomb,
"   you wont have to drive 'em out.
"Peace grips the earth in good manners;
"Earth and water dye the air in your valley." end quote.
          "De Tribus" (Federico
in Sicily, aulentissima
                    ver l'estate,
                              and Fordie:
"A DICtionary
          and learn the meaning of words!"

                              Kuan   光

                    Ming   明

Double it

          Kuan   光

     Ming   明

Durch das Bankhaus Pacelli kompromittiert
and B. Swan thought civil war was the only means of getting
                              (from Spaniards)
          five bucks ($) for one buck's worth of petrol.

He'd been on "one of them boats".

OLYMPIAD

236

A pyre in Athens, by Peregrinus
Who did not share Plarr's point of view,
                                    born in Parion.
Coelum tecto, Deus nec vendit;
Terra lecto, sed largitur
            and that Caritas leads to serenity.
Stead asked Douglas about the rupee . . .
            with their own gods to lead them
nor sin by misnaming
            out of similitude into gathering
"Mortal blame has no sound in her ears".
                Until Rémusat: "Has not", "Aquinas has not
"bien rendue compte
            des connaissances à priori."
"Want to load" (Cocteau)
            "all the rest of it onto you."
            Erigena,
            Anselm,
            Cherbury,
            Rémusat,
            Thiers was against income-tax
                "the portal to inquisition"
And from Psellos
                right down to Degas
No such nuances,
                old what's-her-name stewing perfumes
During summer heat in Byzantium

to the distress of the servitù.
"Russia an ally"
said the old Commissioner (Agra)
Neque aurum diligunt
"that STICKS
in
my
throat."
Gardner, A.G.
Aug. 1, 1914
also specific
Beauclerc the first norman duke who could read,
Half the land, and slaves or how much
belonged to the temples
as Julian noticed ("Apostate")
2 million died for investiture,
Rome; Autun; Poictiers; Benevento
crosse (+) et l'anneau (O)
1075; '77; '78; '87
et le prépuce at Puy en Vellay
"To avoid other views" said Herbert (De Veritate)
"their first consideration"
come in subjecto
lisses
amoureuses
a tenir
EX OUSIAS ... HYPOSTASIN
III, 5, 3   PERI EROTAS

hieron

nous to ariston autou
                as light into water compenetrans
that is pathema
                ouk aphistatai"
                                thus Plotinus
                                        per plura diafana
neither weighed out nor hindered;
                        aloof.
                                1 Jan '58

CI

Finding scarcely anyone save Monsieur de Rémusat
        who could understand him
(junipers, south side) M. Talleyrand
          spruce and fir take the North
Chalais, Aubeterre,
        snow-flakes at a hand's breadth, and rain.
Trees line the banks, mostly willows. Kublai,
Te Te of Ch'eng, called Timur, 1247, came hither
Forest thru ice into emerald

             in   旦   Tan (dawn, that is)

   larix, corayana and berberis,
        after 2 stages A-tun-tzu
           a distance of one hundred *li*
Pinus armandi,
       Talleyrand, Thiers, tried to get sense into princes.
6 to the public; 3%, and then one to the state
        (Simon admits it)
4 letters patent, 5 seals
      after the 4th year of Yung-lo
         12th May, 1406, and a gold belt
            inlaid with flowers, pay for the troops holding
                 passes; rations, chair-coolies, horses.
— "To write of today," sd/ Mr Kennan, "is not scholarship"
      and, going toward slavery, have mislaid family names.
40 years trailer life, non-productive,

                    non-agricultural
                    (Del Pelo Pardi
          came on cunicoli)
                    tho' avoiding the squalor of taxes
                    by cretins imposed;
Not attempting as Peabody, Warren G. "Peabody Coke and
                                        Coal", said
                    to unscrew the inscrutable
"infini" as measured by Renan
                                        "la bêtise humaine."
That one dollar's worth of oil sell at 5 dollars.
                    Talleyrand, Austerlitz, Mme Rémusat:
          "90 francs fee for obtaining gold for
                    a one thousand franc note" (1805) . . .
                    and Cambacérès
A constitution given to Italy,
                    Xmas day of that year, Bonaparte's maximum.
"that intelligent men can believe"
                    non-sectarian   /
Marbois and then Mollien at the Treasury
                    and then Gaudin,
                    Mt Cenis, Simplon, Mme Rémusat
Wouldn't swallow it (i. e. that
                    a great mind could seek glory in war.)
                    1806, 12th December.
"Studies at Jena will be continued,"
                    "Liberty for a small privileged class"
                                        a necessity
Hottenguer, Neuflize, their Nessus

"Were in France" (Mme de Rémusat) "wholly ignorant
        of what was then passing outside."
Gaudin did not pay interest on government credit. Nor did
                                                Kang Hi.
        Mme d'Houdetot never perceived evil in anyone.
"Sort of ignorance," said the old priest to Yeats in a railway train,
        "is spreading every day from the schools!"
Obit 1933, Tsung-Kuan, for Honour.
        Bears live on acorns
                and come raiding our fields.
                                Bouffier,
Elzéard has made the forest at Vergons
                under Kuanon's eye there is oak-wood. Sengper
                                                ga-mu,
To him we burn pine with white smoke,
                morning and evening.
                The hills here are blue-green with juniper,
the stream, as Achilöos there below us,
                here one man can hold the whole pass
over this mountain, at Mont Ségur the chief's cell

you can enter it sideways only, TSO is here named

from the rope bridge, hemp rope? a reed rope?
        and they pay the land tax in buckwheat.
Food was in Tolosa, not chemical, and in Gubbio
L'il Josephine on the radio and a bull-fair
and they had sent the stone door-frames to America
                not in war-time, antiques.
                "No money, no swiss" quoted Wilson (McN.)

KALON KAGATHON, and Marengo,

       This aura will have, with red flash,

       the form of a diamond, or of crimson,

Apollonius, Porphery, Anselm,

       Plotinus EN THEORIA 'ON NOUS EXEI

had one vision only, and if the stars be but unicorns ...

or took the stars for those antilopes.

HS'UAN TSUNG, 1389 natus, painted kittens,

       and Joey said, "are they for real"

       before primitives in the Mellon Gallery,

Washington

"Should", said H. J., "for humanity's credit

                feign their existence

With the sun and moon on her shoulders,

       the star-discs sewn on her coat

         at Li Chiang, the snow range,

                 a wide meadow

and the ²dto – ¹mba's face (exorcist's)

              muy simpático

by the waters of Stone Drum,

          the two aces

Mint grows at the foot of the Snow Range

       the first moon is the tiger's,

         Pheasant calls out of bracken

Rossoni: "così lo stato ..." etcetera

      Delcroix: "che magnifica!"

         (prescrittibile)

he perceived it:

       The green spur, the white meadow

       "May their pond be full;

The son have his father's arm
and good hearing;
(noun graph upright; adjective sideways)
"His horse's mane flowing
His body and soul are at peace."

CII

This I had from Kalupso
             who had it from Hermes
"eleven literates and, I suppose,
                    Dwight L. Morrow"
the body elected,
             residence required, not as in England
"A cargo of Iron"
             lied Pallas
                    and as to why Penelope waited
keinas . . . e Orgei. line 639. Leucothoe
rose as an incense bush,
                    resisting Apollo,
                           Orchamus, Babylon
And after 500 years
                    still offered that shrub to the sea-gull,
Phaecians,
             she being of Cadmus line
The snow's lace washed here as sea-foam

   But the lot of 'em, Yeats, Possum, Old Wyndham

             had no ground to stand on
Black shawls still worn for Demeter
             in Venice,
                    in my time,
                           my young time
             OIOS TELESAI ERGON . . . EROS TE

The cat talks μάω
        (mao) with a greek inflection.
Barley is the marrow of men,
              40 centess' in my time
an orzo.
      At Procope, one franc fifteen for a luncheon
and ten centimes tip for the waiter. Noi altri borghesi
could not go down into the piazza. We thought we could
                    control . . .
And that ye sail over lithe water . . .
        under eyelids . . .
Winkelmann noted the eyelids,
    Yeats two months on a sonnet of Ronsard's.
"Jacques Père" on a sign near Le Portel,
    and belgians would pronounce it.
Eva has improved that line about Freiheit.
    "50 more years on The Changes"
or is said to have said that he could have.
Swan broke his knee cap on landing
    having scaled that 30 foot wall,
  and maintained his serenity,
    another chap hung all night in the trail ropes
and saw two other men fall.
    Took the Z for the tail of the KatZe
vide Frobenius on relative Dummheit of pupil and teacher
"The libraries" (Ingrid) "have no Domvile." Jan 1955
    as was natural
    "pseudos d'ouk . . . ei gar pepneumenos"
seed barley with the sacrifice (Lacedaemon)
But with Leucothoe's mind in that incense

all Babylon could not hold it down.

     "for my bitch eyes" in Ilion

copper and wine like a bear cub's

        in sunlight, thus Atalant

the colour as *aithiops*

          the gloss probably

               oinops

as lacquer in sunlight

        haliporphuros,

            russet-gold

in the air, extant, not carmine, not flame, oriXalko,

              le xaladines

lit by the torch-flare,

        and from the nature, the sign.

Small lions are there in benevolence

        to the left of San Marco

        AISSOUSIN,

           the spirits,

Berenice, a late constellation.

          "Same books" said Tcheou

they ought to be brother-like.

        Crystaline,

          south slope for juniper,

Wild goose follows the sun-bird,

     in mountains; salt, copper, coral,

        dead words out of fashion

KAI ALOGA,

     nature APHANASTON,

      the pine needles glow as red wire

OU THELEI EAEAN EIS KOSMOU

they want to burst out of the universe
amnis herbidas ripas
                        Antoninus;
                        Julian
                        would not be worshipped
"So thick the dead could not fall"
                        Marcellinus
"dead chap ahead of me with his head split
                        could not fall."
                        XXIII, 6, and there also
Assyrios fines ingressus,
            Built granaries, sueta annona,
            naturally labled "apostate".
Quem mihi febricula eripuit,
            Domitian, infaustus
            tried to buy peace with money.

CIII

1850: gt objection to any honesty in the White House
'56, an M. C. from California
    killed one of the waiters at the Willard
22nd. Brooks thrashed Sumner in Camera Senatus
"respectful of our own rights and of others"
    for which decent view he was ousted
   Homestead versus kolschoz
   Rome versus Babylon
no sense of quiddity in the sovreignty
    i. e. the power to issue
The slaves were red herring,
    land not secure against issuers
Emerson, Agassiz, Alcot
   at Hawthorne's funeral
   names of the principal bond-holders
— persuade Spain to sell Cuba
      via Belmont, not via Sickles;
land to all veterans: Mommsen
   160 acres, 33rd Congress
"I see its relation to one thing,
   Hui sees its relation to ten."
Monetary literacy, sans which a loss of freedom is consequent
cunicoli, canalesque
   and the people (min) ate
   caelum renovabat,
    animals dance,
     manes come.

Protocol Jan. 1831: Belgium neutral
in perpetuity
Trying (T. C. P.) 50 years later to keep some of the
non-interest-bearing etc.
in circulation
as currency
Still market, no use to brokers.
France, after Talleyrand started
one war in Europe.
Bismarck: no war after '70, that was his aim
He said: No more after '70
Casimir put Napoleon back on his Column
12th April, Journal des Debats,
1831
that bitch Mme de Lieven
that bitch Mme de Staël
Bolivar dead, who else was there?
Tolosa, 1919, Gubbio,
on pouvait manger
"Europe" said Picabia: exhausted
by the conquest of Alsace Lorraine
T. to Broglie Ap 9, '33
as I recall it there was no such thing as public
opinion (Vienna)
Metternich destroyed Maria Theresa. Maremma
Hroosia,
"tranne nella casa del re"
B. Mussolini
to some chap from Predappio
not yet, so far as I know, written down.

Lugubrious Knole,
                    Capture of Warsaw
Paris, at Palais Royal
            "where they are rather badly off for society"
de Vaux talked of nothing but bullfights
            not only 32 million subjects, but
                    pretend to govern all Europe
That he (the Archbishop) had not quite the grasp
St Leu, Beauharnais, Tascher
                given to M's'lle Hortense by the Citizen Talleyrand
"a sapphire, and a bit of the cross
            true cross, exhumed with Charlemagne's skeleton.
Mme de Genlis:
            six paintings by me; fruits, insects, animals
Bismarck thought centralization bitched France
Ivar Kreuger, according to Lorrimer's paper
            a titan, and more than,
Edishu added a zero to the number of Krauts murdered
                    in Poland
1831, in New York State: that debtors be not imprisoned
"Last superior OUT of his cabinet"
        John Quinn re/ Lansing's departure.
        and at three o'clock in the morning . . .
        my ex-partner
                    "wuz
                    sekkertary
                        of State."
1841 Fillimore: Wolverine built in Pittsburg
            for a lake parity.
Telegraph bill. 3 March '43

"Not with a cold thing"

said Griffith,

"can't move 'em"

ut delectet

Mat Quay read greek in secret. Mr. Beecher

carried some rusty cannon-balls into his pulpit

that were allegedly from Bunker Hill, Boston.

and at Nara, a. D. 784 was an art show:

Hindoo, greek, Persian

90 years from Perry to Sow-face

"the colossal conceit of Americans," said Mr. Griffis, a. D. 1915

Heaven made hearing and seeing men have the rule

cheu

i   regent

Hia caeca ratione agebat

Absolutely drop idea of putting Chase

into the Treasury

"14 killed," Stanton to Buchanan, "greatly below former reports

of a thousand"

Present my Compliments to Miss Lane.

Biddle for conscription even in Eighteen Fourteen

A. J. to Buchanan: unable to perceive that U. S. interests

will be safer in other hands than her own.

from the Hermitage.

Foreign Ministers must drive with 4 horses

and a postillion

St Petersburg '32

"I cannot, I fear, with truth defend

                    the chastity of the Empress,
                              Emperor thinks brits weary of
                                        Constitution,
The french are a singular people.
              Napoleon's taxes less than ½ now at Bergheim."
                    Buchanan got a treaty out of the hRooshuns
"worst the art of man" (speaking of bank system)
                    could devise,
English income tax odious, has risen to seven pence in the
                                        pound
Vic's character without blemish, London 1852
The Daily Telegraph has been bought over
                    and (his "Inaugural")
that men have sunk to consider the mere material value
                    of the Union
a grant from States of limited powers
              nec Templum aedificavit
                              nec restituit rem
but not his fault by a damn sight.
                    Winter in Pontus distressing
              but still at Sulmona the lion heads,
Federico wrote of the Falcon
              and Orsi: "Anch'io sono
                         antichità Siracusana."
Arab coins found in mounds in Sweden
                    under Fortuna
Raleigh noted that Genova's loans were not productive
         "all they have left is their usury"
Wodan ministrat virtutem
              Frico, voluptatem,

                    736

Agelmund reigned 33 years.
"quae a thure
        solebant sacrificiis" . . .
                that was in Tuscany.
In this province is Roma,
                Brennus came here for the wine,
                        liking its quality
Lupus comes itineris, Rothar arianae haeresios —
                edicti prologo
dope already in use
"Puteum de testiculis impleam clericorum"
                        dixit Alchis
would fill full a well with priests' balls,
                        heretics', naturally
Das Leihkapital.
And there is, of course, the Mensdorf letter
                that has had (1958)
                        no publicity.

CIV

Na Khi talk made out of wind noise,
    And North Khi, not to be heard amid sounds of the forest
but to fit in with them unperceived by the game,
    But when the young lout was selling the old lout
           the idea of betraying Mihailovitch
The air of the room became heavy so that young S.
    Resigned from the F. O. and "went into the City" —
Banners they took after Lepanto
      but now obtain "control of the outlets"
        to keep down printed quality

Ling   by ling only:

                semina.
Flames withered; the wind blew confusion

And a $ to look like a franc,
        the franc worth a centesimo
1 fr. 15   Procope,
      Dondo at the Tabarin,
At Moulin Rouge no admittance without a starched collar
      nor with a cap, at the Tabarin.
Degas' eye at La Concorde,
      splintered light, Seurat's,
        or that of Pitagora
Disraeli, Wolff Henry (double ff)

bitching England
and by-passing Parliament;
In metal cylinders, swallowed by camels
who are then killed after passing the frontier
de l'audace, PANURGIA, & heroin.
in Xreia, to dissociate demand from the need.
"Good chaps" said Schmidt
"damn shame we have to fight 'em."
Hate is not born in the trenches
nor among 2nd. lieutenants.
Old Rocke (with an -e terminal not the botanist)
learned Abyssinia,
Sammy's nevvy got the gold out of the palace bed-room
Londres' books neglected,
the French did not learn them.
and there is
no glow such as of pine-needles burning
Without ²muan   ¹bpo
no reality
Wind over snow-slope   agitante
nos otros
calescimus
Against jade
calescimus,
and the jade weathers dust-swirl.
Murare, tradurre:
Pope Nicolo had those two passions.
Gained for the latin tongue
(Valla)
latinitas

Bassinio left greek tags in his margins
                moulding the cadence
Uncle Carlo purged the mouth of that river
                the Rubicon
with russet sails (Wieland)
                at the landing
A lick here, a lick there
                and at least got the torpedo boat overland,
The Pollok was hooked by false promise:
                                "black sea"
"help by the black sea"
                only a pollok could have swallowed that promise
Of the blue sky and a wild-cat,
                                Pitonessa
The small breasts snow-soft over tripod

                       under the cloud
                                the three voices

And stopped (in lucid intervals)
                the digging of metals,
Once gold was
                by ants
                out of burrows
                                not

pao three

                This is not treasure.
Can you tell pao three from pao four, a wild cat:

        da radice torbida
                is no clarity

And who try to use the mind for the senses
                              drive screws with a hammer
                                                      maalesh

Adolf furious from perception.
     But there is a blindness that comes from inside —
they try to explain themselves out of nullity.
"Beg the gentleman to go home AT ONCE
          say I will call on him."
                              THAT is politeness
And the cap for a forester
          showing nuance.
1910: Pears' soap for lamas
                    Les Douze unconscious of Fordie,
Among medicos: Ambroise Paré
          before Zeus, six bluejays before him
          THEMIS against leagues of princes
Said Yo-Yo:
          "What part ob yu iz deh poEM??"
          of the vicinage, by his peers
And to raise up guilds
                    in time of the moon kings
          mitred by consecration of light
"Wash yu feet?
          tread strange lan'."
Luigi in hill paths
          chews wheat at sunrise,
                    that grain, his communion.
And if the stars be but unicorns,
                    light for lasso.
Yseult is dead, and Walter,

and Fordie,
familiares
"And how my olde friend
— eh — eh
HOWells?
can "etcetera
Remy's word was "milésiennes"
William's: monoceros,
vide his book plate.
The production IS the beloved.
And Gladstone took a little packet of tea to
Miss What's-her-name, Palmerston's fancy
but did not sell England
for four million quid to . . . (deleted . . .
Suez Canal shares
Said Hollis (Christopher)
Regius . . . (deleted) Professorships
for falsification
and Coke disappeared from curricula.
Von Bülow got news from the agencies:
France betrayed Talleyrand,
"Pickin' daisies" "He (Wells) won't have
an opinion."
Thus Orage respected belatedly. "Nicht Bosheit"
said Margherita Regina, or one of 'em, "DUMMheit".
Mirabeau had it worse, Ovid much worse in Pontus.
"No sooner in Goa
than they started uprooting spice trees,
Intorcetta's portrait is still there in Sicily
with an unreadable text on his fan

Hence Webster, Voltaire and Leibnitz
     by phyllotaxis
          in leaf-grain
But in Venice more affirmations
     of individual men
From Selvo to Franchetti, than any elsewhere.
Po like a map beneath us
          "Very cleverly drained"
          said the prisoner's escort.
               Larranaga
saw fashion an element:
     No science without clear definitions.
        and there is a style of the period
          "My Chauncey Alcot
     If you'll bee
          my Molly
           O!"
Moral scruple unknown to financiers
          at THAT time
a common custom in business.
Lukie Ionides: will do, a greek will
          ANYTHING
till he gets Twenty Thousand
     (meaning quid sterling)
     after that, he sees that it pays to be honest.
Pulchra documenta
     Bülow from agencies
          "don't waste time getting into papers"
Get the agencies.
     and to summarize:

Gold was in control of the Pontifex,
        standard at Byzance
           and El Melek
until 1204.
      kalos kagathos
Del Mar cites 12 cases of tickets
        as from Iron in Spartan coinage
In splendour of blue-jays
        Cythera PAGGKALA
Mond killed the English Review
        and Ford went to Paris (an interval)
Village festival on the Quatorze
Brits paid out of french pocket
        one whole installment;
Alex, the debts of his soldiers
And as for what happened after the king lost exclusivity
        even Del Mar gasps with astonishment
McNair Wilson, Larranaga, or Tremaine at 2 in the morning
        "Fer some gawd damn fool reason . . .
no more sense than pill box hats where might be Gains-
                        boroughs,"
referring to prescrittibile
          or
What a government usefully COULD do.
False middles serve neither commerce
        nor the NOOS in activity
That fine old word (Stink Saunders' word) "an Independence"

 pen yeh

744

Homestead versus kolschoz,
        advice to farms, not control
tessera, Monreale,
        Topaz, God can sit on.
For 30 years nothing of interest occurred in that country.
but the Burgomeister's Schwager
        mistrusted Fetzen Papier
Where deer's feet make dust in shadow
        at wood's edge.
        curet cogitare perennia
foung houang li i
        varnish and silk is their tribute
Iu's weights are still in the treasury.

CV

Feb. 1956
Is this a divagation:

                    Talleyrand saved Europe for a century
France betrayed Talleyrand;

                 Germany, Bismarck.
And Muss saved, rem salvavit,

             in Spain

                 il salvabile.

       semina motuum

From Sulmona

        the lion-fount—

           must be Sulmona, Ovidio's,
Federico noted the hawk form

        and no one has yet translated "Il Marescalco",

          (Cesena, Zezena de be"e colonne)
Mozart obit aetat 35,

        Christian's hat and gloves so clearly painted

          (Herbiet)
the corridor ½ an inch wide,

             must be somewhere
"moyens d'existence inconnus."

        Anselm "Monologion" scripsit, 1063
"non spatio, sed sapientia"

        not in space but in knowing

          non pares, not equal in dignity

rerum naturas.

       Do not use their mathematics to think with . . .
Lanfranci timuerunt sapientiam,

          were alarmed by Lanfranc's horse-sense.

           Passed that day drawing a grasshopper
"Loans from Tibet" said old Gallagher,

           Patrick, and died in this bughouse?
Sodom on Thames sold out Napoleon

Hou Je   stando nel Paradiso Terrestre

and the sheep on Rham plains have different names

           according to colour,

        nouns, not one noun plus an adjective,
"Meas nugas" my Trifles, said Anselm.
"L'adoravano" said the sacristan, Bari

          "come Santa Lucia"
So it, a stone cupid, had to be stored in the sacristy.
Barocco, anima: stuff left from the 5 & 10

      vagula, tenula

        and with splendours
"non genitus" Caput 57, "discendendo"

      Guido C. had read "Monologion"
vera imago

      and via mind is the nearest you'll get to it,
"rationalem"

      said Anselm.

         Guido: "intenzione".
Ratio,

    luna,

747

speculum non est imago,
mirrour, not image;
Sapor, the flavour,
pulchritudo
ne divisibilis intellectu
not to be split by syllogization
to the blessed isles (insulis fortunatis)
fertur
quasi apes, as bees . . . alvearia,
uranici templi
lumine ut amictus
with light as an army-cloak.
Canterbury well, above Capua
by Anselm's direction,
he said: dig there.
Puteus Cantauriensis
nine miles approx east of Capua
And he said: ". . . eh . . .
I might eat a partridge."
So we scuttled all day
and no partridge
Till the stable boy met a martin
that had caught one.
. . . et sake et soke on stronde . . .
on streame on woden
in stream and forest
all other *libertates*,
consuetudines, Port of Sandwich
justice . . . centralization,
coin is the symbol of equity

Rochester nave built by the lombards,
                    the high hall and the carving
Rufus raised rent 5 to 40
                              usu terrae
Unitas Charitatis,
                    consuetudo diversa,
Having lost the wisdom of Khati
        but for something not brute force in government
"ordine"
            Boamund versus Alexis,
                    that maniac Boniface, Clermont.
& the public extremely excited.
                    George Fifth under the drizzle,
                    as in one November
                    a man who had willed no wrong.
33 years after the Bard's death . . .
                          "Dalleyrand"
800 years after En Bertrans
        "en gatje", had the four towers,
                          "Dalleyrand Berigorrr!"
Urban, an obscenity
            with the rents at 40 from 5,
Charles of the Suevi
            a noose of light looped over his shoulder,
Antoninus declined to be God.
Athelstan on occasion distributed,
            Ethelbald exempted from taxes,
                Egbert left local laws,
                          consuetudines
"And we bjJayzus reject your damn bishops."

Paschal to Anselm.

        At this time was Guillaume de Poictiers,
Henry left 100,000 quid in good coin
                also vessels
Fragmentary:
           (Maverick repeating this queery dogmaticly.
                mosaic? any mosaic.
You cannot leave these things out.
        οὐ θέλει ἔην εἰς κόσμον
but from at least here is the Charta Magna
I shall have to learn a little greek to keep up with this
        but so will you, drratt you.
"They want to bust out of the kosmos"
                   accensio
Anselm versus damn Rufus
"Ugly? a bore,
        Pretty, a whore!"
             brother Anselm is pessimistic,
digestion weak,
        but had a clear line on the Trinity, and
By sheer grammar: Essentia
             feminine
                Immaculata
Immaculabile. Ambrose:
        "First treason: shepherd to flock."
        and they want it apocryphal.
Franks: ten years exemption from taxes
        Valentinian to oust the Alani
        and then Omnia Gallia, Faramond, 425
Pepin, over an altar to Zagreus,

Ethelbald: tax exemptions
>>> Charles to Offa, a belt, one hungarian sword.
Quendrida bumped off brother Kenelm,
>> Egbert left local laws.
>> "Looping the light over my shoulder,"
>>> (Charles of the Suevi)
>> "Drew me over fiery mountains"
As is left in Hariulf's Chronicle. Thus dreamed it.
For a thousand years savages against maniacs
>>>> and vice versa.
Alfred sorted out hundreds; tithings,
> They probably murdered Erigena,
>> Athelstan gon yilden rere, after 925
>>> Aunt Ethelfled had been literate,
>>>> Canute for alleviation of Alp tolls
>>>> Gerbert at the astrolabe
>>>>> better than Ptolemy,
A tenth tithe and circet of corn.
With a Crommelyn at the breech-block
>> or a del Valle,
This is what the swine haven't got
>> with their
>>>> πανουργία

Guido had read the Proslogion
>> as had, presumably, Villon.

CVI

AND was her daughter like that;
Black as Demeter's gown,

                        eyes, hair?
Dis' bride, Queen over Phlegethon,
            girls faint as mist about her?

The strength of men is in grain. Kuan
NINE decrees, 8th essay, the Kuan

 Tzu

So slow is the rose to open.
A match flares in the eyes' hearth,
            then darkness
"Venice shawls from Demeter's gown"
This Tzu could guide you in some things,
                     but not hither,
How to govern is from the time of Kuan Chung
    but the cup of white gold at Patera
Helen's breasts gave that.
              ὁ θεός
runs thru his zodiac,
          misnaming no Caledon,
not in memory,
           in eternity
              and "as a wind's breath
that changing its direction changeth its name",
                    Apeliota

for the gold light of wheat surging upward
                                    ungathered
Persephone in the cotton-field
            granite next sea wave
is for clarity
            deep waters reflecting all fire
nueva lumbre,
                    Earth, Air, Sea
                                in the flame's barge
over Amazon, Orinoco, great rivers.
"But for Kuan Chung we should still dress as barbarians."
And if Antoninus got there, this was hidden

        Kuan, hidden
Ad posteros urbem donat,

                        coin'd Artemis
all goods light against coin-skill
if there be 400 mountains for copper —
            under cinnabar you will find copper —
river gold is from Ko Lu;
                        price from XREIA;
Yao and Shun ruled by jade
        That the goddess turn crystal within her
This is grain rite
            Luigi in the hill path
                        this is grain rite
near Enna, at Nyssa:
                    Circe, Persephone
so different is sea from glen that
                        the juniper is her holy bush

                        753

between the two pine trees, not Circe
>   but Circe was like that
>   coming from the house of smoothe stone
"not know which god"
>   nor could enter her eyes by probing
>   the light blazed behind her
>   nor was this from sunset.

Athene Pronoia,
>   in hypostasis
Helios, Perse: Circe
Zeus: Artemis out of Leto
Under wildwood
>   Help me to neede
By Circeo, the stone eyes looking seaward
>   Nor could you enter her eyes by probing.
>   The temple shook with Apollo
As with leopards by mount's edge,
>   light blazed behind her;
>   trees open, their minds stand before them
As in Carrara is whiteness:
>   Xoroi. At Sulmona are lion heads.
>   Gold light, in veined phylotaxis.
By hundred blue-gray over their rock-pool,
>   Or the king-wings in migration
>   And in thy mind beauty, O Artemis
Over asphodel, over broom-plant,
>   faun's ear a-level that blossom.
>   Yao and Shun ruled by jade.
Whuder ich maei lidhan
>   helpe me to neede

the flowers are blessed against thunder bolt
helpe me to neede.
That great acorn of light bulging outward,
Aquileia, caffaris, caltha palistris,
ulex, that is gorse, herys arachnites;
Scrub oak climbs against cloud-wall —
three years peace, they had to get rid of him,
— violet, sea green, and no name.
Circe's were not, having fire behind them.
Buck stands under ash grove,
jasmine twines over capitols
Selena Arsinoe
So late did queens rise into heaven.
At Zephyrium, July that was, at Zephyrium
The high admiral built there;
Aedificavit
TO APHRODITE EUPLOIA
"an Aeolian gave it, ex voto
Arsinoe Kupris.
At Miwo the moon's axe is renewed
HREZEIN
Selena, foam on the wave-swirl
Out of gold light flooding the peristyle
Trees open in Paros,
White feet as Carrara's whiteness
in Xoroi.
God's eye art 'ou.
The columns gleam as if cloisonné,
The sky is leaded with elm boughs.

CVII

The azalea is grown while we sleep
In Selinunt',
                in Akragas
Coke. Inst. 2..
                        to all cathedral churches to be
                                read 4 times in the yeare
                20. H. 3
                        that is certainty
mother and nurse of repose
                he that holdeth by castle-guard
                                        pays no scutage
And speaking of clarity
                        Milite, Coke, Edwardus
"that light which was Sigier"
                . . . of Berengar his heirs was this Eleanor
all the land stored with ploughs, & shall be at the least as he
                                                received it
quod custod' . . . vendi non debent
Light, cubic
                by volume
so that Dante's view is quite natural;
                (Tenth, Paradiso, nel Sole)
non per color, ma per lume parvente
Custumier . . .   de Normand'
                de la foresta   14
                are yellow-green after sunset   H
in politique capacity a king dies not   3

ancient eit franchies,
ne injuste vexes
progressus ostendunt

Magna Charta, chap XII
periplum, assise in periplum
and Kung also was minister

本 pen

the root is that charter.
"It appeareth in Glanvil"
saving his wainage (his cart)
hominum de vicineto
sacramentum proborum
laicum tenementum
"it appeareth in Glanvil"
"de par le monde"

j'ai connu
the books of a scholler his countenance
H.2 E. 1
to their glory
en temps le roy Henri deux
and that slobbering bugger Jim First
bitched our heritage
OBIT, in Stratford 1616, Jacques Père obit,
In 33 years Noll cut down Charlie
OBIT Coke 1634 & in '49

Noll cut down Charlie
Puer Apulius . . . ver l'estate
Voltaire could not do it;
the french could not do it.

they had not Magna Charta
in ver l'estate, Queen of Akragas
resistent,

       Templum aedificavit
         Segesta
hospitality . . . of the ancient ornaments and
       commandations of England
          ii. Inst. xxi
nec alii boscum,
     high-wood is called saltus;
       in Fleta, maeremium
qui utlagatus est
   and a literacy in these auncient authors
     to understand auncient statute . . .
against who fishes with kidells and skarkells
or makes that several which ought to be common
. . . from the sheepes back 9 tenths of our export
      (note to cap. 25)
so that after one set of damned scoundrels (tonsured)
another set of damned scoundrels
      (untonsured)
the foulest of all these Jimmy Stuart.
   Coke: the clearest mind ever in England
vitex, white eglantine
    as tenthril thru grill-work
     wave pattern at Excideuil
A spire level the well-curb,
    Mme Pierre bought a lamb in that market.
Atque in re publica maxime conservanda sunt iura belli . . .
    is called butlerage

                    paid only by merchant strangers (cap. xxx)
wooll woolfels & leather
            hearth silver abolished
                    naught new imposed until Mary
of allome, Scacarrio Rot. 319
            in the Pope's dominion
                                    iii s. iiii d
on currants was against law
            in commun ley . . .
                    ad mesure,
Laws of Edgar: ex omni satrapia   xxxv
            a circuit of perambulation
sil ne fuit dizein
            quod trithinga teneatur integra
                    decemvirale collegium
exceptis viris religiosis et . . .
                    vide Bracton
sub colore donationis
                    his testibus . . .
                        were call'd chartae.
That is our PIVOT
                    Statute de Merton:
                                    canons regular
seven miles from the city of London . . .
            between him and the Prior of Bingham
                on the morrow after the feast of St Vincent
            18 H. 3 according to Bracton
& this Helianor was of the daughters, heirs
            of Raymond Berengar
            and sister of Arch. Cantaur

                            759

                    de la plus beale
& of brain-wash
            1st/ the symbol/
                        corruption of Symbol
then the invasion of Bede's time
        and the hog-wash with King James
                his "version"
till in 1850 to unfashion the lingua latina;
        to drive truth out of curricula.
                    Coke's quotes might have told something.
Alex, Antoninus in blot-out
                        and Randolph,
not to distreine corne in sheafes
                Edward "Mirror of Princes"
                Statute of Merton, Cap. Five.
5 groats to an ounce of silver
            not subject to forrein lawes
                One thousand two sixty seven
                King Henry's 52
in the Utas of St Martin
        "as well high as low"
                Sapiens incipit a fine
Box hedge, the garden in form,
            heliotrope, kalikanthus, basilicum
the red bird, that is a cardinal,
            lark almost out of season
had been a field full at Allegre
            as 40 rising together,
                    the short tails.
Was new coin 1560,

'65, dutch weavers in Norwich
at terms, whores in St Paul's,
Trinity, Michaelmas,
Hillary is from Jan 23rd.
Each wench to a pillar
"as do the Serjeants at lawe".
To use grain for food only;
build no more houses in London
de heretico comburendo
Bacon for, Coke opposing.
In a white sheet in the Savoy
500 marks, be imprisoned
Sir Henry (1628) Martin gave sentence.
Invasion of the rights of his subjects
3 months to *habeas*
B. 18.
The tapestries were still there in Chaise Dieu,
the sky's glass leaded with elm boughs
Marlowe greeks it μὴ ὄν
Avon's man
says it in english
and if the stone can be perfect
Gaudier has left us three Ninas,
Diana crumbles in Notre-Dame des Champs
but the bronze must be somewhere,
Amphion not for museums   or stone.
but for her mind
like the underwave
Not the glitter 2 fathoms inshore,
the coral light sifting slowly mid sea-fans

                              the great algae
                  color prediletto
the crystal body of air
                  deep green over azure
Sirenes σῆραγξ as crystal Σειρήν
            dark hippocampi θελκτήριη
                                        god's antennae.
Norfolk tumbler, a small sort of greyhound
                        to Cecil;
Planted 500 mulberries —
            that was Hatfield —
                    and vines from south of the Channel
But had enclosed common pasture
            Gondemar "devil in dung-cart"!

            Flaccus' translator wore the crown
            The jew and the buggar dragged it down:
            "Devil in dung-cart" Gondemar
            And Raleigh's head on King James' platter."
"That the dead will not fawn to advance themselves"
                        1621, December eleventh.
So that Dante's view is quite natural:
            this light
                    as a river
            in Kung; in Ocellus, Coke, Agassiz
                    ῥεῖ, the flowing
                    this persistent awareness
Three Ninas from Gaudier,
            Their mania is a lusting for farness
            Blind to the olive leaf,

                        762

not seeing the oak's veins.
Wheat was in bread in the old days.
(1.46 after mid-night)
Alan Upward's seal showed Sitalkas.
Coin was in Ambracia;
The caelator's son, named Pythagora.

CVIII

COMMINUIT
      there is frost on the rock's face
nurse of industry (25 Edward III)
    BRUM
"alla" at Verona
      of courage
having none hath no care to defend it

           pen yeh

Enrolled in the ball of fire

          as brightness

             clear emerald
for the kindness,
      infinite,
        of her hands
From the Charter to the Petition   1628
    in June and toward twilight
        DROIT FAIT
Statutum Tallagio
      Lambarde on Valla
          "all monopolies"
"nor against his will into Ireland"
        autarchia
not cloth from out of the Realm
    Owse, Wherfe, Nid, Derwent,

Swale, Yore & Tine
      Post Festum Sancti Hilarii
mults des mals et disherisons
           18 E. 1   a. d. 1290
ne curge de S. Edward
      prochainement
and his father H. 3 before him
      ne quis injuriam —
           salvum conductum
                 18 die Jul. 11,   18 E.1
      die decimoctavo
was 15 000 three score.
      Divers had banished
but the usuries, no King before him.
      Holl fol 285
      Wals hypod
      Florilegius Dunstable
Angliae exeuntibus,
      and Uncle Carlo
        and, from Taufers, Margherita
No officer of ours or our heirs'
      take corn, leather or cattle
      without assent of the party
               cujus bona
Et Forestae
      per la grace de Dieu
          Dangleterre
      to be published
      25 Edward
Devant eux en judgement

                    cestascavoir
                    et en amendement
                                    oient a guier
& if contrary shall be undone
            this nient tenus
and read per an, deux foits
                    twice a year
mises ne prises   1272
        raised into precedent   25
                                                             ————
                                                             1297

Confirmationis
        Chartorum
Cap. VI bitched by Disraeli
de la maletot des leyes
                40 shillings
nous lettres ouverts
        nostre fits a Londres le x jour Doctobre
                    the five and 20th year
Customes 6 shillings 8 pence
                dimidium marcum trecentis pellibus
aliorum liberorum
                        34th year
                    nullum tallagium
                    (or tailogium)
                    in pleno parliamento
& no increase in burocracy
                    or to, or for, any subject
et vacua nulla,
            any infringement
                nihil capiatur

                        766

our pardon of Bohun of Hereford;
                    John de Ferraris
and that this be read in the churches
                    Bohun, Felton Ferraris
                    Defenders
                                        Henry III
                                        1216-'72
                        E. I. 1272-1307

Articul: a son people
CESTASCAVOIR
                    & that they be read 4 times the year
                    Sheng Yu
Michael, Xmas, Easter, Saint John
                    & be tried locally
prison, ransom, amerce
                    according to trespass
and Charles kept this seven years under the hatches
                                        1634-'41
Felton's knife was a tenpenny
articuli super Chartas
                    28th Edward
Soient esleus
            . . . trois prodes chevaliers
                    ou autres avisés
for "Vierge" see Fleta, 12 miles round about the King's house.
Hastings Dover Hithe Rumney Sandwich

by reason of the narrownesse
                    of the sea there

sheriffs elective

where shrivality is not in fee
ou viscount nest my de fee
In those inquests next neighbors
    "that they be most sufficient"
and is against packing juries
    et malveyes procurers   Elfynge
                                        Cler

De lum bank et lauter   Domus
    against William of Helmswell, parson   Com
Be marked with a leopard's head
    no worse than the touch of Paris
                Articuli twenty
Nor set any stone in gold
    except it be natural
    28 Edward I, a. D. 1300
auxy soit signe teste de leopard
    and false stone not set in true gold
    Pertaine to the King onely
    to put a value to coin
And to make price of the quantity
    Cap xx
and of 12 graines in mid-ear
    frumento in mediae spicae
    magnalia coronae
ELIZABETH
    Angliae amor,
    ad valorem reducta.
To take wood to melt ore
    non extat memoria
    . . . ardendam, fundendam

& souls of the dead defrauded

                  35 Edward

send or cause to be sent out of the

                  Kingdom

and that the seal be in custody of four men dignioribus

                                & the prior

alien abbots may visit;

              not export

                  by means whereof daily almes was decayed

. . . to Paragots alone

              10 000 marks

                  alienigenae superiores

the brocars of Rome promote caitifes

                  learning decayeth

                            Rot, parl 50 E. 3

damnable customs introduc of new in Roma.

That grosbois is oak, ash, elm,

                  beech, horsbeche & hornbeam

but of acorns tithe shall be paid

For every lamb a penny

              time out of mind

                  one lira per sheep nel Tirolo

sale must be in place overt

        not in a backe-room

& between sun-up & sun-down

                  dies solaris

ut pena ad paucos

            metus ad omnes perveniat

of 2 rights the more ancient preferred

              caveat emptor

HORSFAIRE from 10 of the clock before noon
              until sunset
the queenes dominions
              Phil, Mar
Colour, with one speciall mark at the least
              of every such horse, mare, colt, gelding
              on paine of default 40 shillings
              ridden openly for one hour
              and after 10 in the morning
as might be for Cadilacs, Fords & such other
              ridden, led, walked or kept standing
& in free markets to the book-keeper one penny
                                        no toll

Coke, Iong Ching
              responsabili
par cretance del ewe which is
              french for floodwater.
Who for bridges
              reparando;
For every new cottage 4 acres
              Stat. de 31 Eliz.

                              Angliae amor.

CIX

Pro Veritate . . .
   curtilagia teneant,
     enough land about each of them
16 foot and a halfe to the pole
     exceptions if sailor, etc
town, seaside or brickworks
     Idlenesse, mother of pickings
      EPARXON
Do sell the same in the realme and buy english
   not carry coin, plate or masse out of the country,
Donaison, denizen
   8H. 6 for cash only in exchange
   5 H. 4. three months credit
    and books not brought in bound.
No wight could pinch at his (Littleton's) writing
   long in the making,
      vocabula artis
Neither ought legal terms to be changed,
      Bracton:
Uncivil to judge a part in ignorance of the totality
      nemo omnia novit
In men's hearts on the rock of reason
   and they could not have been
     "excused jury service"
had there been no juries in his, The Confessor's, time.
Amenities are from Ambracia
   veigne en Court

and Sellaio
                    painted that goddess
le Concord del fine
                    Coke
                    συμβαίναι
                    in the 43rd of Elizabeth
The *fine* cannot omit ascun chose
                    continuance solonques le purpot
                              CHARDE dit estre certaine.
                    in quex le terre demeure
                                                  (liver dit)
certainty engenders repose
                    not for the sake of some leasehold but for clarity
"de ses vicines".
                    Time mother of Manors
Nor can the King create a new custom
                    in the fine print
                    tempora non regum
by a hawk, a pair of gilt spurs or similia
Cope is a hill
dene: a valley, arundinetum
drus is a thicket
                    Si nomina nescis perit rerum cognitio
                    nemo artifex nascitur
Ten families in pledge and a chief pledge
Though the bishopric be dissolved
                    a city remaineth

Tuan　端　　　et consuetudo

"In grateful resentment to Wadsworth, 20 shillings
                        May 15th,
                                Town House in Hartford
Charles, God's Grace, '62
                        Brewen, Canfield,
                                a Body politique
                                        and meere mocion
Ordeyned, heirs, successors, Woollcott, Talcot, perpetual
Seal, Governor, Deputy and 12 assistants
                        2nd. Thursday, May and October
Oathes, Ship, transport and carry
                        under their common seal
and not hinder fishinge
                for salting
                        by Narrowgancett
and on the South by the Sea
                        Mynes, Mynerals Precious Stones Quarries
                                As of our Mannor East Greenwich
                                        in Soccage, not Capite
One fifth of all oares Gold and Silver
                23rd April, Westminster
                                HOWARD
Wing like feldspar
                        and the foot-grip firm to hold balance
Green yellow the sunlight, more rapid,
Azaleas by snow slope.
afraid he will balk and not sign mobilization,
                        got, said Monro, to get rid of him
                                        (Eddie)
He has been around in the hospitals

773

Who for bridges

          reparando

For every new cottage   4 acres

         Stat de 31 Eliz.

                Angliae amor

And false stone not to be set in true gold

to the king onely to put value

         and to make price of the quantity

auxy soit signe teste leopard

Clear deep off Taormina

         high cliff and azure beneath it

form is cut in the lute's neck, tone is from the bowl

Oak boughs alone over Selloi

        This wing, colour of feldspar

               phyllotaxis

Over wicket gate

      INO Ινώ Kadmeia

Erigena, Anselm,

        the fight thru Herbert and Rémusat

Helios,

     Καλλἲαστράγαλος Ino Kadmeia,

San Domenico, Santa Sabina,

           Sta Maria Trastevere

             in Cosmedin

Le chapeau melon de St Pierre

    You in the dinghy (piccioletta) astern there!

DRAFTS & FRAGMENTS OF
CANTOS CX-CXVII

CX

Thy quiet house
The crozier's curve runs in the wall,
The harl, feather-white, as a dolphin on sea-brink

I am all for Verkehr without tyranny
      — wake exultant
              in caracole
Hast'ou seen boat's wake on sea-wall,
           how crests it?
What panache?
      paw-flap, wave-tap,
         that is gaiety,
Toba Sojo,
    toward limpidity,
         that is exultance,
   here the crest runs on wall
che paion' si al vent'
       ²Hăr-²la-¹llü ³k'ö
    of the wind sway,
The nine fates and the seven,
     and the black tree was born dumb,
The water is blue and not turquoise
When the stag drinks at the salt spring
     and sheep come down with the gentian sprout,
can you see with eyes of coral or turquoise
    or walk with the oak's root?

Yellow iris in that river bed

      yüeh$^{4.5}$

      ming^2

      mo$^{4.5}$

      hsien^1

      p'eng^2

Quercus on Mt Sumeru

    can'st 'ou see with the eyes of turquoise?

      heaven   earth

        in the center

          is

        juniper

The purifications

    are snow, rain, artemisia,

    also dew, oak and the juniper

And in thy mind beauty, O Artemis,

    as of mountain lakes in the dawn,

Foam and silk are thy fingers,

      Kuanon,

and the long suavity of her moving,

    willow and olive reflected,

Brook-water idles,

    topaz against pallor of under-leaf

The lake waves Canaletto'd

    under blue paler than heaven,

the rock-layers arc'd as with a compass,

    this rock is magnesia,

Cozzaglio, Dino Martinazzi made the road here (Gardesana)

Savoia, Novara at Veneto,
Solari was in that—
Un caso triste e denho di memoria

"Had I ever been in one?" i.e. a cavalry charge,
Uncle G. : "Knew when I came out that
there wd. be one hell of a row
in the Senate."
Knox came in, Lodge said: "Have you read it?"
"For the last time" he thought it was, till
Bettoni, like Galliffet
                    (Ibukerki).
Cypress versus rock-slide,
        Cozzaglio, the *tracciolino*
            Riccardo Cozzaglio.
        At Oleari, the Divisione Sforzesca
        disobeyed into victory,
        Had horses with them.

Felix nupsit,
            an end.
In love with Khaty
        now dead for 5000 years.

Over water bluer than midnight
        where the winter olive is taken
Here are earth's breasts mirroured
                        and all Euridices,
Laurel bark sheathing the fugitive,
            a day's wraith unrooted?
        Neath this altar now Endymion lies

KALLIASTRAGALOS
Καλλιαστράγαλος

新 hsin¹

        that is, to go forth by day

新 hsin¹

That love be the cause of hate,
        something is twisted,
Awoi,
      bare trees walk on the sky-line,
      but that one valley reach the four seas,
mountain sunset inverted.

La Tour, San Carlo gone,
        and Dieudonné, Voisin
Byzance, a tomb, an end,
      Galla's rest, and thy quiet house at Torcello
"What! What!" says the auzel here,
"Tullup" said that bird in Virginia,
        their meaning?
That war is the destruction of restaurants
       Quos ego Persephonae

止 chih³

not with jet planes,
The holiness of their courage forgotten
       and the Brescian lions effaced,
Until the mind jumps without building

chih³

and there is no *chih* and no root.
Bunting and Upward neglected,
all the resisters blacked out,
From time's wreckage shored,
these fragments shored against ruin,

and the sun jih⁴·⁵

new with the day.
Mr Rock still hopes to climb at Mount Kinabalu
his fragments sunk (20 years)
13,455 ft. facing Jesselton, Borneo,

Falling spiders and scorpions,
Give light against falling poison,
A wind of darkness hurls against forest
the candle flickers
is faint
Lux enim—
versus this tempest.
The marble form in the pine wood,
The shrine seen and not seen
From the roots of sequoias

ching⁴
pray 敬 pray

There is power

Awoi or Komachi,
the oval moon.

Notes for CXI

I, one thing, as relation to one thing;
      Hui sees relation to ten.
20 shillings to Wadsworth
        "in resentment." Town house in Hartford.
Roche-Guyon stoned to death at Gisors.
       Power to issue, au fond,
               to tax.
Directory cd. have made bulwark of Italy
post-bag B.
        Austerlitz
          Banque de France
             Mme de Genlis
Lannes did not enjoy sight of a battlefield.
Whole lesson of Talleyrand
            Wu
            Hsieh (heart's field)
            Szu
Enlarged his empire
        diminished his forces,
Ten years a blessing,
        five a nuisance,
that was Napoleon
with constitutional guarantees
        April 22nd.
"Very few interested"
        N. to Talleyrand, "in civilization."
So that Alexander asked Talleyrand what to do about France.

And "to change the meaning of words themselves from one
conference to another."
Oct. 31st, Wien

And 600 more dead at Quemoy—
they call it political.

A nice quiet paradise,
Orage held the basic was pity
compassione,
Amor
Cold mermaid up from black water—
Night against sea-cliffs
the low reef of coral—
And the sand grey against undertow
as Geryon—lured there—but in splendour,
Veritas, by anthesis, from the sea depth
come burchiello in su la riva
The eyes holding trouble—
no light
ex profundis—
naught from feigning.
Soul melts into air,
anima into aura,
Serenitas.

Coin'd gold
also bumped off 8000 Byzantines
Edictum prologo
Rothar.

From CXII

... owl, and wagtail

and huo³-hu², the fire-fox

Amṛta, that is nectar

            white wind, white dew

Here from the beginning, we have been here

               from the beginning

From her breath were the goddesses

          ²La ²mu<u>n</u> ³mi

If we did not perform ²Ndaw ¹bpö

          nothing is solid

without ²Mùa<u>n</u> ¹bpö

        no reality

Agility, that is from the juniper,

rice grows and the land is invisible

By the pomegranate water,

            in the clear air

               over Li Chiang

The firm voice amid pine wood,

           many springs are at the foot of

               Hsiang Shan

By the temple pool, Lung Wang's

       the clear discourse

           as Jade stream

玉   Yü⁴

河   ho²

Artemisia
Arundinaria
Winnowed in fate's tray

 neath

luna

CXIII

Thru the 12 Houses of Heaven
        seeing the just and the unjust,
        tasting the sweet and the sorry,
Pater Helios turning.
"Mortal praise has no sound in her ears"
Θρῆνος   (Fortuna's)
And who no longer make gods out of beauty
Θρῆνος   this is a dying.
Yet to walk with Mozart, Agassiz and Linnaeus
    'neath overhanging air under sun-beat
Here take thy mind's space
And to this garden, Marcella, ever seeking by petal, by leaf-vein
    out of dark, and toward half-light

And over Li Chiang, the snow range is turquoise
Rock's world that he saved us for memory
        a thin trace in high air
And with them Paré (Ambroise) and the Men against Death
Tweddel, Donnelly,
           old Pumpelly crossed Gobi
"no horse, no dog, and no goat."

"I'd eat his liver, told that son of . . .
and now bigod I have done it"
          17 Maggio,
               why not spirits?
But for the sun and serenitas
        (19th May '59)

H.D. once said "serenitas"

                    (Atthis, etc.)

        at Dieudonné's

                 in pre-history.

No dog, no horse, and no goat,

The long flank, the firm breast

             and to know beauty and death and despair

and to think that what has been shall be,

            flowing, ever unstill.

Then a partridge-shaped cloud over dust storm.

The hells move in cycles,

           No man can see his own end.

The Gods have not returned. "They have never left us."

           They have not returned.

Cloud's processional and the air moves with their living.

Pride, jealousy and possessiveness

        3 pains of hell

and a clear wind over garofani

          over Portofino 3 lights in triangulation

Or apples from Hesperides fall in their lap

        from phantom trees.

The old Countess remembered (say 1928)

        that ball in St. Petersburg

and as to how Stef got out of Poland...

        Sir Ian told 'em help

          would come via the sea

(the black one, the Black Sea)

        Pétain warned 'em.

And the road under apple-boughs

                    mostly grass-covered
And the olives to windward
                    Kalenda Maja.
Li Sao, Li Sao, for sorrow

          but there is something intelligent in the cherry-stone
Canals, bridges, and house walls
                              orange in sunlight
But to hitch sensibility to efficiency?
               grass versus granite,
For the little light and more harmony
Oh God of all men, none excluded
and howls for Schwundgeld in the Convention
                              (our Constitutional
                    17 ... whichwhat)
Nothing new but their ignorance,
                    ever perennial
Parsley used in the sacrifice
          and (calling Paul Peter) 12%
          does not mean one, oh, four, 104%

Error of chaos. Justification is from kindness of heart
          and from her hands floweth mercy.
As for who demand belief rather than justice.
And the host of Egypt, the pyramid builder,
               waiting there to be born.
No more the pseudo-gothic sprawled house
               out over the bridge there
                    (Washington Bridge, N.Y.C.)
               but everything boxed for economy.
That the body is inside the soul—

                    the lifting and folding brightness
                        the darkness shattered,
                            the fragment.
That Yeats noted the symbol over that portico
                            (Paris).
And the bull by the force that is in him—
            not lord of it,
                mastered.
And to know interest from usura
(Sac. Cairoli, prezzo giusto)
        In this sphere is Giustizia.
In mountain air the grass frozen emerald
            and with the mind set on that light
                saffron, emerald,
                    seeping.
"but that kind of ignorance" said the old priest to Yeats
    (in a railway train) "is spreading every day from the schools"-
to say nothing of other varieties.
Article X for example—put over, and 100 years to get back
                        to the awareness of
                    (what's his name in that Convention)
And in thy mind beauty,
            O Artemis.
As to sin, they invented it—eh?
                to implement domination
eh? largely.
            There remains grumpiness,
            malvagità
Sea, over roofs, but still the sea and the headland.
And in every woman, somewhere in the snarl is a tenderness,

A blue light under stars.
The ruined orchards, trees rotting. Empty frames at Limone.
And for a little magnanimity somewhere,
And to know the share from the charge
                    (scala altrui)
God's eye art 'ou, do not surrender perception.

And in thy mind beauty, O Artemis
                    Daphne afoot in vain speed.
When the Syrian onyx is broken.
                    Out of dark, thou, Father Helios, leadest,
but the mind as Ixion, unstill, ever turning.

CXIV

"Pas même Fréron

      hais personne

            pas même Fréron,"

"I hate no-one," said Voltaire

"not even Fréron."

And before Mr Law scarcely 300

      and now 1800 great vessels

and he, John Law, died in Venice in poverty.

        We far from recognizing indebtedness.

         "not even Tom Pick"

"You respect a good book, contradicting it—

      the rest aren't worth powder."

Amid corridors and ambassadors

      glow worms and lanterns, and this moving is

               from the inward

     o di diversa natura (Giordano Bruno)

and in these triangular spaces?

And is here among serious characters

      and not reasoning from a belly-ache.

Or that Ari. might have heard about fishes,

      thank Alex.

Falls white *bianco c(h)ade*

    yet sentient

      sees not.

Their dichotomies (feminine) present in heaven and hell.

    Tenthrils trailing

caught in rocks under wave.

Gems sunned as mirrors, alternate.
These simple men who have fought against jealousy,
        as the man of Oneida.
    Ownership! Ownership!
There was a thoughtful man named Macleod:
        To mitigate ownership.
And the literature of his time (Sandro's, Firenze) was
        in painting.
Governed by wood (the control of)

 mu⁴·⁵

Another by metal (control of)
        Fu Hi, etcetera.

This is not vanity, to have had good guys in the family
        or feminine gaiety—quick on the uptake
        "All the same in a hundred years."
        "Harve was like that" (the old cat-head
                re a question of conduct.)
        "the appointed when nothing can stop it—
        unappointed when nothing can kill you."
Even old Sarah,
        quick on the uptake

snobism—niente—
    the *tribù*.
Armes et blasons!
    me foot!!
Al's conversation—reputed.

Old Joel's "Locke" found in Texas
and Del Mar vaguely on Assay Commission (H.L.P.)
    if it was Del Mar.
Tanagra mia, Ambracia,
    for the delicacy
        for the kindness,
The grass flower clings to its stalk under Zephyrus.
Fear, father of cruelty,
    are we to write a genealogy of the demons?
And on July 14th said:
      "That lizard's feet are like snow flakes"
        τετραδάκτυλος
      (pale young four toes)
ubi amor, ibi oculus.
But these had thrones,
   and in my mind were still, uncontending—
not to possession, in hypostasis
   Some hall of mirrors.
      Quelque toile
"au Louvre en quelque toile"
    to reign, to dance in a maze,
To live a thousand years in a wink.
     York State or Paris—
Nor began nor ends anything.
Boy in the fruit shop would also have liked to write something,
but said: "bisogna esser portato."
The kindness, infinite, of her hands.
     Sea, blue under cliffs, or
William murmuring: "Sligo in heaven" when the mist came
    to Tigullio. And that the truth is in kindness.

From CXV

The scientists are in terror
        and the European mind stops
Wyndham Lewis chose blindness
        rather than have his mind stop.
Night under wind mid garofani,
        the petals are almost still
Mozart, Linnaeus, Sulmona,
When one's friends hate each other
        how can there be peace in the world?
Their asperities diverted me in my green time.
A blown husk that is finished
        but the light sings eternal
a pale flare over marshes
        where the salt hay whispers to tide's change
Time, space,
        neither life nor death is the answer.
And of man seeking good,
        doing evil.
In meiner Heimat
        where the dead walked
        and the living were made of cardboard.

CXVI

Came Neptunus
        his mind leaping
                like dolphins,
These concepts the human mind has attained.
To make Cosmos—
To achieve the possible—
Muss., wrecked for an error,
But the record
        the palimpsest—
a little light
        in great darkness—
cuniculi—
An old "crank" dead in Virginia.
Unprepared young burdened with records,
The vision of the Madonna
        above the cigar butts
          and over the portal.
"Have made a mass of laws"
            (mucchio di leggi)
Litterae nihil sanantes
        Justinian's,
a tangle of works unfinished.

I have brought the great ball of crystal;
        who can lift it?
Can you enter the great acorn of light?
        But the beauty is not the madness

Tho' my errors and wrecks lie about me.
And I am not a demigod,
I cannot make it cohere.
If love be not in the house there is nothing.
The voice of famine unheard.
How came beauty against this blackness,
Twice beauty under the elms—
                To be saved by squirrels and bluejays?
                        "plus j'aime le chien"
Ariadne.
                Disney against the metaphysicals,
and Laforgue more than they thought in him,
Spire thanked me in proposito
And I have learned more from Jules
                                (Jules Laforgue) since then
deeps in him,
                and Linnaeus.
                        chi crescerà i nostri—
but about that terzo
                third heaven,
                        that Venere,
again is all "paradiso"
        a nice quiet paradise
                over the shambles,
and some climbing
                before the take-off,
to "see again,"
the verb is "see," not "walk on"

i.e. it coheres all right
                even if my notes do not cohere.
Many errors,
            a little rightness,
to excuse his hell
                and my paradiso.
And as to why they go wrong,
                    thinking of rightness
And as to who will copy this palimpsest?
            al poco giorno
                        ed al gran cerchio d'ombra
But to affirm the gold thread in the pattern
                        (Torcello)
al Vicolo d'oro
            (Tigullio).
To confess wrong without losing rightness:
Charity I have had sometimes,
                I cannot make it flow thru.
A little light, like a rushlight
                to lead back to splendour.

Addendum for C

The Evil is Usury, *neschek*
the serpent
neschek whose name is known, the defiler,
beyond race and against race
the defiler
Τόκος   hic mali medium est
Here is the core of evil, the burning hell without let-up,
The canker corrupting all things, Fafnir the worm,
Syphilis of the State, of all kingdoms,
Wart of the common-weal,
Wenn-maker, corrupter of all things.
Darkness the defiler,
Twin evil of envy,
Snake of the seven heads, Hydra, entering all things,
Passing the doors of temples, defiling the Grove of Paphos,
neschek, the crawling evil,
        slime, the corrupter of all things,
Poisoner of the fount,
    · of all fountains, *neschek,*
The serpent, evil against Nature's increase,
Against beauty
            Τὸ καλόν
                    formosus nec est nec decens

A thousand are dead in his folds,
                        in the eel-fisher's basket
            Χαῖρη! Ω Διώνη, Χαῖρη
        pure Light, we beseech thee
    Crystal, we beseech thee
Clarity, we beseech thee
                        from the labyrinth
Sero, sero! learned that Spain is mercury;
that Finland is nickel. Late learning!
S...... doing evil in place of the R.........
"A pity that poets have used symbol and metaphor
and no man learned anything from them
    for their speaking in figures."

All other sins are open,
Usura alone not understood.
Opium Shanghai, opium Singapore
"with the silver spilla...
        amber, caught up and turned..."
                                Lotophagoi

[Circa 1941]

Now sun rises in Ram sign.
   With clack of bamboo against olive stock
We have heard the birds praising Jannequin
   and the black cat's tail is exalted.

The sexton of San Pantaleo plays "è mobile" on his carillon
"un' e due . . . che la donna è mobile"
   in the hill tower (videt et urbes)
And a black head under white cherry boughs
   precedes us down the salita.
The water-bug's mittens show on the bright rock below him.

[*Circa 1941*]

Notes for CXVII et seq.

For the blue flash and the moments
                    benedetta
the young for the old
                    that is tragedy
And for one beautiful day there was peace.
          Brancusi's bird
                              in the hollow of pine trunks
or when the snow was like sea foam
          Twilit sky leaded with elm boughs.
Under the Rupe Tarpeia
               weep out your jealousies—
To make a church
               or an altar to Zagreus Ζαγρεύς
Son of Semele Σεμέλη
Without jealousy
               like the double arch of a window
Or some great colonnade.

M'amour, m'amour
                what do I love and
                        where are you?
That I lost my center
                fighting the world.
The dreams clash
                and are shattered—
and that I tried to make a paradiso
                                terrestre.

La faillite de François Bernouard, Paris
or a field of larks at Allègre,
        "es laissa cader"
so high toward the sun and then falling,
        "de joi sas alas"
to set here the roads of France.

Two mice and a moth my guides—
To have heard the farfalla gasping
        as toward a bridge over worlds.
That the kings meet in their island,
        where no food is after flight from the pole.
Milkweed the sustenance
        as to enter arcanum.

To be men not destroyers.